EDINBUR
FOR UNDER FIVES

A Handbook for Parents with Young Children

9th Edition

Compiled by local members of the National Childbirth Trust

Published by Edinburgh for Under Fives

1st edition 1987, reprinted 1987
2nd edition 1989
3rd edition 1991
4th edition 1993
5th edition 1995
6th edition 1997
7th edition 2000
8th edition 2002
9th edition 2004

Edinburgh for Under Fives Committee 2003-4

Kathleen Taylor (convenor)
Kaye McAlpine (co-ordinator)
Sue Mclean (treasurer)
Kathy McGlew
Claire McIntosh
Jennifer Bruce

Principal Editor & Layout Design: Kaye McAlpine
Associate Editor: Kathleen Taylor
Efuf Logo: Ann Ross Paterson
Map: Shin Young Hwang

Printed by: D & J Croal Limited, Haddington, 01620 828404

Research Team 2003/4:
Alice Arthur, Lesley Baillie, Rhona Bean, Zoë Black, Sue Broadway, Jennifer Bruce, Juliette Carpentier, Naomi Crowley, Valery Devlin, Alison Harrison, Mark Hornsey, Nicky Laing, Kaye McAlpine, Claire McIntosh, Denise McKay, Elspeth MacKenzie, Sue Mclean, Clare McLeod, Morag MacLeod, Jane Marriott, Sarah Matthews, Shani Mason, Wendy Moncur, Nathalie Nunn, Fiona Smart, Jacqui Sproul, Nicky Sommer, Kathleen Taylor, Heike Ulferts, Fiona Whybrow – and all their 'under fives'.

INTRODUCTION

Welcome to the 9th edition of Edinburgh for Under Fives. As well as an abundance of information on places to go, or where to eat, there are tips and information on everything from childcare to healthcare. You will find all the inspiration you need for your under five to enjoy and make the most of this wonderful city.

If you have been somewhere you like and it is not included, or indeed somewhere which has disappointed you, please let us know as your comments and input are invaluable. This book is produced by people like you – mothers, fathers, carers of small children and we would like to thank these volunteers for their hard work, tenacity and efficiency in bringing us the best of what Edinburgh has to offer.

By purchasing this guidebook you are helping the National Childbirth Trust. Any profit generated after printing costs and expenses, will be donated to the charity. We are also able to sponsor antenatal teachers throughout their training.

If you would like to contact us, you can write or email:

Edinburgh for Under Fives
PO Box 012345
Edinburgh EH9 2YB

Email: info@efuf.co.uk
Web: www.edinburghforunderfives.co.uk

If you would like information on becoming a member of the National Childbirth Trust, see the inside back page.

CONTENTS

Activities for Children

ART & CRAFT

Although they are not numerous, there are art and craft classes available for under 5s in Edinburgh, outside a nursery environment. The following venues run classes for younger children.

Artskool

73 Viewforth EH10 4LL
Contact: Susie Wilson
Tel: 229 6885

Class times: Tue 10.15, 13.30 for 3-5 yrs; 15.45 for 4-6 yrs. Wed 10.15, 13.45 for 3-5 yrs; 15.45 for 4-6 yrs. £4.20/class, bookable in termly blocks in advance.

Fun experiences in art and craft for young children in the home of a practising artist. Children explore colour, line, shape, texture and composition through painting, drawing, papermaking, model making and printmaking. For children 3-6 yrs. Classes last 45 mins, with groups of around 6 children/class. Adults are welcome to stay in a separate room where they can have coffee; there is a toy box for younger children. Holiday workshops available for older children.

The Ceramic Experience

Hopetoun St EH7 4ND
Contact: Anna St Clair
Tel: 556 0070
Email: ceramicx@freeuk.com
Web: www.ceramicx.biz

Opening times: daily 10.00-17.30

Ceramic painting studio for families, where babies' and children's footprints can be put onto anything from tiles to teapots. Clay imprints can also be produced in a variety of finishes.

There is a café and two soft play areas. Seating for 150 and plenty of room to run around. Separate party room. Nappy changing facilities available for use by male and female carers. Free parking available. Premises accessible for pushchairs, with ramps and wide doors. Adults can choose to paint as well or can just relax while children play in the ball pool.

The Craft Kitchen

23 Columba Rd EH4 3QZ
Contact: Susie Lumsden
Tel: 538 0947
Email: thecraftkitchen@blueyonder.co.uk

Offers classes for adults and children, birthday parties, nights out and private bookings. A wide variety of classes is offered, ranging from silk, glass and fabric painting, to mosaics, paper making, felt making and lots of techniques for making cards using stamping and embossing, lace, punch art and collage. Special drop-in or 1 hour sessions are arranged for pre-school children. During term time there are lots of classes for adults during the day and for children after school. In the holidays all ages are catered for. Discounts available for block bookings and for children participating with an adult. All classes are offered by appointment and must be booked in advance. Contact venue for more information.

Doodles Ceramics Work Shop

29 Marchmont Cres EH9 1HQ
Contact: Holly Peters
Tel: 229 1399
Email: doodlescw@aol.com
Web: www.doodlesscotland.co.uk

Opening times: Tue-Thu 11.00-21.00, Fri, Sat 10.00-18.00, Sun 12.00-18.00

An opportunity for children to make ceramic gifts for parents, grandparents etc, decorated with foodsafe paint. Friendly, helpful staff are available for hands-on advice. If your child finishes their project ahead of time, there are books and toys to amuse them. Free juice for children/tea and coffee for adults. Baby hand and foot prints are a speciality.

Toilet facilities. No nappy-changing room, but there is space for changing. There is no place to breastfeed in private. Premises accessible by single and double pushchairs.

Edinburgh Rudolph Steiner School Parent and Toddler Group

60 Spylaw Rd
Edinburgh EH10 5BR
Tel: 337 3410

Opening times: Mon-Fri 10.15-12.30, Mon-Thu 13.30-15.30

See *Parent and Toddler Groups* for further information

This parent and toddler group offers a range of baking and simple crafts as well as other nursery/parent and toddler activities. Breastfeeding is welcome, although there is not a private area for feeding.

The Netherbow

43-45 High St EH1 1SR

Puppet shows and storytelling performances for under 5s. Workshops available, including some for under 5s. Nappy changing on ground floor near reception. See also *Annual Events*.

St Bride's Centre

10 Orwell Ter EH11 2DZ
Contact: Robert Murray
Tel: 346 1405

A range of workshops for children, including arts and crafts, singing and dance are available throughout the year. Contact centre for more details. See also *Annual Events*.

BALL SPORTS

Enjoy-a-Ball

Various venues through city
Contact: Warwick Dredge
Tel: 333 2286
Mob: 07966 362088
Email: dredge@enjoy-a-ball.com
Web: www.enjoyaball.com

Sports coaching programme for 4-9 year olds. No more than 10 children per class. The programme is divided into four stages. Stage 1 – Bee Bops is for 4 and 5 year olds and introduces them to a formalised sports environment. Fun and creative games are used to enable the children to learn basic sporting skills in a non-threatening and unintimidating sporting environment. Also aims to develop the child's confidence, concentration and social skills. Children are presented with a certificate at the completion of a stage and reports are given to parents. All equipment is provided. Children attend one hourly class per week. Classes are held in local sports, church and community centres on Mon-Fri afternoons and on Sat mornings. Free trial lesson available.

COMPUTERS

Whizzkids

Multimedia Learning Centre
19 Morningside Drive
Edinburgh EH10 5LZ
Tel: 447 5893

Fun and educational computer classes for children aged 3+ yrs. Computer based activities are used to teach pre-school children basic language and maths skills. Classes are held on an individual or small group basis at £5/½ hr. Classes are booked in monthly blocks.

COOKERY CLASSES

Cookery classes for younger children can be fun with enjoyable results!

Currie and Balerno High Schools

Contact: Margaret Knight, Assistant Community Programme Manager
Tel: 477 7733

Fun with Food, for 3-5 yrs. Classes run for 8-10 weeks and must be booked and paid for in advance. Days and times may vary from term-to-term. Places are limited. Telephone contact for more details.

DANCE

Classes for younger children (ie 2½-4½ yrs), usually teach music and movement. This may include nursery rhymes and simple dancing – hopping, skipping, toe-pointing, mime and moving in time to music. Socialising, learning to wait your turn etc, are key elements in all dancing classes. Footwear is sometimes light shoes, available from any decent shoe shop, more often ballet shoes. There are many local dance classes, some of which are list-

ed here, others may be found through friends' recommendations, ads in local libraries, community centres, shop windows and the local press.
Choosing the right class for your child can be difficult; it's worthwhile investigating the teacher's qualifications, class content studio facilities etc. The Royal Academy of Dance has a registration system for teachers. Contact the RAD for a list of local registered teachers. Tel: 020 7326 8000 or contact them by email via their website: www. rad.org.uk.

DANCE TEACHERS REGISTERED WITH THE ROYAL ACADEMY OF DANCE

Buckstone Youth Dance

Tel: 445 3892 (waiting list secretary)

Ballet (RAD) from pre-school year. Modern and Tap (BTDA) from primary 1. Jazz from primary 4. £2.25/class for girls and boys living in the Buckstone area. Teachers are also registered with the British Theatre Dance Association.

Central Scotland Ballet School

29 Hamilton Cres
Maddiston FK2 0NW
Contact: Jacqueline Clark
Tel: 01324 716425

Basic Ballet and movement to music for 2 1/2+ yrs. Sat classes at Rosebery Hall, S Queensferry. £2/class, pay for 10 week term. Teachers exams in Ballet. Also ISTD registered.

Dance for All at the Theatre School

106 St Stephen St EH3 5AQ
Tel: 226 5533

Dance classes for children 2 1/2 -4 yrs. General nursery dance; a fun introduction to dance steps, rhythm and co-ordination, mime, songs and creative dance.
4-5 yrs pre-primary Ballet; a gentle introduction to more structured dance steps and sequences, alongside free expression and creative dance, rhythm and co-ordination exercises.
Tap dancing classes from 4 1/2 yrs. Jazz classes available from 5 yrs.
Nappy-changing facilities. Breastfeeding welcomed, but no private breastfeeding location. Accessible by single pushchairs.
After-school classes and all day Saturday. Phone for full details.

Edinburgh Dance Academy

65 Orchard Brae Ave EH4 2UR
Tel: 343 1015
Email: edinburghdance@aol.com
Web: www.edinburghdanceacademy.co.uk

Ballet from 3yrs+. Classes are held in venues throughout Edinburgh and the Lothians. Under 3s wear pink short-sleeved leotard, pink tu-tu, pink socks and pink satin ballet shoes. Contact for current details, venues and requirements.

EH Dance UK

TF3, 4 Kings Rd EH15 1EA
Tel: 669 8047
Mob: 07976 585479
Email: lindadixondance@hotmail.com
Web: www.ehdance.co.uk

Classes in ballet, tap and jazz in the Craigmount area. Classes start at age 3 where the emphasis is placed on fun and the children are encouraged to learn the basics of balance, movement and interaction with other children. Phone for current prices.

Jane Goulding School of Dance

Falla View
Ampherlaw
Nr Carnwath ML11 8LH
Tel: 01555 840126
Mob: 07740 585614

Edinburgh classes for under 5s are held on Tue-Fri at Balerno Community Centre.
Ballet 3+ yrs. Dress: all pupils wear leotards and ballet shoes. Please phone for current prices.

Lothian Dance Academy

10 Promenade Ter
Portobello EH15 1DT
Contact: Morag Phillips
Tel: 669 9073

Pre-school classes for 3 and 4 year olds. Ballet and Tap are informal and fun at this stage and consist of runs, skips, galops, mime and gesture, learning to share, working with partner, in groups and much more. Classes held at various locations throughout the city. Phone for current prices and locations.

Manor School of Ballet

Manor School of Ballet

Tel: 334 0399

Contact: Mrs Noel Platfoot (Director)

Music and movement for ages 2 1/2-4 yrs. Ballet (4 1/2+ yrs). 45 min classes £3/class.

Classes are held at:

Marchmont St Giles Church, Kilgraston Rd; Old Parish Church, High St, Corstorphine; Belgrave Hall, Belgrave Rd, Corstorphine; St Serf's Church, Goldenacre; and Inverleith Church, Ferry Rd.

In terms of dress, the youngest pupils wear normal clothes, plus ballet shoes, which the school sells at a reasonable price. Children start to wear leotards at age 3 1/2 yrs. The school employs several teachers who are all RAD and ISTD registered. See also *Activities for Parents*.

Morningside Dance Academy

Morningside Dance Academy

Contact: Sonja Messer B.Phil (Hons), Principal

Tel: 661 0844 or 477 4344

Classes held at The Grange Studio, 9b Grange Rd and 11-23 Morningside Dr. Ballet, Tap, Modern, drama and Jazz dancing from age 3 to Majors. RAD and BTDA syllabus to Examination Standard.

OTHER DANCE TEACHERS

Pamela Allam AISTD, BTDA

Tel: 01259 742973

Nursery Ballet for pre-school children. Older children do Ballet and Tap.

Classes are held on Thursdays at St Columba's Church, Blackhall. Classes last 45 mins. 3 x 10 wk terms. All classes accompanied by a pianist. Fully qualified staff. Registered teacher recognised by the Council for Dance Education and Training. Enrolment by phone.

Dance Base

National Centre for Dance
14-16 Grassmarket EH1 2JU
Tel: 225 5525
Web: www.dancebase.co.uk

Dance Base is a fully accessible building offering state-of-the-art facilities, with four dance studios. Creative Dance for under 5's and 'Dance a Story' classes run throughout the year and encour

age children to express themselves through movement games, facial expressions, using props, action songs and story-telling in a non-competitive environment. Children under the age of 5 must be accompanied by an adult. Adults are encouraged to take their socks and shoes off and join in with their children. Phone or email centre for details of class times and prices.
Dance for 2-5 yrs, Wed 11.00-12.00, Thu 14.30-15.30.
Through simple games children and parents explore movement together, using stretching, facial expressions and hand gestures. Saturday class 2-5 yrs 10.00-11.00. This is for the whole family to enjoy; bring brothers and sisters too! Children can join in as soon as they can walk! All classes £20 for block of 4 classes, or Pay-on–the-day £2.50 (£1/extra child). See also *Activities for Parents.*

Dancercise

Portobello Swim Centre
Contact: Louise Mackinnon
Tel: 669 9916

Dance classes for all ages. Under 5s Fri 16.00-17.00.

Dancing for Fun

St Bernard Centre
Stockbridge Parish Church
Saxe Coburg St
Contact: Kate Wright
Tel: 01620 860 788

Dance class for 3-5 year olds held on Mondays 15.30-16.30, which aims to enable the children to express themselves, experience a sense of space and freedom and the joy of dance and to begin to listen to their bodies to find more inner and outer balance. £4/class. Free trial session.

Edinburgh Dance Centre

Westfield Halls
Westfield Ave EH11 2QE
Tel: 337 0748

Dance classes for 2½+ yrs and adults in fully equipped studios with bars and mirrors. Qualified teachers giving classes in: Flexibility/Stretch, Modern, Ballet, Tap, Jazz, Disco, Latin, Ballroom and Tae Kwon Do etc. Changing room. 'Stagecoach' also operates from the Dance Centre, offering song, dance and drama.

Mhairi Hogg School of Dancing

Contact: Mhairi Hogg MBATD
Tel: 449 3035

Classes held in Colinton Mains Community Centre and Oxgangs Neighbourhood Centre. Nursery Tap classes are held for 3-5 yrs. Highland and Modern Dance classes for 5 yrs upwards. A class leotard is worn, plus Tap or Ballet shoes. Enrolment by phone.

ENVIRONMENT

Currie and Balerno High Schools

Contact: Margaret Knight
Tel: 477 7733

Green Tots course for 3-5 year olds, which explores nature and the environment. Involves arts and crafts work and activities such as growing woodland boxes. Courses run for 8-10 weeks and must be booked and paid for in advance. Days and times may vary term-to-term. Crèche available if booked in advance. Phone contact for current prices and times.

GYMNASTICS

Gymnastics classes are popular for the under 5s and classes accommodating this age group are generally available in Edinburgh. When choosing a class, convenience is usually the prime consideration. However, it is well worth checking on the teacher's qualifications for teaching pre-school children, the facilities available and on their insurance cover, in the event of an accident.
All British Amateur Gymnastics Association (BAGA) coaches will charge a set amount to all children who attend their classes. This is paid to the Association for insurance purposes. This sum will be paid irrespective of the cost of the course. Anyone working with young children, ie nursery groups etc, might be interested in taking the Scottish Gymnastics Coaching Award for pre-school gymnastics and movement. For information, a copy of the syllabus, and general advice on gymnastics classes, contact Scottish Gymnastics Association, via their website: www.scottishgymnastics.com.

Ainslie Park Leisure Centre

92 Pilton Drive
Tel: 551 2400

Gym Nippers programmes for under 5s. Run on block course. Contact centre for details.

Craiglockhart Tennis & Sports Centre

177 Colinton Rd
Tel: 443 0101 Sports Centre
Tel: 444 1969 Tennis Centre

Gym Nippers pre-school programme for under 5s. Under 3s must be accompanied by an adult. Course is run on a 9 wk block. Priority is given to children already on the programme. There is a Gymnastic Link Transition Programme to allow children to progress from Pre-school to 5+ yrs gymnastics Wed 15.30-16.30. Classes run by qualified staff. Crèche Mon, Tue, Wed, Thu to fit in with centre programme; pre-booking essential. See *Activities for Parents.*

Currie and Balerno High Schools

Contact: Margaret Knight, Asst Community Programme Manager
Tel: 477 7733

Gym and Games Fun for Kids for 3-5 yrs. Classes run for 8-10 wks and must be booked and paid for in advance. Days and times may vary term-to-term. Crèche available if booked in advance. Phone contact for current prices and times.

Drumbrae Leisure Centre

30 Drumbrae Ter
Tel: 312 7957

Gym Nippers on Saturday mornings. Gymnastics for older children also. Must be booked. Contact centre for details.

Gracemount Leisure Centre

22 Gracemount Dr
Tel: 658 1940

Gym tots Wed 10.00-10.45, 10.45-11.30 £2.50/class. Mini gymnastics available for 3-5 yrs Mon, Wed 13.00-14.00 and 14.00-15.00, £2.50/class, block of 6 wks. Possible waiting list. Crèche Mon, Wed and Fri 9.15-10.45 and 10.50-12.15. Sports Camp during school holidays.

Gymini

Eric Liddell Centre
Morningside Rd
Contact: Fiona
Tel: 334 3657

Gymnastics classes for toddlers onwards. Classes are held in a large, bright room with rubber matting, lots of equipment and friendly and imaginative teachers. Room is on top floor of building – lift available. Nappy changing facilities available. Not much space for pushchairs but these can be left downstairs. Café on ground floor of centre for parents waiting for 3-5year olds.

Parent and toddler classes: Tue 9.30-10.10 and 11.05-11.45; Thu 9.30-10.10.

Classes for 3-5year olds: Tue 10.15-11.00, 13.00-1345, 13.50-1435; Thu 10.15-11.00, 11.05-11.50, 13.00-13.45 and 13.50-14.35.

Jack Kane Sports Centre

208 Niddrie Mains Rd
Tel: 669 0404 or 664 4710

Pre-school gymnastics Tue 9.45-10.30 (18 mths-3 yrs); 10.45-11.30 (18 mths-3yrs); 13.00-13.45 (3-5 yrs); 13.45-14.30 (3-5 yrs). Further details from centre.

Kirkliston Leisure Centre

Kirklands Park St
Kirkliston
Tel: 333 4700

Gymnastics classes for under fives held on Mondays. Parent and toddler class (18 mths or older): 11.00-11.45. 3 and 4 year olds class: 10.00-10.45 and 14.15-15.00. Classes usually booked in a block of 6-8 weeks. Contact centre for current prices. Crèche available but must be booked in advance and costs £3.00/session (or £1.80 with a LAC).

Meadowbank Sports Centre

London Rd
Tel: 661 5351

Gym Nippers programme offers young children the chance to learn balance, movement and co-ordination along with music and action songs, all in a fun, creative environment. Classes are available for: 18mths-3 yrs (children must be accompanied by an adult), 3-5 yrs, 4-5 yrs, P1, P2. Courses are arranged via block bookings and can be booked in advance. Contact venue for further details.

Musselburgh Sports Centre

Newbigging
Musselburgh EH21 7AS
Tel: 653 6367

Gymnastics classes Wed 15.30-16.15, Fri 13.30-14.15 (18mths-3yrs, parents must stay); Wed 16.15-17.00 and 17.00-17.45, Fri 14.15-15.00, 15.00-15.45 (3-5 yrs). £2.10/class booked in advance. Waiting list. Teacher is BAGA approved coach. Crèche £1.90. Details from centre.

Oxgangs Kindergym

Pentland Community Centre
Oxgangs Brae EH13 9LS
Tel: 445 5559

45 min session for children accompanied by parent/carer. Meets Mon-Thu 9.30 and 10.30 and some afternoons. Booking in blocks of 4 weeks. £1.50 annual centre membership and £2.00/session. Concessionary rates and some free places available. Children with special needs / disabilities especially welcomed.

Portobello Indoor Bowls and Leisure Centre

20 Westbank St
Portobello EH15 1DR
Tel: 669 0878

Gymnastics classes for 18 mths-3 yrs (children must be accompanied by parent/carer): Mon 9.30-11.15 and 10.15-10.30; Fri 9.00-10.15, 10.20-11.05. Ages 3-5 yrs - Fri 11.15-12.00. £2.30/ session.

Tumbletots

Contact: Jo Letelier Lobos
Tel: 01875 320066
Web: www.tumbletots.com/edinburgh
Classes held at: Cluny Church Centre, Cluny Dr, Morningside – Mon, Tue, Fri
Inverleith Church Hall, Ferry Rd – Tue
Murrayfield Parish Church – Wed
Queen Margaret Hall, Linlithgow – Thu
Tumbletots' specially designed programme is divided into 3 age ranges, which helps develop co-ordination, balance, climbing skills and agility. All with appropriate equipment. Supervision is by specially trained staff. Parents stay with under 3s.
There are 3 different ability levels: Gymbabes – crawling - walking. Play, exploration and learning in a safe environment; Tumbletots – for children who can walk confidently. Sessions based round 'activity stations'; and Gymbobs – 5-7yrs
Membership and insurance £15.00/yr (includes t-shirt, 'Right Start' magazine 6 issues/yr and insurance cover). £4.50/each 45 min session, paid in advance in 5-8 week blocks, after 1 trial session (paid).

Wester Hailes Education Centre

5 **Murrayburn Dr**
Tel: 442 2201

Toddler gymnastics classes for 3-5 year olds held on Saturdays 12.00-13.00. Cost £1. A waiting list applies. Contact the centre for more details.

JUDO

Shishi Kai Judo

Eric Liddell Centre
15 Morningside Rd
Contact: Jim Syrett
Tel: 447 7859
Email: jim@gymini.freeserve.co.uk

Judo classes for children aged 4 years onwards. The class for 4-5 year olds is held on Fridays 1600-1645. There is a waiting area for parents/carers and it's possible to view the class. First session free. Child/coach ration is 8:1. All coaches qualified, registered and child protection vetted. Contact Club for prices and more information.

MUSIC

Young children love music. However, in most cases under 5s are not able to specialise in a particular instrument – their hands are not big enough, they don't have the lung power etc. One of the main exceptions to this is the violin. Half-sized instruments retain tonal qualities, while being of a good size for little hands.
Most of the music classes mentioned below, therefore, teach listening skills and moving in time to music. It is highly advisable to book in advance for all classes.

Baby Music

Contact: Jane Crewe
Tel: 2293667 (Birth Resource Centre)

Action songs, rhymes and lullabies for babies up to 1yr.
These are very popular classes , so places are limited: please call for venue, times, cost and to reserve a place. Concessions are available. Affiliated to the Pre-school Music Association.

Music for Fun

5 Willowbrae Ave
Contact: Nina Craighead
Tel: 620 0685

Finger rhymes, action songs, dancing and musical games, and percussion playing for children from 3 yrs to school age. Run by former primary school teacher in her home. Classes are on Mon & Wed 13.45-14.30. £2/class. Payment is by class each week – there's no payment required if the child is absent. A cup of tea/coffee is provided in the kitchen for whoever brings the child to the class.

Daisy's Music Time

Held in Wardie Parish Church Hall
Primrose Bank Rd EH5 3JE
Contact: Di McGuire
Tel: 662 1243

Music and Fun for babies and toddlers. For children 6 mths-3½ yrs. Runs in terms, with classes on Tue & Wed mornings. Parent/carer stays with child for the session. Breastfeeding welcomed, but no specific nappy-changing room – the cloakroom area is used. Venue accessible by double and single pushchairs. Ample on-street parking adjacent to the venue. Phone for current times and further information.

Dough-Doh Music Club

3 Seaforth Drive
Contact: Carol Freeman
Tel: 332 4540

Educationally motivated music club for ages 2-5 yrs. Established 1994, this club is taken by Carol and Laraine, two experienced teachers. Meet the Dodo family! Listen, learn and move to unique Dodo stories, tongue twisters, rhymes and songs. Children develop natural rhythm through use of percussion instruments (eggs, bells, sticks) and to love music with our keyboard. Classes last 40-50 mins. Information pack and testimonials on request. This is a mobile service and is suitable for schools, nurseries, playgroups etc.

Jack and Jill – Music Fun for Tots

Contact: Jill Reeves (MusBHons, PGCE, Music Therapist)
Tel: 667 9664 / mob. 07729 719756

Lap rides, finger plays, action songs, dancing, playing simple percussion instruments, and listening to live music – interactive musical fun and learning for tots (ages 3 mths-4 yrs) and their accompanying adults. Children with special needs welcome. Classes are held in Marchmont St Giles Church, Kilgraston Rd, on Wed and Fri mornings during term time. £3.25/class, payable termly.

Edinburgh Young Musicians

Contact: Jean Murray
Tel: 226 3392
Email: admin@e-y-m.org.uk
Web: www.e-y-m.org.uk

Musical play classes for children, starting in their final pre-school year, leading to instrumental tuition, choirs and orchestras for older children. Classes provide a general introduction to music, developing the child's sense of rhythm, sense of pitch, listening skills, co-ordination and imagination.
Classes are held at James Gillespie's High School, Lauderdale St.

Jo Jingles

Contact: Joanne Goodall
Tel: 443 4196
Web:www.jojingles.co.uk

Music and movement classes for various age ranges (9mths-2yrs, 2-3 yrs and 3-5 yrs). Includes action songs, nursery rhymes and playing of musical instruments. Some songs are familiar, others are new, so there's something to keep the participating parent/carer on their toes. Also available for Birthdays (see *Birthdays & Celebrations*)
Current classes held in various venues throughout the city, including Murrayfield, Craiglockhart, Corstorphine, Cramond, Blackhall and Oxgangs. Different classes for different age groups: classes are tailored to those children who attend, so you might find groups such as 6 mths-walking, 9 mths-2 yrs, 2-3 yrs, 3-5 yrs and so on. Contact Joanne Goodall for current times and class groups. More venues may be included in 2004/5. Breastfeeding welcomed. Nappy changing facilities available.

Mini Minstrels

18 Bonaly Cres
Contact: Hazel Stewart
Tel: 441 3750

Music sessions for 3-6 yrs. Singing, musical games, instruments, and development of musical skills through fun.
3 yrs: various times on Tue, £2.50/30 mins. Max 6 in class.
Pre-school year; Wed or Thu £3.00/45 mins. Max 8 in class.
P1: Wed or Thu 16.00, £3.25/50 mins. Max 10 in class.

Mrs Furryboots

Contact: Clare Hannah
Tel: 665 7931
Email: mrsfurryboots@btinternet.com

Music making classes for babies, toddlers and pre-school children. There are two baby groups – for 1-2 yrs and 2-3 yrs – which last 30mins each and where parents/carers stay with the child. There is also a 3-5 yrs group which lasts 45 minutes, and children can be left or parent/carer can stay, whichever suits the child best.
Activities include singing, dancing, playing instruments, games to develop pitch and rhythm and an introduction to simple notation through words with beats.

At the start of each session, Mrs Furryboots makes sure she has on her magical musical furryboots which help her make music. No private breastfeeding area or specific nappy changing facility.

Music with Mummy

8 Greenbank Loan EH10 5SH
Contact: Carolyn Watson
Tel: 447 7033

Lively approach to music for children aged 3 and under. Structured programme that encourages listening skills, sense of rhythm through music and games – and having fun! Has been running since 1992. Weekly 1/2 hr sessions, limited to 8 children (accompanied by parent/carer). £2.50/session, payable 1/2 termly in advance. Held in teacher's home. Facilities for storing pushchairs. Please phone for current times.

St Mary's Music School

25 Grosvenor Cres
Contact: Monica Wilkinson
Tel: 538 7766

Music classes for children in their final pre-school year, including musical games, singing, listening, and use of simple percussion instruments. Classes are on Sat 9.00-13.30. £4.75/class.
Also classes for older children, including group instrumental lessons for beginners. There is generally a waiting list.

SIGNING

Sing and Sign

Contact: Roz Coe
Tel: 554 4574
Email: rozcoe@madasafish.com
Web: www.singandsign.com

Classes are aimed at 7-18 month olds (& their mums/dads etc!) and run in a course of up to 12 weeks (during term times). Classes last 45 mins, and signs are taught through songs & rhymes which are specially written or adapted to target signs relating to babies' routines & interest. Musical instruments, props, puppets & pictures are used to capture babies' & mums' attention & the aim of the classes is to enhance parent-baby communication by using signs (as well as having a bit of fun along the way). Classes held in the West End and also Trinity/Leith: phone for current prices.

Tinytalk UK

Contact: Susan Kane
Tel: 476-5158

Tinytalk UK provides fun classes for babies and young toddlers (0-2yrs) using special signs, adapted from British sign language. These are taught through singing and action songs and can be used by babies to begin to express their feelings, wishes and needs before they can talk.
Classes comprise 1/2 hour of signing and singing and 1/2 hour of playtime and refreshments. Classes cost £4/hour (including coffee/biscuits)
Classes run on Tuesdays 9.30-10.30 at Morningside Parish Church and on Fridays 9.30-10.30 and 10.45-11.45 at Wardie Parish church.

VIOLIN LESSONS

Julia Fowler

1F1 Belford Rd
Tel: 220 1453

Classes (3-4 yrs) offering rhythm training, simple percussion and singing, music and movement leading on to lessons, taught with a version of the Suzuki method, although Ms Fowler is not registered with the Suzuki Institute. Stress is laid on learning to listen, as children learn to play by ear. Parental involvement is essential. Tuition in groups of up to 4. £5-£7.50/ 1/2 hr lesson, according to size of group. Small brothers and sisters welcome.

PLAY, SOFT PLAY & FUN CENTRES

Soft play centres vary greatly in terms of size and availability of areas for younger children – where some may have some great facilities for older brothers and sisters, under 3s may be confined to a ball-pit – ideal if they're happy, not so great if they're not. It might be wise to avoid planning your first visit to a soft play centre during school holidays, or on school half-days, as they can become extremely busy, and the noise and general good-natured mayhem might overawe a young first-timer. Please note that not all the soft play centres are listed: as with other sections, some venues did not respond to enquiries.

Agenda

92 St John's Rd
Corstorphine

Tel: 316 4466

Although primarily a restaurant, Agenda does have a soft-play area, consisting of multi-level play, a slide into a ball-pit, cargo nets etc. There are large soft shapes to amuse younger children, but the equipment for young toddlers (tables and chairs, tiny basketball hoop etc), which is set apart from the soft-play unit, was looking rather tired at the time of visiting. The down side is that the soft play is in a room which you can't view directly from the restaurant (consequently you might find yourself abandoned with other people's children who are not being supervised). The up side is that this is one of the few soft plays where you can enjoy a decent cup of coffee, tea etc. while your children play.

Bonnyrigg Leisure Centre

King George V Park
Park Rd
Bonnyrigg
Tel: 663 7579

Pleasant soft play area with imaginative layout. Includes features such as ballpool, slide, rat run, giant castle and a multitude of play shapes.
Reasonable prices – 80p/$^1/_2$ hr. Ideal to hire for small groups (£15.00/hr).

Castle Gyle

Gyle Shopping Centre
Tel: 476 7766

Large soft play, ball pool and slide; home corner, playdough, toys and games to suit different ages of children (ages 2-8 yrs accepted). Situated near the central entrance to the shopping centre. £3.40/hr. Phone for current opening hours.

Clambers

Royal Commonwealth Pool
21 Dalkeith Rd EH16 5BB
Tel: 667 7211

Opening times: Mon-Fri 10.00-18.00, Sat and Sun 10.00-17.00. Check availability at reception
This multi-level play area has 3 levels of slides, tubes and lots of safe surfaces to clamber on and over. Suitable for 3-8 yrs. Parents and carers must stay in the surrounding area – or you can join your child inside the play area.
There is a toddler (under 3s) area within Clambers, where children must be accompanied by a parent or carer. Access times for this area are: Mon-Thu 10.00-18.00; Fri 10.00-13.00; Sat & Sun 10.00-12.00. Under 3s are not admitted at all during school holidays. Available for birthday groups (see *Birthdays & Celebrations*)

Clown Around

Units 2&3
109 Restalrig Rd EH6 7NY
Tel: 553 7676
Mob: 07976 053690

Opening hours: daily 10.00-18.00. Phone for current charges
A fairly new soft play centre, which has the additional attraction (in our case certainly!) of trampolines. There's a toddler area, which has a multi-level soft play unit, along with soft shapes and interactive items, such as musical notes on one of the walls. The other multi-level area is for 4-10 yrs, and has rat runs, a slide, a large ball pit, moveable 'obstacles' etc. There's also a games consul area. Nappy-changing facilities available.
There are 2 locations with tables, from which you can see the play areas. There's a café, so you can relax with a tea or coffee while you watch the antics. While the food is pretty much run of the mill (fish & chips, burgers, filled rolls etc), it is freshly prepared. Breastfeeding welcomed. Birthday parties catered for (see *Birthdays & Celebrations*). The unit has access for disabled visitors,

and a controlled entry/exit arrangement.

The Happy Castle

Bankmill
Valleyfield Rd
Penicuik
Tel: 01968 675638
Fax: 01968 675911

Opening times: daily, 10.00-18.00.
Admission: £3.50/hr (ages 1-12 admitted).
Go through Penicuik town centre and after town hall on the left, follow the road round Bridge St, turn left into Valleyfield Rd, The Happy Castle is sign-posted. Then turn right and continue on under the narrow bridge, bear left and you will find the car park; the entrance is on the right.
There's a separate area for under 3s, with soft play, slides, ball pool and scramble nets – excellent fun for climbers, but less mobile babies would be happier (and more accessible) at the entrance. During busy times it would be advisable to stay close to younger children, as the older children can be boisterous if they sneak in.
There's a huge multi-storied soft play extravaganza for children up to 12 yrs, containing aerial slides, rope bridges, free fall and snake slides.
Café
High chairs, breastfeeding welcome, bottles heated, nappy-changing facilities
Private rooms for parties, special rates for group bookings.
Good seating arrangements mean that parents and carers can enjoy their tea or coffee while keeping an eye on the children. Themed selection of children's meals; also toasties, baked potatoes etc. Jugs of diluting juice available at reasonable prices.

Jelly Club

Peffermill Rd
Tel: 652 0212
Email:info@jellyclub.co.uk
Web: www.jellyclub.co.uk

Opening times: daily, 10.30-18.30.
Admission: £3.50/0-2 yrs; £3.95/3-4 yrs; £4.50/ 5-12 yrs, No charge for adults.
The Jelly Club underwent an extensive refurbishment in 2002, and now offers more equipment and increased security (there's now an electronic entry/exit format).
The five play zones are aimed at different ages. Two soft play areas with ball pit and slides, one for 0-3 yrs (also has small chutes, soft shapes and rockers), one for 4-12 yrs. Adventure maze area for 4-10 yrs with climbing sections, walkways, slides etc. 'Jelly Village' for 2-7 yrs provides cars and tractors for pedalling around a road system, with petrol pumps and traffic lights for make-believe play. There's two large bouncy castles with slides and nets, one for 2-6 yrs, one for 6-12 yrs. There's also a small garden seating area. Rocking chairs are available for babies accompanying older siblings.
There's usually some supervision in all play zones. Parents not allowed in bouncy castle or adventure maze. Shoes required for some zones and socks for others. Under 3s may find it a bit daunting and under 4s may be frustrated at being excluded from various zones. It's advisable to phone in advance to check if there are large school parties booked in, and it's best to avoid busy times (Sat, Sun and lunch times). No booking required except for groups. Wheelchair/pushchair access to the main seating area. Nappy-changing surface in toilet for the disabled & in the ladies.
Café
High chairs, breastfeeding welcome, bottles and food heated
Seating throughout the play area so parents/carers can see their children. Usual food selection (chips, sandwiches, pannini, pasta), children's menu (chips, nuggets, pasta), and snacks at reasonable prices. There's an extensive menu chalked on boards, but some items aren't always available. Birthday parties hosted in separate rooms.

Junglee Fun

115 North High St
Musselburgh EH21 6JE
Tel: 653 0666
Web: www.junglee-fun.com

Opening times; daily, Mon-Fri 9.30-16.30; Sun 12.00-16.30 and for parties. Phone for current charges.
Soft play centre/café, which offers a brightly coloured environment with soft play shapes, small ball pool, climbing units and jungle-themed toys. Caters for children aged 0-6 yrs. Due to the enclosed layout of the play area, parents/carers can relax in the café area while also being able to supervise their children. If there are older brothers or sisters, there's a Playstation 2 in the café to keep them occupied – although it may well prove to be very popular! Nappy-changing facilities, child-friendly toilets with potties and booster seats. Premises are accessible to pushchairs. No smoking policy throughout. Space for storing pushchairs. Available for party hire: pre-booking required.
Café
High chairs, bottles heated, breastfeeding welcome

Café serves light meals such as baked potatoes, toasties, etc as well as home baking, tea, coffee, juice etc.

Kirkliston Leisure Centre

Kirklands Park St
Kirkliston
Tel: 333 4700

Scampers Soft Play. Currently available two times a week, Tue 13.00-16.00; Fri 14.00-16.00. Phone centre for more information.

Little Marco's

Marco's Leisure Centre
51-95 Grove St
Haymarket
Tel: 228 2141

Opening times: daily, 12.00-17.00 weekdays; 10.00-19.00 weekends

Admission: all children £5/ 1 1/2 hrs. Playgroup or other outing £3/child/ 1 1/2 hrs play (for groups of 10+ children): playleaders must stay with children.

Children's indoor adventure playground with lots of large play apparatus, such as a bouncy castle, slides, tunnels to crawl through, soft play area, and a large ball pool. Suitable for children 31-55" tall – under this size at parents' own risk. Under 3s may find the centre daunting at first. With under 4s, pick a quiet time, as over 5s can be overpowering. Wheelchair and pushchair access is available by lift. Toilets are nearby. Both Ladies and Gents have nappy-changing surface. Parties hosted.

Lounge (ground floor)

£, tables suitable for clip-on seats, breastfeeding welcome, bottles heated, licensed

Counter service bar/café with large comfy seating area. Food served includes quiche, burgers, salads, soups etc. Vegetarian dish available. Children's menu. Space for pushchairs. Toilets nearby.

Meadowbank Sports Centre

139 London Rd
Tel: 661 5351

Opening times: daily, 9.00-20.00.

Soft play opening times: Mon 13.30-14.30; Tue, Thu 9.30-11.30, 13.30-14.30; Wed, Fri 10.30-11.30; Sat, Sun 10.30-11.30, 12-30-13.30.

Admission: £1.70/hr. Group hire £19/hr (max. 20 children)

There is ramped access to the sports centre and the automatic entrance doors are wide enough for a double pushchair. The lift offers access to all facilities and is suitable for use by parents with young children and people with disabilities. There are toilets on all floors and nappy-changing facilities are available.

The soft play area provides fun and entertainment in a safe area for the under 5s, and equipment is suitable for children with special needs. As this area is unsupervised, parents and carers must remain with their children at all times. The area can be booked for private parties.

Musselburgh Sports Centre

Newbigging
Tel: 653 6367

Small soft play area for under 5s, which costs £1.25/ 1/2 hr.

SKATING

Murrayfield Ice Rink Ltd

Riversdale Cres
Murrayfield EH12 5XN
Tel: 337 6933

Sessions: daily from 14.30. Best times for under 5s and their families are beginners sessions Mon, Fri 17.00-19.00. Group tuition Wed 17.00-19.00 and Sun 12.00-13.45 (this is a certificated Learn to Skate session with instruction from resident coaching staff). Family skating Thu 19.00-21.00 and Sat 10.00-12.00. Groups can be taken w/day mornings by prior arrangement with resident instructor. Beginners sessions, including skate hire cost from £3. Group and UK Learn to Skate sessions cost £3 plus £1 for skate hire. Skates available from children's size 5. Wheelchair access and toilet facilities for the disabled. Shop sells all manner of skates and accessories. Café open most sessions serving hot drinks, hot snacks, toasties, etc. Hot drinks and snacks from machines at other times.

SWIMMING

Most babies love moving in water once the initial fear of being uncovered has gone. Swimming is an excellent way of exercising the body, and more and more parents are introducing their children to the pleasures of water early in life. Safety is obviously a motivating factor. Opinions vary as to when to start your child off (6 mths is probably the average), but whenever you start, here are a few things to remember:

- Have a healthy respect for the dangers of water.
- Always stay near your child when in or near water.
- Allow at least 1 hour after a feed before entering the water.

- Respect your child's wishes. Do not force youngsters into the water if they dislike it. Wait and try again in a week or so.
- Babies get chilled easily. Take them out of the water at the first signs of cold. 10 mins in the water is enough for the first times, and no more than 30 mins at other times.

What to Wear

There are various companies producing swimsuits and shorts with in-built nappy, ranging from 3-36 mths. Disposable swim nappies are available, but they're expensive. Ordinary nappies are not suitable.

Buoyancy Aids

Small arm bands are available. The type with 2 or more air chambers and non-returnable valves are the safest. The triangular type with a flat section next to the body will stop your child wobbling too much. These aids are available from swim centres, sports shops, Early Learning Centre, Jenners toy dept, and so on. Other buoyancy aids, such as body vests and inflatable ring seats, are available. You might find that these are more suitable for young babies and aids such as these also come in several sizes. Remember that arm bands and inflatable rings are not lifesavers. Early classes are intended to develop your child's confidence and pleasure in the water. They teach some of the basic skills leading towards learning to swim, and show parents how they can help their children. As regards a proper stroke, experts say that it is better to let under 5s develop their own way of swimming through playing regularly in water: perfecting a stroke can come later. In fact, the longer you leave it, the quicker they learn. The Amateur Swimming Association offers the following useful publications by mail order:

- 'Water Activities for Adult and Child' – £2, plus p&p of £1
- 'Teach Your Child to Swim' (Usborne Pubs) – £5.99, plus p&p

Send your order and remittance to: ASA Swimming Times Ltd, 2 Kingfisher Enterprise Park, 50 Arthur St, Redditch, Worcs B98 8LG (Tel: 0800 220 292 or 01527 514 288). Alternatively, check bookshops or the EDL service for copies.

Swimming in the Sea

Edinburgh's beaches from Cramond to Musselburgh are generally reasonably clean. However, standards can change from season to season, so always check before going into the water, and always obey the notices posted – just because it looks clean doesn't mean it's safe. The Scottish Environment Protection Agency (SEPA) monitors and reports on water quality (see www.sepa.org.uk for latest results) of other recreational waters as well as those which are EC recognised. Some of these beaches in urban areas can be affected by sewage debris and have higher bacterial concentrations during and immediately after heavy rain, caused by storm sewer overflows and run off from streets.

Another source of information is Friends of the Earth Scotland's website – www.foe-scotland.org.uk, where information regarding the state of all 60 EC bathing waters in Scotland can be found.

East of Edinburgh, water quality is generally better, although sewage treatment improvements are still required in the Longniddry area, which may also affect Seton Sands. EC bathing waters at Seton Sands, Gullane, Yellowcraigs, North Berwick (West Sands and Milsey Bay which is east of the harbour), Dunbar (East and Belhaven Bay), Whitesands, Thorntonloch, Pease Bay and Coldingham all meet European water quality standards. Some are exceptionally clean.

Belhaven Beach is good to play on, but there are strong currents and it is not safe for bathing. Other beaches away from towns are generally safe to play on but simply do not have official EC recognition because they are too sparsely used.

Beaches which are most suitable for toddlers are: Gullane, Seacliffe and Yellowcraigs. All have toilets (no charge for use), Gullane (Apr-Sept). Seacliffe Beach, non-EC, is one of the cleanest and safest beaches on the Lothian coast.

- Remember, sea water can be extremely cold, even on sunny days.

Family Swimming During the Summer Months

Wester Hailes runs family sessions. Schools with pools, such as Trinity Academy, Currie High, the Royal High, Queensferry High, Dr Bell's Primary, Portobello High, James Gillespie's and Gracemount High, may all offer evening family swimming sessions: contact the Community Education programme for current information, Tel: 469 3250.

Some of the city's private gyms and hotels have pools that offer swimming classes and activities for children but these can be extremely expensive. See Yellow Pages for full listings.

SWIMMING POOLS

General Notes & Information

The pools in this section are all local authority run. For details of the City Council Leisure Access Scheme (LAC) which gives reduced admission rates to cardholders, see *Activities for Parents*.

- The water temperature ranges from 80-84°F.

- All pools have showers and hairdryers. Most hairdryers take 20p coins.
- In general the admission charge entitles you to unlimited swimming time. However, when pools are busy e.g. during school holidays, they may run sessions of limited duration, usually 40 mins.
- The pools all sell armbands, shampoo sachets, soap, combs and goggles.
- All pools without cafeterias have hot and cold drinks machines and sweet/snack machines.
- Spectators are allowed into all Council pools, free of charge.
- During school holidays and at w/ends, most of the pools have fun play-sessions with toys, inflatables etc.
- Children under 8 must always be accompanied by an adult at all Council pools. The number of children whom an adult can accompany is currently in debate, and the safety ratio may differ in some pools in the near future.

At Council pools, lessons are *very* popular and must be booked in advance. There are three main booking periods.

- August – for the period August to January;
- December – for the period January to July
- June for Summer holiday courses.

Customers who have made main bookings in either August or December are offered priority booking for any other courses, within that period. However, new customers can still apply for any remaining spaces in the new course.

- In August and December course places are offered on a first come first served basis. You should expect long queues which form ahead of opening time.
- For details of the school holiday activities and play sessions, contact the Edinburgh Leisure Head Office, Tel: 650 1001 for a current seasonal leaflet or your local sports/swim centre.

Ainslie Park

92 Pilton Dr EH5 2HF
Tel: 551 2400

Opening times: Mon-Thu 07.30-21.15, Fri 07.30-20.30; Sat/Sun 08.00-17.00.

Free car park beside centre.

Modern leisure centre. Amenities include a large pool (25m x 8 lanes), shallow teaching pool, spa pool and splash pool, sports hall, pulse centre and crèche. There is an extensive range of activities and coaching sessions.

Changing area: mixed, with 3 large family cubicles. Coin-operated lockers (50p returnable deposit). Wall-mounted hairdryers, play pens, changing tables, and high chairs are available, as are safety seats to assist in changing with children.

Learner pool starts with a gentle water-filled slope leading into a shallow pool, which is very suitable for introducing small babies and toddlers to the water. At one end there's a jet-pressurised water system, which older toddlers and children enjoy.

Entrance to the spectator area overlooking the pool is through the sitting area.

Parent and child sessions are held throughout the week and aim to familiarise the baby/toddler with the environment of water. No booking necessary. Classes are available for pre-school children. Lessons are very popular and have to be booked in advance. Full programme available from centre.

Balerno – See Currie and Balerno High Schools

Bonnyrigg Leisure Centre

King George V Park
Park Rd
Bonnyrigg EH19 2AW
Tel: 663 7579

Opening times: daily, 9.00-22.00. Reduced opening hours during public hols 10.00-18.00.

Pool admission: adult £1.75; child/concession £1.

Pool available for private booking £37/hr.

Free car parking for up to 80 cars.

This modern centre includes a leisure pool, consisting of upper and lower lagoon, and special water features such as water cannons, geysers, spa pool, slides and water mushrooms. No spectating area. Centre also has 'Knights and Princesses' soft play area, and a games hall. Programmed sessions include swimming lessons, gymnastics and martial arts among others.

Crèche: Opening times: Mon-Fri 9.45-11.15.

Changing area: mixed family changing is available, with coin-operated lockers and nappy-changing facilities. There are no cafeteria facilities, but a wide range of snacks is available from vending machines. Tables, chairs, and high chairs are provided in the conservatory.

NB: parents/carers may only supervise a max of 2 children under 8 yrs in the swimming pool.

Currie and Balerno High Schools

Tel: 477 7733
Contact: Margaret Knight, Asst Community Programme Manager

Parent and Toddler Swimming Classes for pre-school children.

Classes run for 8-10 weeks and must be booked and paid for in advance. Days and times vary term-to-term. Places are limited. Family sessions are available throughout the entire year at both schools as follows:
Balerno High School: Tue and Fri 18.15-18.55, and 19.10-19.50; Sat 15.15-15.55 and 16.10-16.40.
Currie High School: Wed 18.05-18.45. Advanced booking is advised (Balerno HS, Tel: 477 7733. Currie HS, Tel: 449 5922).

Dalry Swim Centre

Caledonian Cres EH11 2AL
Tel: 313 3964

Opening times: Mon-Thu 8.00-9.00, 12.00-15.00, 17.00-19.40; Fri 8.00-9.00, 12.00-13.40, 17.00-19.40; Sat 12.00-15.40; Sun 9.00-15.40. Ladies only swimming Tue 18.30-20.30. Other times also – contact the centre.
Admission: adult peak £2.60/ off peak £2.10 (Leisure Card Holder £2.10/£1.50 respectively). Under 5s and primary school children free. Older children (up to 18) £1.30.
On-street parking available, but area is very busy.
Victorian 23m (25 yd) swimming pool with changing cubicles and coin-return lockers upstairs. Nappy-changing facilities and play pens on poolside. Ample space for parking pushchairs. Purpose-built changing, shower and toilet for people with disabilities.
Antenatal swimming exercise session 9.00-9.40 and Parent and Child sessions 9.40-10.20 on Tuesdays. These sessions are supervised by friendly, qualified coaching staff, from whom advice and assistance is available. No booking necessary. New pulse centre due to open October 2003. Full programme available from centre. Staff fully trained to service the special needs of under 5s and the parents. NB the water can be on the chilly side!

Drumbrae Leisure Centre

Drumbrae Ter EH4 7SF
Tel: 312 7957

Opening times: Mon-Fri 8.00-22.00; Sat 9.00-15.30; Sun 9.00-15.30.
Admission: adult peak £2.40/ off peak £1.80; child £1.20. Under 5s and all children of primary school age free. All children under 8 must be accompanied by an adult.
Opened in 1999, this centre is close to various bus routes and has a good-sized car park. Built all on the same level, the large, bright swimming pool is worth visiting just for the amazing view. Centre recently won an award from Practical Parenting magazine as one of the most child-friendly pools in the UK.
Pushchair park (50p refundable). Multi-purpose hall for various activities including gymnastics, GymNippers and birthday parties. There's also a pulse centre. Numerous toilets with changing facilities throughout the centre.
Changing areas:
mixed, with family and facilities for the disabled. Coin-operated lockers require 50p coins (refundable). Changing area is open to the swimming pool, so care should be taken with over-enthusiastic children: a poolside barrier is erected at certain times to prevent children charging straight out of the booths and into the water.
Adult and Child swim session Mon 9.30-10.00 and Wed 11.00-11.30: sessions to develop water safety and confidence, for children 4 mths-4 yrs, accompanied by an adult in the water.
Learn to Swim programmes for pre-school children 3½-5 yrs who are confident in the water, adult and child (under 2) and adult and child (2-4) in 10 week blocks. Contact venue for information on dates and prices.
Crèche:
Opening times: Mon-Fri 9.15-12.30; Tue, Thu 13.00-15.00. £3/session (1½ hrs) or £2 with a Leisure Card. Bookable 7 days in advance.
Cafeteria:
£, high chairs (4), serves cold snacks
Opening times: Mon-Fri 9.00-14.00. There are also vending machines selling drinks, chocolate bars etc. The seating area is near to the pool viewing area.

Dunbar 'Splash' Leisure Pool - **See *Out of Town Trips*.**

Glenogle Swim Centre

Glenogle Rd
Stockbridge EH3 5JB
Tel: 343 6376

Opening times: core hours 8.00-19.40, but public swimming times vary greatly due to classes and other activities – contact centre for details.
Admission: adult standard £2.60/£2.10, off-peak £2.10/£1.50; Under 5s and primary school children free. Secondary school children £1.30.
Car parking: on-street metered parking.
Victorian 23m (25yd) pool in listed building with changing cubicles around the edge of the pool. Ample space for parking pushchairs. Many stairs to cash desk and pool, but help is available from helpful staff. Nappy-changing and play pens at poolside.
Parents and Child swim sessions on Mon 9.40-10.20 all year, plus

Wed 9.40-10.20 in Winter, supervised by qualified staff. Ante-natal exercise session Mon 9.00-9.40 all year, plus Wed in Winter. Play session with floating toys 12.00-14.00 on Sat.
Swimming classes: comprehensive programme from 4+ yrs on Tue, Thu, Fri afternoons and Sat mornings. Blocks of 8x25 mins, must be booked in advance. No crèche.

Gracemount Leisure Centre

22 Gracemount Dr, EH16 6RN
Tel: 658 1940

Opened in 2000, this swimming pool and fitness centre provides swimming lessons, tots classes and ante-natal exercise – full programme available from the centre. Nappy-changing facilities (M&F). There is an area for private breastfeeding. Premises are accessible to double pushchairs. Lift access to upper floor.
Crèche:
Opening times: Mon, Wed, Fri 09.15-10.45 and 10.50-12.15 (2 sessions). £2.50/child (LAC holders £1.50). Must be booked 7 days in advance.

Leith Victoria Swim Centre

Junction Pl EH6 5JA
Tel: 555 4728

Car parking: parking, including parking for disabled, at the Bonnington Rd entrance.
Lift available, changing for the disabled, and access to 23m (25 yd) Victorian swimming pool. Spectating facilities available. Variety of facilities to suit all abilities: contact reception for current details.
Crèche:
Opening times: Mon-Fri 9.00-12.00, booking system in place. No cafeteria, but drinks etc available from vending machines. Pushchair corner, where they can be locked to a rail: chain and padlock available at reception if you leave deposit.

Leith Waterworld

377 Easter Rd, EH6 8HU
Tel: 555 6000

Opening times: Term time: Fri/Sat/Sun: 10.00-17.00 (out of water by 16.45). During school holidays: Mon-Sun: 10.00-17.00 (out of water by 16.45).
Parent and toddler classes: Fri 10.15-11.00; Adult aqua fit class: Fri: 11.15-12.00.
Admission: Adult: £3.40; Junior £2.40; Under 5's Free; Family ticket (2 adults and 2 children) £9.00; Parent and toddler class: £2.60; Adult aqua fit class: £2.00. The Island soft play session: £1.20 for 1 hour session; Multi-sensory Play session: £1.20, carers free.
Pool has sloping 'beach' style entrance, wave machines, fast flow channel, spa pool, flumes for toddlers and older children, river run and bubble beds. Family changing areas, including nappy changing facilities and facilities for people with disabilities. Soft play area for toddlers and children aged 3-8years.
Multi-sensory area for children with disabilities: This area has been designed to be both subtle and relaxing, whilst providing stimulating sounds and textures. It features a choice for a variety of disabilities and can accommodate up to 15 people (including carers) at a time.
Party room available for hire.
Waterworld no longer has a café but there are vending machines available.

Loanhead Leisure Centre

George Ave
Loanhead EH20 9LA
Tel: 440 4516

Opening times: vary considerably from day to day, and at different times of the year – contact centre for current hours.
Car parking: free car parking, with designated parent and child spaces.
Admission: adult £2.20; child £1.10. Family ticket (2 adults and up to 4 children) £5.80.
This modern leisure centre has a 25m pool, with adjoining toddler pool with slides and a viewing gallery. Parents may only supervise a maximum of 2 children each in the pool. Water tends to be nicely warm for children during parent and child sessions.
Changing areas:
mixed family changing is available, with nappy-changing facilities.
Crèche:
Opening times: Mon/Tue 9.30-12.30, Wed 9.30-14.00, Thu/Fri 9.30-11.30. 90p/child, bookable in hourly sessions. When the crèche is closed, the area can be used for nappy-changing and feeding.
Drinks and snacks can be bought from vending machines, and there are tables, chairs and high chairs.

Musselburgh Sports Centre

Newbigging EH21 7AS
Tel: 653 6367

A modern sports centre, offering a wide range of facilities, such as a pool, health suite and café. A swim for under 5s costs 30p. Children's swimming classes, including lessons for under 5s, are

available – contact centre for details.
There is no private area for breastfeeding.
Crèche
Opening times: Mon/Wed/Thu 9.00-11.00, Tue .
Café has high chairs. Centre accessible to double pushchairs.

Portobello Swim Centre

57, The Promenade EH15 2BS
Tel: 669 6888

Access is well thought out, with a ramp to front entrance, automatic doors which are wide enough for double pushchairs. Secure pushchair parking at reception (padlocks available for refundable deposit). A lift gives access to first floor/café.
Changing area;
2 family changing rooms with baby seat and nappy-changing unit. Play pen/nappy-changing unit/high chair in both ladies' and gents' changing rooms.
Swimming classes for children. Pre-school (31/2-5 yrs, confident in water); adult and child (2-4 yrs); adult and baby (4 mths-2 yrs). Classes also available for children with special needs. All lessons take place in the centre's small pool. Spectating area for parents/carers.
Crèche:
Opening times: Mon-Fri 9.00-12.00 (0-5 yrs), £3/child (LAC holder £2).
Cafeteria:
Children's menu, high chairs, breastfeeding welcome, facilities to heat baby food and to warm milk.

Royal Commonwealth Pool

Dalkeith Rd
Newington EH16 5AE
Tel: 667 7211

Opening times: Mon-Fri: 6.00-21.30; Sat: 6.00-8.00 then 10.00-21.30; Sun: 10.00-16.30
Admission: Under 12s are free and there are reduced rates for under 18s. For current adult admission prices, please phone.
Car parking: limited – the overflow car park can also be crowded at peak times, so it is advisable to leave plenty time for parking before lessons.
Built for the 1970 Commonwealth Games, facilities include a large competition-sized 50m pool, shallow teaching pool, and diving pool. Other facilities include a fitness centre with exercise and weight machines, separate male and female saunas, a coffee concession and a crèche. For reasons of hygiene, pushchairs must be left in the foyer. Padlocks and chains are provided – keys can be obtained from cash desk. The entire building is a no smoking zone.
In both the main pool and the teaching pool children under 8 must be accompanied in the water by an adult.
Changing areas;
Down a steep flight of stairs. Lift access to changing level available. Female changing area has high chairs, which you can take into your cubicle. There are also play pens, nappy bins and a nappy-changing table. Hand hairdryers are available. Coin-operated lockers – 50p returnable. Fathers/male carers can have high chairs transferred to their area on request. There is a table for dressing babies in the male changing room. Pushchairs are available downstairs for sleeping babies.
Teaching pool is usually occupied by young children, and many parents change their babies' clothes on the wide shelf with padded mats surrounding the pool, so they stay uncovered for the minimum time. The teaching pool temperature is 30°C every morning Mon-Fri. Chairs on the pool side.
Parent and baby sessions held every weekday am. Under 1s at 10.00 and under 2s at 10.30. Parents and babies introduced to early water skills under the supervision of an instructor. Parent and child lessons are also available – contact centre for current information.
Swim classes for under 5s are available during term times and must be booked and paid for in advance. Pre-school classes for 3-5 year olds are held mornings and afternoons everyday. Classes for over 5s run during term times, Sat mornings and in the Summer holidays.
There is also a soft play area. 'Clambers', for 3-8 yrs, is Edinburgh's largest multi-level adventure play area, with slides, tubes, ball pit and lots of soft surfaces. During term time, under 3s can enjoy 'Clambers' accompanied by their parent/carer.
Toilets available upstairs and down.
Coffee Outlet
High chairs (4), breastfeeding welcome, bottles heated, no-smoking, parties hosted
Current opening times (subject to change): Mon-Fri 1000-1800 and Sat/Sun 11.00-17.00. Hot food is available up to 17.15 during the week and 1600 at the weekend.

There is a spacious seating area in front of the coffee outlet or beside Clambers. Both areas overlook the main swimming pool and there is a relaxed atmosphere and plenty of room for children to run around. The area is also fully accessible for pushchairs and prams. The coffee outlet sells snacks and hot food and there are various vending machines selling snacks and drinks. There are toilets nearby with nappy changing facilities although these are not always as clean as they could be.

Warrender Swim Centre

Thirlestane Rd
Marchmont EH9 1AP
Tel: 447 0052

Opening times: daily, but times vary from day to day. Full programme is available from centre – or telephone in advance to check times.

Admission: adult peak £2.60 (LAC holder £2.10)/ off peak £2.10(LAC holder £1.50). Under 5s and primary school children free. Older children (under 18s) £1.30.

Car parking: free on-street parking.

Bright, airy Victorian pool with changing cubicles around the pool. Coin-operated lockers – 50p returnable. Play pens, high chairs, and nappy-changing tables beside the pool. There's also a wide bench suitable for changing nappies. Prams/pushchairs may be left in the foyer.

Parent and child sessions on Wed 9.45-10.30. No booking necessary.

Classes: blocks of 8 swimming lessons available for babies, children and adults must be booked in advance.

Ante-natal swimming session Wed 10.30-11.15. Full programme available from centre. Play fun session on Sat 13.00-14.00 with mats, toys and inflatables. No crèche.

Wester Hailes Swimming Pool

Western Hailes Education Centre
5 Murrayburn Dr
Wester Hailes EH14 2SU
Tel: 442 2201

Opening times: Mon, Tue, Thu, Fri 9.30-21.10; Wed 9.30-18.00 (women only 18.00-20.10); Sat 10.30-16.30; Sun 9.30-16.30.

Admission: adult £1.80; child 90p. 10p key deposit

Modern pool with amenities including: a 25m pool; a children's pool; and a diving pool with springboard and highboard. The children's pool is graded in depth, so small children can touch the bottom at one end. There is a frog house with slide into the water. Under 4s must be supervised on the slide. Nappy-changing facilities available on the pool side. In the Summer, there's an early morning family swim 8.50-9.30. When the leisure pool is really busy it operates on session times.

Changing area:

in the female changing area, there's a separate facility which includes mats, play pen and high chairs. These items are available on request in the male changing area. Lockers lock automatically on closure, so beware of locking the key inside! There is a powder room with mirrors, and hairdryers are available. A lockable pushchair bay is also available.

Classes: a comprehensive programme of swimming lessons for ages 3 yrs+ is available. These must be booked in advance. Details on request.

Crèche:

Opening times: Term time only Mon-Fri 8.00-17.00. Prebookable. 50p/session.

Cafeteria:

£, high chairs (2), bottles heated, parties hosted, seats 200

Opening times: Mon-Fri 9.00-21.00; Sat/Sun 10.00-16.00. Self-service cafeteria overlooking pool, offering an inexpensive range of snacks and meals. Wholefood and vegetarian options available on weekdays. The staffroom may be used on request for breastfeeding. Prams and pushchairs allowed inside. Take-aways available. Toilets by cafeteria.

PRIVATE SWIMMING CLASSES

There are a number of private swimming teachers who run classes at various venues throughout Edinburgh. Many of these have long waiting lists and have preferred not to be listed in this guide. The following offer classes for under 5s.

Swimming Nature

Tel: 0870 900 8002
Web: www.swimmingnature.co.uk

Swimming classes held in Edinburgh University Aquatics Centre, Holyrood Rd. Class sizes are small and instructors work in the water following a modular programme that can be easily followed by children and their parents. Fun, games, stories and rewards are used to encourage and stimulate the children to love the water. Free trial lesson offered. Call centre for information and to make a booking.

Waterbabies Edinburgh

Contact: Hugh Davidson
Tel: 312 7520
Mobile: 07958 631220
Email: hugh@waterbabies.co.uk
Website: www.waterbabies.co.uk

Swimming classes for babies from birth onwards. Fully qualified STA instructors teach water confidence and safety techniques with babies swimming above and below the water's surface. Classes are small and held throughout Edinburgh in private, warm-water pools. Contact Waterbabies for information about prices and course times.

Activities for Parents & Carers

Making time for yourself as well as for your children is very important. The aim of this section is to provide you with some starting points and ideas of the types of community classes, education and training opportunities, and sports facilities in the area. Many of the centres listed have crèche facilities and we have listed those we know about – but it is always worth checking with the venue. There are many possibilities open to parents with young children – thanks to evening classes, open/flexible learning opportunities and a wealth of community based initiatives to help parents to extend their horizons and have a break from childcare. If the venues are unable to provide childcare, there is a range of private crèches/nurseries that can offer flexible childcare. For full listings, see *Childcare* and *Pre-school Play and Education.*

COMMUNITY EDUCATION CENTRES

These centres provide a broad range of formal and informal activities and classes. There are opportunities to study for qualifications, keep fit, or learn a new craft or skill. Many provide a crèche. The majority of these centres are schools, community schools or resource centres. Many run programmes under the management of the City of Edinburgh Council's 'Adult Community Education Programme'. Classes start in September, January and April. For further information on classes, contact Community Education on 469 3250. See also *Sport and Leisure* in this section.

Cameron House Community Centre

Cameron House Ave EH15 5LF
Contact: Susan Ferguson
Tel: 667 3762

Daytime classes with crèche. Yoga and keep-fit.
Toddler Group on Fridays 10.30-12.30; small friendly group. Phone venue for further information on classes etc.

Carrickvale Community Education Centre

Stenhouse St W
Edinburgh EH11 3EP
Tel: 443 6971

Daytime classes with free crèche, such as art and crafts, languages, computing and other miscellaneous classes. There are also currently 2 Parent and Toddler groups, running Thu and Fri 9.30-11.30. Phone centre for information on any class or group.

Castlebrae Family Centre

Castlebrae Community High School
2a Greendykes Rd
EH16 4DP
Centre Leader: Lyn Tarlton
Tel: 661 1282

Centre providing range of activities for babies and young children, but also adult education classes. Contact centre for details.

Clovenstone Community Centre

54 Clovenstone Pk
Tel: 453 4561

Variety of social and educational activities which cater for local residents of all ages. Free crèche – mainly for women's activities. Programmes on request.

Craigmount Community Centre

Craigmount High School
Craigs Rd
Tel: 339 1884/8278

Wide range of activities, including arts and crafts, alternative therapies and miscellaneous groups. Women's discussion group. Free crèche (under 5s), usually staffed by two people. Also Sat 9.00-13.00, there's a class for Japanese children (3+ yrs) in their own language and culture, and an English class for their parents, with crèche (0-3 yrs).

Craigroyston Community Centre

1a Pennywell Rd
Tel: 332 7360

Various classes – with crèche provision – run throughout the year. Full details are available from centre.

Craigroyston Community High School

Craigroyston Under 5s Centre
Contact: Linda McDonald
Tel: 477 7801

Under 5s centre where people may come to play and learn with their children. Adult day and evening classes also run, with cover provided for the children of adult learners as appropriate.

Currie and Balerno High Schools

Contact: Margaret Knight, Asst Community Programme Manager
Tel: 477 7733 or 449 5922

Comprehensive programmes of learning and recreational opportunities are offered throughout the year at the dual sites of Currie and Balerno high schools. The combined resources of the schools allow for the provision of a wide range of day, evening and weekend classes, courses and community activities. Crèche places are available at both schools for children of adult students attending morning classes/activities. Please book crèche requirements when enrolling for day class. Contact the above nos for details of current classes etc.

Drummond High Community High School

41 Bellevue Pl
Tel: 556 2651

Wide variety of day and evening classes. Vocational courses also available. Contact venue for availability of crèche.

Duncan Place Resource Centre

4 Duncan Pl EH6 8HN
Contact: Rohan Seilman
Tel: 554 1509

A range of adult education classes, daytime and evening. Crèche facilities for daytime classes. Adult clubs are also run, as are Fri afternoon classes for older children. Contact centre for more information.

First Step Community Project

37 Galt Ave
Musselburgh EH21 8HU
Contact: Prisca Kemp or Cathy Carstairs
Tel: 665 0848

Variety of classes and courses, such as: computing; cookery; stress management; assertiveness; art; women's group; Dad's group; and positive parenting. Crèche available on Wed 9.30-11.30 (£1 charge) for class participants. Contact project for more details.

Fort Community Wing

N Fort St, Leith EH6 4HF
Contact: Nancy Richardson (9.30-13.00)
Tel: 553 1074

Various classes run throughout the year. Phone to find out what is currently available and whether crèche facilities are available.

Gilmerton Community Centre

4 Drum St, Gilmerton
Contact: Lea Taylor
Tel: 664 2335

Groups specific to women are run, such as a women's interest group, and also a support group. Free crèche with experienced staff. A playgroup also runs Mon-Thu – contact centre for all current details or playgroup application form.

Lasswade High School Centre

Eskdale Drive
Bonnyrigg, Midlothian EH19 2LA
Contact: David Hand
Tel: 663 8170/7171

Various discussion and interest groups from the area meet. New members are welcome, so phone centre for current information.

Lochend YWCA

198 Restalrig Rd S
Contact: Lilian Watson
Tel: 554 3400

Activities for centre users vary from term to term, but adult education groups, computer groups, discussion groups and health groups are typical – a crèche is usually provided. Phone for current information.

St Bride's Centre

10 Orwell Ter EH11 2DZ
Contact: Faye Ward
Tel: 346 1405

Programme of classes, activities, shows and popular films during term time and holidays. Crèche available with some morning adult classes. Café with enclosed children's play area open Mon-Fri 10.00-16.00. Nappy changing facilities. After school club for 4-8 yrs, Thu 17.00-18.30 during term time.
Classes available vary, so contact centre for current information.

South Bridge Resource Centre

Infirmary St
Edinburgh EH1 1LT
Tel: 556 2944

Daytime classes in computing, dressmaking, pottery and some others. Crèche available. Other classes may be available. Phone for details.

South Queensferry Community Centre

Joint Sites: Community Centre, Kirkliston Rd, S Queensferry & Rosebery Hall, S Queensferry
Contact: Steve Stewart
Tel: 331 2113

Various classes: Pottery, Mon 12.10-2.10, Tue 9.30-11.30; Arts & Crafts Wed 9.30-11.30 at the Community Centre site.

Badminton Tue 9.15-11.10, at Rosebery Hall site. All with crèche: 75p/first child, 50p/subsequent children.
There are also playgroups at both sites (Mon-Fri at the Community Centre; Mon, Wed, Fri at Rosebery Hall). Childminder's group Thu 9.30-11.30. Toy Library Fri 10.00-12.00.

Southside Community Centre

117 Nicolson St
Edinburgh EH8 9ER
Conact: venue
Tel: 667 0484

Class with free crèche (0-5yrs); must be pre-booked. Yoga Tue 10.00-12.00. Southside Sunshine Club (for 0-3 years) Wed 10.00-12.00. Other classes available. Classes can vary from term to term, so phone for information. Other groups, such as Parents and Tots may also meet – phone for current information.
Centre Cafeteria
Opening times: Mon-Fri 10.00-14.30
£, high chairs (2), breastfeeding welcome, bottles heated
Café serving snacks and wholesome lunches. Menu incl. dish of the day. Meals served 12.00-14.00. Children's portions; vegetarian dishes.

Stevenson College Community-based ESL Section

Duncan Place Resource Centre
4 Duncan Pl EH6 8HW
Tel: 535 4630
Fax: 535 4633

Community-based classes (held in schools and community centres all over the city) for adults permanently resident in Edinburgh who speak English as a second language. Crèche (0-5) for some classes.

Tollcross Community Education Centre

Tollcross Primary School
Fountainbridge
Contact: Pauline Fordyce
Tel: 229 8448

General day activities, including lip reading, craft classes, Gaelic Mother and Toddlers Group, Tollcross Parents Group. Free crèche for some daytime Adult Education classes.

Wester Hailes Education Centre

5 Murrayburn Drive
Edinburgh EH14 2SU
Tel: 442 2201

Modern community school providing opportunities for all ages to study or play. Amenities include library, art, drama/music studios, technical workshops, swimming pools, gymnasium, racquet sports hall, and cafeteria. Variety of classes including computing, languages, SQA subjects etc; adults may be integrated with older school pupils. Recreational classes are adult only. Rainbow Crèche (0-5yrs) for children of parents or carers who are taking classes/activities. Early registration for crèche is recommended.

YWCA Roundabout Centre

4b Gayfield Place EH7 4AB
Tel: 556 1168/557 4695

This is a small community centre committed to the eradication of racism.
Providing training and support for volunteers. Rainbow People – friendship network and support group for parents and carers of children of mixed race/dual heritage. Women's Personal Safety Action Group. Advice & Information for anyone seeking advice on volunteering, adult education, training events. Also runs a 'Budget Cookery' course. Crèche.
Other groups and classes, depending on needs. Contact centre for details.

EDUCATION & TRAINING

Edinburgh offers a huge variety of education, training and 'new direction' courses. There are also opportunities to learn a practical skill, craft or sport through the Adult Community Education Programme run by the City Council at schools throughout the city. If a venue has a crèche available, this is always mentioned in the entry.

Adult Learning Project

184 Dalry Rd
Edinburgh EH11 2EP
Contact: Stan Reeves
Tel: 337 5442

Courses, programmes, projects and events. Linking adult education and social action, incl. social and national politics, history, women's studies, language and writing, multicultural work and literacy.

Careers Scotland

(2 addresses in Edinburgh)

Cairncross House, 25 Union St EH1 3LR
Tel: 556 4110
Fax: 557 6736

Atholl House
2 Canning St EH3 8EG
Tel: 228 7520
Fax: 2292541

Information on careers, education and training. Individual career counselling services for employed and unemployed adults. Children welcome. Other premises are used, on outreach basis, for those who are out of town. Write or phone for an appointment.

Edinburgh College of Art

Lauriston Pl
Tel: 229 9311

Courses in art and design, architecture and town planning. Some evening classes available.

Employment Service

Disability Service Team
24-26 Torphichen St EH3 8JP
Contact: Jane Bruce (DST Manager)
Tel: 456 5330

Primarily for individuals with disabilities or health problems looking to return to work. Services include assessment, work preparation, job matching and practical assistance to take on employment through Access to Work.

Heriot-Watt University

Riccarton Campus EH14 4AS
Tel: 451 3451
Web: www.hw.ac.uk

Established university with excellent reputation in science, engineering, mathematics, computer science, management, finance, languages and built environment. Check website for details of courses available at undergraduate & postgraduate level.
Pinocchio's Nursery at Heriot-Watt is open Mon-Fri (0-5 yrs): Tel: 451 5236.

Jewel and Esk Valley College

Milton Rd Campus, 24 Milton Rd E
Eskbank Campus, Newbattle Rd, Dalkeith
(Also offers courses in Haddington at Alderston House)
Tel: 660 1010 for sites
Tel: 0845 850 0060 for a prospectus
Web: www.jevc.ac.uk

Wide range of educational, vocational and leisure courses. Scottish Wider Access Programmes for mature students moving on to higher education. Swimming pool and gymnasium at Milton Rd. Open learning options available. No crèche facilities.

Lasswade High School Centre

Eskdale Dr
Bonnyrigg
Tel: 663 7171/8170
Contact: Community Education Worker

A variety of daytime/evening classes for adults. Contact centre for current syllabus.

Learn Direct Scotland

Freephone: 0800 100 900
Web: www.learndirectscotland.com

Offers careers advice and course information. Advisors can give objective course information and subjective advice over the phone. LDS also provides details of other similar organisations and can forward individuals' details regarding the Government's Individual Learning Account, and can advise and explain about other sources of course funding.

Moray House Institute

Faculty of Education,
University of Edinburgh
Old Moray House, Holyrood Rd
Tel: 651 6138

Courses leading to qualifications in teaching, community education and sport and leisure. Undergraduate and post- graduate courses available. University has nursery provision.

Napier University

10 Colinton Rd
Tel: 0500 35 35 70
Email: info@napier.ac.uk
Web: www.napier.ac.uk

Full-time undergraduate, postgraduate and part-time prospectuses available from the Information Office. Flexible learning through Credit Accumulation and Transfer Scheme (CATS), as well as open learning facilities and courses, summer school and a wide range of short courses.

NISUS Scotland

121 Giles St
Director: Susan Godfrey
Tel: 554 5656

Full-time courses in Information Technology for unemployed women aged over 25 with low or no qualifications. ESF and CEC funded in partnership with Edinburgh's Telford College. EWTC also offers 'Quaytech' training - cost-effective IT skills training to both voluntary and private sectors, which is open to men and women. In addition, EWTC provides 'Flexit' – a drop-in IT training programme in hourly blocks for men or women with disabilities or health concerns.

The Number Shop

188-190 The Pleasance
Tel: 668 4787

The Number Shop is part of the City of Edinburgh Council's Community-Based Adult Education Service and provides free help with arithmetic and maths. Tuition is available to adults who want to improve their numeracy skills and to feel more confident with numbers for everyday use. Just drop-in or phone for an interview with a member of staff.

The Office of Lifelong Learning

University of Edinburgh
11 Buccleuch Place
Tel: 650 4400
Web: www.lifelong.ed.ac.uk

Offers a Return To Learning programme. Courses specifically designed for adults or those who fall into the 'mature student' category: course structures include 'New Horizons', 'Access' and 'Stepping Stones'. For more information contact RTL secretary at the above address. Evening classes on a wide range of subjects also run – contact centre for prospectus and information.

The Open University in Scotland

10 Drumsheugh Gdns
Tel: 225 2889
Web: www.open.ac.uk/scotland

The OU offers a wide range of courses, diplomas, degrees and professional qualifications. With the support of a personal tutor, you study by part-time open learning, which fits, around your family and work commitments. For many OU courses, you don't need to have qualifications. Contact the OU Course Choice Team for further information and a prospectus.

Play Scotland

Midlothian Innovation Centre,
Pentlandfield,
Roslin, Midlothian EH25 9RE
Contact: Helena Brown
Tel: 440 9070
Fax: 440 9071
Email: helenabrown@playscotland.fsnet.co.uk
Web: www.playscotland.org

A charitable organisation which provides advice and information to both its members and the public about play, funding opportunities, play provision and play training. Also acts as a pressure group to persuade others that play is important for children and young people and conduccts and stimulate research into play provision in Scotland.

Queen Margaret University College

Clerwood Terrace
EH4 4LX
Admissions contact: Alan Butchart
Tel: 317 3247

A range of full-time, part-time, distance learning, post-registration and continued professional development courses. Undergraduate and postgraduate degrees are available in the areas of health care, theatre arts and cultural management, communication and information, business and management, science and social sciences.

Scottish Pre-school Play Association (SPPA)

Head Office
45 Finnieston St,
Glasgow G3 8JU
Tel: 0141 221 4148

SPPA provides practical help with all aspects of running your pre-school group. It provides information and advice on setting up and running your group, competitive group insurance, and a range of pre-five publications and training opportunities. For membership information contact SPPA Centre.

Office covering City of Edinburgh:

264 St Vincent St,
Glasgow G2 5RL
Tel: 0141 221 9388

Local support service for playgroups, toddler groups, under fives groups and nurseries.

Scottish Wider Access Programme (SWAP)

57 George Square
Tel: 650 6861
Freephone: 0800 731 0949

Wide range of access courses to prepare adults, over 21, who do not have the standard entrance qualifications for study in further or higher education. Successful completion of an access course at an appropriate level guarantees a place at a range of colleges and universities. Part-time and flexible programmes may be available.

Second Chance to Learn

Edinburgh University Settlement
The Old Fire Station
27 East Norton Pl, London Rd EH7 5DR

Courses for adults with few or no qualifications who want to return to work or find a new direction for their lives. Courses include SQA modules in communications, numeracy and IT. Courses in child development, parenting, behaviour and play (all SQA) also available. Other venues at Craigmillar, Wester Hailes, Pilton and South Edinburgh. Free crèche.

Stevenson College of Further Education

Bankhead Ave EH11 4DE
Tel: 535 4700 (Information Centre)
Email: info@stevenson.ac.uk
Tel: 535 4725 (Information on funding and support services)
Email: studentservices@stevenson.ac.uk
Web: www.stevenson.ac.uk

Offers a wide range of courses on a full-time, part-time, evening and flexible learning basis. Courses are designed to help achieve your ambitions whether they involve returning to work or education, gaining formal qualifications or developing your career. Student support team can arrange childcare and may be able to help with fees for after schools clubs, nurseries and childminders. Contact the information centre on the above number for further information.

Edinburgh's Telford College

Crewe Toll
Tel: 332 2491
Tel: 332 2424 (Course Information Line – 24 hr service)
Email: mail@ed-coll.ac.uk
Web: www.ed-coll.ac.uk

Wide range of courses in general education, vocational skills and general and recreational interest suitable for preparing to go back to work or wishing to maintain skills and interests. Large open learning programme and a range of other attendance patterns – ask if shorter hours are possible. Some subject areas have 'drop-in' facilities which increases flexibility.
Nursery has 80 places, split into 4 rooms of 20 children (2-5 yrs). Opening times are 8.30-4.30 during term-time only. For more information phone 315 7476 and ask for Lynn McNair or Mike McMillan.

University of Edinburgh

Old College, South Bridge
Tel: 650 1000

Special prospectus for mature students. Entrance qualifications for degree courses may differ for mature students. The University has a nursery (6wks-5yrs). Tel: 667 9584, for information from nursery manager. See also Centre for Continuing Education.

Women onto Work (WOW)

137 Buccleuch St Edinburgh EH8 9NE
Tel: 662 4514
Email: mail@womenontowork.org

Courses in Craigmillar, greater Pilton, Wester Hailes, South Edinburgh and citywide. For women who have been out of paid employment, to look at options for employment or further study. Also for women from an ethnic minority or with a disability. Full childcare provided.

Workers Educational Association (WEA)

34b Thistle St North West Lane
Contact: Elizabeth Bryan or John McCaughie
Tel: 225 7772

Scottish-wide voluntary adult education organisation which works locally to encourage access to learning through life. Free, friendly and informal courses in confidence building, returning to learning, social and political studies, and the arts. Courses can be tailored to meet needs of groups.

FILM & MEDIA

Edinburgh Media Base

25a S W Thistle St Lane
EH2 1EW
Tel: 220 0220
Email: info@edinburghmediabase.com
Web: www.edinburghmediabase.com

Non-profit making organisation which offers training courses in all aspects of film making and production; also provides an equipment hire service. Sliding rates dependent on earnings.

SPORTS & LEISURE

We outline below only the centres that are run by local councils and offer reasonably priced facilities, membership and regular crèches. There are a number of health, fitness and sports centres springing up the length and breadth of the city. These usually charge a joining fee, and thereafter have a monthly payment scheme. Full details in the Yellow Pages. It's worth checking local press for up-to-date information, or indeed phoning around, as this market is very competitive and many clubs run short-term special offers for new memberships. Check the crèche facilities – there have been past examples of crèches running only for a short term and then being closed as a means of membership recruitment: if documentation mentions a crèche is planned, again proceed with caution. However, many established private clubs have established crèche facilities – which are as popular as those run within the centres run by local councils: always book your crèche place in advance.

Leisure Access Scheme

Edinburgh Leisure, which runs facilities for the City of Edinburgh Council, offer this scheme, giving access to a wide range of benefits and discounts to all Edinburgh Leisure facilities, including sports, swim and golf centres. Currently, the scheme's Leisure Access Cards cost £35 (at time of writing); concessionary groups pay between £2 and £8. There are activity prices for cardholders and non-cardholders at peak and off-peak time. Children always pay the lowest price available. You do not need a Leisure card to use facilities but if children (under 18s) or adults want to book in advance they must have one. Application forms are available from all sport and swim centres, local libraries and Edinburgh Leisure Head Office at 23 Waterloo Pl, Tel: 557 5457.

Parents and carers who are Leisure Cardholders are entitled to use on-site crèche facilities at reduced rates. For information about the crèches contact the crèche Co-ordinator on the Waterloo Pl number above. All centres can provide information about their prices, current activities and the coaching they offer. Programmes do tend to vary throughout the year, so it is advisable to check details in advance.

Edinburgh Leisure's Sports and Service Development Section, based at Meadowbank Sports Centre provides an information point for sport and recreation opportunities within Edinburgh. Will advise on classes, crèche facilities etc, Tel: 652 2178.

DANCE

Dance Base

National Centre for Dance
14-16 Grassmarket EH1 2JU
Tel: 225 5525
Web: www.dancebase.co.uk

Offers classes and workshops in a wide range of dance styles, from ballroom to belly-dancing! All ages and abilities. Also classes in Tai Chi, yoga, Pilates and Alexander Technique. See *Activities for Children* for main entry.

Edinburgh Dance Academy

65 Orchard Brae Ave
EH4 2UR
Tel: 343 1015
Email: edinburghdance@aol.com
Web: www.edinburghdanceacademy.co.uk

Ballet, Modern, Jazz and Tap lessons. Pilates-based body conditioning classes for mothers. See also *Activities for Children.*

Manor School of Ballet

Contact: Mrs Noel Platfoot (director)
Tel: 334 0399
Fax: 334 0399

Tap classes for beginners up to advanced. Keep-fit classes and ballet classes for beginners up to advanced. See *Activities for Children* for full entry.

SPORTS & LEISURE CENTRES

Ainslie Park Leisure Centre

92 Pilton Drive
Tel: 551 2400

Wide range of coaching and activity classes, including aerobics, body conditioning and sculpture, body systems, circuit training, fitness/weight training (recently refurbished gym), badminton, gymnastics, judo, step, yoga and swimming lessons for children and adults of all ages and ability. Antenatal, postnatal and aquafit exercise classes. 'Women Only' evening every Mon 18.00-22.00. Programme available from centre.

Crèche:

Mon, Tue 9.00-13.00; Wed 9.00-13.30; Thu, Fri 9.00-12.30. £3 or £2 for Leisure Access Cardholders. Must be booked in advance.

Staffed by qualified crèche workers.

Bonnyrigg Leisure Centre

King George V Park
Bonnyrigg EH19 2AD
Tel: 663 7579

Opening times: Mon-Sun 9.00-22.00 incl. most public holidays (reduced opening hours 10.00-18.00)
This centre offers a leisure pool consisting of upper and lower lagoon and special water features, and exercise studio, fitness suite, sauna and outdoor 5-a-side and tennis courts. Programmed sessions include aerobics, step, martial arts and fitness classes. Leisure Access Card scheme in operation offers discounts for concessionary groups. Crèche Mon-Fri 9.45-11.15; pre-booking essential up to 7 days in advance. Free parking. Range of snacks available from vending machine. Mixed family changing available. Coin-operated lockers and nappy changing facilities.

Countryside Ranger Service

Hermitage House
Hermitage of Braid
69a Braid Rd, Morningside
Tel: 447 7145
Email: ranger@cecrangerservice.demon.co.uk
Web: www.cecrangerservice.demon.co.uk

Guided walks and special events programme based on various themes for all the family all year round. Phone for information and programme – rangers are very helpful. Details of women's walks programme advertised in local notice boards and local press – especially 'Herald and Post'.

Craiglockhart Tennis & Sports Centre

177 Colinton Rd
Tel: 443 0101 (Sports Centre)
Tel: 444 1969 (Tennis Centre)

Opening times: Mon-Thu 9.00-23.00; Fri 10.00-23.00; Sat, Sun 9.00-22.30
City's main public centre for racquet sports, with indoor tennis, badminton and squash. Coaching in aerobics, step, weight training, keep-fit and trampolining. Well equipped weights gym. Outdoor facilities include tennis courts and boating pond. Easy access for pushchairs. Programme available from centre. The tennis facilities include 6 indoor courts and 8 outdoor, with a main centre court. Tennis coaching classes available by block booking or drop in for 'women only' sessions: Mon, Wed 9.30-11.00, 11.00-12.30 and Fri 10.30-12.30. Free car parking at the tennis centre; short walk down two flights of stairs to the main centre.
There are crèche facilities at the main centre for under 5s only. £3 (£2 Leisure Access Cardholders): run by qualified staff, must be booked in advance. Phone centre for details.

Dalry Swim Centre

Caledonian Cres
Tel: 313 3964

Range of exercise and aquafit classes and swimming classes. Antenatal class Tue 9.00-9.40. Sauna. Full programme available from centre. No crèche facilities.

Drumbrae Leisure Centre

30 Drumbrae Ter
Tel: 312 7957

Modern leisure centre offering a wide range of activities, including sports coaching and swimming lessons, exercise classes, women-only sessions. There is a 'pulse centre' with easy to use equipment. Centre is all on one level, which makes for all-round easy access. Full programme with current times etc available from centre. Crèche facilities available – best to book ahead. Centre also has a café and vending machines.

Glenogle Swim Centre

Glenogle Rd
Tel: 343 6376

Leisure Centre with pool, sauna, gym and wide range of fitness classes, such as Yoga, Pilates and Bodybalance. Comprehensive Programme of swimming lessons for adults and children. Antenatal exercise session Mon 9.00-9.40 all year, plus Wed 9.00-9.40 in winter. Full programme available from the centre. No crèche.

Gorgie Dalry Community Association

22 McLeod St
Contact: Jim Young
Tel/Fax: 337 3252

Mon-Sat 9.00-18.00 (plus some evenings); Sun 11.00-19.00 (staffed only when classes are on).
Formed from an amalgamated sports centre/community association – activities include football, basketball, tennis, hockey, badminton cricket, self-defence and general keep-fit classes. Can also host one-off social and community events. Crèche (under 3s). Call centre for full details.

Gracemount Leisure Centre

22 Gracemount Dr
Tel: 658 1940

Facilities include multi-purpose games hall hosting badminton, basketball, 5-a-side football, volleyball, gymnastics, trampolining, indoor hockey, short tennis, table tennis, martial arts, and fitness studio. Crèche. A wide range of fitness classes for all ages and abilities are available. 'Women only' evening Wed 18.00-21.00. Sports camps during school holidays. Programme available from centre. Good access with lift and ramps to all floors. Crèche Mon, Wed and Fri 9.15-10.45, 10.50-12.15; cost £2.50, Leisure Access Cardholders £1.50. Must be booked (up to 7 days in advance). Café and vending machines on site.

Inch Community Centre

255 Gilmerton Rd
Tel: 664 4710

Exercise class Fri 9.15-10.15, £1.50/class. Free crèche.

Jack Kane Sports Centre

208 Niddrie Mains Rd
Tel: 664 4710 or 669 0404

Centre has facilities for badminton, martial arts, football, basketball, pulse centre, free weights, hockey, gymnastics. Programme available from centre. No crèche.

Kirkliston Leisure Centre

Kirklands Park St
Tel: 333 4700

Multi-purpose sports hall. Outdoor tennis and 5-a-side facilities. 'Women only' sessions. Crèche available and breastfeeding welcome. Nappy changing facilities. Good access, all on one level. Free car parking. Play area for older children to the rear of building.

Lasswade High School Centre

Eskdale Dr
Bonnyrigg, Midlothian EH19 2LA
Tel: 663 7171 (Main Office)
Tel: 663 8170 (Community Education)
Tel: 660 1933 (Sports Centre)

Facilities include main sports hall, 2 squash courts, weight training room, fitness suite, activities studio, gymnasium, lounge, cafeteria, outdoor facilities, indoor football and rugby. Also a variety of daytime/evening classes for adults.
Kiddie Trampers and Kiddie Kartwheels are available for 2½ year olds to 5 year olds.
Crèche morning sessions Mon-Fri 9.00-12.00; afternoon sessions 1.00-3.00/3.45; staffed by qualified nursery nurses, £1.20/session. Shoppers' Crèche available at a higher cost of £2.30. Book 7 days in advance from 9.00 am daily.

Leith Victoria Swim Centre

Junction Pl
Tel: 555 4728

Swimming pool, sauna, pulse centre, fitness programme including women only sessions, beauty therapy and a variety of relaxation classes. Hot and cold vending machines. Crèche available Mon-Fri 9.00-12.00 (phone to book). Car parking, including disabled parking, at Bonnington Rd entrance. Lift available with disabled access to pool and Pulse Centre. Full details of current hours and programme of events available from reception.

Leith Waterworld

337 Easter Rd
EH6 8HU
Tel: 555 6000

Adult aqua fit classes Fri 11.15-12.00; £2.00/class
Parent and toddlers classes Fri 10.15-11.00 ; £2.60/class

Loanhead Leisure Centre

George Ave
Loanhead
Tel: 440 4516

This modern leisure centre has a swimming pool, fitness suite, exercise studio and outdoor 5-a-side and tennis courts. Contact centre for details of exercise classes and other activities. Crèche facilities available.

Meadowbank Sports Centre

139 London Rd
Tel: 661 5351

Opening times: Mon 9.30-22.30 (last booking 21.30), Tue-Sun 9.00-22.30.
Excellent centre on 3 floors. Facilities for over 30 sports including badminton, squash, yoga, aerobics, step, fitness centre and running track. Ramped access and automatic doors wide enough for a double pushchair. Lift for disabled centre users and parents with small children. Full programme available from centre.

Musselburgh Sports Centre

Newbigging
Musselburgh EH21 7AS
Tel: 653 6367

Modern leisure centre offering squash, multi-purpose sports hall, bodyworks gym, meeting room, dance studio and lounge area, plus swimming pool, health suite with sauna, steam room, spa and café. Wide range of activities, including: hockey, volleyball, badminton, squash, table tennis, basketball, trampolining, and judo. Fitness classes include step, aerobics, aquafit and body conditioning. Programme available from centre.
Crèche coincides with step and aerobic classes, although parents can use any facilities at these times. Advisable to book up to 7 days in advance.

Portobello Indoor Bowls and Leisure Centre

20 Westbank St
Portobello EH15 1DR
Tel: 669 0878

Winter: indoor bowls and fitness classes. Adults' and children's classes in a wide range of activities.
Summer: indoor bowling and a wide range of activities for adults and children. Good access, with lift to first floor. Breastfeeding welcome. Nappy changing facilities. Catering -contact centre for function / bar / cafeteria details.

Portobello Swim Centre

57 The Promenade
Portobello
Tel: 669 6888

Wide range of facilities, including Turkish baths. Also pulse centre with cardiovascular and resistance equipment. Make an appointment for induction. Alternatively, you can just go for a swim. Aquafit ante-/postnatal classes. Pay as you go swim lessons for adults. Café on 1st floor, accessible by lift.
Crèche (0-5 yrs), Mon-Fri 9.00-12.00. Cost £3 (non-leisure cardholders and £2 Leisure Access Cardholders). Always 2 experienced crèche workers on duty. During crèche times, centre offers adult swimming classes for all abilities and fitness classes (including step and aerobics) for men and women in the fitness centre.

Queensferry High Recreation Centre

30 Ashburnham Rd
S Queensferry
Tel: 319 3222

Opening times: Mon-Thu 16.30-22.00; Fri 16.00-22.00; Sat 10.00-17.00; Sun 9.00-17.00. For opening hours during school holidays, please contact centre.
Casual bookings welcomed for badminton, table tennis, 5-a-side football, basketball, short tennis, pool and pulse centre. Adult coaching lessons in swimming, aquafit, aerobics, step, fitness training, subaqua and badminton. Contact centre for details of times, prices and booking information.
Children's activities include swimming lessons, tots tennis, short tennis, holiday activity camps. See also *Birthdays & Celebrations*.

Ratho Community Centre

1 School Wynd
Ratho EH28 8TT
Contact: Dave Stewart
Tel: 333 1055

Keep-fit, Fri 9.30-11.00. £2.50/session. Crèche (under 5s) £1/child or £1.50 for 2 or more. Staffed by the appropriate no. of crèche workers. Coffee bar facilities available.

Royal Commonwealth Pool

Tel: 667 7211

The pool offers a wide range of activities/swimming sessions with something to suit all the family. Programme available from centre. Crèche (5 and under); Leisure Cardholder £2, non-holder £3. (Mon-Fri 9.00-12.00). Two experienced crèche workers on duty at all times. Can be booked in advance if you are attending a course of activity/swimming lessons.
You can also use the crèche, if there are spaces available, when using pool or fitness room. See *Activities for Children* for full entry.

Saughton Sports Complex

Stevenson Dr, Balgreen
Tel: 444 0422

Sports complex with outdoor facilities for football, 5-a-side football, tennis, hockey and running track with floodlights; run in safety and meet new training partners. Suitable for all levels and supervised by a qualified coach. Small pulse gym.

South Queensferry Community Centre

Joint Sites - Community Centre, Kirkliston Rd, S Queensferry & Rosebery Hall, S Queensferry
Tel: 331 2113
Contact: Steve Stewart

Badminton Tue 9.15-11.15, at Rosebery Hall site. Crèche available; 75p/first child, 50p/subsequent children. Enquiries on the above no. between 8.30-14.30, Mon-Fri.

Warrender Swim Centre

Thirlestane Rd
Marchmont EH9 1AP
Tel: 447 0052

Full range of classes available including aquafit, antenatal, parent and child. Masters swimming lessons also available. Sauna. Yoga classes, Pulse Fitness Suite with full range of resistance and cardiovascular fitness equipment. Full programme available from centre. No crèche facilities

Wester Hailes Education Centre

5 Murrayburn Drive
Edinburgh EH14 2SU
Tel: 442 2201

This community leisure centre offers a programme of aerobics, aquafit and other activity classes for adults. Women-only swimming on Wednesday evenings. Crèche available (only open term times, not open in the evening). Phone for details.

Annual Events

ANNUAL EVENTS

A vast range of events are hosted in and around Edinburgh. Some have a long history, others are more recently established events. We have also listed some of the holiday clubs which are available. Keep an eye on local press for details of others. When there's a lot going on, we've listed the information by location: 'in the city', 'close to home', and 'further afield'. For more information, why not go online – sites such as www.edinburg.org or www.eventful-edinburgh.com may prove helpful.

JANUARY- MARCH

The start of the year can be a bit of an anti-climax: Christmas is over, the lights are down in the city and the outlook could seem a bit bleak. However, there are always lots to go and see …

PANTOMIMES & PLAYS

The panto season extends over the Winter season. If you are thinking about going to one, why not consider waiting until after Christmas, otherwise the outing might just become part of the exciting blur leading up to Santa's visit. Venues such as the King's Theatre, the Royal Lyceum, Theatre Workshop and the Netherbow stage traditional pantos and also more contemporary shows.

Although some of the pantos have famous names heading the bill, they tend to appeal to an older audience and they can be a bit long for under fives. Plus remember that the jokes tend to become more adult in the evening performances! Probably more suitable for under 5s are shows such as those from 'The Happy Gang' or 'The Singing Kettle'. See press for details and *Places to Visit*, for addresses and facilities.

Snowdrops at Dalmeny House

Dalmeny House
Nr S Queensferry
Tel: 331 1888
Web: www.dalmeny.co.uk

Although the house is only open in the Summer, the gardens are opened specially on a Sun during Feb/Mar for Snowdrop Day – the exact date depends on when the snowdrops come out! Impressive display on Mons Hill. Backpacks, wellies and warm socks recommended. Refreshments available in the tearoom.

This is a charity event and all funds raised benefit St Columba's Hospice, The Queen's Nursing Institute of Scotland and The Garden Fund of the National Trust for Scotland. Try going online for current information.

EASTER EVENTS & EASTER BREAK LEISURE SCHEMES

IN THE CITY

Easter Egg Rolling

Holyrood Park
Park Rangers' office
Tel: 556 1761

At Dunsapie Loch in Holyrood Park, Easter Sunday. This is an unofficial, but extremely popular event.

Craiglockhart Tennis & Sports Centre

Tel: 443 0101

Tots tennis (3-5 yrs) £6.50/4 days. Booking essential.

Edinburgh Zoo

Easter Treasure Trail
Tel: 334 9171
Web: edinburghzoo.org.uk

Easter Sunday, Monday. Two age groups: 7 and under, 8 and over. 'Follow the animal clues and find a chocolate surprise'. No extra charge. No booking necessary. Zoo holds other special events on a daily basis during school holidays, such as brass rubbing, touch tables and information talks.

St Bride's Centre

10 Orwell Ter
Tel: 346 1405

Contact centre for current information regarding children's summer programmes. Events are run for children aged 4+ years.

CLOSE TO HOME

Easter 'Eggcitement'

Almond Valley Heritage Centre
Livingston Village
Tel: 01506 414957
Web: www.almondvalley.co.uk

During a fortnight over Easter, 10.00-17.00.

Lambs, chicks and other baby animals to see; egg painting, bonnet making and an Easter Trail. Standard admission charges apply (see *Out of Town Trips: W Lothian*).

Easter Egg Specials

Bo'ness and Kinneil Railway
Tel: 01506 822298
Tel: 01506 824356 for information on this special event
Web: www.srps.org.uk

From Edinburgh, travel along the M9, leave at J3 and follow the A904 to Bo'ness. The railway is situated near the town centre, behind Tesco's car park.
Easter w/end, Fri-Mon, 7 journeys per day, starting at 10.30. Last train 16.30
This event has slight variation per year, but includes the likes of face painting, children's entertainment, a colouring competition, a hunt-the-easter-egg game and an easter bonnet competition. During the train ride, the Easter Bunny distributes eggs. Charges vary from usual rates – adult/ child £7, under 2s free; family saver (4 seats) ticket usually available c. £25

Hopetoun House

South Queensferry
Tel: 331 2451
Web: www.hopetounhouse.com

Lots of arts, crafts and entertainment for the children including a chick hunt throughout the house itself. Other planned events include a Summer fair, teddy bear's picnic etc. Contact venue for dates and prices.

FURTHER AFIELD

Easter Egg Extravaganza

Traquair House
Innerleithen EH44 6PW
Tel: 01896 830323
Web: www.traquair.co.uk
Email: enquiries@traquair.co.uk

Easter Sunday, 14.30 onwards.
Over 3500 mini eggs hidden in the maze for under 10s to hunt out and eat! Other entertainment also available, which varies from year to year. Ground admission charges apply.

Easter Fun

New Lanark Visitor Centre
Tel: 01555 661 345

Easter Sunday and Monday 12.00-16.00. Activities usually include a treasure trail and Easter Bunnies distributing eggs around the centre.

Currie and Balerno Community Schools Partnership

Tel: 477 7733
Contact: Margaret Knight, Asst Community Programme Manager

Offers several programmes, usually for 3-4 yr olds and 4-immediate pre-school aged children. For the younger age range, the programme incorporates early learning skills in a range of creative and physical activities; for older children, there is a variety of fun, educational and recreational activities for children about to start primary school in the Autumn of the current year. Mid-morning juice and biscuits are included in course fees.
It is recommended that children in both activities wear old clothes in case of paint spillage etc. All children must be toilet trained.
Also pre-school swimming classes for children who will be starting primary school in the Autumn of the current year. Parents are not required to be in the pool.
Booking recommended, although activities may also be booked on a daily basis.

APRIL-MAY

IN THE CITY

Edinburgh International Science Festival

Web: www.sciencefestival.co.uk

This is the largest science festival in the world. Various venues throughout the city, including the Science Play Centre at the Assembly Rooms. Programme becomes available at the beginning of March. Interesting, gooey and exciting events for all ages from 3yrs upwards. See programme for details of shows - pick one up from bookshops throughout the city or from The Hub, tel: 473 2070. Best to book well in advance.

NCT SALES

NCT Centre
University Health Service
5th Floor
5 Bristo Square EH3 9AL
Tel: 668 3257
Web: nct-edinburgh.freeserve.co.uk

Edinburgh North and South Branches hold annual sales of nearly new nursery equipment, children's and maternity clothes and toys. A small percentage from the sale goes to NCT funds, the rest to the seller. First sale of the year is usually in Spring and sales are held approximately 8 times a year. Venues vary. Contact the NCT centre, or see press for details.

Balerno Children's Gala

Tel: 449 5582
Contact: Brian Conway

Last week in May. Week starts with a procession of floats and crowning of the Gala Queen. Many events held around the village during the week leading up to the gala day, including bike races for all ages and a pet show. There are children's races, bouncy castles, a disco magic and puppet shows and many stalls representing local clubs on the day. 13.00-17.00 in Malleny Park (or the High school, if raining).

Lauriston Castle grounds, Cramond

Tel: 336 2060

Lauriston Castle hosts a series of Summer events. To keep everything dynamic, the programme usually changes from year to year, so contact Castle for information. However, for the last few years, they have hosted a teddy bears picnic every second year: next one due 2005. Usual charges for castle itself.

Royal Highland Show

Royal Highland Centre, Ingilston
Edinburgh EH28 8NF
Tel: 335 6200
Web: www.royalhighlandshow.org.uk

Thu-Sun 3rd week in June.
Showground open 8.00-20.00 Thu-Sat, 8.00-19.00 Sun
Approximate admission prices: £16 for adults (£10 student/ senior citizens concessions) Accompanied children under the age of 16 free. Reduced prices after 16.00. Disabled visitors are not given concessionary rates but their carer receives free entry. See media or website for advance booking. Car parking is £4 per vehicle per admission.
Special buses usually run from Edinburgh out to the showground (phone Traveline for details: 225 3858)
There's a huge range of attractions available within the showground and the show does offer specific activities etc especially for children, although the very size of the place might be a little overwhelming for them at first. It makes no difference to children that the cattle, sheep, horses, poultry etc are the country's finest – it's fun just to see them up close! Each year there are unique attractions, so the show has an individual input every year.
The show has a crèche with registered staff, and also provides a breast feeding area, along with bottle warming facilities.

Scottish International Children's Festival

Imaginate
45a George St
Edinburgh EH2 2HT
Tel: 225 8050
Web: www.imaginate.org.uk

Held at various venues around the city for one wk (Mon-Sun) May/June. This is Britain's largest performing arts festival for children. Aimed specifically at 3-14yrs, with weekend afternoon shows programmed so that the majority of the family can be catered for ie. a show for ages 3-6yrs will run simultaneously with one for, say, 5-12yrs. Venues are chosen for child friendliness. Venue cafés provide child orientated menus during festival run. free childcare for babies and toddlers - book your place(s) when you book a performance, details of crèche available on booking. Programmes available beginning of April.

CLOSE TO HOME

Day Out with Thomas at Bo'ness and Kinneil Railway

Tel: 01506 822298
Tel: 01506 824356 for information on this special event.
Web: www.srps.org.uk

From Edinburgh, travel along the M9, leave at J3 and follow the A904 to Bo'ness. The railway is situated near the town centre, behind Tesco's car park.
Over a long weekend in mid-May. First train leaves at 10.30, last train leaves at 16.30. Engines wear a 'Thomas' type face. There's a bouncy castle, a children's roundabout, face painting, an inflatable slide – and the Fat Controller is usually around just to keep everyone on their best behaviour! There's no advance booking so it's probably best to get there early. Adult/child £7, under 2s 7 free; family ticket (4 seats) c.£25.

FURTHER AFIELD

Links Market

Town House, Kirkcaldy
Contact: John Haggart
Tel. 01592 417843
Web: www.fifedirect.org.uk (look under 'Leisure')

Kirkcaldy Esplanade. This historic fair lasts 6 days, starting on Wed before 3rd Fri in April. Reputedly the longest street funfair in Europe - perhaps in the world, and April 2004 saw its 700th anniversary. Numerous rides and stalls for under 5s. Wed from

14.30, Thu-Mon from 13.00. Well worth the 40 min drive across the Forth Bridge! Trains from Waverley and Haymarket.

Spring Fling

Summerlee Heritage Park
Coatbridge
Tel: 01236 431261

3 day festival for children on May Bank Holiday w/end. Free entry.

JUNE-JULY

IN THE CITY

Currie and Balerno Community Schools Partnership

Tel: 477 7733
Contact: Margaret Knight, Asst Community Programme Manager

Summer break programmes for toddlers through to pre-schoolage. Also offer swimming classes. See 'Easter' entry for full information.

Edinburgh Zoo

Tel: 334 9171
Web: edinburghzoo.org.uk

Special events throughout the Summer. Check the zoo's website for up-to-date details.

St Bride's Centre

10 Orwell Ter
Tel: 346 1405

Contact centre for current information regarding children's Summer programmes. Events are run for children aged 4+ years.

CLOSE TO HOME

Lifeboat Week

Tel: 01620 892197
Contact: North Berwick Tourist Information

Take A198 to N Berwick. Regular bus and train services.
North Berwick, last week in July. All kinds of fundraising events and an opportunity to see Blue Peter III, the only Scottish based lifeboat to be funded by Blue Peter.

Museum of Flight

East Fortune Airfield, East Lothian
Tel: 01620 880308
Web: www.nms.ac.uk/flight or www.scotwings.co.uk

There's usually a festival of flight show in mid-July. 2003 saw the centenary of flight celebrated, but whatever the date, these shows are spectacular events for anyone interested in aviation. July plays host to Scotland's largest civil air show with fantastic air displays. Recent inclusions included an evening event with flights choreographed to music. Peripheral attractions usually include stalls, bouncy castle, refreshments etc. The museum recommends ear plugs for young children. Only guide/hearing dogs permitted entry.
Ticketed events, expect to pay £10/adult. A family ticket (2A + 3C) costs approx £30. Under 5s free. Discounts available on advance online bookings and for NMS members.
In general, the Museum of Flight has ample car parking facilities. There are nappy changing facilities in the toilet facilities for the disabled visitors. The Parachute café offers a range of fresh snacks and treats.

Queensferry High Recreation Centre

30 Ashburnham Rd
S Queensferry
Tel: 319 3222

Centre runs holiday activity camps. Contact venue for details.

GALAS/FESTIVALS

Many local Galas that are held in the city and the Lothians take place in June. These may be the principal annual event that annually draws a community together and they are well worth supporting – although due to changing local demographics and funding difficulties many are finding it hard to continue. We have listed just a few of them.

Clermiston and Drumbrae Children's Gala

Contact: Karen Keil
Tel: 339 4149

Location: Drum Brae Leisure Centre. Usually held on the 2nd Sat in June. However, 2004's Gala will take place in Sep to coincide with the 50th anniversary of the building of Clermiston. Attractions and events usually include a parade, a fun fair, magicians, clowns etc. Day finishes with a children's disco.

Corstorphine Fair

Contact: Corstorphine Fair Committee
c/o 42/5 Gogarloch Syke
Edinburgh EH12 9JB
Web: www.corstorphinefair.org.uk

Main location: St Margaret's Park. Biennial event on 1st Sat in June - due 2004/2006. A large, extremely well-supported community event with many stalls (100+ in 2002) and attractions such as a bouncy castle, pony rides, face painting, funfair rides, puppets, dancers and displays, plus a handy NCT feeding and changing tent. The celebrations last around a week and include a duck race and an 'Open Doors' day event on the days running up to the fair day itself.

Davidson's Mains Gala Day

Contact: Susan Robertson
Tel: 336 2572
Web: www.dmainsgala.org.uk

Location: Lauriston Castle grounds. 3rd Sat in June. A traditional gala, complete with a parade along Davidson's Mains Main Street, leaving the War memorial at 11.30, with the Gala Queen-elect riding in a horse-drawn carriage. After the Queen's crowning there's plenty of family orientated entertainment laid on, including pony rides, a bouncy castle, 'Thomas' rides and stalls.

Gorgie Dalry Gala Day

Tel: 337 3252 (community centre)
Contact Jim Young

Murieston Park. 2nd w/end in June, Sat 12.00-16.00. Puppet shows, children's entertainers, clowns, theatre for children and many shows free.

Kirkliston Gala

Contact: Leisure Centre
Tel: 333 4700

Kirkliston Leisure Centre. 2nd Sat in June. Parade through village. Displays, bands, model railway and races.

Leith Festival

Web: www.leithfestival.com

Leith Festival is a Community Festival for the people of Leith and North Edinburgh. The festival runs from Sun-Sat at the beginning of June.

In recent years the Festival has grown and now offers something for the under-fives throughout the week, mostly during the day, in various venues in Leith. You can find out more about the festival by listening to Leith FM, the Festival's own radio station which broadcasts on 87.7fm during the festival week (subject to licence). The Festival ends with a walking parade down Leith Walk commencing at noon. The parade finishes at Leith Links with a traditional gala day with stalls, funfair, hot air balloon, football competitions, a tug of war and live music. Look out for the programme usually published just after Easter or go online.

Meadows Festival

Contact: Meadows Festival Association
PO Box 1053
Edinburgh EH7 5YA
Tel/fax: 620 9108 (24 hrs)

Sat and Sun beginning June. A popular festival, with stalls, funfair, puppets, children's competitions, face painting, live music etc. Free crèche. Feeding / changing tent run by NCT. This is a long-running event (2004 will see its 30th anniversary), but various set-backs always seem to threaten its ongoing existence.

Stockbridge Festival

Contact: Ken Hyde
Tel: 557 1925

Weekend at end of June. Street party in St Stephen St all day Sat. On Sun at 15.00 the famous duck race takes place – ducks are launched off the bridge across the river – stand down on the river path beside Pizza Express to get a close-up view! Ducks for sale in the previous weeks in local shops such as Stockbridge Bookshop and the Baillie pub. Events during the preceding week such as quizzes, fun fair in Inverleith Park etc.

CLOSE TO HOME

Bo'ness Fair Day

Take M9 out of Edinburgh. Come off at J5 and follow the signs to Bo'ness on the A904. Alternatively, take A90 out of Edinburgh, then follow the A904 out through Newton to Champany Corner on the A904. Turn right and follow the road to Bo'ness. 2nd Fri in July. Reputedly the largest fair in Scotland. Extremely well supported and a good example of a traditional 'Fair-day'. It's worthwhile taking a trip through prior to the actual fair,to see the impressive house frontages which decorate the homes of the children involved. The Queen is chosen from one of the town's schools, so the focus is on a different part of the town each year.

AUGUST-SEPTEMBER

August is Edinburgh's busiest month of the year, as people from all over the world descend upon the city for the Edinburgh International Festival and the Fringe. The city's population is said to double in August. There are breathtaking numbers of official events – and almost the same amount of street entertainers, although licensing is reducing their numbers year on year. Free snippets of acts can be seen on the main stage in Princes Street gardens during the day and evening. So hold on to your toddler, turn up and enjoy yourselves!

IN THE CITY

Edinburgh Festival Fringe

180 High St
Contact: Fringe Office
Tel: 226 5257
Web: www.edfringe.com

Cited in the Guinness Book of Records as the largest Arts Festival in the world! A myriad of events, such as puppet shows, magic, drama and music at venues throughout the city. The programme lists events by age group. Programme free from the Fringe Office and other venues round the city - bookshops are the best bet for picking one up.

Fringe Sunday

180 High St
Contact: Fringe Office
Tel: 226 5257
Web: www.edfringe.com

Location: The Meadows. 2nd Sun of Festival 11.00-17.00. This is an exuberant melange of what's on offer throughout the Fringe: it's bright, loud and tends to reflect the essence of what the Fringe is about. It's also extremely busy, so hold on to small hands! There is normally a handy NCT feeding and changing tent.

Edinburgh International Book Festival

137 Dundee Street Edinburgh EH11 1BG.
Tel: 228 5444
Tel: 624 5050 (box office)
Email: admin@edbookfest.co.uk
Web: www.edbookfest.co.uk

Location: Charlotte Square. Mid Aug. 9.30-21.30 daily. Europe's largest book event. Plenty for children of all ages, including including events especially for 0-5s. There's a dedicated Children's Bookshop, workshops, storytelling from favourite authors, demonstrations from illustrators and even visits by well loved characters. Tickets can be booked in advance or on the day, but popular events do sell out very quickly. Some events are free. Cafés on site. Log on to the website, where there's specific info about the Children's Book Festival.

Edinburgh International Festival

The Hub, Castlehill, Royal Mile
Tel: 473 2000
Web: www.eif.co.uk

Held in venues throughout the city. The reputation has taken Edinburgh's name to all parts of the globe. Events include theatre, puppet shows, dance, opera and music – some shows may be suitable for under 5s, it all depends on the programme. Full programme available from end of March onwards – again, check your nearest bookshop for a copy. What might be of more interest is the Fireworks Concert, held at the end of the Festival (see below).

Festival Cavalcade

Procession of floats, pipe bands, members of Tattoo etc on 1st Sun of festival. Starts at Waterloo Pl at around 14.30, proceeds along Princes St and arrives at the Grassmarket at approx 16.00. Very popular, so arrive early to secure good viewpoint. May be a little long and loud for some under 5s. See local press for information.

Festival Fireworks

A spectacular farewell to the Festival! Music, 'son et lumière' fireworks display free to the public. The castle and the castle rock provide a dramatic backdrop. For a seat at the concert performed by the Chamber Orchestra in Princes St Gardens, book very early at The Hub (it's done by postal ballot and the closing date's in May!). Small children may be wary of the loud noise and the crowds, which can be very heavy around Princes St, George St and The Mound. Quieter locations, still with great views, are around Bruntsfield Links and Inverleith Park - take a radio as at least one local station has coverage - so you can hear the music while watching.

Edinburgh Mela

Contact: The Arts Quarter
Gateway Theatre, Elm Row
Edinburgh EH7 4AH
Tel: 557 1400
Web: www.edinburgh-mela.co.uk

Location: Pilrig Park. Last weekend in Aug / 1st weekend in Sept. The Edinburgh Mela is a long established celebration of multiculturalism. The park is transformed with stalls, sculptures and artworks. Music, puppet shows and performers. Children's workshops vary each year, but they are mostly best suited to older children. The fun is for all the family however and most events are free. Other events around city in week running up to w/end. For information, try going online.

Edinburgh Military Tattoo

Tattoo Office, 32 Market Street
Edinburgh EH1 1QB
Tel: 225 1188 (Box Office)
Fax: 225 8627
Email: edintattoo@edintattoo.co.uk
Web: www.edinburgh-tattoo.co.uk.

Location: Edinburgh Castle Esplanade. First 3 wks in Aug. Famous event including pipes, drums and massed bands, as well as international music, theatre and dance. There's a different theme each year. Performances start late; Mon-Fri 21.00, Sat 22.30, but there's additional early shows on Sat at 19.30 (book early as it's very popular). Quite ambitious event to take under 5s to, due to the length of show and the bangs and crashes that can be part of the displays, but they go free if they sit on an adult's knee. Seating is hard and can be cold – take a cushion along! Tickets half-price at dress rehearsal. Blankets and refreshments advised.

NCT Sponsored Toddle

NCT Centre
University Health Service
5th Floor
5 Bristo Square EH3 9AL
Tel: 668 3257
Web: nct-edinburgh.freeserve.co.uk

A fun event for families with pre-school children, to raise funds for Edinburgh NCT.

Scotland Yard Summer Festival

Contact: Alison Harper
Tel: 557 8199

King George V Park, Canonmills. Variable dates in Aug. Family festival, with stalls, activities and music.

CLOSE TO HOME

Almond Valley Heritage Centre

Livingston Village
Tel: 01506 414957
Web: www.almondvalley.co.uk

'Yesterday's Harvest'. Last Sun in Aug. 10.00-17.00. See how the harvest used to be gathered, as some of the old machinery is dusted off and put to work. Join in with tattie howkin and stookin hay. You can try making your own corn dollies ... rolling in the haystacks available too!

'Railway Shuntabout', last weekend in Aug. See the special trains on the narrow-gauge railway and keep your eyes peeled for some of the centre's more unusual engines.

Day Out with Thomas

Bo'ness and Kinneil Railway
Tel: 01506 822298
Web: www.srps.org.uk

Fri, Sat and Sun in Aug. Fares as in May entry. Contact Scottish Railway Preservation Society for exact dates.

Vogrie Festival Day

Contact: Yvonne Anderson
Tel: 271 3353

Vogrie Country Park. 2nd Sun in mid-Aug. 11.00-17.00. Large event throughout grounds includes puppet shows, magicians, music, model railway, funfair and much more! Phone for current entrance prices.

FURTHER AFIELD

Traquair Fair

Traquair House
Innerleithen EH44 6PW
Tel: 01896 830323
Email: enquiries@traquair.co.uk
Web: www.traquair.co.uk

1st weekend in Aug. Entertainment for all the family. Recently, themed fairs have opened up new dimension to this well-established event. Entertainment on offer includes the likes of theatre, live music, street entertainers, clowns, workshops, crafts etc. Children's entertainment includes well known children's musicians (the likes of Mr Boom, Jo Jingles etc) magicians, face painting, art workshops, a mini train, swing boats and so on. Special entrance prices for this weekend. Expect to pay in the region of £14/adult, £8/child. £38/family (2A & 3C). Under 5s free . Advance purchase discounts available.

OCTOBER-NOVEMBER

IN THE CITY

Scottish International Storytelling Festival

43-45 High Street
Contact: The Netherbow
Tel: 556 9597

Web: scottishstorytellingcentre.co.uk

Various venues throughout the Lothians, end Oct-mid Nov. A two week feast of storytelling from the oral tradition for all the family. Booking essential.

Fireworks Extravaganza

Meadowbank Sports Centre
Contact: Gary Hanley, Duty Manager at the stadium
Tel: 661 5351

Large well organised display. Popular with an older audience but may prove a bit overwhelming for under 5s.

Smaller fireworks displays organised by local Scout or Round Table groups are advertised locally. See press for details. For information on firework displays, phone City of Edinburgh Council Recreation Dept, tel: 529 7844.

CLOSE TO HOME

Spooky Happenings

Almond Valley Heritage Centre
Tel: 01506 414957
Web: www.almondvalley.co.uk

Runs for 2 wks during Oct. Open 18.00-21.00 on Hallowe'en. Special events include ghost hunts, a 'trail of terror', monster masks makes, and other Hallowe'en horrors. Certain to scare the adults! Standard admission charges.

Wizards and Witches Rides

Bo'ness & Kinneil Railway
Tel: 01506 822298
Web: www.srps.org.uk

The weekend nearest Hallowe'en. £7 per person. Children under 2 free. Family ticket (4 seats) £25.Trains run from 10.30 and run every hour until 16.30. Enjoy (or otherwise!) a train ride, complete with a visit to the Witches' Cavern.There's also a magic show, and prizes awarded throughout the weekend for the best fancy dress.

FURTHER AFIELD

Traquair Christmas Fair

Traquair House, Innerleithen,
Peeblesshire, EH44 6PW
Tel: 01896 830323
Email: enquiries@traquair.co.uk

Last Sat & Sun in Nov.
An opportunity to combine Christmas shopping with a day out (if you are so inclined!). Santa usually has a presence here, and there are other attractions for children such as a puppet show. Ease yourself into the festive shopping spree, with a mooch around craft stalls and some mulled wine. Free entry to the house and grounds. For information, contact Traquair house by the means above.

DECEMBER

IN THE CITY

Edinburgh's Capital Christmas

Tel: 529 4310
Web: www.capitalchristmas.co.uk

End of Nov-24 Dec. A varied programme of street theatre, a parade, shopping opportunities in the themed Christmas market in Princes Street Gardens, and perhaps best of all for under 5s, the switching on of the Christmas lights. See local press near the time for details.The city's Hogmanay celebrations run-on almost seamlessly from this event (see 'After Christmas' section).

Edinburgh Zoo

Tel: 334 9171
Web: www.edinburghzoo.org.uk

Usually hosts a Santa weekend, the weekend before Christmas, with Santa roaming around the Zoo from 11.00am - 4.00pm - children can get a gift from his sack for £1.However, it is not certain whether this weekend may run 2004/5. Please check with the Zoo.

CLOSE TO HOME

Santa Barge Trips

Edinburgh Canal Centre, Ratho
Tel: 333 1320
Email: info@bridgeinn.com
Web: www.bridgeinn.com

Santa Cruises run each w/end from the beginning of Dec until Christmas week when they become daily. Cruises are 1 hr long and times vary from early morning until evening. Santa comes on-board and and distributes gifts for the children: there are mince pies and coffee for parents so you don't feel too left out. Booking essential! Cost: around £7.50

Santa Special Weekends

Almond Valley Heritage Centre
Livingston Village
Tel: 01506 414957
Web: www.almondvalley.co.uk

4 w/ends prior to Christmas. Visit Santa's farmyard cottage, enjoy a nativity scene with the animals, and make traditional Christmas decorations. There are also narrow gauge railway trips to the 'North Pole'. Standard admission prices apply with extra charge for Santa visit.

Santa Steam Trains

Bo'ness and Kinneil Railway
Tel: 01506 822298
Web: www.srps.org.uk

4 w/ends leading up to Christmas. Sat and Sun 10.30; 12.00; 13.30; 15.00. Santa visits each child with a gift during the 50 min journey,. Tea/coffee and mince pies for adults, fruit for children. Trains are well decorated and friendly staff lead the festive singing. An enjoyable outing for all. Booking essential. Contact railway for prices.

AFTER CHRISTMAS

Edinburgh's Hogmanay

Email: hogmanay@edinburgh.gov.uk
Web: www.edinburghshogmanay.org

Venues all over the city centre. 29th Dec-4th Jan. This event has become Britain's biggest (and busiest!) street party. Includes a carnival and funfair and other indoor and outdoor events, some ticketed and some free. There's also the torchlight procession, kids' Hogmanay, a food fair and live music. Events around Princes St and the High St on Hogmanay can be extremely crowded, require street passes (which are in limited number), and would probably prove overwhelming for an under 5.

Sled Dogs

Holyrood Park

1 Jan. Afternoon. Wrap up warmly and take a trip to Holyrood Park where you can watch sled dog racing. The dogs themselves seem very attractive to young children – maybe it's because of their eyes – many have blue or mis-matched ones. The races are for fun, and there's a relaxed, friendly atmosphere.

Birthdays & Celebrations

POINTS OF INTEREST

Several venues specialise in organising parties and the *Eating Out* section identifies those restaurants willing to host parties: and remember, if you have a favourite local eatery that we haven't listed, it's always worth asking. Contact the management for details of numbers, food and facilities. Many church halls, public halls, schools, community centres and sports clubs will hire out their premises for an afternoon; again, it's always worth asking in your area.

For full details of venues, check out the relevant main entry in other section. Remember weekends tend to be busier. Younger children may be quite frightened if it is too crowded, especially in the more energetic venues. In addition, you may have to book well in advance for a weekend slot.

PARTY VENUES

Ainslie Park Leisure Centre

Tel: 551 2400

Parties last 2 hrs – 1 hr swimming or in the games hall and 1 hr eating – bring your own food. Bouncy castle available. See also *Activities for Children.*

Almond Valley Heritage Trust

Livingston Village
Tel: 01506 414957
Web: www.almondvalley.co.uk

Special birthday party package includes admission to all features of Mill Farm and the Heritage Centre (free admission to all adults helping at the party). Exclusive use of party room for 2 hrs (time to organise your own games too); your own tractor & trailer ride, and an exclusive booked session in the soft play area. Traditional birthday tea of sandwiches, sausage rolls, buns, etc is provided; just take the cake. Vegetarian and special diets can be catered for. Disposable tableware, party hats, tooters, balloons and badges. Partygoers are welcome to stay on at the farm afterwards. Parents can buy teas/coffees in the café next door. The charge for this package is £4.50/child. Min 10 children, £20 deposit required. Party bags can be provided for £2/child. See also *Out of Town Trips.*

Balerno High School

Tel: 477 7733

Swimming parties (lifeguard supplied, balls, floats and goals available). Also football or other ball games in the gym. Offers a variety of venues for a birthday tea. Parents supply the food and drink and organise the games. See *Activities for Children.*

Biggar Puppet Theatre

Jill & Ian Purves
Tel: 01899 220631
Email: admin@purvespuppets.com
Web: www. purvespuppets.com

Special birthday party option is offered by this well-established company. Parties take place at 12.45, followed by a performance at 13.30. Buffet (provided) and performance ticket is £10/head (Min. 10 people but that can include the adults). You need to provide the cake. They do the washing-up! See also *Out of Town Trips.*

Bonnyrigg Leisure Centre

Tel: 663 7579

Hall and soft play room can be hired for parties. Children spend 1 hr in soft play, and then1 hr in hall, eating and playing party games. A bouncy castle can also be set up in the hall. Self-catering – a kitchen is available for preparing food and they tidy up the mess!

Contact reception to book and for current prices. See also *Activities for Children.*

Broxburn Swimming Pool

Tel: 01506 775680

Soft play and pool parties hosted. The soft play option is hosted in the 'Pirates Cove' soft play area. Party price (£36) ensures 2 hrs exclusive use (you need to provide the party treats etc). A blend of soft play and swimming is also available, costing £50 for 2 hrs. Max no. is 20. See also *Out of Town Trips*

Bubbles

Livingston Leisure Pool
Tel: 01506 777870

Offers 'Space Bugs' soft play party, for children up to age 7– two hours of fun on slides, chutes, ball pool and on soft shapes. Venue provides a party menu, which is served in a designated eating area. Parties cost £6/child. Package includes food, take-home bags, invitations, thank you cards and party photograph. £20 deposit required when booking. See also *Out of Town Trips*

Caper House Play Barn

East Kilbride
Tel: 01355 579836

Birthday parties hosted, contact venue for details. See *Out of Town Trips*.

Castle Gyle

Gyle Shopping Centre
Tel: 476 7766

Large soft play, ball pool and slide; home corner, playdough, toys and games to suit different ages of children (ages 2-8 yrs accepted). The whole room can be booked for parties: Mon-Sat 18.15-19.45, Sun 17.15-18.45. Room hire is £48 for 1 1/2 hrs with a deposit of £10 (max 24 children). Either take your own food or party food can be ordered from Burger King. See *Shopping*.

The Ceramic Experience

Hopetoun St EH7 4ND
Contact: Anna St Clair
Tel: 556 0070
Email: ceramicx@freeuk.com
Web: www.ceramicx.biz

Each child paints an item either in acrylics (which can be taken away on the day, but item is not food safe) or the item can be glazed (this needs to be fired and picked up a day or so later). Venue provides the food – and does all the clearing away afterwards! Contact for current details. See also *Activites for Children*.

Charlie Chalk Parties

Available at Brewsters pubs, including Newhaven Quay in Edinburgh. Includes time in the soft play area, choice of main course and juice, visit to the ice cream factory; plus balloon, goodie bag, invitations and a special birthday cake (for parties of more than 8) .
Supervision and maximum numbers vary with each location. Phone venue for a booking form and price options.

Brewsters
Newhaven Quay
Newhaven Pl
Tel: 555 1570

Cheeky Chimps Parties

Freeport Shopping and Leisure Village
Tel: 01501 762104

Cheeky Chimps soft play area is situated within the shopping malls. Parties last 1 1/2 hrs (1 hr in soft play, then 1/2 hr in party room). One adult required per 4 children.
Cost £5/child with a party box (hot or cold meal) included or £3.50 if self catering. Deposit of £2/child required.

Min 10 and max 30 children. If your child is a member of the Banana Club, there is 10% off the price. See *Shopping*.

The Children's Party Cruise

Edinburgh Canal Centre
The Bridge Inn, Ratho
Tel: 333 1320/1251
Email: info@bridgeinn.com
Web: www.bridgeinn.com

A children's party on board a cruising canal boat restaurant. A tape disco is provided, take your own tapes (a disco can be organised for extra). A video player is available at no extra cost and there is plenty of space to play. Bridge Inn supply the food, but you can take a cake or any other food. Min 20 people, max 36, for a 2 hr cruise on the Union Canal – £8/person.
See *Places to Visit, Eating Out*.

Clambers

Royal Commonwealth Pool
Tel: 667 7211
Fax: 662 0265

Two party options are offered at the Royal Commonwealth Pool. The soft play option is held in Clambers, which has 3 levels of soft play,. The other option is a pool visit. The RCP staff will provide the catering, balloons, and the invitations. A dedicated party host for the day is also provided and if requested in advance, will do face painting as well as play party games. A visit from Edi B (Edinburgh Leisure's bear mascot) can also be arranged. Clambers Party costs £7/child: pool parties – price on written application. Mascot appearance £12.50. Parties must be booked in person, at reception: a non-refundable deposit is also required at time of booking. Minimum 10 children, maximum 35. See also *Activities for Children*.

Craiglockhart Tennis & Sports Centre

177 Colinton Rd
Tel: 443 0101

Parties last 2 hrs and include hire of bouncy castle. This facility is only available at weekends: cost £40. You take your own food and entertainment. Please book in advance.

Dalkeith Country Park

Tel: 654 1666
Website: www.dalkeithcountrypark.com

Parties in café in the stable block or take your own food and eat at the picnic tables around the park. Large outdoor play area in the trees. See *Out of Town Trips*.

Deep Sea World

Battery Quarry
North Queensferry KY11 1JR
Tel: 01383 411411
Email: info@deepseaworld.com
Web: www.deepseaworld.com

The party includes a 1 hr guided tour of the centre with a dedicated party host, touching starfish and sea anemones in the rock pools with the divers, a journey along the world's longest underwater tunnel to view the sharks, fish, eels and the birthday board displaying the birthday child's name and age. Look out for the divers at feeding time. The last 1/2 hr is spent in the Lagoon café, with Shaky the Shark where there is a choice of hot or cold food and a surprise gift for the birthday child. All children get face painting, floating balloons and themed goodies.

Parents provide the cake. Additional goodie bags are available from £2.

Cost is £9.95/child (2 adults get in free, min 10 children). Deposit of £20 required. Themed pirate and tropical parties are also available for an extra £10. Members get a 10% discount. See *Out of Town Trips*.

Doodles Ceramics Work Shop

29 Marchmont Cres EH9 1HQ
Contact: Holly Peters
Tel: 229 1399
Email: doodlescw@aol.com
Web: www.doodlesscotland.co.uk

Opening times: Tue-Thu 11.00-21.00, Fri, Sat 10.00-18.00, Sun 12.00-18.00

Doodles can cater for parties of any age group, from first birthdays and beyond. Although 25 is the maximum no. of children which can be accommodated, there is no minimum requirement.

Drumbrae Leisure Centre

Tel: 312 7957

Pool party, football and other activities are available, as well as a bouncy castle option. Take your own birthday feast. Contact reception for current details.

Easylife Nanny Agency

Tel: 553 2657
Mobile: 07870 855291
E mail: info@easylifena.co.uk
Website: www.easylifena.co.uk

Contact for current details of children's birthday parties. See also *Childcare*.

Edinburgh Zoo

Tel: 314 0324 (for party info)
Web: www.edinburghzoo.org.uk

Zoo offers a 'design your own party' option, which provides a range of 'meal deals', activities such as party games or crafts, and an animal walkabout (ages 3-5 yrs can currently choose from the giraffes, the penguins, the monkeys, the rhinos or the pygmy hippos). Times for a party vary: in Mar-Sep the zoo offers start times between 15.00 and 16.00 Mon-Fri, Sat & Sun 13.00-16.00; times for Oct-Feb are 14.00 or 14.30 only. Phone number above for current options, cost information etc.

The Fairy Shop

37-39 Morningside Rd
Tel: 466 7474

Parties themed around the magical world of fairies and wizards. A fairy queen welcomes guests to one of the two party rooms (one large, one small depending on size of group). Parties last 1 1/2 hrs and include: invitations, wizard and fairy costumes, party tea, party bags and games (with prizes). Just take your own cake. Party concludes with a fairy story and each child gets to make a magical wish. Staff include nursery nurses and trainee teachers. Cost £7.99/child, min 10, max 18. Suitable for 3-8 yrs.

Gorgie City Farm

51 Gorgie Road
Tel: 337 4202
Email: gorgiefarm@compuserve.com

A party with a difference which includes a visit to see and feed animals, party tea (choice of menu and a vegetarian option if requested) and for an additional charge, pony rides around the farm (weather permitting). After tea there is music and games. Please take appropriate clothing if weather is bad. Adult supervision is provided throughout the party and only 2 parents/carers are required to stay for the duration (due to lack of space in the party room).

Min 10 and max 15 children. Cost £6.50 or £7.50/child (dependent on menu option); includes hats, balloons, blowers and a party bag. Bring your own cake. For pony rides the cost is £10 per party extra.

Gorgie/Dalry Community Association

22 Mcleod St EH11 2NH
Tel: 337 3252
Fax: 346 0772

Offer the options of a traditional party with games etc, or an activity-based party (football, unihoc or basketball). Centre will provide party food, with staff on hand to help serve refreshments. Parties last for 2 hrs, with a min of 10 and a max of 30 children. Contact centre for current details.

Gracemount Leisure Centre

Tel: 658 1940

Parties last 2 hrs – 1 hr in the hall playing games, football, or on the bouncy castle then 1 hr for eating and party games, etc in the function room. Bring your own food. Cost £27.00. See also *Activities for Children*.

Happy Castle

Penicuik
Tel: 01968 675638

Two private rooms with a castle theme. Duration 1 hr 45 mins. Min 10, max 40 children. Cost includes play facilities, hot meal with choice of food, jelly and ice cream and a party bag. Phone for current prices. See also *Out of Town Trips*.

In the Pink

66-68 Hamilton Pl
Tel: 226 4408

Venue contains a shop and party room for 40+ children. Theme parties available: princess/knights, ballet, fairies, teddy bears' picnic. Room has a fairy castle mural and a pink bouncy castle. For older children there are disco parties, girl makeovers/make-up parties. Highchairs and nappy changing facilities available. The shop is 'unashamedly pink' with wands, wigs, glitter and kitsch. Contact venue for more details.

Jack Kane Centre

Tel: 669 0404

Birthday party facilities available at the weekends for a 2 hr period. For the under 5s there is a bouncy castle in a room with soft mats on the floor and walls; tables can be laid out, you take the food. Payment is for facility hire only: cost £40 for up to 15 children, deposit of £20 on booking. See *Activities for Parents*.

Jedburgh Deer and Farm Park

Camptown,
Jedburgh TD8 6PL
Tel: 01835 840364
Email: mervinslaw@ecosse.net
Website: www.aboutscotland.com/jedforest

Several party packages available ('bronze', 'silver 'or 'gold') from £12. All include entrance to the farm park and facilities, plus a birthday tea and present box. Tractor safaris and owl handling are also available. Min 10 children. 10% deposit required on booking. See *Out of Town Trips*.

Jelly Club

Tel: 652 0212
Website: www.jellyclub.com

Party format includes 1 hr 20 mins of play in the play centre, excluding the climbing wall. An assistant and a party room is allocated to each group for the duration (you can leave belongings in there and use it as a base for the children to return to). Parental supervision is required in a ratio of 1 adult to 5 children. No food or drink (except birthday cakes) may be brought in but parents may purchase drinks or snacks from the café. There are different play areas according to age. Those suitable for under 5s include a ball pit and slide (0-3 yrs), an adventure maze (4-10 yrs) and the Jelly Village (3-7 yrs). Min 8 children, no max. Individual needs and special diets catered for. There are various safety rules about children's dress to be considered. Contact venue for current prices.

Note: at weekends the Jelly Club can get very busy with as many as 5 parties going on simultaneously. This may be daunting for nervous youngsters. If you are not hampered by pushchairs, try and book the balcony area to allow you a better view of the vast ground floor as the children scatter in all directions! See also *Activities for Children*.

Kirkliston Leisure Centre

Tel: 333 4700

Take your own food and games to this centre. The 2 hr party includes use of a bouncy castle for 1 hr, then everyone moves into the multi-purpose room for the second hour, where the grown ups can set out food, etc on tables. Alternatively, just hire the multi-purpose room for 1 1/2 hr. Cost £40 for 2 hr party; £24 for 1 1/2 hr hire of room party. Max 20. Booking in advance is essential.

Linlithgow Leisure Centre

McGinley Way
Tel: 01506 775440

The leisure centre can offer a soft play area, followed by use of the dance studio area for your own catering. Alternatively, hire the 5 aside hall for a kick about. Cost £33.50 for soft play, etc (max 20 children); £23.50 for sports hall only. Booking in advance is essential.

Little Marco's

Tel: 228 2141

Parties last 2 hrs during which the group have exclusive use of one or more tables (one table seats a max of 10 children). Parents are required to supervise the party proceedings. Recommend midweek parties for under 5s when it is quieter. Contact venue for current prices etc. See also *Activities for Children*.

Loanhead Leisure Centre

Tel: 440 4516

Two party options available. The Bouncy Fun Party (costs £35.65) includes use of a bouncy castle and a multitude of soft play shapes. Tables and chairs can be set out for your party tea (you provide the food). Adjoining kitchen is also available.
Swimming parties can also be held, with giant inflatables and play shapes. Cost £56.60 for max 40 children. The hall can be hired simultaneously to cater for your party. Contact centre for more details on times and prices.

Mariner Leisure Centre

Camelon
Tel: 01324 503750

Birthday parties available, contact centre for details. See *Out of Town Trips*.

Meadowbank Sports Centre

Tel: 661 5351

Soft play area can be booked per hr for private parties, playgroups, etc. The café upstairs can reserve tables and there are 3 party menus to choose from.

Musselburgh Sports Centre

Newbigging
Tel: 653 6367

Soft play parties cost £28.80/hr. Max 20 children. Food can be provided by centre's café, contact centre for various menus and prices. Alternatively, take your own food: charge for room for own catering £9.30/hr. See also *Activities for Children*.

North Berwick Sports Centre

Tel: 01620 893454

Birthday parties available, contact centre for details. See *Out of Town Trips*.

Play Action Team

Tel: 529 7910 – Octobus
Tel: 529 7905 – Towdabout

Octobus is a colourful, fun-filled play activity bus, available for private hire for events such as children's birthday parties, fairs and gala days. Age and number restrictions apply and hire charges vary according to the event, location and day required.
Towdabout is a mobile play area with play equipment suitable for 3-7 yrs. It is available for private hire at events such as children's birthday parties, fairs and gala days.

Portobello Swim Centre

Tel: 669 6888

The small pool is available for birthday party bookings (exclusive use) on Sat, Sun for £25/hr. Spectating area. Café can provide the party food.

Queensferry High and Recreation Centre

Ashburnham Rd
S Queensferry
Tel: 319 3222

The High School has facilities which can be hired out at evenings or weekends. Party deals include bouncy castle parties or 5 aside parties. The Recreation Centre can offer the hire of a room for your own entertainment or 5 aside parties. The fee is currently set at £25. Booking in advance is essential.

Wester Hailes Education Centre

Tel: 621 8303

A 'Birthday Tea' can be supplied for your swimming party. Soft play area also available to hire plus the coffee lounge for your own catering or food can be provided. Contact centre for details. See *Activities for Children*.

PARTIES AT HOME

There's a lot to remember if you decide to hold your child's party at home. We hope the following will help. Useful books with lots of ideas are available in libraries. The main criteria are: plan ahead; and allow plenty of time – everything takes longer than you think (or any book states!)

This may serve as a checklist:

- Balloons – for front door, rooms and party bag presents
- Banners
- Cakes – tins, decorations, candles (try musical or relighting candles), candle holders
- Fancy dress – hats and masks
- Invitations – handing these out at least 2 weeks before the party gives everyone enough warning
- Music – for party games
- Party bags – usually contain a small present, sweets or fruit, balloon and cake. An alternative to party bags is to do a lucky dip of presents such as board books, crayons, bat & ball, or nursery rhyme tapes. Hide the presents in shredded newspaper and get each child to take their pick
- Prizes for games – pass the parcel keeps everyone happy with a gift for each child that unwraps a layer. Do the same for each child that is out of the game during musical bumps or statues.
- Streamers and tooters – take care with party poppers as they may frighten young children.
- Tableware – plates and napkins can be replaced by themed boxes (eg Action Man's jeep, Cinderella's carriage or Noah's Ark), which can hold a covered cup & straw, scoop for crisps or chips and space for sandwiches or other food. Some children are so taken with these boxes that they will ask to take them home afterwards!
- Table cover – an idea if you are short of chairs is to spread the cover on the floor and have a picnic, keep cloths or paper towelling close by for spills.

BUYING AND HIRING

A&D Hire & DIY Garden Centre

9 Featherhall Ave
Corstorphine
Tel: 334 2348

Mon-Fri 9.00-17.00, Sat-Sun 10.00-13.00
Small bouncy castles for home indoor/outdoor use. Phone for current prices.

Bennetts Bouncy Castles

9 Meadowplace Rd EH12 7TZ
Tel: 334 4545 (24hrs)
Email: bennettshire@blueyonder.com
Web: www.bennettshire.co.uk

Bouncy castles delivered and set up from £45. All sizes from 10' x 10', suitable for indoor use or in your garden with a shower cover. Specialised designs for under 5s.

Jenners

Good selection of hats, masks and other dressing-up requirements. Also lots of small gifts. See *Shopping*.

John Lewis

Large choice of paper tablecloths, serviettes, cups, plates. Also good selection of small gifts and stationery stocking fillers. See *Shopping*.

Monkey Business

167 Morrison St
Tel: 228 6636
Web: www.smiffys.com

Mon-Wed, Fri-Sat 9.30-17.00; Thu 9.30-18.30; Sun 12.00-16.00
Quality costumes to buy or hire, plus a large selection of hats, masks, wigs and jokes, and novelties (although many are geared towards a more adult market). Helium balloons, plus gas cylinders for hire. Fireworks stocked all year round.

Pickwicks

44 Raeburn Pl
Stockbridge
Tel: 332 5078

Range of party paraphernalia, including hats, balloons, party bag gifts and some table decarations and tableware.
Also at:

10 Shandwick Pl
Tel: 226 4663

Party Land/Birthdays

Unit 9
Gyle Shopping Centre EH12 9JY
Tel: 339 7309

Good selection of tableware, themed party ware, gifts, balloons – including helium ones. Also stock wigs, party bag fillers, some soft toys etc.

Also at:

Unit 30
Cameron Toll Shopping Centre EH16 5TB
Tel: 0131 664 8076

Unit 9
Fort Kinnaird,EH15 3RH
Tel: 669 9905

115 Princes St EH2 3AA
Tel: 2261906

Party Mania

30 West Nicolson St
Tel/Fax: 667 6020
Website: www.partypartyparty.co.uk

Mon-Sat 9.00-18.00
Tableware, party bag fillers, decorations, poppers, confetti, wigs, hats and helium balloon table decorations. Helium gas tanks (from £20) can also be hired to fill your own balloons. Accessible with pushchairs.

Party Pieces

Freepost (RG910)
Child's Court Farm
Ashampstead Common
Berkshire RG8 7BR
Tel: 01635 201844
Fax: 01635 201911
Web: www.partypieces.co.uk

Takes the strain out of organising children's parties. Colour catalogue with around 500 products to choose from, including: invitations, games, balloons, party bag fillers and tableware (including themed boxes with a cup, straw & napkin) at very reasonable prices. Next day delivery service available if orders received before 2pm. Order by post or online.

The Finishing Touch

See *Catering and Cakes* section in this chapter.

Toys R Us

Party bag gifts, cups, plates, etc on various themes. Party bag fillers. See *Shopping*.

Tridias

Tel: 0870 443 1300
Web: www.tridias.co.uk

Themed tableware, invitations and party bag fillers etc. Toys and gifts also available. Express delivery option available.

Woolworth's

Party bag gifts, tableware, sweets, toys and other party accessories. Range varies in terms of choice from branch to branch. See *Shopping*.

CATERING AND CAKES

Most parents provide their own food for 'home hosted' parties and there are books in the library to inspire you. Colours and shapes make the food interesting although many children will only want to eat sweets and crisps. Try not to overestimate the amount you need, children are usually there for the fun rather than the food. Most of the supermarkets can, with prior warning, provide trays of buffet food, such as sandwiches. Or why not try your local deli or sandwich shop?
Cakes are usually the centrepiece of any party and again libraries often have books with easy to follow recipes and ideas. A number of shops hire out cake tins and instructions. However, if you don't feel ambitious enough to tackle one, Edinburgh seems to be teeming with people with novelty cake making businesses.

Local bakers, confectioners and many supermarkets supply cakes, or try asking around for a volunteer from parents. The following firms have something special to offer:

The Cake and Chocolate Shop

12 Bruntsfield Pl
Tel: 228 4350
Website: www.cakeandchocolateshop.co.uk

Mon-Fri 9.00-17.30 Sat 9.30-17.00
Will make cakes to any design (the only limit is your imagination) and there are lots of books of photographs to give you ideas.

The Finishing Touch

17 Patrick's Sq
Tel: 667 0914
Mon-Sat 10.00-17.30

Over 40 novelty tins to hire, plus numbers, letters, squares, hexagons, etc. Good instructions. £1/night., with a £10refundable deposit/tin. Also every imaginable utensil and ingredient for cake decorating. Lots of other party paraphernalia too including party toys, masks, wigs and an extensive range of ribbons.

Paper Lace

29 South St
Dalkeith EH22 1AH
Tel: 663 2491
Email: Place138@aol.com
Novelty cake tin hire. Also balloons and balloon delivery. Accessible to pushchairs.

Studio One

71 Morningside Rd
Tel: 447 0452
Email: studioonecookshop@yahoo.co.uk

Mon-Fri 9.30-18.00 Sat 9.30-17.30 Sun 12.00-16.00
Tin hire: £2/night, £10 deposit. Letters, numbers, hearts, squares, etc.

ENTERTAINMENT

Many of the entertainers we contacted felt that their acts weren't suitable for under 5s and stressed that there was nothing worse than granny giving a running commentary to tots. It is most important when looking for an act to tell them the age span of the children and whether you have seen them before, as many entertainers have several routines. Some may even run the whole party if you want.

Those listed below have acts/services suited to the under 5s age group.

Carries-Matic Theme Parties

Contact: Carrie Todd
Tel: 0131 336 3673
Mob: 07952 945 749
Email: carriesmatic@yahoo.co.uk

Specially designed party entertainment to suit your occassion, using stories, poems, song, dance, puppets, face-paint, balloons and games to give an interactive and educational experience. Using your own venue, prices are £50 for one hour and £60 for two hours. Parties suitable for all ages from tiny tots to teens and there are a wide variety of themes available including; Ballet, Wizards, Pink Princesses and Native American Indian. You can choose your own theme too.
Carrie is a professionally trained dancer, ex-dance and drama teacher and children's theatre director, and now mother. She has been vetted by Disclosure Scotland and passed to work with children.

Cartoon Hire

118 Braid Rd
Tel: 447 5059
Email: tommy.simpson@virgin.net

Over 50 films to choose from; Disney, Star Wars, etc etc. Tommy brings along a projector and large screen.

Gary James and Stone the Crow

46 Easter Drylaw Bank EH4 2QN
Tel: 332 8321
Mobile 0793 272 8695
Email: g.james@blueyonder.co.uk

Children's entertainer, magic, balloon modelling, 'Punch and Judy' style show. Full (2 hour) party packages are also available.

Flotsam and Jetsam Puppets: the Blue Dress Shows

24 Blackwood Cres
Contact: Aileen Finlay
Tel: 662 9834
Mob: 07813 705 840
Email:
flotsam_and_jetsam_theatre@btopenworld.com

Lively puppets and gentle stories specially designed to appeal to younger children (ages 2 and upwards). Puppeteer and storyteller Aileen Finlay will come to your party wearing her magical blue 'story dress'. The dress has many pockets and in each one are puppets and props waiting to come out and tell their stories. Lots of joining-in fun and a special surprise for the birthday child. Call for a brochure and current prices. Educational shows based around the seasons are also available to playgroups and nurseries.

Gordon's Magic and Puppet Show

Gordon Morris
7 Royal Park Ter
Tel: 652 2189
Email: gordon@puppet23.freeserve.co.uk

Entertainment for birthday parties and other events with puppets, magic, balloon animals and organised games. Packed with chances for party guests to participate in the action.

Jack Martin

21 Bruntsfield Gdns
Tel: 229 4147

Jack and his wife Jill have been entertaining children for nearly 40 yrs. They try out all their new material on their 4 grandchildren! A 50 min 'Birthday Show' for 3-8 yrs in the Edinburgh district costs £55. The show consists of various string puppets (including chickens, clowns, and even Elvis) which juggle, play piano and sing. There is also loads of magic with the children as 'helpers'. To round off there is a 'politically correct' 'Punch and Judy' show with Punch doing the dusting! A truly 'Jolly Mixture' show.

Jimmy Craig

11 Barry Rd
Kirkcaldy
Tel: 01592 261706

This experienced fun magician provides prize winning fun filled magical entertainment for children. He specialises in shows suitable for children of playgroup age and up.

Jo Jingles

Contact: Joanne Goodall
Tel: 443 4196
Email: joannegoodall@tinyworld.co.uk
Web: www.jojingles.co.uk

Jo Jingles is available for birthday parties, for children up to 5 yrs old. Sessions last 30 or 45 mins, and include musical instrument playing, nursery rhymes and action songs. Weekly classes also available in venues throughout Edinburgh and West Lothian. Contact for current prices. See also *Activities for Children*.

Kids & Co

Contact: Fiona
Tel: 334 4309
Mobile: 0771 8919125

Fiona specialises in stress free parties. She can organise everything from the venue, birthday cake, catering and party bags. You can choose from various themes and her team will supervise the games and entertain the children. Best of all the tidying up is included in the price.

Magic Bob

Main St
Gordon
Tel: 01573 410363
Email: magicbobquiletti@btinternet.com
Website: www.magicbob.co.uk

This popular magician performs a variety of colourful, cheerful shows which children and adults love. Lots of good humour and audience participation with souvenirs for all partygoers. Traditional yet innovative.

Mr Boom

Andy Munro
The Old Repeater Station
Libberton
South Lanarkshire
Tel: 01555 841168
Email: info@mrboom.co.uk
Website: www.mrboom.co.uk

The children's one-man band from the moon has been visiting Planet Earth for some 17 years now. He's written a wealth of science based songs well known to several generations of youngsters. He's a popular draw at fund raising concerts and visits schools and nurseries with his enchanting singing and dancing show for young children. Sing along all together now! Dance in a pixie ring! Be a planet going round the sun! If Mr Boom's there, you'll have lots of fun.

Story Teller Scotland

Contact: Linda Bandelier
Tel: 554 8771
Email: info@storytellerscotland.co.uk

Song and storytelling programmes for children's parties and nursery schools. Probably most suitable for 4+. Contact Linda for fees and to discuss content.

Tricky Ricky

Ricky McLeod
41 Broomhall Pl EH12 7PE
Tel: 334 7671
Email: ricky@trickyricky.com
Web: www.trickyricky.com

Multi award-winning children's entertainer & magician. Magic, songs and lots of fun, including Bingo the real puppet dog!

NOTES

Childcare

INTRODUCTION

The aim of this section is to provide you with some information on childcare options if you return to work, studies, or need some help looking after your child. If your circumstances are particularly difficult, your local Social Work Department may be able to assist. Choices include taking your child to a childminder or employing someone to come to you. Private nurseries are detailed in Pre-school Play and Education.

The search for and selection of the right childcare can be extremely stressful, and while you should try to be clear about what you want for your child, you may find that you have to make unexpected compromises in order to get it right. Give yourself as much time as possible so that you do not feel unnecessarily pressured to make a decision. If you feel happy and relaxed about your childcare arrangements, then you can use your time away from your child much more effectively. While your child may seem so vulnerable and to need only you, remember that other adults outside the family can be a very positive part of their life.

Talk to as many people as you can about their experiences of childcare: their good accounts will reassure you and their 'horror stories' will help you be aware of what to look out for. There is an informal local network of nannies and childminders and you may find what you are looking for via word of mouth.

For information and support about returning to work, your local NCT branch may have a working mothers' group, or you could contact:

Edinburgh Childcare Information Service

PO Box 777
Edinburgh EH4 4JY
Tel: 270 6060 (Mon-Fri 08.30-16.00)
Fax: 270 6069
Freephone: 0800 0320323
Email: childcareinformation@edinburgh.gov.uk
Web: www.childcarelink.gov.uk

As part of the Government's National Childcare Strategy, the City of Council runs the Childcare Information Service. The service aims to provide comprehensive, impartial advice and information to parents and carers in or seeking to return to employment or training.

Information is regularly updated and includes details of current vacancies and charges. Lists and profiles of childcare provision can also be tailored to meet each family's specific needs, such as services for a particular age group or geographical area.

On a freephone number, parents and carers can now contact one telephone helpline to find out about the most suitable childcare for their family's needs (see above). Information is available on all different types of registered childcare – whether provided by the independent, voluntary or statutory sectors, including: childminders; independent nurseries; local nurseries; out of school care; playgroups; crèches and holiday play-schemes.

Parents at Work

1-3 Berry St
London EC1V 0AA
Tel: 020 7253 7243
Tel: 020 7490 2414 (24 hour answer phone for free fact-sheets on childcare and flexible working)
Tel: 020 7253 4664 (helpline for low income families)
Fax: 020 7253 6253
Email: info@parentsatwork.org.uk
Web: www.parentsatwork.org.uk

Parents at Work help children, their parents and employers with information about childcare and flexible working; advise on workplace violence, maternity rights and tax credits, and benefits, tax credits and childcare for parents of children with disabilities.

AU PAIRS & 'MOTHER'S HELPS'

If you do not need someone to take full responsibility for your child/ren on a regular basis, but feel that you need some help in the home with general work as well as childcare, a mother's help may fit the bill. Mother's helps do not need any qualifications or experience and you can specify what you want them to do to help you, but remember the emphasis is on the word 'help'.

An au pair is a young, single person (aged between 17 and 27) who comes to the UK in order to learn English. They live with a host family and should have the opportunity to study, and in return for board and lodging with a room of their own and a reasonable allowance (about £50+/wk), they should help in the house for up to 5 hours a day 5 days a week. So, there should be at least 2 free days per week, and the help can include light housework and childcare.

These conditions are laid down by the Home Office: au pairs from the European Union do not need work permits and may stay as long as they like; au pairs from outside the EU must apply for a visa which is valid for two years. Call the Home Office

Immigration Department on Tel: 020 8649 7878 (www.ind.homeoffice.gov.uk) for more details, such as the countries included in the au pair scheme.

You will probably find when you are looking for childcare, that many well-meaning acquaintances suggest having an au pair. However you should think very carefully about whether this form of help would suit you. Au pairs are not qualified in childcare and their main reason for being with you is to learn about the language and the country, not to care for your children. Whilst many au pairs have extremely successful placements, you must remember that you have a responsibility as a host family: many au pairs are desperately unhappy as they are asked to work very long hours, and are treated as a servant rather than as one of the family. Their English may be limited on arrival; they can be very young and inexperienced, not only in domestic matters, but in life in general. You may find yourself having to explain to them the most basic elements of childcare, as well as possibly having to deal with unanticipated issues, such as anti-social behaviour, romantic dramas, homesickness, etc. Many parents find that, although they have help with housework, childcare and babysitting, they have also acquired the equivalent of an extra (teenage) child with all the responsibilities that entails!

Au pairs are not a cheap solution for regular childcare if you have very young children, but they can be perfect as a help around the house or for part-time care for older children.

Au pairs can be found through agencies or contacts with the language departments of local schools, colleges and universities.

The Edinburgh Au Pair Agency

Carrick Cottage, The Walled Garden
Rosewell
Midlothian EH24 9EQ
Contact: Anne Hunter
Tel: 440 0800
Email: aupairs@rosewell.co.uk

This agency may answer your queries on au pairs. Their au pairs (male and female) are between 20 and 27 years of age, with a basic/average level of spoken English, completed Secondary School education (many are graduates), and with evidence of having a genuine interest in children and some experience of caring for them. Three types of placements are available depending on the amount of hours you would like your au pair to work. There is a small registration fee and a one-off placement fee.

BABYSITTERS

Some of the nanny agencies can also help you find babysitters, although this is an expensive option. You can, if you wish, employ a neighbouring teenager to babysit but bear in mind that he or she must be over sixteen. Current rates are £4.50+/hr, more after midnight and if you are out late you should ensure that they get home safely.

Babysitting Circles

These are groups of parents who get together to provide a babysitting circle. To find out about circles in your area ask neighbours, parent and toddler groups, local parents, your Health Visitor, or your local NCT group. All these circles are organised on a purely informal basis and it is up to you to decide if you are happy with the way the circle is run. Many arrange for the parents and the children to meet together at regular intervals so that you can get to know each other better and if the circle is large enough similar families are matched together so that a new mother with one baby, for example, can avoid the happy bedtime chaos of a larger family with toddlers and older children!

Babysitting Agencies
(see also Nanny Agencies in this chapter)

Babybusters

Contact: Natalie
Tel: 337 3421

This is a small group of women qualified and/or experienced in childcare who are available for babysitting evenings and occasional daytimes. Parents pay a registration fee at the beginning, but rates thereafter are very reasonable.

First Hand

(formerly known as Edinburgh Sitters)
39 Broughton Place
Tel: 557 3121

This project aims to provide a regular reliable sitter service to lone parents and carers of children and young adults with disabilities in Edinburgh and to promote, provide and support volunteering opportunities. Includes a Saturday group for children of lone parents and befriending for young adults with disabilities. This is a valuable service for those who really need it and volunteers are always needed.

Home Agency

36 McLaren Rd
Edinburgh
Contact: Sarah
Tel: 468 4200

Babysitters, cleaners and ironers provided. All babysitters have childcare experience (some qualified) and are genuinely interested in working with children. Registration fee (which includes first 10 placements), reasonable charges thereafter.

Night and Day Nannies

Contact: Fiona Dickson
Tel: 339 1584 or 539 1687
Email: fiona@nightandday.fsnet.co.uk

Initially conceived as a babysitting service, this agency run by a NNEB qualified mother, now offers placements from full time nannies through to babysitters.

CHILDMINDERS

Childminders care for children in their own homes. They can offer a child a homely, family environment; most will have had first-hand experience with their own children, and may well be involved with the local toddler/play groups and schools, which may be an advantage for your child later on.

Childminders are self employed and are legally required to register with the Social Work Department Registration and Inspection Service. Registration involves health, police, fire and home safety checks and is reviewed regularly. Registration is not, however, an evaluation of their skills as a childminder – these are for you to assess. Childminders are approved to care for a maximum of five children under 8 yrs, of whom no more than three are under 5 yrs and two under 2 yrs, and these figures include their own children. You must use a registered childminder: if in doubt ask to see a registration certificate, and check that it is up to date.

How to Find a Childminder

A list of all registered childminders is available from the Childcare Information Service (270 6060 or Freephone 0800 0320323). Your health visitor may have a list (check it is up-to-date) and other parents who use a childminder may know of any local vacancies.

How Much Will it Cost?

Rates vary according to area, but across Edinburgh the average rate is £3.50/hr per child. Rates for part-time places may carry a premium, and some minders offer a reduced rate for siblings.

Childminders are responsible for their own tax and National Insurance payments and also for Public Liability and Accident Insurance cover. You should check that they are either covered by their domestic insurance or that they have a special childminder's insurance policy. Payment for holidays and sick pay vary: often a childminder will not charge if unavailable due to holidays or illness, but if you do not attend you should pay the normal rate or at least a percentage of it.

Choosing a Childminder

You will need to decide where you want your childminder to be based: someone close to home may mean that your child can make friends locally which will carry on to school, and enforced change in the long term is less likely to be necessary if your childminder is willing to continue caring for your child once he or she has started school. It is also more convenient to have someone nearby who can take your child, if say, you are ill. Alternatively, you may prefer a childminder who lives closer to your place of work.

Once you have selected the names in your chosen area from the list, you will need to phone around to find out who has vacancies. Be prepared to find few vacancies – in many areas in Edinburgh demand outstrips supply. Most childminders are very helpful in telling you of any vacancies they are aware of, so do ask. Always visit anyone who sounds suitable in their home and prepare yourself with a list of information for the childminder about you and your child and also questions you want to ask about the childminder. You need to establish the practicalities of hours, rates, holidays, sick pay, overtime (if required) and notice and whether you need to provide food and nappies. You might also want to think about the following during your visit: Will your child have plenty of play opportunities – indoors and outdoors? Will there be outings to the park, playgroup, library etc? Will your child be able to rest during the day? If so where? What are the arrangements for meals and snacks? Are there other children for your child to play with and are they happy, settled and busy? What time will be set aside for you to discuss your child with the childminder? Will your wishes for the care of your child be accepted and respected? When you do decide ensure you have a written contract summarising your agreement with the childminder.

Scottish Childminding Association

Suite 3
7 Melville Terrace
Stirling FK8 2ND
Tel: 01786 445377
or contact: Enid Lowe, Tel: 0131 449 4614
Web: www.childminding.org

This is a Scottish organisation which promotes good quality childcare within a home environment. It provides support, advice and information to all who are interested in childminding. It produces several useful publications for parents and childminders, including 'Selecting a Suitable Childminder' (free with A5 sae), the SCMA Code of Practice (£5.00), Pay and Conditions leaflet (£1.00), and Childminding Contracts (£3.00 for 5), postage & packing extra.

NANNIES

You may prefer to employ someone to look after your children in your own home. Nannies may 'live in' or 'live out'. The choice between these options will depend on the nature of your childcare needs, your available accommodation, how you feel about having someone in your home and also on your financial resources. Nannies are not required to be registered in the same way that childminders are, so you must follow through on references thoroughly. It is worth thinking beforehand about the sort of person you are looking for and to specify your requirements with regard to training and qualifications, experience, age and so on.

Conditions of Service

Be clear in your own mind about your conditions of service in terms of hours, holidays, pay, duties, sick pay and so on. Must your nanny be able to drive, be a non-smoker, understand a vegetarian diet, allergies, observe certain religious practices and so on? In the case of live-in help you should also think about any restrictions you wish to place upon the use of your home, such as having friends to stay, using the phone, etc. Apart from looking after the children, duties can include babysitting, cooking, light housework and so on. Be realistic: if you have one young child who sleeps for a couple of hours each day then it is reasonable to ask the nanny to fill that time with light housework, but if there are active toddlers or young children around then they must take priority with the nanny over time-consuming domestic chores. Rates vary widely depending on qualifications and experience: full-time live-out care can range from £190+/wk net, or £4.75+/hr part-time. Live-in pay can be less (£160+), but don't forget to take account of the 'hidden' domestic costs. When deciding what to pay take into account training, experience, number of children and level of responsibility required. Remember too the additional cost to you of National Insurance contributions and income tax payments, which can equal up to one third of the person's take-home pay. When you do appoint someone, it is up to you to contact your local Inland Revenue office to let them know you are an employer, and they will send you the necessary paperwork for you to fill in.

Finding a Nanny

The following suggestions may help you find the right person:

- Local contacts or friends may be able to recommend someone suitable – nannies usually know other nannies, or parents with children at private nurseries may hear that a member of staff is looking for a move. Take advantage of anyone's experience of employing a nanny – ask them about what they like about their nannies, and if there is anything they would have done differently.
- You can place advertisements in the Scotsman and/or the Evening News on Fridays (contact the papers at least two days in advance). Be prepared for a good number of responses, but if response is by phone in the first instance have a short list of questions handy to filter out unsuitable candidates quickly and only interview those who meet your criteria of experience and qualifications. You could also place notices in health centres where they have a general notice board, or you could look further afield by placing an advert in e.g. The Lady.
- If you seek someone with childcare qualifications, but don't mind if they do not have experience, contact the local colleges which offer childcare training (Jewel & Esk Valley, Tel: 660 1010, Stevenson, Tel: 535 4600, West Lothian College Tel: 01506 418181) – the final term (Apr/May) is the best time to do this.

You may also wish to use an employment agency and there are a few in the Edinburgh area which specialise in finding nannies. They usually charge a registration fee and then once they have your details they try to match you with someone suitable. If you are looking for a part-time nanny, some will try to set up a nanny-share scheme with other clients. All candidates should have been thoroughly interviewed and references checked by the agency, but the final responsibility to ensure the nanny's suitability and to double check references is with you. If you do appoint someone, you then pay a substantial appointment fee to the agency. If you use an agency, find out before signing up what they offer in terms of service to you: some provide useful fact packs on registration which will help you with interviewing, contracts, conditions of employment, tax and National Insurance etc. They should also give some sort of guarantee to find a temporary cover if you need it. Go for an agency that you feel will give you a dependable service, but remember it can only be as good as the nannies on its books, and if, as can sometimes be the case, they cannot come up with anyone suitable, it will be back to you to find someone.

Interviews

Ask all candidates to send you their CV in advance or, if that's not possible to bring it with them to the interview – this will give you a good starting point. Prepare your list of questions in advance and don't feel embarrassed to ask searching questions – you need to find out as much as you can in a very short time! Don't forget to give the candidates a chance to ask you questions and to tell you about themselves – they need to assess whether you will be the right family for them too and you can find out a lot about someone by listening carefully to what they have to say. Be sure to obtain references from previous employers or from college tutors and follow them up (even if it means phoning Australia!) – again have a short list of questions ready to ask referees but also give them an opportunity to volunteer their own information.

Contract

It is important to have mutual expectations clear at the outset. A written contract stating the terms and conditions of service and the duties and responsibilities of the job is very helpful in preventing problems later on, or at least making them easier to sort out, for both parties and the law requires employers to provide certain written particulars.

We have listed a couple of agencies below: please bear in mind that although there are more, some did not respond to the questionnaires

NANNY AGENCIES

Butterfly Personnel

7 Earlston Pl
Edinburgh EH7 5SU
Tel: 659 5065
Email: enquiries@nanny-agency.net
Web: www.nanny-agency.net

Established in 1998 and registered with the Care Commission, this agency specialises in providing permanent/temporary nannies and babysitters. It also provides emergency cover staff to many nurseries and private homes. Staff are fully interviewed, reference checked and cleared through Disclosure Scotland. They carry photo ID cards. No registration fee required.

Family Circle Recruitment

37 Comiston Rd
Edinburgh EH10 6AB
Tel: 447 9162
Fax: 447 7037
Mobile: 07970 442428

The childcare division provides all aspects of temporary and permanent childcare cover including nannies, emergency cover, nursery staff, maternity nurses, child friendly housekeepers and also 'after school club' help.

OTHER SOURCES OF HELP WITH CHILDCARE

The Childcare Listing (Scotland)

26 Coltbridge Terrace
Edinburgh
EH12 6AE
Tel: 337 7001

The Childcare Listing (Scotland) is a fortnightly publication set up to match the needs of parents and childcarers. Subscribe to the Listing and advertise your childcare needs for FREE. It is designed for people needing childcare – nannies, childminders, nanny shares, after school carers and babysitters – and for childcarers looking for work.

Edinburgh Crèche Co-op

297 Easter Rd
Edinburgh EH6 8LH
Tel: 553 2116

Specialises in delivering flexible, professional childcare services including setting up and running crèche facilities, training, consultancy and staff cover. You need to provide a suitable room and the crèche workers are vetted, trained and experienced in organising stimulating and educational play activities, with an emphasis on child-centred care. It has full public liability insurance and complies with all relevant legislation and can be fully operational with only a few days notice.

First Hand

(formerly known as Edinburgh Sitters)
39 Broughton Pl
Edinburgh EH1 3RR
Tel: 557 3121

This project aims to provide a regular reliable sitter service to lone parents and carers of disabled children and adults in Edinburgh, and to promote, provide and support volunteering opportunities. The project now also offers support to families with children under 3 under the Sure Start initiative. There is a high demand for their services and although priority may be given in special cases, there is a very long waiting list. Sitters are matched to specific families for a regular on-going arrangement. This is a valuable service for those who really need it and volunteers are always needed.

Family Circle Recruitment

See *Nannies* in this chapter.

North Edinburgh Childcare

Crèche Services
18b Ferry Rd
Edinburgh EH4 4BL
Contact: Nancy Wyse
Tel: 311 6934

Provides a one-stop childcare facility which gives quality, affordable crèche cover to enable parents to access local opportunities. The playbus is safe, stimulating and above all, fun. It is available for bookings by any group or organisation who are planning an event – anytime, anywhere, on a one-off or for a regular event and can accommodate up to 12 children between the ages of 0-12yrs (under 1s can be catered for if there are less than 6 other children). Rates are on a sliding scale.

One Stop Childcare

17 Calder Gro
Edinburgh EH11 4LZ
Tel: 476 7800

One Stop Childcare's crèche service is designed to respond to the needs of a broad range of clients. Childcare can be provided in and outside Edinburgh, either on a long or short term basis or for a one-off event. One Stop will provide, or come to, a suitable location and supply play materials and a healthy snack.

Social Work Department

Tel: 556 6787

The Social Work Department can help with childcare in the form of Children's Centres, day carers and places at specially approved private nurseries. The service is free but is only available to families who are in need of help for social, financial or health reasons.

Eating Out

The experience of eating out with young children often lies somewhere between fun and enthusiastic chaos! Needs vary according to age and our researchers endeavoured to check all the various requirements. A newborn will be quite content in a car seat, but in a matter of months a high chair is a priority, then, before you know it, the location of the toilet is the first requisite for toilet training toddlers – the list goes on.

If you are choosing a meal for a special occasion you are always best to book first, mentioning that you will have children under 5 yrs (and that you found the restaurant listed in this book). Check that the facilities you need will be available (high chairs may be reserved, for example). Several hotels and family restaurants have special promotions at the weekend, such as under 5s eating free or special children's entertainment, so it's worth checking.

Hours

We have listed the opening hours. For those restaurants which open late into the evening, we've listed the 'curfew' times for children, where the venue noted them. If you're booking for a party including children, it's worthwhile mentioning the fact when booking, as some places have earlier curfews than others, although 20.00 is a popular cut off point.

Pricing

We have used the pound symbol (£)– to represent the approximate price of an adult main course. £: under £5, ££: £5-10, £££: over £10.

High chairs

We have asked how many high chairs, clip-ons and booster seats there are, but bear in mind that the high chairs may well all be occupied. Make sure that staff know you require one so that they can help you; they might not always notice you struggle with a small fractious tot! And don't be afraid to mention any problems with the high chair to the staff – you might be surprised how many do not have restraints.

Nappy-change surface

What constitutes a 'good changing surface' to a parent and to a manager with no children may be very different. A shelf with a rim is easy to install and does not take up much space, and is much more acceptable than crawling around on the floor of a public toilet. On the other hand, it is a pleasant surprise to find that an increasing number of places keep a supply of disposable nappies and wipes tucked away in case of emergencies – ask if you are desperate, and you may strike lucky!

With the role of fathers increasingly acknowledged, more places are trying to offer changing facilities outwith the ladies' toilets, and this is indicated in the text by 'M&F'.

No-smoking Area

Many restaurants now provide no-smoking areas. Some have gone one step further and prohibit smoking throughout the entire eating area. This is indicated in the text.

Licenses

Generally, restaurants can only serve alcohol with food.

Parties hosted – Contact management for details, or see *Birthdays and Celebrations*.

Prams

Some places do not allow prams or pushchairs. The entries indicate if there is space inside to store them (perhaps folded).

Toilet Access

Access should be reasonable, we have said if there are stairs or other hazards.

Play and Provisions

Details of special provisions for young children were included in the questionnaire and are indicated in the listings, e.g. children's menus or half portions, baby foods, the availability of play equipment, toys, etc.

Fast Food

Details of the most popular chains are at the end of *Eating Out*.

Please let us know of any other places where your family have enjoyed a meal, and of any good or bad experiences in places included here – email us via our website edinburghforunderfives.co.uk or write to PO Box 012345, Edinburgh, EH9 2YB.

CENTRAL EDINBURGH

Bean Scene

67 Holyrood Rd
Tel: 557 6549

Opening hours: Mon-Sat 8.00-20.00; Sun 10.00-20.00

£, high chairs (3), breastfeeding welcome, no-smoking, baby food and bottles heated, nappy-changing room, seats 30.

Trendy but chilled out coffee house near the site of the new Parliament and Holyrood Palace. It sells a variety of light snacks and tapas. Kids' bags containing a sandwich, juice, fruit, biscuit and crisps are another option. The atmosphere is relaxed (there are several large sofas) and extremely child friendly – there are drawing materials, toys and videos available and free baby wipes and nappies in the changing room. There is a side entrance if you want to avoid steps at the door. Space to park prams inside.

Bella

7 Hanover St
Tel: 225 4808

Opening hours: Mon-Sat 10.30-23.00; Sun 12.00-23.00

££-£££, high chairs (6), breastfeeding welcome, can provide hot water for heating bottles and baby food; no-smoking area, nappy-changing facility (F only), licensed, seats 114.

Popular city-centre eatery. Quick, friendly service, vegetarian dishes, children's menu, crayons and colour-in place mat to help pass the time. Pushchairs can be taken in, if folded.

BhS Restaurant

64 Princes St
Tel 226 2621

Opening hours: Mon-Wed 9.00-17.30; Thu 9.00-20.00; Fri-Sat 9.00-18.00; Sun 11.00-17.00

£, high chairs (6), booster seats (2), breastfeeding welcome, bottles heated, nappy-change surface, no-smoking area, seats 200.

Large, spacious self-service cafe/restaurant. Level access from Rose St entrance but can also be accessed from main store via escalator to centre of eating area. Extensive choice from snacks to lunches, including vegetarian dishes and carry out items; large children's menu and half portions available for under 12s. Children's meals come in decorative lunch/picnic boxes for under £2. Baby food available, or will warm food brought in by parents. Each high chair comes with a disposable bib, very handy if you find you have forgotten yours. Toilets and feeding and nappy-changing room (M&F) up a floor (3 flights of stairs).

Brodies Coffee Houses

Ottakar's Bookshop (1st floor)
57 George St
Tel: 220 2943

Opening hours: Mon-Sat 9.00-18.00: Sun 11.30-16.00

£, high chairs (2), breastfeeding welcome, bottles heated, nappy-change surface, no-smoking, seats 100.

Handily located self-service cafe on 1st floor of Ottakar's bookshop, accessed by stairs or a lift. Offers a varied menu and accommodates most tastes, includes light snacks and home baking (including, perhaps, the best scones in Edinburgh). Child portions and carry-out food available. Tables in corners and balcony offer some privacy breastfeeding mothers. Toilets and changing room near restaurant. Willing and helpful staff. Space to park pushchairs unfolded.

Browns Restaurant and Bar

131-133 George St
Tel: 225 4442

Opening hours: Mon-Sun 11.00-23.00

££-£££, high chairs (8), breastfeeding welcome, children's menu, baby food and bottles heated, nappy-changing facilities (M&F), no-smoking area, licensed, seats 270.

Spacious restaurant at the West end of George St. Owing to licensing laws children are not allowed in the bar area, but under 5s are welcome in the restaurant. Crayons and books for children to colour in and a free portion of ice cream for children at the end of their meal.

Cafe Rouge

43 Frederick St
Tel: 225 4515

Opening hours: Mon-Sat 10.00-23.00

££, high chairs (8), breastfeeding welcome, nappy-changing facilities, no-smoking area, licensed, seats 140.

A few steps up to entrance, then all on one level. As the name suggests, there's a French accent to the menu. Table-service and daily specials. 'Menu pour les enfants' includes choice of items, juice and dessert for one price. Half portions available. Nappy-changing in toilet for disabled.

Chisholms Restaurant

Caledonian Hilton Hotel
Princes St, W End
Tel: 222 8900

Opening hours: Mon-Sun breakfast and dinner; Mon-Sat lunch (please telephone to confirm restaurant's current hours)

£££, high chairs (4), breastfeeding welcome, bottles heated, no-smoking area, licensed, seats 120.

Table-service in plush surroundings. Family Sunday Brunch every Sunday 12.00-15.00, with children's play area and live music – great for a special family occasion. Large range of food and snacks throughout day. Space to park pushchairs and prams. Crayons and paper provided if requested. During off peak hours entry is gained through main hotel door.

Debenhams

4th Floor, The Castle View Restaurant
Princes St
Tel: 225 1326

Opening hours: Mon-Fri 9.30-16.30; Sat 9.00-17.00

£, high chairs (5), breastfeeding welcome, bottles heated, nappy-change surface, no-smoking, seats 96. Feeding bowls, bibs and wipes, free baby food.

Large self-service restaurant with friendly staff and (as its name suggests!) excellent views of castle. Impressive range of high-chairs to suit both babies and toddlers. Varied menu including hot food (with children's options), salads and baking. Children's menu with 'fun sheet' on back for colouring-in. Children's 'pick and mix' and packed lunch boxes. Toilets and Mother's rooms nearby at lifts.

The Elephant House

21 George IV Bridge
Tel: 220 5355

Opening hours: Mon-Fri 8.00-23.00; Sat, Sun 9.00-23.00

£, high chairs (2), breastfeeding welcome, no-smoking area.

A useful cafe stop on the way into town from the Meadows. The Elephant House is a self-service coffee house with good range of coffees, baking and lunches. Children enjoy the 'elephant' shortbread. Wonderful display of all things 'elephant' to keep toddlers amused; they also love the elephant seats at the front of the cafe in the no-smoking area. Magazines and children's books at rear. Toilets on the same level as the cafe and nappy-changing (M&F) in the toilet for the disabled.

Est Est Est

135 George St
Tel: 225 2555

Opening hours: Mon-Sun 12.00-23.00

££, high chairs (12), breastfeeding welcome, bottles heated, nappy-change surface (M&F), no-smoking area, licensed, seats 200.

This eatery aims to combine great food, cool surroundings and a positive attitude towards families. Popular with people without children too, the restaurant manages to cater for all ages. There is a children's menu, although half portions of the main pasta dishes always go down well, and while they are waiting for their food, children can crayon on the table cloth (don't try this at home!). Children can also make their own pizzas.

The Filling Station

235 High St
Tel: 226 2488

Opening hours: Mon-Sun 12.00-00.00

££, high chairs (4), tables suitable for clip-ons, breastfeeding welcome, bottles heated, nappy-change surface (M&F), licensed, seats 122.

Children welcome in the eating area of this bar/restaurant. Car theme throughout, fun atmosphere, TV and video provide entertainment for both parents and children. American, Mexican and Italian food, children's portions. Nappy-changing area adjacent to toilet for the disabled.

Frasers Restaurant

5th Floor, 145 Princes St

Opening hours: Mon, Wed, Fri 9.00-17.00; Tue 9.30-17.00; Thu 9.00-19.00; Sat 9.00-17.30; Sun 11.00-16.30

£, high chairs (3), breastfeeding welcome, no-smoking area, bottle and food warming items provided, seats 116.

Self-service restaurant with easy access from lifts. Spacious eating area, children's menu. Toilets located adjacent to the restaurant.

Garfunkels

29-31 Frederick St
Tel: 225 4579

Opening hours: Mon-Sun 12.00-23.30

££, high chairs (12), tables suitable for clip-ons, breastfeeding welcome, bottles heated, nappy-change surface (in F toilets only, but alternative arrangements can be made for men with under 5s), no-smoking area, licensed, parties hosted on weekdays.

Comfortable, table-service restaurant serving a wide range of food. Also offers a children's menu. All children under 10 receive a bag containing 'goodies'. Toilets downstairs in basement.

Gennaro

64 Grassmarket
Tel: 226 3706

Opening hours: Mon-Sun 12.00-00.00

££, clip-ons (2), breastfeeding welcome, bottles heated, licensed, seats 60.

Traditional Italian restaurant which welcomes families. Varied menu with children's portions available. No prams, pushchairs folded. One lively toddler made dinner even more lively when one of the clip-ons was attached to a wobbly table, so do check! Seating outside continental style. If not too busy, waiters like to entertain children, allowing parents to enjoy their meal in peace. Carry-out food available.

Gurkha Brigade

9a Antigua St
Tel: 556 6446

Opening hours: Mon-Fri 12.00-14.30, 17.30-23.00; Sat 12.00-14.30, 17.30-00.00

£, high chair (1), breastfeeding welcome, private space available, seats 40.

Friendly Nepalese restaurant welcomes families at all times. Children's snacks and meals such as chicken salad, fish and chips also available.

Chef welcomes children in the kitchen to see food being prepared. Space for pushchairs. No nappy-changing facilities.

Hard Rock Cafe

20 George St
Tel: 260 3000

Opening hours: Mon-Sat 12.00-late, (under 14s must be seated by 20.00)

££, high chairs (6), booster seats (6), breastfeeding welcome, bottles heated, nappy-change facilities (M&F), no-smoking area, licensed, seats 150.

Busy and informal family restaurant, with a focus on US and Tex/Mex food. Good access for prams, and there are small booths available for family gatherings, or if you prefer some privacy for breastfeeding. Colour-in books, crayons and balloons for children, also plasma screens and fairly loud music to keep them amused. Staff friendly and welcoming to children.

Hendersons

94 Hanover St
Tel: 225 2131

Opening hours: Mon-Sat 8.00-22.30; Sun 9.00-21.00 during Festival

££, high chairs (4), tables suitable for clip-ons, breastfeeding welcome, bottles heated, nappy-change surface (M&F), no-smoking area, licensed, seats 180.

Basement buffet restaurant (access down stairs), serving broad range of vegetarian and vegan food. Children's menu for £3.50. Healthy food displayed so children can choose what they want. No chips! Several dishes contain nuts, so do check if allergies are an issue. Quiet alcoves make pushchair access tricky, but they're good for breastfeeding if you prefer some privacy. Staff available to help with pushchairs. Carry-out service available. Books and crayons can be provided.

The Hub

Castlehill
Tel: 473 2067
Email: thehub@eif.co.uk

Opening hours: Sun, Mon 9.30-18.00; Tue-Sat 9.30-22.00

£, high chairs, breastfeeding welcome, nappy-changing, no smoking.

Fixed menu and light snacks, children's portions available. Spacious inside, with a mix of low sofas and regular tables and chairs. There's also seating outside on the terrace. Pushchairs and prams welcome. Toilets and nappy changing facilities near to restaurant, towards the rear of the ground floor.

Jenners

48 Princes St
Tel: 225 2442

Jenners is popular, but can be daunting when negotiated with a pushchair. For easiest access, enter by Rose St next to the Barber's Shop and take the lift up. If this takes you too far from the areas you want, & you don't want the perfumery/beauty dept first, enter the store by the side entrance of S St David's St. As with all entrances (except the Rose St lift option), this involves negotiating a few steps. This brings you into the Menswear area. Go towards the rear of the store (Men's Designer Dept) and this gives you access to the large lift, which makes for easier pushchair transport.

There are 4 restaurants to choose from in store.

Toilets, nappy-changing and feeding room all located on 3rd floor.

Cafe 2 - Ground Floor

Opening hours: Mon, Wed 9.15-17.00; Tue 9.45-17.00; Thu 9.15-19.00; Fri-Sat 9.15-17.30

£, breastfeeding welcome, no-smoking.

Coffees, teas, soft drinks, sticky pastries etc. Small café on entrance-level mezzanine above Menswear dept. Ideal for a quick bite, but it can be busy and the stools aren't ideal for small children.

Kenningtons Restaurant - 1st Floor

Opening hours: Mon, Wed 9.15-17.00; Tue 9.45-17.00; Thu 9.15-17.00; Fri-Sat 9.15-17.30

££-£££, high chairs, breastfeeding welcome, bottles heated, licensed.

Most formal of the store's restaurants. No-smoking throughout, with table-service. Child's menu available.

Princes St Restaurant - 2nd Floor

Opening hours: Mon, Wed 9.15-17.00; Tue 9.45-17.00; Thu 9.15-19.00; Fri, Sat 9.15-17.30

£-££, high chairs, breastfeeding welcome, bottles heated, licensed. Access through the food hall.

Busy self-service restaurant on two levels. Mainly no-smoking (smoker's area is to the left after the pay area). Choice of salad bar and dishes of the day. Good selection of teabreads and cakes. The made-to-order hot dish are brought to your table.

Bistro on 5 - 5th Floor

Opening hours: Mon, Wed 9.15-17.00; Tue 9.45-17.00; Thu 9.15-17.00; Fri, Sat 9.15-17.30

£-££, high chairs, breastfeeding welcome, bottles heated, licensed, no-smoking.

Self-service cafe/bistro. Can be accessed by 3 lifts (the largest comes opens on to the hair salon – turn right for the restaurant). Selection of snacks, soup and dishes of the day. Cakes and scones, etc. Some tables are set up on a dais area, but the few steps are negotiable by a pushchair. The made-to-order hot dishes are brought to your table. This cafe can be quieter when the others are busy, outwith weekends and Xmas period.

The Place to Eat - John Lewis

St James' Centre
Tel: 556 9121

Opening hours: Mon-Wed 9.30-5.45; Thu 9.45-19.45; Fri 9.30-19.45; Sat 9.30-18.15; Sun 11.00-17.00

£-££, high chairs (6), breastfeeding welcome, bottles and baby food heated, feeding and changing facilities available (M&F) on same floor, no-smoking, licensed, seats 280.

Large, busy self-service restaurant and espresso bar on level 4. Fantastic views over the city from large windows. Vegetarian dishes available, as well as children's portions and children's lunchboxes. Small selection of baby food available to buy. Plenty of room for prams and pushchairs. Staff will assist with getting trays to tables, and will bring heated baby food, etc to you at your table. Bibs, bowls and spoons available if required. Easy access from lifts. Also easy access to fantastic baby facilities, 'the loos with the views' for the under 5s. Children made most welcome everywhere, but the smaller espresso bar with its temptingly low furniture and glass walls is probably more suitable for babies and older children than lively toddlers.

Lower Aisle Restaurant, St Giles Cathedral

Parliament Sq, High St
Tel: 225 5147

Mon-Fri 8.30-16.30 (19.30 during the Edinburgh Festival); Sun 10.00-14.00; Sat 10.00-16.30 during the Festival

£, high chair (1), tables suitable for clip-ons, breastfeeding welcome, bottles heated, no-smoking area, seats 70.

Spacious self-service restaurant down a flight of stairs, uncluttered with simple furniture. Soup, rolls, light snacks, variety of vegetarian dishes, vegan diet catered for. Children's portions available. Fraternised by the legal profession. It often gets very busy, especially after services. Friendly staff. Toilets: Gents on ground floor, no nappy-changing facilities, but bench in Ladies toilet - down five steps.

Marks and Spencer's Cafe Revive

91 Princes St
(M&S Ladies and Children's Wear Shop)
Tel: 225 2301

Opening hours: Mon, Tue 9.00-17.30; Wed, Fri 9.00-17.30; Thu 9.00-19.30; Sun 11.00-16.30

££, high chairs (3), breastfeeding welcome; no smoking; seats 80; nappy-changing room (M & F), toilets, mother and baby room on ground floor.

Self-service cafe at the rear of the basement floor, accessed by lift or stairs. Large selection of tempting sandwiches, cakes, scones and light snacks. No baby food or children's portions available, but jugs of hot water are provided to heat jars or bottles. The café is adjacent to displays of clothes, and although the café is partially paneled off, lively toddlers (with sticky fingers) can be a bit of a liability. Toilets and nappy-changing are up one floor (lift), where there is also a mother and baby room for mothers to breastfeed in private if desired. Space for prams and pushchairs. See main entry under *Shopping*.

also at

54 Princes St
Rose St Level
(M&S Menswear, Food and Home Shop)

Mon, Tue 9.00-17.30; Wed, Fri 9.00-17.30; Thu 9.00-19.30; Sun 12.00-16.30

££, high chairs (3), breastfeeding welcome; no smoking; seats 40; nappy-changing unit (M & F), toilets adjacent to the cafe.

Café situated at the back of the store, accessible by lift from the main store or by automatic door entrance from Rose St. Serving similar snacks and sandwiches as the main cafe at 91. Nappy changing room is cramped, and can be awkward for larger pushchairs: it's more or less impossible to access with a traditional pram or double pushchair.

National Portrait Gallery

Queen St Cafe
1 Queen St
Tel: 624 6241

Opening hours: Mon-Sat 10.30-16.30; Sun 14.00-16.30

£, high chairs (2, no reins), breastfeeding welcome, no-smoking area, licensed, seats 60.

Self-service cafe with light snacks and vegetarian dishes. Prefer pushchairs folded. Toilets on same floor. Nappy-changing facilities in the larger toilet for the disabled.

Pizza Hut

46 North Bridge
Tel: 226 3038

Opening hours Mon-Thu 11.30-22.30; Fri, Sun 11.30-23.30; Sat 11.30-00.00

££, high chairs (4), breastfeeding welcome, bottles heated, nappy-

change surface, no-smoking area, licensed, seats 150.
Some seating downstairs. Access by staircase. Toilets are down 2 flights of stairs. Selection of toys for babies and children. All restaurants have a children's menu which has suggestions from the adult menu plus a healthy salad bar. Games and comic free with every child's meal, salad bar. Ground floor seating. Carry out food available. See also *Eating Out - West.*

Refresh!

1 Waterloo Pl
Tel: 557 4171
Opening hours Mon-Sat 8.00-18.00; Sun 10.00-17.00
£, high chairs (3), breastfeeding welcome, bottles heated, no-smoking area, seats 70.
At the east end of Princes St. Light snacks, including French bread pizzas, sandwiches and baked potatoes, all prepared on the premises. Very helpful staff. Carry-out food, delivery in the city. Toilets down quite a long flight of stairs.

Royal Museum of Scotland

Chambers St
Tel: 225 7534
Opening hours Mon-Sat 10.00-16.30; Sun 13.00-16.30
£, high chairs (3), breastfeeding welcome, bottles and baby food heated, no-smoking area, parties hosted, seats 80.
Two cafes – Café Delos in main hall and the other at the rear of the building; access from Lothian St.
Café Delos is pleasant, airy and spacious with (occasionally erratic!) waitress-service, selling light snacks and home-baking. Ample space for pushchairs. Toilets and changing facilities on same floor. The cafe at the rear of the main building (the old Tearoom) is now known as 'Soupson'. It serves soup, salads, sandwiches and children's' snacks. Range of soft drinks as well as teas, coffees etc. Filter coffee comes in 2 strengths. High chairs (3) and booster seats (4) are available. Space to park pushchairs if folded.

Spoon

15 Blackfriars St
EH1 1NB
Tel: 556 6922
Opening hours Mon-Sat 8.00-18.00. Festival 8.00-22.00
£, highchair (1), breastfeeding welcome, bottles and baby food heated, no-smoking; seats 24.
Welcomes children with open arms. Paper, crayons, felt tips and finger puppets. Space to park pushchairs unfolded. Snacks and variety of larger dishes, including vegetarian. Emphasis on fresh seasonal ingredients.

Starbucks Coffee Company

There are more than 13 outlets (as we go to press) in Edinburgh! In the city centre the following outlets offer coffees, muffins and lively atmosphere. Facilities vary at each one and the following are possibly more convenient if you are in town with babies and young children.
Opening hours vary, with the majority open between 8.30-19.00 Mon-Sat and Sun 9.00-17.00.

Haymarket - Palmerston Pl
East End -30a George St (Corner of Hanover and George St) and Castle St
Old Town - High St at the corner of the Tron
Princes St - 120a Princes St
Stockbridge - Bakers Pl
West End - 106 George St

£, breastfeeding welcome
Some (including Princes St and Castle St) have nappy-changing facilities and high chairs.
Of these branches, the Princes St outlet at 120a has a wonderful view and is a relaxing place to spend time with visitors; particularly if the armchairs at the window are free as you have a wonderful view of Edinburgh Castle. The back area is more private and has very comfortable chairs for breastfeeding. However, the cafe is up two flights of stairs and there are no plans at present to install a lift. Staff are welcome and friendly and if you are able to leave a pram or pushchair downstairs to go up and ask for help, they will assist. Also at
85 George St; Lothian Rd and Exchange Cres – these outlets are more focussed on the office market and do not have high chairs.

NORTH EDINBURGH

Acorn Centre

Leith Methodist Church
1 Junction Pl
Tel: 555 4153
Opening hours: Tue 10.00-14.00; Sat 10.00-12.00
£, high chair (1), breastfeeding welcome, nappy-changing facilities, seats 64, no-smoking.
A little haven in Leith although it's only open 2 days a week. The staff are very friendly and accommodating. Children well catered for, either by making up sandwiches to their taste or smaller portions from the menu. Space for pushchairs.

Brewsters

51-53 Newhaven Pl
Tel: 555 1570

Opening hours: Mon-Sat 11.00-23.00; Sun 12.00-23.00; Fun Factory 11.00-21.00

££, high chairs (9), booster seats (5), breastfeeding welcome, bottles heated, nappy-changing room (M&F), licensed, no-smoking area, parties hosted, seats 200.

Large family-orientated restaurant by the Travel Inn on Newhaven Harbour. Children's meal includes visit to the ice cream factory to choose their own sweets to top the ice cream. Baby food available to buy. Large choice for adults (including 'weight watcher' coded items). The restaurant is on one floor. One area adjacent to the bar is a 'child free zone', but with Charlie Chalk's Fun Factory on site there is plenty to keep toddlers occupied. Simple system of ordering and paying first means that a quick escape can be made without having to wait for the bill. Mother and Toddler group held on Mon, Wed and Fri 10.30-11.30 (except in the school holidays).

Cramond Brig

Queensferry Rd
Tel: 339 4350
www.cramondbrig.org.uk

Opening hours: Mon-Sun 11.00-23.00; Fri-Sat 11.00-24.00

££, high chairs (7), breastfeeding welcome, bottles heated, nappy-changing room (M&F), table-service, licensed, seats 122.

No longer as family oriented as it was, but still welcoming to children. Children's menu, colour-in posters and pens. Eating areas on 3 levels with stairs between them. Space for prams and pushchairs.

Dean Gallery: Café Newton

Belford Rd
Tel: 624 6200
Email: enquries@natgalscot.ac.uk

Opening hours: Mon-Sun 10.00-16.30

£, high chairs (3), breastfeeding welcome, no-smoking, licensed, seats 30.

Art deco style ground floor cafe, with lovely coffee and cakes, and a tasty and interesting lunch menu with dish of the day and a variety of vegetarian dishes. Half portions available for children.

Giuliano's on the Shore

1 Commercial St, Leith
Tel/Fax: 554 5272

Opening hours: Sun-Thu 12.00-22.30; Fri-Sat 12.00-23.00

£££, high chairs (12), tables suitable for clip-ons, breastfeeding welcome, bottles heated, nappy-changing room, licensed, parties hosted, seats 120. Carry-out food available.

Recently refurbished. Children are the mainstay of this lively Italian restaurant where they can even make their own pizzas, but grown-ups are well catered for too! Half portions available and they promise they can cater for any diet. Crayons and books available. Access good. Toilets on ground floor.

Howies

4/6 Glanville Pl, Stockbridge
Tel: 225 5553
Website: www.howies.uk.com

Opening hours: Mon-Sun 12.00-14.30, 18.00-22.00

££, highchairs (2), clip-on (1), breastfeeding welcome, no smoking area, licensed, seats 65.

Contemporary styled restaurant, with a relaxed feel. Part of an independent chain, originating in Edinburgh, but now with premises in Aberdeen and Dundee. Toilets are downstairs, but toilet for disabled is on ground floor. All Howies restaurants have changing facilities. It can get pretty busy at lunchtime, but friendly staff are never pushy. As they only have a couple of highchairs and one clip-on, it makes good sense to book ahead, so a chair is at the table when you arrive. The chef will prepare children's meals to order. Occasional promotions, such as 'kids for £2' offer, plus they usually have a 45 minute lunch promise, with key dishes marked as such on the menu. Staff are happy to warm baby food or bottles, and we've always found that they're patiently indulgent to tiny diners. Oh, and they do rather nice puddings! See *Eating Out – West*.

Lauriston Farm Restaurant

69 Lauriston Farm Rd
Tel: 312 7071

Opening hours: Mon-Sat 11.00-23.00; Sun 12.00-22.00

££, high chairs (16), breastfeeding welcome, bottles heated, changing area (M&F), no-smoking, seats 240.

Open and spacious restaurant, recently refurbished, with children's menu, and using the order and pay at once policy, which means you can leave quickly if you have to! There is a small indoor play area, and a bigger outdoor one, although under 5s will probably need adult supervision on it. When we went, on a Saturday lunchtime, service was pleasant and speedy.

Malmaison Brasserie

1 Tower Pl
Tel: 468 5000

Opening hours: Mon-Sun 10.00-22.00

££, high chairs (2), breastfeeding welcome, licensed, seats 65

(Brasserie) 40 (Café).
Friendly hotel by Leith Docks, welcoming to children, but posh enough to please the grandparents. Varied menu with good choice for vegetarians. When we went the mussels were excellent. Half portions available. Good access. Space for prams and pushchairs. Nappy-changing table in disabled toilet.

Mariachi

72 Commercial Quay, Leith
Tel: 538 0022
Opening hours: Mon-Sun 12.00-23.00
££, high chairs (5), breastfeeding welcome, bottles and baby food heated, licensed, seats 150. Bright, glass-fronted Mexican restaurant with relaxed atmosphere facing Victoria Quay in semi-pedestrianised area. Spacious with plenty of room for pushchairs. Staff exceptionally welcoming and helpful, very child friendly, with quick service an added bonus. No specialised changing facilities but toilets are roomy and clean. They do a buffet lunch on weekdays, 12.00 - 14.30. Children's food, toys & crayons. Parties hosted.

Peacock Inn

Lindsay Rd, Newhaven
Tel: 552 8707
Opening hours: Mon-Sat 12.00-21.45; Sun 12.30-21.45
££, high chairs (6), breastfeeding welcome, licensed.
Large table-service family room in this inn on the Forth. Extensive bar menu including soup, salads, fish, steak. Children's menu. Haddock and chips very good!

Pizza Express

1 Deanhaugh St
Tel: 332 7229
Opening hours: Mon-Thu 11.30-23.00; Fri-Sun 11.30-00.00
££-£££, high chairs (10), breastfeeding welcome, nappy-changing facilities (M&F), no-smoking area, licensed, seats 110 inside, 50 outside by Water of Leith.
Pizzas galore in stylish surroundings by Water of Leith walkway. Crayons and paper usually materialise on the table pretty quickly if you have a toddler, and balloons sometimes are a 'goodbye' gesture. Friendly staff. Toilets with changing facilities downstairs. See also *Eating Out – West.*

Scottish National Gallery of Modern Art Café

72 Belford Rd
Tel: 332 8600
Opening hours: Mon-Sun 10.00-16.30
£, high chairs (3), clip-ons (1), breastfeeding welcome, feeder beakers, no-smoking, licensed.
Access by lift to self-service café in basement. Delicious home-cooked soups, hot meals, salads and great cakes. Also vegetarian meals. Half portions of soup and meals available. Outdoor terrace for fine weather, where children can run around in the garden. The only down-side is that it can be very busy during lunch-time.

Telford Arms

78 Telford Rd
Tel: 332 4647
Opening hours: Mon-Sun 11.00-20.00
££, high chairs (4), tables suitable for clip-ons, breastfeeding welcome, children's menu, nappy-changing surface (M&F), no-smoking area, licensed, seats 200.
Families are warmly welcome in the lounge area of this bar. There is a fixed but varied menu plus a children's menu, with table-service. Accessible to wheelchairs.

Terrace Café

West Gate, Royal Botanic Garden
Tel: 552 0616
Website: www.rbge.org.uk
Opening hours: Mon-Sun 10.00-17.00 (Apr-Aug 9.30-18.00)
££, high chairs (7), breastfeeding welcome, bottles heated, nappy-change surface (M&F), licensed, seats 80 inside, 80 outside.
A very popular pleasant meeting place for parents and toddlers, situated next to Inverleith House. The menu includes healthy home made hot meals and salads plus children's lunch boxes. Pushchairs allowed in the café but it is courtesy to leave them just inside the door when it is very busy. Nappy-changing facilities in toilet for the disabled. Often extremely busy at lunch-time, and the queueing/payment system can result in a long time spent queueing with a hungry child in tow if you're by yourself.

EAST EDINBURGH

Asda Wal-Mart

100 The Jewel
Tel: 669 9151

Opening hours: Mon-Sat 8.00-22.00; Sun 9.00-19.00

£, high chairs (6), breastfeeding welcome, nappy-change facilities (M&F), no-smoking, seats 120.

There is such a thing as a free lunch! This bright spacious, good value café offers free baby food (when buying an adult's meal), bibs and bottle warming. Hot water is available for heating jars. The children's menu offers a choice of hot or cold meals with vegetarian options. A variety of hot meals are available. Carry-out food available. Play area (charge for use) next door for 3+ yrs.

Chiquito

6 Kinnaird Park
Newcraighall
Tel: 657 4444

Opening hours: Mon-Thu, Sun 12.00-22.00; Fri-Sat 12.00-23.00

££, high chairs (4), booster seats (3), breastfeeding welcome, nappy-change facilities (M&F), licensed, all non-smoking apart from bar area, seats 103.

Spacious, bright restaurant with relaxed atmosphere. There is comfortable booth seating available, handy for babies in car seats. Staff are welcoming and will happily heat baby food and bottles. There is a children's menu and staff will sing 'Happy Birthday' if you are celebrating. Children's birthday parties hosted.

Costa Coffee

WH Smiths
Fort Kinnaird
Newcraighall
Tel: 669 1351

Mon-Fri 10.00-19.00; Sat 10.00-17.30; Sun 11.00-17.30

£, high chairs (2), breastfeeding welcome, bottles and baby food heated, nappy change (M&F), no-smoking, seats 60.

This small self-service coffee shop is located on the first floor within WH Smiths, with easy access by lift. It offers a variety of hot and cold sandwiches including pannini and toasties, and also has a large selection of pastries and cakes. Ample room for prams and pushchairs next to your table.The staff are friendly and helpful. Take-away food available if you are in a rush!

Esquires Coffee House

Clinton Cards
Fort Kinnaird
Newcraighall.
Tel: 669 5019

Mon-Fri, Sun 10.00-18.00; Sat 0.900-18.00

£, high chairs (4), breastfeeding welcome, bottles and baby food heated, nappy change facilities(M&F), no-smoking,seats 50.

This airy, self-service café is located above Clinton cards, the largest card and soft toy shop in the UK – hence its popularity with children. Easy access by lift. It serves a good selection of light snacks including soup of the day with a roll, which is a popular choice for young children. There's also fresh fruit juice, Italian milkshakes, smoothies and cakes. Parents are welcome to bring their own food and drinks for toddlers and children. Crayons and colouring books are provided.Carry-out food is available. Space for folded pushchairs and prams.

Giuliano's

18/19 Union Pl
Tel: 556 6590

Mon-Sun 12.00-02.30

££, high chairs (7), breastfeeding welcome, nappy-change facilities (F only). bottles and baby food heated, children's menu and child portions, no-smoking area, licensed, table-service, carry-out available, seats 170.

This large, very friendly Italian restaurant has a relaxed atmosphere and is welcoming to children and babies. Colour-in books and crayons provided. Tables near the entrance have room to park pushchairs and are no-smoking.

Java Junction Coffee Shop

B&Q Warehouse
Newcraighall Rd
Tel: 669 4545

Mon-Sat 8.00-17.00; Sun 9.00-17.00

£, high chairs (2), breastfeeding welcome, no-smoking, nappy-change facilities (M&F), seats 44.

This small self-service coffee shop tucked in the back of the enormous B & Q warehouse is a rest spot for the DIY enthusiast (or otherwise!). It offers a variety of hot and cold snacks, all day breakfasts (with vegetarian option) and a dish of the day. Half portions are available for children. It is easy to park shopping trolleys, prams or pushchairs next to the tables. Carry-out food is available. Babies love the lighting display in the main warehouse.

Luca's
32-38 High St
Musselburgh
Tel: 665 2237
Mon-Sat 9.00-22.00; Sun 10.30-22.00
£, high chairs (5), breastfeeding welcome, no-smoking area, nappy-change facilities (M&F) seats 115.
As well as the famous ice cream, to eat in or take out, the café serves full menu from toasties and pannini to pizzas and all day brunches. Childrens portions available. Spacious two floored premises – ground floor has capacity to seat 72. Easy pushchair access to ground floor.

Starbucks Coffee Company
Borders Books
Fort Kinnaird
Newcraighall
Tel: 657 9768
Mon-Sat 09.00-21.30; Sun 10.00-19.30
£, no high chairs, clip on seats (1), breastfeeding welcome, bottles and baby food heated, nappy change (M&F), no-smoking, seats 80.
This small café has a relaxed atmosphere and friendly staff. It serves light snacks including sandwiches and pannini with interesting and unusual fillings, muffins, biscuits, cakes etc. Crayons and paper are available on request, and books can be brought up from the book shop to look at. It is situated on a mezzanine level with easy lift access. Space for folded pushchairs, prams can be placed in hallway. Carry out food is available.

Vittoria Restaurant
113 Brunswick Street (Leith Walk)
Edinburgh
Tel: 556 6171
Mon-Sat 10.00-23.00; Sun 12.00-23.00
££, high chairs (6) ,breastfeeding welcome, nappy change facilities(M&F), bottles and baby food heated,two large no-smoking rooms,seats 200, licensed,
Friendly Italian restaurant happy to serve anyone anything, from a coffee to a full meal. Pizzas and pasta available, vegetarian meals, burgers, chips, sandwiches, ice-creams. Children's menu and half portions available,Free crayons and colour-in pictures available. Carry-out food available. There's space for prams outside, folded pushchairs inside. Full disabled entrance and toilet. Parties hosted and welcomed.

SOUTH EDINBURGH

Annabelle's and Annabelle's II
27 Sciennes Rd
Tel: 667 0700
Mon-Fri 8.30-17.00; Sat 10.00-15.00
£, high chairs (2), breastfeeding welcome, nappy-changing facilities, no-smoking, seats 30.
Friendly café with fresh food for lunches, snacks and afternoon tea. Space for folded pushchairs, but not prams. There are large windows so pushchairs and prams can easily be seen if left outside. Carry-out service.

The Balmwell
39-41 Howdenhall Rd
Tel: 672 1408
Mon-Fri 12.00-14.00, 17.30-21.30; Sat-Sun 12.00-21.30
££, high chairs, breastfeeding welcome, nappy-changing facilities, no-smoking, licensed.
'Carvery' style resturant. Children's menu available. Large beer garden.

394 Bistro
394 Morningside Rd
Tel: 447 9287
Mon-Sat 9.45-17.00
££, high chairs (2), breastfeeding welcome, half portions for children, no-smoking, licensed, seats 40.
Wholesome food and a no-smoking policy. Basement area, room for pushchairs if folded. There is an alcove table which seats 6 and is slightly away from the main customer area – phone in advance to book it!

Braid Hills Hotel
Buckstone Bistro
134 Braid Rd
Tel: 447 8888
Mon-Sat 11.00-20.00; Sun 12.30-20.00
££, high chairs (3), breastfeeding welcome, bottles and baby food heated, nappy-changing surface (F), no-smoking area, licensed, seats 70.
Families are welcome in the bistro, children's menu available. A wide choice of food in lovely surroundings without being too costly. Waitress-service. No prams.

Brattisani's

85/87 Newington Rd
Tel: 667 5808

Mon-Sun 9.30-11.30 (teas and coffees), 11.30-23.00 (meals)

£, high chair (1), breastfeeding welcome, bottles heated, seats 60.

A fish and chip shop fronts this friendly restaurant and this is reflected in the menu. Waitress service. Children's portions served.

Café Artista

94-96 Marchmont Crescent
Tel: 443 7526

Mon-Fri 08.00-19.00; Sat 09.30-19.00; Sun 11.00-18.00

££, high chairs (2), breastfeeding welcome, bottles heated, totally no-smoking, licensed, seats 40.

A warm and friendly café welcoming children in the true Italian style, serving Italian inspired meals and snacks. Toys, books, crayons and pens, children's art exhibition wall and seasonal competitions. Space for pushchairs. Additional seating outside in the summer.

Café Grande

184 Bruntsfield Pl
Tel: 228 1188

Mon-Wed 9.00-22.00; Thu-Sat 9.00-23.00; Sun 10.00-18.00

££, high chairs (1), clip-ons (2), breastfeeding welcome, bottles heated, changing mat and potty provided, no-smoking area, licensed, seats 50.

Friendly waitress-service café/bistro where children are welcome. Breakfasts, coffees, cakes and light meals served. Children's menu available. Pushchairs allowed (folded) but prams must be left outside. Box of toys, books and crayons provided.

Café South

8 Newington Rd
Tel: 668 4422

Tue-Fri 12.00-14.00

£, high chairs (2), breastfeeding welcome, bottles heated.

This friendly café serving light meals and snacks is part of a hotel with a family friendly policy.

De Niro's Ristorante

140 Nicolson St
Tel: 662 4185

Mon-Sun 12.00-23.30

££, high chairs (2), clip-ons (1), breastfeeding welcome, bottles heated, no-smoking area, licensed, seats 70.

Families are welcome in this Italian restaurant before 19.00. Books and lollipops available and children can help to make their own pizza.

Edinburgh Festival Theatre

Café Lucia
13/29 Nicolson St
Tel: 662 1112

Mon-Sat 10.00-17.30; depending on shows Sun 16.00-

£, high chairs (2), breastfeeding welcome, no-smoking, licensed (for children until 20.00), parties hosted, seats 60.

This self-service café offers light snacks and half portions for children. It is part of the theatre and has show material displayed like 'Playdays' and 'The Singing Kettle'. Toilets and nappy-changing room (M&F) are one floor up, lift available.

Elephants and Bagels

37 Marshall St
Tel: 668 4404
Website: www.elephant-house.co.uk

Mon-Fri 08.30-17.00; Sat-Sun 09.30-17.00

(Later closing in summer)

£, high chairs (1) , breastfeeding welcome, bottles heated, no-smoking area, seats 40.

The sister café of The Elephant House, this is Edinburgh's first and foremost bagel shop, serving a variety of bagels with all kinds of fillings, as well as other light snacks. Crayons, pens and paper provided, children's art exhibited – and there's a large collection of elephants. Space for pushchairs. Toilets are downstairs. Additional seating outside in the summer. Children's parties by prior arrangement.

The Engine Shed Café

19 St Leonard's Lane
Tel: 662 0040

Mon-Thu 10.30-15.30; Fri 10.30-14.30; Sat 10.30-16.00; Sun 11.00-16.00

(Check opening hrs during holiday periods)

££, high chairs (5), tables suitable for clip-ons, breastfeeding welcome, bottles heated, nappy-changing surface (M&F), no-smoking, seats 60.

Run by Garvald Community Enterprises, the café houses a bakery, as well as bright, cheerful vegetarian café on the 1st floor, accessed by lift or stairs. Reasonably priced menu changes daily and children's portions are available. All the food is made on the premises. Carry-out service, delivery within the City and outside catering available. Children made very welcome. Relaxed atmosphere and friendly staff. Toilet for the disabled on the ground floor and toilets adjacent to café.

Moveable nappy-changing unit suitable for use in Ladies or Gents.

Favorit

30 Leven St
Tel: 221 1800
Mon-Sun 8.30-01.00
££, breastfeeding welcome, licensed.
Trendy American retro style café/bar offers coffees, brunches, snacks and drinks; useful for a coffee stop. Front area is no-smoking until 17.00. Toilets on the same level, but no nappy-changing facilities.

also at:
19 Teviot Pl
Tel: 220 6880
Mon-Sun 8.30-03.00
Same style and approach as the Leven St Café; toilets are downstairs.

Kaffe Politik

146 Marchmont Rd
Tel: 446 9873
Mon-Sun 10.00-22.00
££, high chairs (1), breastfeeding welcome, carry-out service, nappy-changing facilities (M&F), bottles heated, licensed, seats 30.
Table-service café/bistro with fixed menu, light snacks and vegetarian dishes. Children can have half portions of menu items. Space for pushchairs folded, but not prams.

Lorette's Coffee Shop

94 Mayfield Rd
Tel: 667 3028
Tue-Fri 9.00-16.00; Sat 9.30-15.30
£, high chair (1), breastfeeding welcome, no-smoking, seats 24.
Small, friendly café serving home-cooked food for lunches and light snacks. No space for prams but pushchairs can be taken inside. Children made very welcome.

Luca's

16 Morningside Rd
Tel: 446 0233
Mon-Sun 9.00-22.00
£, high chairs (4), breastfeeding welcome, bottles heated, nappy-changing facilities (M&F), no-smoking, seats 50 upstairs and 15 on ground floor.
Homemade pizza, pasta, milkshakes and the 'famous' ice-cream; children's menu available with half portions of many dishes. Access to upstairs is by a spiral staircase; prams and pushchairs can be left downstairs. Toilets are located on the ground floor.

Parrots

3 Viewforth
Tel: 229 3252
Tue-Thu 18.00-22.15; Fri 17.30-22.15; Sat 17.00-22.15 (no curfew for children, parents judgement accepted!)
££, high chair, breastfeeding welcome, no-smoking.
Families welcome, relaxed approach to parties including children. 723 parrots (counted by a little boy!) of different shapes and sizes to entertain children. Table-service with a large variety of ethnic dishes, fixed menu items, pasta, vegetarian dishes and snacks. Staff very friendly to children. Limited floorspace for pushchairs. If booking, it is helpful to mention that your party will include children as some tables are more suitable for them than others.

Pasquale's

169 Gilmore Pl
Tel: 228 3115
Mon-Fri 12.00-14.30, 17.00-0.00; Sat-Sun 17.00-0.00
££, breastfeeding welcome, licensed, bottles heated, seats 60.
Very friendly Italian restaurant and pizzeria serving food that children (and their parents!) love. Children very welcome and can have half portions from main menu. Space is limited so pushchairs should be folded.

Sherry's

372 Morningside Rd
Tel: 447 9217
Mon-Sat 9.00-17.00
£, high chairs (2), breastfeeding welcome, totally no-smoking, licensed, seats 44.
Very pleasant, friendly coffee shop. Home-baking and cooking. Pushchairs allowed but prams must be left outside (large window near tables for easy viewing). Toilets downstairs.

The Square Centre Café

Nicolson Square Methodist Church
25 Nicolson Sq
Tel: 662 0417
Mon-Fri 8.30-15.30
£, high chairs (4), clips ons (1), booster seats (2), tables suitable for clip-ons, breastfeeding welcome, bottles heated, nappy-changing facilities (M&F), no smoking, seats 100.
Spacious self-service café. Scones, cakes and filled rolls served throughout the day. Cooked breakfast 8.30-11.00. Hot meals, salads and vegetarian option served from 12.00. Smaller portions

available for children. Disabled/pram access round the back of the café.

The 1924 Café and Cards

The Eric Liddle Centre
15 Morningside Rd, Holy Corner
Tel: 452 3325
Mon-Sat 9.00-16.00
£, high chairs (2), tables suitable for clip-ons, breastfeeding welcome, bottles heated, nappy-changing surface (M&F), totally no-smoking area, disabled access, seats 40.
Friendly café serving homemade soups, snacks and homebaking. Plenty of room for pushchairs and prams. Located within Eric Liddell Centre, focus for community care, arts and education projects.

Ti Amo Restaurant

16 Nicolson St
Tel: 556 5678
Mon-Sun 12.00-23.30
££, high chairs (2), clip-ons (1), breastfeeding welcome, bottles heated, no-smoking area, licensed, seats 140.
Families welcome in this Italian restaurant before 19.00. Books, crayons, paper, toys and lollipops available and children can help to make their own pizza. The fishpond is an additional attraction!

WEST EDINBURGH

Agenda

92 St John's Rd, Corstorphine
Tel: 316 4466
Mon-Sun 10.00-19.00
££, high chairs (6), breastfeeding welcome, bottles and baby food heated, nappy-changing (M&F), children's menu and child portions, large play room, no-smoking area, licensed, table-service, seats 90.
Modern hotel with a restaurant which has a separate play room with a large soft play area, some toys for younger children and video games and playstation for older children. However, if you have younger children, it may be best to stick to 'school-time' visits; if there are more boisterous 5+ years children in the area, there's not a lot of space left for tinies in the actual soft play. You can't see into the area from the restaurant, so be prepared to eat and then play, or to spend some time going from the table into the playroom. If booking a table in advance, remember to request a table near the playroom, as there's an adjoining restaurant area where people without children usually sit.
Food tends along the British bistro/bar classics, such a thai fish cakes, club sandwiches, and so on. The menu does change fairly regularly, although the children's one is fairly static and fairly predictable. Pram and pushchair access via entrance from car park– inside there's plenty space to park prams and pushchairs but if it's busy folded is preferred. Child-sized sinks in toilets are a delight for children.
From 10.00-12.00 you can have a coffee while children play, from 12.00-15.00 you must order food, from 15.00-17.00 usually ok to come for a play and coffee and from 17.00-18.30 need to order dinner. No children allowed in the restaurant after 20.00 and no children allowed in the bar. Contact hotel for details of children's parties. If you have brought your car, remember to obtain a token from your server to exit the car park.

Apex European Hotel

90 Haymarket Ter
Tel: 474 3456
Mon-Sun 10.00-14.30, 19.00-122.00
££, high chairs (2), breastfeeding welcome, bottles heated, children's portions offered, nappy changing rooms (M&F), non smoking, licensed, seats 42.
Stylish, modern hotel in the west of the city offering brasserie-style menu. No dedicated children's menu but very accomodating to families and will cook a child's meal to order where possible.

Bar Roma

39A Queensferry St
Tel: 226 2977
Sun-Thu 12.00-24.00; Fri-Sat 12.00-1.00
££, breastfeeding welcome, high chairs, nappy-changing, seats 200.
Friendly and spacious Italian restaurant. Children's portions are available. It can be very busy at lunchtimes.

Barnton Thistle

Queensferry Rd, Barnton Roundabout
Tel: 339 1144
Mon-Sat 12.00-14.30, 18.30-21.00; Sun 12.00-14.30, 18.30-21.00
££, high chairs (3), tables suitable for clip-ons, bottles heated, licensed, parties hosted, seats 120.
BB's restaurant has a variety of dishes to appeal to most tastes.

Brasserie at Norton House

Norton House Hotel, Ingliston (opp showground)
Tel: 333 1275
Mon-Sun 12.00-14.30, 18.00-21.30
££, high chairs (8), breastfeeding welcome, bottles and baby food heated, no smoking, licensed, seats 60.

Contemporary styled restaurant with conservatory overlooking the hotel grounds. Children's menu available.

The Bridge Inn

The Edinburgh Canal Centre, Ratho
Tel: 333 1320/1251
Mon-Sat 12.00-20.00; Sun 12.30-20.00
££, high chairs (8), clip-ons (5), breastfeeding welcome, bottles heated, nappy-change surface (nappies and wipes provided), licensed,, seats 120. In addition, there are 2 canal boats, each of which seat 36 passengers.
Inn has a family area, a play area and patio. There's *a* varied menu – including large children's menu. Outdoor play area with carousel. Resident family of ducks live beside the canal. Rosie and Jim Canal Safety Campaign promoters. Parties hosted.

also:

Pop Inn

Mon-Sun 12.00-18.00
Informal lounge bar with relaxed and family dining, part of the Bridge Inn.

Coffee and Cream

235 St John's Rd
Tel: 539 7008
Mon-Sat 8.30-17.00
£, high chair (1), breastfeeding welcome, feeder beakers, available.
Children of all ages are welcome. Coffee shop offers scones, toasties, etc. Children's menu and child portions available. Friendly staff are happy to help out and table-service is a bonus.

Cuba Norte

192 Morrison St
Tel: 221 1430
Mon-Sun 12.00-20.00
££, breastfeeding welcome, bottles heated, licensed, seats 150.
Spacious, friendly bar/café decorated in Cuban style. Serves Cuban and vegetarian (including vegan) food. Chef will cook to order for special requests. Toilets are down one flight of stairs. No nappy-changing facilities.

Ramada Jarvis Hotel

Ellersly Rd
Tel: 337 6888
Mon-Sun 10.00-19.00
££, high chairs (4), breastfeeding welcome, bottles heated, licensed, no smoking, seats 60.
Friendly country house hotel with garden. Children made very welcome, under 3s eat free.
3-5yrs can enjoy a 3 course meal for £3. Books and crayons available. A bedroom will be offered for nappychanging, or should a mum prefer to breastfeed in private.

Filmhouse Café Bar

88 Lothian Rd
Tel: 229 5932
Mon-Sun 10.00-21.00
££, highchairs (2), breastfeeding welcome, nappy-changing facility (M&F), no-smoking area, licensed, seats 150.
Busy café/bar serving light snacks, vegetarian and vegan food with a fixed menu and a daily special. A relaxed and informal atmosphere, so well suited to families. Limited space for pushchairs.

Gyle Shopping Centre - Food Court

Tel: 539 9000
Mon-Wed, Sat, 8.00-19.00; Thu, Fri 8.00-20.00; Sun 8.00-17.30
£-££, high chairs (10), breastfeeding welcome, bottles heated, nappy-changing room (M&F), self-service, no-smoking, seats 680.
The food court is upstairs and is accessible by a lift, stairs and an escalator. It offers a wide range of foods including baked potatoes, sandwiches, fish and chips, pizzas, dish of the day options etc, all provided by different franchises. The up side is that there's plenty choice, the downside is that you may have to queue a couple of times. Toddler seats with play tables are situated along the left wall as you leave the lift. Nappy changing room further along the same side, as are food/bottle heating facilities.

Holiday Inn – Edinburgh North

Queensferry Rd
Blackhall
Tel: 311 4920
Mon-Sun 18.30-22.00
£££, high chairs (5), tables suitable for clip-ons, breastfeeding welcome, bottles heated, feeding and changing room, family area, garden, no-smoking area, licensed, seats 80.
Inventive children's menu provides plenty of choice. Children under 12 eat free from children's menu if accompanied by 2 adults. There is an outdoor play area for use at Sunday lunch times with chute, tunnel, etc.

Jimmy Chungs

20 Grindlay St
Tel 228 8688
Mon-Sun 11.45-14.45, 17.00-22.45
££, highchairs (10), breastfeeding welcome, bottles heated, nappy

change room (M&F), no smoking area, seats 200, licensed.
Chinese buffet restaurant with lively atmosphere. Children made very welcome by friendly staff. All-you-can-eat three-course lunch only £4.99(children £2.99) so booking recommended.

Khukuri

8 W Maitland St
Tel: 228 2085
Mon-Fri 12.00-14.00, 17.30-23.30; Sat 12.00-14.00, 17.30-24.00; Sun 17.00-23.00
££, high chairs, breastfeeding welcome, bottles heated.
Friendly Nepalese restaurant serving fixed menu meals. Chef can adapt dishes. Children's portions available. Toilets downstairs. Staff welcome family dining.

Lazio Restaurant

95 Lothian Rd
Tel: 229 7788
Mon-Thu 17.00-01.00, Fri-Sun 12.00-03.00
££, high chairs (3), breastfeeding welcome, bottles heated, licensed, seats 60.
Families are welcomed at this restaurant. Varied menu, children's portions available. Folded pushchairs only. Toilets on ground floor. Crayons and pencils supplied so children can add drawing to the 'gallery'.

Old Orleans

Fountain Park, Dundee St
Tel: 228-8339
££, high chairs (6), boosters seats (6), breastfeeding welcome, bottles heated, children's menu, nappy changing rooms (M&F), non smoking area, licensed, seats 250.
Located within popular leisure complex next to multiplex cinema and bowling alley. Fun children's menu offering Tex-Mex and Cajun dishes. Crayons available for children to draw inbetween courses. Available for children's parties

Pizza Express

32 Queensferry St, West End
Tel: 225 8863
Mon-Sun 11.30-20.00
££-£££, high chairs, breastfeeding welcome, bottles and baby food heated, nappy-changing facilities (M&F), no-smoking area, licensed.
Pizzas galore in stylish surroundings. Crayons, paper and balloons are available to distract impatient young diners. Children's portions available. Restaurant can cater for children's parties if given prior notice. Friendly staff.See Also *Eating Out – Central.*

Pizza Hut

113-117 Lothian Rd
Tel: 228 2920
Mon-Thu 12.00-22.30;Fri-Sat 12.00-23.00
££, high chairs (6), booster seats (2), breastfeeding welcome, bottles heated, nappy-change surface (M&F), no-smoking , licensed, seats 96.
Family restaurant. Crayons, toys and balloons available. Toilets on ground floor. Ice cream factory very popular with young ones. Hosts children's parties. See also *Eating Out – Central.*

St. Bride's Community Centre

10 Orwell Ter
Tel: 346 1405
Mon-Fri 10.00-15.30; Sat 10.00-16.00
£, high chairs (2), breastfeeding welcome, bottles and baby food heated, children's parties hosted, non-smoking, nappy changing room.
Child friendly café offering hot meals and home bakes at great prices. There is a large soft play area, reading corner and toys for children. Plenty space for pushchairs.

St. George's West Church

Shandwick Pl
Tel: 225 7001
Email: gwest@dircon.co.uk
Mon-Sat 10.00-15.30
£, high chairs (2), clip-ons (1), breastfeeding welcome, no-smoking, children's menu available, baby food and bottles heated, nappy-changing surface, parties hosted, seats 90.
In addition to great value hot meals and cakes, this restaurant now has a children's play area. Access also by lift at side entrance on Stafford St. Offers space for pushchairs if folded.

Traverse Theatre

10 Cambridge St
Tel: 228 5383
Mon-Sat 10.30-20.00; Sun 17.00-20.00
£, high chairs (2), breastfeeding welcome, bottles heated, nappy-changing room (M&F), no-smoking area, licensed, seats 56.
Centrally located, a large, open café/bar with friendly and welcoming staff. Wide range of vegetarian dishes and home-baking; children's portions are available. Lift to café, bar and theatres. Newspapers and board games.
There's a good wine list and American and continental beers are available at the bar. The atmosphere is very relaxed; an ideal place for parents with young children to enjoy a drink, a coffee and something to eat. Space for prams and pushchairs.

Verandah Restaurant

17 Dalry Rd, Haymarket
Tel: 337 5828
Mon-Sun 12.00-14.30, 17.00-24.00
£££, high chairs, tables suitable for clip-ons, breastfeeding welcome, bottles heated, licensed, seats 44.
A friendly Indian restaurant with a very high culinary standard. Varied menu including vegetarian options. Special lunch menus available. Children's portions served, and crayons and colouring books provided to keep little ones amused. Carry out food available. Free home delivery service.

FAST FOOD

There are many fast food outlets in Edinburgh. We have listed Burger King, McDonald's and Kentucky Fried Chicken outlets below. The universal nature of these eateries means that you know what to expect in terms of food, environment etc. Most offer children's themed meals, nappy-changing facilities, and may host children's parties: contact venue for more details. All offer sit-in and take-away meals. Where 'drive-thru' is available, we have also noted this.

BURGER KING

£, highchairs, breastfeeding welcomed, tables suitable for clip-ons. Either no-smoking, or with a no-smoking area. All have nappy-changing facilities.
The outlet at the Gyle has the advantage of the good toilet and nappy-changing facilities of the centre.

Gyle Shopping Centre
Tel: 317 1561
Mon-Wed, Sat 9.00-19.00; Thu, Fri 9.00-20.00; Sun 9.00-17.30

Milton Rd (at Big W)
Tel: 6690558
Mon-Sun 8.00-22.00

10-15 Princes St
Tel: 557 4575
Sun-Thu 8.00-23.00; Fri, Sat 8.00-00.30
Parties hosted.

118 Princes St/Castle St
Tel: 220 1644
Mon-Sat 8.00-22.00; Sun 10.00-22.00
Parties hosted.

Waverley Station (inside main travel centre area)
Tel: 557 9128
Mon-Sat 6.00-00.00; Sun 8.00-00.00

KENTUCKY FRIED CHICKEN

£, highchairs, breastfeeding welcomed, tables suitable for clip-ons, no-smoking areas, nappy-changing facilities.
As the name suggests, the emphasis is on fried chicken meals, including buckets, tortilla wraps and burgers, although muffins etc are also available, plus children's themed meals with toys and cartons of juice.

Craigleith Retail Park
South Groathill Ave
Tel: 343 3101
Mon-Fri, Sun 11.30-22.30; Sat 11.00-23.00
'Drive-thru' available.

36 Nicolson St
Tel: 662 9533
Sun-Thu 11.00-23.00; Fri, Sat 11.00-00.00

McDONALD'S

£, highchairs, breastfeeding welcomed, tables suitable for clip-ons, bottles heated, no-smoking areas, nappy-changing facilities.
Some have a children's area, with small tables and chairs, some with tvs showing Cartoon Network. Frequent promotional toys, including film tie-ins. 'Happy Meals' available for children.

Builyeon Rd
S Queensferry
Tel: 331 5981
Mon-Sun 7.00-00.00
'Drive-thru' available.

1 Glasgow Road, Corstorphine
EH12 8HW
Tel: 334 9789
'Drive-thru' available.

99 Gorgie Park Rd
EH14 1NG
Tel: 337 1869
Sun-Sat 8.00-00.00
'Drive-thru' available.

Kinnaird Park
Newcraighall EH15 3RD
Tel: 657 5363
Mon-Sun 8.00-00.00
'Drive-thru' available.

59 London Rd
EH7 6AA
Tel: 659 5841
Mon-Sun 8.00-00.00
'Drive-thru' available.

Newbridge Ind Estate, Newbridge
EH28 1PW
Tel: 335 0148
'Drive-thru' available

Unit 12, Princes Mall, Princes Street
EH1 1BQ

137-138 Princes St EH2 4BL
Tel: 226 3872
Mon-Sun 7.30-24.00

Seafield Road,
63 Craigentinny Avenue North
EH6 7LJ
'Drive thru' available

3-5 South St Andrew St
EH2 2AU
Tel: 558 9348

74 Telford Rd EH4 2NF
Tel: 315 3447
Mon-Sun 8.00-23.00
'Drive-thru' available. Children's parties hosted.

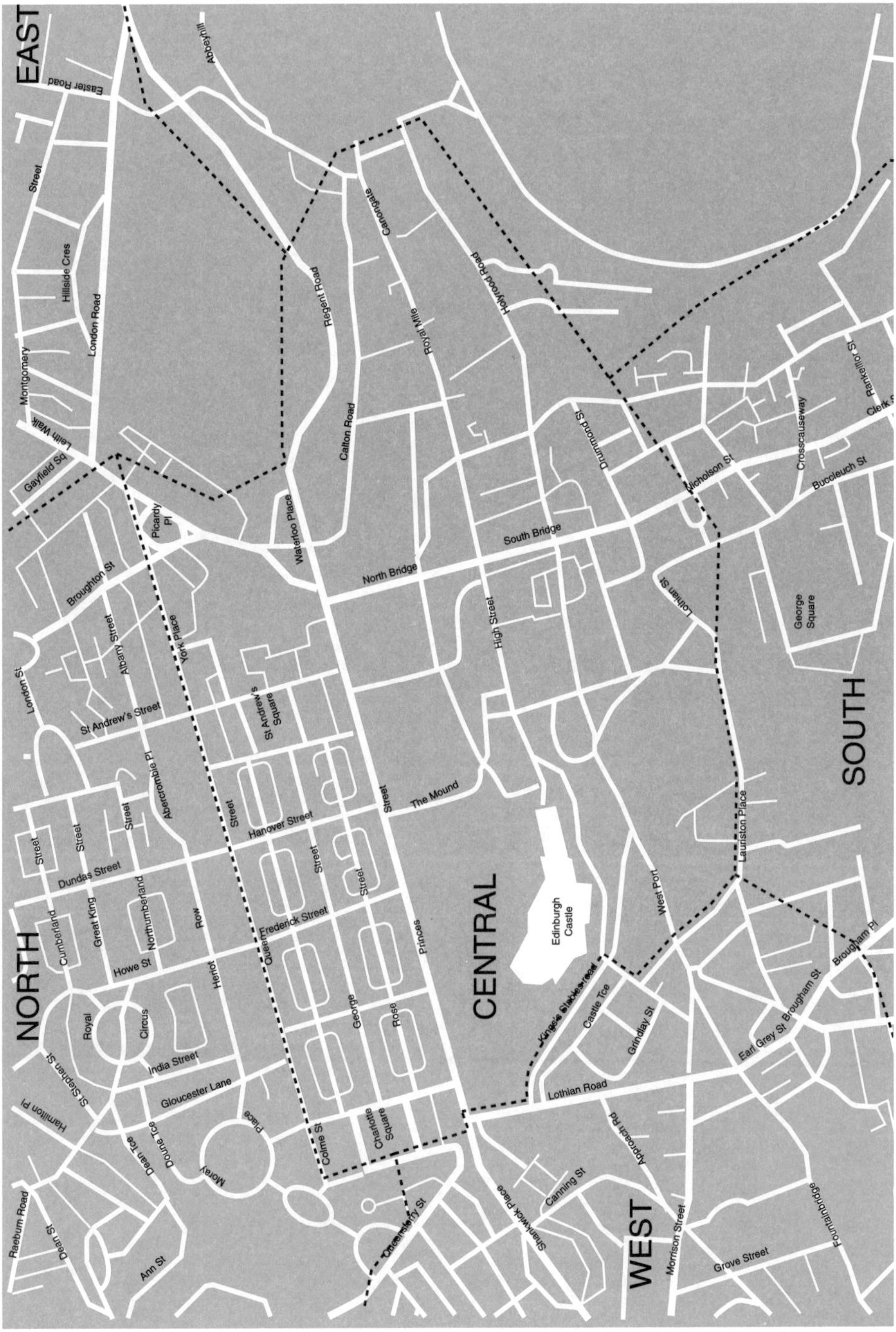

EAST
NORTH
CENTRAL
SOUTH
WEST
Easter Road
Abbeyhill
Montgomery Street
Hillside Cres
London Road
Leith Walk
Gayfield Sq
Picardy Pl
Broughton St
London St
Albany Street
York Place
St Andrew's Street
St Andrew's Square
Waterloo Place
Regent Road
Calton Road
Canongate
Royal Mile
Holyrood Road
North Bridge
South Bridge
High Street
Drummond St
Nicholson St
Crosscauseway
Rankeillor St
Clerk St
Buccleuch St
Lothian St
George Square
Lauriston Place
West Port
Brougham Pl
Brougham St
Earl Grey St
Lothian Road
Grindlay St
Castle Tce
King's Stables Road
Edinburgh Castle
The Mound
Princes Street
Rose Street
George Street
Hanover Street
Frederick Street
Queen Street
Heriot Row
Abercrombie Pl
Dundas Street
Great King Street
Northumberland Street
Cumberland Street
Howe St
Royal Circus
India Street
Gloucester Lane
St Stephen St
Hamilton Pl
Raeburn Road
Dean St
Ann St
Dean Tce
Doune Tce
Moray Place
Colme St
Charlotte Square
Queensferry St
Shandwick Place
Canning St
Approach Rd
Morrison Street
Grove Street
Fountainbridge

For Free

This section is a quick-reference guide to having fun for free. Indoors and out, there are lots of places to go with Under 5s that don't cost anything, excepting, perhaps, your transport there and back.

INDOORS

IKEA crèche and soft play area

There's no height restriction, but obviously children are left at their parents' discretion. There's also the play lay-outs in the children's section. IKEA offers complementary teas & coffee from 9.30-10.00, so if you're intending browsing, you might like to make use of this – though you'll need nerves of steel to walk out without at least one purchase!

Ocean Terminal Shopping Centre

Weekend and bank holiday events for children include storytelling in a wigwam, and bands of pirates roaming the shopping centre! There is also a giant chess board to play with, that has toddler-size pieces.

STER CENTURY CINEMA – OCEAN TERMINAL

Children's films on Sat and Sun morning. Admission: Children £2, accompanying adults free.

The Mussel Inn

61 Rose Street, Edinburgh.
Tel: 225 5979
££, high chairs, breastfeeding welcome.
Grown-up but child friendly seafood restaurant that likes to encourage children to try eating shellfish, so it gives it to them for free, followed by a free ice-cream too.

Museums & Galleries

The following museums and galleries have free entry

Museum of Childhood

Newhaven Heritage Museum

The People's Story

Queensferry Museum

Royal Museum

Museum of Scotland

Prestongrange Industrial Museum

North Berwick Museum

Dunbar Under Ground

The Dean Gallery

National Gallery of Scotland

Scottish National Gallery of Modern Art

Scottish National Portrait Gallery

Brass Rubbing Centre

Although some of these are more suited to older under 5s, places like the Royal Museum or The Museum of Scotland are packed with things to catch young children's eyes. Remember too that the Royal Museum and the Museum of Scotland have a dedicated area for eating packed lunches. Although this is used by schools during visits, it's also available to the public, so you don't have to eat in the cafés.

Art galleries can prove fascinating for some children – the Lichtenstein, with its bright colours, in the ground floor corridor of the Scottish National Gallery of Modern Art always grabs the attention on our visits!

HOLISTIC

Baby Massage Classes at the Royal Infirmary

Contact: Joanne McCormick
Tel: 242 2601
Please call only on Mon 14.00-19.30, Tue 14.00-19.30, Thu 14.00-16.00 in order to talk to Joanne,
A course of 6 hour long sessions, with about six mums and babies. The course is run by a midwife.

OUTDOORS

Gorgie City Farm

Trainspotting – from the bridge in Princes Street Gardens

Royal Botanic Garden: we always have fun searching for the dinosaurs that (apparently!) live there. No luck in spotting them yet, but the nosy squirrels and the ducks seem to be a good substitute

Looking at the boats at Cramond, Musselburgh, Granton, South Queensferry and Leith harbours.

Vogrie Country Park.

Dalkeith Country Park in winter.

Parks & Playgrounds – if it's a nice day (and it's feasible!) why not walk a little bit further and visit a less familiar playpark.

Holyrood Park, Salisbury Crags and Arthur's Seat: loads of space to run, run, run. There are signets at some points of the year, frogs crossing the roads at others. On Ne'er Day, there's sled dog racing.

Lauriston Castle grounds.

Why not have a glance through *Annual Events* – many of the events listed in this section have free entry.

NOTES

Healthcare

This section includes local NHS, voluntary and complementary health care facilities, but cannot claim to be comprehensive; it should however be able to direct you to sources of more detailed information.

EMERGENCY CARE

If your child requires urgent medical attention:
Dial 999;
or,
contact your GP;
or go direct to:
Royal Hospital for Sick Children
Sciennes Rd
Tel: 536 0000

GENERAL PRACTITIONER SERVICES

If you think your child has a medical problem the normal first contact is your GP. As well as treating most common conditions and referring your child on to a specialist, (should this be necessary), most GPs in Edinburgh provide special services for under 5s. These include a Child Health Surveillance Programme, often in conjunction with your health visitor, in which your child will be called for routine medical and developmental checks. In addition, your GP is likely to undertake your child's basic immunisation programme.

New to the Area?
Lothian Health Board (see 'Useful Addresses' in this chapter) or Capital Information Points (in libraries and throughout the city) can provide a list of local GPs.

Want to change your GP?
You can do so by registering and completing a form with a new doctor of your choice. If you have difficulty finding a GP who will accept you as a patient, contact the Health Board (see 'Useful Addresses' in this chapter) which has an obligation to find a GP.

Night Care?
GPs offer 24 hr care but you may not always be seen by a GP from your own practice if you require treatment between 18.00 and 8.00, or at weekends or public holidays. Many local GPs utilise a co-operative service at these times which means that the duty doctors attend the patients of several different surgeries. You may be asked to attend a local treatment centre rather than receive a home visit.

HOSPITAL SERVICES (EXCLUDING MATERNITY)

Royal Hospital for Sick Children
Sciennes Rd
Tel: 536 0000

Orientated to the needs of children in all areas of the hospital. Clinics, waiting areas and the accident and emergency department are all stocked with toys and books etc for all ages.
Resident facilities are available for parents wishing to stay with their child in hospital. These comprise of separate areas, which are not directly part of the clinical setting and some accommodation on the wards, including a small number of child and parent cubicles with en suite facilities. All parents who wish to stay with their child can do so and attempts will be made to find beds for as many as possible. Priority is given to parents of very sick children, parents who travel long distances and breastfeeding mothers. Parent sitting rooms, kitchen, laundry and bathroom facilities are all available.
Visiting is permitted on a 24 hr basis for parents/guardians. Other visitors are welcome until 19.00 at the discretion of the ward charge nurse. An adult must accompany visiting children at all times and take responsibility for their behaviour.
Play staff are available in all the clinical areas to ensure that play is encouraged and maintained during a child's stay in hospital. The play specialists within the team can assist the child to understand the treatments and investigations they are undergoing while in hospital. Volunteers support professional staff within Sick Kids. For example, they may support the play specialists to ensure that the children's recreational needs are met. They guide families around the hospital, take the mobile library around the wards, befriend a child, read bedtime stories to the children in the evenings or even assist with fundraising.
Preoperative Play Coordinators run pre-admission visits for children who are due to have surgery. These are recommended in order to alleviate stress and anxiety surrounding a hospital admission. Visits can also be organised for small groups of nursery/primary school children wishing to find out more about hospitals.
With prior arrangement the hospital nursery can accommodate a number of young children of parents visiting the hospital. The nursery is open Mon-Fri 7.20-18.00. For further information contact Carolyn Hedley, Play Services Coordinator, Tel: 536 0000, Bleep: 241.

St John's Hospital at Howden

Howden Rd W
Livingston
Tel: 01506 419 666

West Lothian Healthcare (NHS) Trust offers a holistic approach to ill children aged 0-16 yrs and their families. Parents are welcome to stay and their needs are accommodated where possible on the ward. Siblings are welcome but appropriate adult supervision is appreciated. Visiting times for parents are open. For friends and relatives the hours are 11.00-19.00 and at the discretion of the Ward Sister.

There is a playroom staffed by play leaders during the week and open at the weekend, nursing staff permitting.

There a wide range of clinics where your child's condition, treatment and care is assessed by paediatricians and nursing staff. There are play facilities coordinated by play leaders when available.

Children's Community Nursing provides specialist nursing care for children in their own homes. They work closely with hospital staff, GPs, health visitors, special schools and many other agencies to help provide the child and family with holistic care. The team comprises of 5 specially trained nurses who cover the whole of West Lothian, one of whom is based in the Child Development Centre and specialises in caring for children with neuro developmental problems.

ANTENATAL CARE

As soon as you think you are pregnant you should visit your GP. Usually you will be asked to choose where you would like to have your baby, at home or in hospital. You can arrange a home birth directly with community midwives, Tel: 536 4278.

Basic facts to bear in mind are your preference and comfort, your medical history, the consultant's policies and hospital facilities. A mother's requests will be met (circumstances permitting) in all of the units.

Simpson Centre for Reproductive Health

Royal Infirmary of Edinburgh – Little France
51 Little France Crescent
Tel: 536 1000

Maternity services in Lothian are now community based, with most women receiving care in their local area. Antenatal care is provided by the local midwifery team, your GP or, if necessary, a consultant obstetrician. This mean that most women only attend hospital for the birth of their baby. Postnatal care is provided at home by the local midwifery team.

Information

The midwives based in your local area will provide advice in relation to all aspects of pregnancy, birth and postnatal care. In addition, a leaflet 'Your Baby – Your Choice' is available in many outlets in the community to help you make decisions about your care. The midwives at your local clinic and parent education sessions should be able to provide you with any further information you require in relation to your care.

Parent Education Sessions

Provided by the midwifery team (with the support of other healthcare profesionals) within your locality, parent education sessions cover various aspects of pregnancy up to and including the birth of your baby, although they may not be entirely all-encompassing. The midwife will also discuss the arrangements for your care following the birth of your baby.

Feeding Your Baby

Information about feeding your baby will be provided by the midwifery team as part of your antenatal care; breastfeeding is encouraged. The Simpson Centre for Reproductive Health has 'Baby Friendly' status awarded by UNICEF for its support of breastfeeding. There is a weekly drop-in clinic on a Tuesday from 1200-1400 on the ground floor of the centre, for those with breastfeeding problems, or contact the NCT Centre, Tel: 668 3257.

Facilities for Childcare

There are two play areas situated on the ground floor of the centre. A selection of toys and children's books is available. Parents are asked to keep children under supervision at all times.

Neonatal Unit

The unit provides specialist care for 44 babies. Parents are encouraged to visit and to participate in their baby's care; siblings are also welcome. There is accommodation available for parents, with priority given to those whose babies are acutely ill or whose babies have been transferred to the unit from another hospital. There is a play area for children stocked with toys and books. Parents are asked to keep visiting children under supervision at all times.

Simpsons Special Care Babies

A voluntarily run charity set up by parents and friends who have had babies in the unit. Raises funds to provide equipment and facilities for the unit, to complement and enhance those provided by the NHS.

St John's Hospital at Howden

Howden Rd W
Livingston
Tel: 01506 419 666

West Lothian Healthcare (NHS) Trust offers a holistic approach to midwifery care encompassing a full range of maternity services, as well as water birth, home birth and domino care.

Antenatal appointments
At your first appointment with the midwife at the health centre, a full range of written information relating to health in pregnancy, screening tests, parenting skills and options for delivery will be discussed and given to you. Your midwife will also plan with you the frequency and content of antenatal visits for the rest of your pregnancy.

Antenatal Classes
Antenatal classes both at your local health centre and at the hospital will be offered to you. Community midwives facilitate these with other health professionals such as health visitors and physiotherapists. Courses vary from: women only classes, women and partner classes, teenage classes, aquanatal classes and hypnotherapy classes.

Special Care Baby Unit
The unit provides holistic care for 14 babies. Breastfeeding is encouraged and necessary facilities are provided. Parents and siblings may visit anytime but supervision of children is required. Parents may stay if accommodation is available.

ANTENATAL CLASSES AND SUPPORT

Association for Improvements in the Maternity Services (AIMS)

40 Leamington Ter
EH10 4JL
Contact: Nadine Edwards
Tel: 0131 229 6259
Tel: 0870 765 1433 (Helpline)
Web: www.aims.org.uk

AIMS provides information and support to parents about their choices in maternity care. A range of booklets on how to make the right decision for you, the second and third stages of labour, home birth, water birth, having twins etc, plus quarterly journal are available. Send SAE for free publications list. Birth pool available for hire.

Birth Resource Centre

Contact: Nadine Edwards, Andrea McLaughlin, Deborah Purdue
Tel: 229 3667 or 229 9035

The centre provides classes for parents during pregnancy and after birth, including yoga for pregnancy, birth preparation workshops for women and their partners, postnatal discussion groups, baby massage, baby music, post natal yoga for parent and baby, and other events. The weekly yoga classes provide practical skills including breathing awareness, relaxation, stretches and movements. These address both physical and emotional issues that arise during pregnancy. The day workshops prepare women and their partners to meet the challenge of labour and birth with confidence and the postnatal groups support women and their families after birth. All sessions provide parents with the information they need to enable them to make decisions about their pregnancies, birth and care of their babies, as well as an opportunity to meet others in similar circumstances. Birth pools, birthballs, library and newsletter available.

National Childbirth Trust

NCT Centre – Edinburgh
University Health Service
5th floor
6 Bristo Square EH8 9AL
Tel: 668 3257
Tel: 0870 444 0907 (NCT Breastfeeding Line 8.00-22.00)

NCT antenatal classes give parents the chance to discuss and to become informed about all aspects of pregnancy, birth and life with a new baby. Relaxation, breathing techniques, massage and different birth positions are practised and explained, enabling parents to approach the birth confidently. Breastfeeding education is included as part of the antenatal class package and support continues postnatally.
Venues vary. Couples Course £126, Refresher Course £55, Short Course £78 Concessionary fee is half full fee.

Scottish Birth Teachers Association

Contact: Nadine Edwards
Tel: 229 6259

2 yr training and occasional study days. List of SBTA teachers available.

Lothian Home Birth Support Group

Contact: Ruth Kirkpatrick
Tel: 445 1507

Offers support and information.

POSTNATAL SUPPORT

Community Midwives
Community midwives visit you at home after the birth of your baby and will attend the delivery if you have a home confinement. They will visit every day until the baby is 10 days old (or for longer if there are any problems).

Health Visitors
Health visitors are nurses with special training in all aspects of family health and particularly that of children and older people. Usually they are associated with a GP practice or community clinic but work closely with other health care professionals. Their knowledge of child development, behaviour and health will offer any advice or reassurance you need. In addition, your health visitor should be a valuable source of local knowledge. A health visitor will visit you on the 11th day after the birth of your baby. Regular contact is maintained through home visits, visits to the baby clinic and by telephone during working hours. He or she will monitor your baby's development and growth through assessments, weighing and hearing tests and will also guide you through immunisation.
Your health visitor will help with problems up until the age of 5 (when the school nurse takes over responsibility), covering a wide range of areas such as sleep problems, speech therapy referrals, crying babies etc. You do not have to have a health visitor, although one will automatically be assigned to you, but you may need to sign a form confirming it is your wish not to have this help. If you are not happy with the relationship you have with your health visitor you can approach another who can advise you on how to change. Health visitors are also concerned with the health and welfare of parents. Health visitors often run clinics and support groups for first time mothers, breastfeeding support, well men, well women, etc.

Gorgie/Dalry Community Health Project

Springwell House, Ardmillan Ter
Tel: 537 7530

Local project identifying and responding to a range of health needs and issues within the local community. Offers counselling, alternative therapies such as homeopathy, reflexology and aromatherapy massage, plus a variety of group work such as adult and child yoga, women's health and a Sure Start funded project for young parents aged 16-24 yrs with children 0-3 yrs. The group meet on a weekly basis and offer support to one another. Crèche facilities available. Call for information.

La Leche League

Tel: 01875 320991, contact: Sandra Thomson
Tel: 01506 414010, contact: Caron Howden
Web: www.laleche.org.uk

Breastfeeding support and information. Monthly group meetings for pregnant and breastfeeding mothers and their babies. Telephone counselling from trained volunteers who have personal breastfeeding experience. They also run toddler group for mothers breastfeeding older children.

NCT Centre

University Health Service
5th floor
6 Bristo Square EH8 9AL
Tel: 6683257
Tel: 0870 444 0907 (NCT Breastfeeding Line 8.00-22.00)
Web: www.nct-edinburgh.freeserve.co.uk
Please phone for new hours

The NCT offers extensive postnatal support in the form of local groups of parents who meet on a regular basis. If you go to NCT antenatal classes your name will be given to your local group representative who should contact you around the time your baby is due, if not before. She will give you details of local meetings and may be able to advise you whom to contact if you have any specific problems. The NCT centre will tell you who your local group representative is if you are not an NCT member. You are welcome to join a postnatal support group even if you have not been to NCT antenatal classes. Activities include coffee mornings or afternoons, evening talks, discussion groups, bumps and babies groups, baby massage, fund-raising events, picnics, local newsletter, etc. Members receive the quarterly magazine 'New Generation'.
The NCT also provides information, support and encouragement for breastfeeding through its network of breastfeeding counsellors who have all breastfed their own children and been through intensive training. They can also arrange the hire of electric breast pumps and valley cushions
A breastfeeding counsellor is usually available at the NCT centre during opening hours and any mother with a query about

breastfeeding can call into the NCT centre.

Postnatal Depression

It is not uncommon for women to feel depressed any time in the first year postnatally. Do not hesitate to ask for help; contact your GP or health visitor for support and advice. Support groups are frequently run for mothers with postnatal depression and your health visitor will be able to advise you.

Postnatal Depression Project

Wallace House, 3 Boswall Rd
Tel: 538 7288

8a Palmerston Pl (drop-in centre)
Tel: 220 3457 (support line)

You can contact the project directly as well as health visitor, GP and other health professional referrals. It offers a range of services to families suffering with postnatal depression including: couple and individual counselling, women's therapy groups, art therapy and baby massage classes. All services supported with crèche facilities.

DENTAL CARE

All dentists providing NHS care can be found on a list held by Lothian Health Board (see Useful Addresses in this chapter), or at your post office or library. The majority of children go to a family dentist for treatment but in certain circumstances your child could be treated by the Community Dental Service. Community dentists have a responsibility to provide dental health education in nurseries and schools, they also monitor the dental health of children through a screening programme.
Mother are entitled to free dental treatment throughout pregnancy and until the baby's 1st birthday. Children under 18 yrs are also entitled to free dental care. It is recommended that the first check up is at about 2 yrs, but if you take your child to the dentists with you on your visits they will become used to the surgery from a very early age.
The average concentration of fluoride in Lothian's water supply does not exceed 0.2 parts per million, too low an amount to benefit the teeth. Dentists may recommend that children take fluoride drops or tablets which are available free from many dentists or baby clinics. If you decide to give your child fluoride supplements make sure that only a pea-sized amount of fluoride toothpaste is used on the brush.

Community Dental Service

Duncan St Dental Centre

16 Duncan St
Tel: 667 7114

Provides information about all aspects of dental health and is happy to provide leaflets and advice for projects at nurseries.

COMPLEMENTARY HEALTH CARE

There is a wide range of complementary/alternative therapists offering a variety of therapies in the Edinburgh area but not all of these would be suitable for children or pregnant women. Most of these services are offered privately by individual practitioners and fees for consultation and treatment vary widely. Practitioners advertise in local directories or can be located via their national professional body. It is strongly recommended that you check that any therapist is registered with their appropriate professional body. Please remember that an entry is not necessarily a recommendation.
It is also sensible to advise any therapist of any conventional medical treatment you are undergoing prior to commencing therapy and vice versa. It would not be practical to attempt to include an exhaustive list of therapies/therapists in a publication such as this. If you are unable to find a local practitioner or a particular therapy your local library will be able to direct you to a national organisation you can contact. You may also be able to obtain further information from the following local resources.
And remember, you can also request an NHS referral to the Homeopathic hospital if you think this would be helpful for you or your child. while the hospital is in Glasgow, it operates outreach clinics in St John's at Howden. However, the waiting list may be extensive.

Aveva Natural Remedies

9 Gillespie Pl, opposite Barclay Church
EH01 4HS
Tel: 228 3234
Web: www.aveva.co.uk
Opening hours: Tue-Thu 10.00-18.00, Fri and Sat 10.00-17.00

Consultations 6 days/wk for all the family, pregnant women, new mothers, toddlers and children up to 12 yrs. Shop selling homeopathic remedies, scottish grown organic herbs, natural products, natural nappies, skin care, beauty products and information including books. Self-help classes and workshops on homeopathy, baby massage, active/natural birth, relaxation, nutrition, natural medicine and yoga. Home visits available.

Baby Massage
Contact: Linda Bendle
Tel: 447 3060

Baby massage classes are suitable from birth to crawling. Possible benefits - may help to relieve colic and constipation; promote relaxation and sleep; strengthen immune, respiratory, circulatory, nervous and cardiovascular systems.

Discover Chiropractic
240 Queensferry Rd
Tel: 332 0063
Email: blackhall@discoverchiropractic.co.uk
Opening hours: Mon,Wed 8.00-11.30 and 14.30-18.10; Tue, Thu 14.00-18.10, Fri 8.00-11.30; 3rd Sat each month 10.00-12.00

Chiropractic care may help with many childhood ailments such as sleeplessness, hyperactivity, vomiting, ear/nose/ throat infections, Erbs Palsy and Shaken Baby Syndrome.
Child friendly family run business, focused on family care. Consultations available from birth. Toys/books/videos available. Nappy changing room with nappies provided. Breastfeeding welcome, premises accessible to pushchairs. Usually a member of staff can look after children during a parent's consultation.

The Edinburgh Natural Health Centre
1 St Colme St (behind Charlotte Sq)
Tel: 220 8205
Opening hours: Mon-Sat 9.00-18.00

Acupuncture, Chinese herbal medicine, homeopathy, nutrition, and hypnotherapy. Free initial consultation for guidance if requested. Courses and lectures. Consultation by appointment.

Glovers Integrated Healthcare
10 William St
Tel: 225 3161
Email: gloversIHC@aol.com
Web: www.glovers-health.co.uk
Opening hours: Mon-Fri 10.00-17.00

Homeopathic consultations and remedies available. Also mail order service.

Homeopathic Clinic
Dalkeith Medical Centre
24 St Andrew St
Dalkeith EH22 1AP
Tel: 561 5510

Homeopathic treatment is available on the NHS at clinics held at both Dalkeith Medical Centre and the Firrhill Medical Centre in Edinburgh. Patients referred by their GPs are able to consult homeopathically-qualified doctors. Treatment is free. All enquiries and referrals to Dalkeith Medical Centre.

Ewan Kenny, Craniosacral Therapist
Energetics
14a Broughton St EH1 3LY
Tel: 557 9567
Email: enquiries@energetics.uk.com

Craniosacral therapy is a gentle 'hands on' treatment. Sutable for all ages, it may prove particularly useful for many infant problems such as colic, breathing difficulties, restlessness and irritability.

Medicalternative
Waterside House
19 Hawthornbank Lane EH4 3BH
Tel: 225 5656
Email: reception@medicalternative.com
Or julie-anne.taylor@virgin.net (for advanced hypnotherapy)
Opening times: 8.00-19.00.

Private health care centre which encompasses both conventional and alternative care. You can walk in off the street and see a qualified GP (no referral or appointment needed). There are numerous alternative therapists, all highly qualified and specialists in their own field. Breastfeeding welcomed. Nappy changing facilities.

Massage Therapies
30A Hermitage Gardens
Edinburgh EH10 6AY
Contact: Benedetta Gaetani d'Aragona
Tel: 447 4421
Opening hours: 9.00-21.00

Specialising in prenatal, perinatal and postnatal massage as well as massage instruction for partners. Prices – 55 mins/£30; 85 mins/£40 and home visits: £35-40. Free parking.

Napiers Dispensary

18 Bristo Pl
Tel: 225 5542
Web: www.napiers.net
Opening hours, shop: Mon 10.00-18.00; Tue-Fri 9.00-18.00; Sat 9.00-17.30; Sun 12.30-16.30

Baby/child herbal clinic: Wed 9.00-13.00 (fortnightly) and Thu 09.30-13.00 by appointment
£20 for first consultation; thereafter £18.

also at:

35 Hamilton Pl
Stockbridge, EH3 5BA
Tel: 315 2130
Web: www.napiers.net
Opening hours, shop: Mon 10.00-18.00; Tue-Sat 9.00-17.30

Baby/child herbal clinic: Fri 9.45-16.45 by appointment.
£20 for first consultation; thereafter £18.
Baby/child homeopathic clinic: Wed fortnightly 9.30-12.45 by appointment
£20 for first consultation thereafter £15. Approx £3 per remedy.
Consultations in herbal medicine, aromatherapy, osteopathy, homeopathy, acupuncture and counselling. The mother and baby herbal clinics provide a range of therapies which can be of use to pregnant women, babies and children. Herbal medicine is especially gentle for babies and children and may prove useful in treating, for instance, colic, sleep problems, cradle cap, glue ear, coughs and catarrh.
The shops stock a range of herbal remedies, health food supplies, vitamins etc; from tea to encourage breast milk to creams for nappy rash. Mail order is available through the website.

The Osteopathic Practice

1 Wester Coates Avenue EH12 5LS.
Contact: Tom Kelman
Tel: 346 0134
Mob: 07866 299 250
Email: tom_kelman@hotmail.com
Practice times: Mon to Fri: 9.00-18.00

Tom Kelman is a Registered Osteopath who holds a post graduate Diploma in Paediatric Osteopathy and who specialises in paediatric and family care. He offers experienced advice, treatment and management for many childhood problems ranging from: unsettled, crying or colicy symptoms following a difficult birth, to children with developmental delay, cerebral palsy, autism or epilepsy. May also help mums with gentle and effective relief from aches and pains before or after a birth.

The Whole Works Complementary Health Centre

Jackson Close
209 Royal Mile
Edinburgh EH1 1PA

Contact: Rob Ritchie (Manager)
Tel: 225 8092
Opening hours: 9.00-20.00

Offers a range of complementary health therapies and counselling, including cranial sacral therapy, homeopathy, chiropractic, acupressure and herbal medicine.

USEFUL ADDRESSES

This list is not intended to be exhaustive but it may help point you in the right direction if you are seeking further information locally. See also Support Groups in Help & Infromation section. For further information check with your local health professional, NCT Group, library or community centre.

Action for Sick Children (Scotland)

172 Leith Walk EH6 5EA
Tel: 553 6553
Email: asc2k@lineone.net

A charity for all children in hospital and for adults caring for them. Information for parents with babies in special care units. Parent packs to help children prepare for a hospital visit. Hospital playbox for loan to local playgroups which helps parents to prepare children (3-6 yrs) for a hospital visit; includes toys, books, real medical equipment and mini uniforms.

Family Planning Centre

18 Dean Ter
Tel: 332 7941 and 343 6243

Lothian Health Board

Stevenson House
555 Gorgie Rd
Tel: 537 8400

Lothian Health Council

21 Torphichen St EH3 8HX
Tel: 229 6605
Email:
Lothianhealthcouncil@lhc.lothian.scot.nhs.uk
Web: www.lhc-online.org

Provides advice and information on the NHS and support to anyone wishing to complain about NHS services or treatment. Also monitors local health services to identify gaps in provision or areas of good practice and consults on proposed changes to health services.

Lothian NHS Board Library and Resource

Deaconess House
148 The Pleasance
Tel: 536 9451/2/3
Opening hours: Mon 13.00-16.30; Tue-Wed 9.30-16.30; Thu 9.30-18.30; Fri 9.30-13.00

Can provide leaflets and posters on a wide range of health issues free of charge. Resources for teaching and training purposes are also available for loan. The centre has several databases which have information about specific conditions and related support and self-help groups. These are updated regularly and information can be printed out on request.

Royal Life Saving Society UK

Tel: 01759 773994
Or contact:
Linsey Watson
Scottish Eastern Branch
17 Station Rd, Loanhead EH20 9RQ

Provides courses in baby resuscitation called 'Save a Baby's Life'. These are invaluable to any parent, carer, babysitter or grandparent, or anyone who will be in sole charge of an infant. They are organised periodically and for a small fee, currently £5, you will be taught life saving skills on a manikin, (it is recommended that you attend without children). Courses last 2 hrs and cover action in an emergency, drowning, choking, breathing stopped, heart stopped. Additional information for technique required for children aged 1+ yrs can be provided in the form of a short display at the end. Contact the above phone number for details of these or their other life saving courses, or send an SAE to Linsey Watson. If you have 10 or more people interested, Linsey would be able to provide you with your own training session or for individuals advise when the next organised course will take place.

Sick Kids Friends Foundation

Royal Hospital for Sick Children
Sciennes Rd

Raises funds to further interests of the child health services in the RHSC.

SNIP - Special Needs Information Point

Royal Hospital for Sick Children
14 Rillbank Ter
Contact: Shirley Young
Tel: 536 0853 (24hr answerphone)
Fax: 536 0853
Minicom: 536 0360
Email: Snip@btinternet.com
Web: www.snipinfo.org

Information for parents, carers and professionals about children with special needs.

Help and Information

This section is meant to be a starting point if you are looking for help or advice. It is not all-encompassing, but we have tried to list the names and addresses of organisations that can provide you with information, advice and support.

HEALTH

For help with specific medical conditions please refer to the chapter on Health Care or contact SNIP (Special Needs Information Point based at the Sick Kids Hospital in Edinburgh) who can provide information, contact addresses and support.

Special Needs Information Point (SNIP)

14 Rillbank Ter
Royal Hospital for Sick Children
Edinburgh EH9 1LN
Tel/Fax: 536 0583
Text phone: 536 0360
Email: Snip@btinternet.com
Web: www.snipinfo.org

BENEFITS / SOCIAL SECURITY INFORMATION

There's a good deal of information online. Two helpful websites are:

Parents at work

www.parentsatwork.org.uk
Has a wide range of information including factsheets about things like tax credits and flexible working.

www.dwp.gov.uk/lifeevent/benefits/index.asp
provides details of the different types of benefits available and how to make a claim.

Other sources of information are:

Benefits Agency

38 Castle Ter
Tel: 229 4311
General information and advice about social security and child benefits.

LOCAL SOCIAL SECURITY OFFICES:

Edinburgh City
38 Castle Ter EH3 9SJ
Tel: 229 4311
For Postal Districts EH1-4, 8-10, 16-20, 22-26, 37

Edinburgh East
275 Portobello High St EH15 2AQ
Tel: 657 7400
For Postal Districts: EH15-16, 21, 31-36, 39-42

Leith
199 Commercial St EH6 6QP
Tel: 555 8000
For Postal Districts: EH4-7

Edinburgh West
8 Clifton Ter
Tel: 01506 772000
For Postal Districts: EH11-14, 28-30

Westerhailes
Westerhailes Plaza EH14 2SP
Tel: 01506 772 000
Postal Districts: EH11-14

CHILD TAX CREDIT

For help or information regarding child tax credit, contact the helpline or write to the office (addresses given below). You will need your NI number (and your partner's if the claim was joint). The help line can be extremely busy, but it's still quicker than writing.

Tax Credits Helpline (for those living in GB)

Tel: 0845 300 3900
Textphone: 0845 300 3909

(for those living in NI)
Tel: 0845 603 2000
Textphone: 0845 607 6078

Helplines are open daily, 8.00-20.00 (except Christmas Day, Boxing Day, New Year's Day and Easter Sunday).

Postal Addresses

(for those living in GB)
Inland Revenue
Tax Credits Office
Preston PR1 0SB

(for those living in NI)
Inland Revenue
Tax Credits Office
Dorchester House
52-58 Great Victoria St Belfast BT2 7WF

For information regarding Child Benefit, there's a national number: 0870 155 55 40.

The City of Edinburgh Council Advice Shop

86-87 South Bridge EH1 1HN
Tel: 225 1255

Consumer advice, debt advice and advice on welfare benefits.

SOCIAL WORK

The City of Edinburgh Council Department of Social Work HQ

Shrubhill House
Shrub Pl, Leith Walk
Tel: 554 4301
Tel: 0800 731 6969 Emergency Social Work Service - out of hours

As well as the HQ listed above, There are 12 social work centres throughout the city, all open Mon-Thu 8.30-16.30, Fri 8.30-15.30. Social workers also work out of hospitals.

Social Work Centres

Central

Victoria St Social Work Centre
11 Victoria St EH1 2HE
Tel: 226 6731

North East

Giles St Social Work Centre
9-11 Giles St EH6 6DJ
Tel: 553 3835

Craigentinny Social Work Centre
Loaning Rd EH7 6JE
Tel: 661 8291

Leith Social Work Centre
St John's House
71 Constitution St EH6 7AF
Tel: 553 2121
North West

Westfield House Social Work Centre
Westfield House
5 Kirk Loan EH12 7HD
Tel: 334 9933

Muirhouse Cres Social Work Centre
34 Muirhouse Cres EH4 4QL
Tel: 343 1991

West Pilton Gdns Social Work Centre
8 West Pilton Gdns EH4 4DP
Tel: 529 5400

South East

Craigmillar Social Work Centre
111 Peffermill Rd EH16 4AL
Tel: 656 9800

Captain's Rd Social Work Centre
40 Captains Rd EH17 8QF
Tel: 529 5300

South West

Springwell House Social Work Centre
1 Gorgie Rd EH11 2LA
Tel: 313 6785

Oxgangs Path Social Work Centre
4 Oxgangs Path EH13 9LX
Tel: 445 4451

Murrayburn Gate Social Work Centre
5 Murrayburn Gate EH14 2SS
Tel: 442 4131

Citizens Advice Bureaux

Web: www.adviceguide.org.uk

A free, confidential service providing general advice and information on topics such as housing, family, employment, benefits and consumer issues. Offers money advice and debt negotiation, representation at employment and social security tribunals, some court representation. Appointments usually last 45 minutes. Most offices have legal clinics on a weekly basis.

EDINBURGH CENTRAL

58 Dundas St
Tel: 557 1500 (public line)
Fax: 557 3543

Opening times: Mon, Tue, Thu 9.30-16.00; Wed 9.30-13.00 (last appointment 11.45), 18.30-20.00 (appointment only)
Legal advice, information and general appointments.

GORGIE/DALRY
137 Dundee St
(Above Fountain Bridge Library)
Tel: 474 8080 (advice line)
Tel: 474 8081(to make appointments)
Opening times: Mon 13.30-16.00, 17.30-19.00 (appointments only);Tue 10.15-12.45, 13.30-16.00;Wed 13.30-16.00;Thu 10.15-12.45,13.30-16.00. Closed Fri

LEITH
166 Gt Junction St
Tel: 554 8144
Opening times: Mon, Tue 9.30-15.30; Wed 9.30-12.00; Thu 9.30-15.30, 18.00-19.30 (legal advice appointments)

PILTON
661 Ferry Rd
Tel: 332 9434
Opening times: Mon, Wed, Thu 9.30-12.30; Tue 9.30-15.30; Fri 9.30-12.00

PORTOBELLO
193 Portobello High St
Tel: 669 7138
Opening times: Mon, Tue, Thu 9.30-3.30; Wed 9.30-12.00, 18.30-19.45. Closed Fri

Gingerbread Edinburgh and Lothians Project Ltd

Gingerbread House
19 Chester St EH3 7RF
Tel: 220 1585
Email: GINGERBREADEDIN@aol.com
Opening times: Mon-Fri 10.00-16.00
Information and advice centre for lone parent families. It also provides 4 after school clubs (in Dalry, Leith, Tollcross and West End), and cover for in-service days, school holiday play schemes, and holiday information packs for lone parents.

Granton Information Centre

134-138 West Granton Rd
Tel: 551 2459 (24 hrs answering machine)
Email:enquiries@GIC.visps.com
Information and advice on benefits, debts, housing, employment etc. Also available for development of local self-help/support groups. Youth and disability rights.

The Rights Office

Southside Community Centre
117 Nicolson St EH8 9YG
Tel: 667 6339
Advice sessions: Mon and Wed 10.00-15.30
Independent advice and representation on welfare benefits, disability rights, employment rights, debt and housing.

MEDIA LISTING

The Scotsman Group

108 Holyrood Rd
Tel: 620 8620 (reception)
Tel: 620 8888 (advertising)
Web: www.scotsman.com

The Scotsman

National daily morning paper, carries birth announcements. Has daily section with details of exhibitions, theatres, art galleries, etc. Church Service information on Sat. Weekend section on Sat with 'What's on' information

Evening News

Daily afternoon and evening paper full of local news. 'Daily Plan-It' has details of events. Also carries daily cinema programmes. Theatres, sales, fêtes etc also listed, especially on Fri.

Scotland on Sunday

Scottish Sunday paper. Has events page.

Edinburgh Herald and Post

Tel: 620 8888 (advertising)
Tel: 620 8705 (editorial)
Email: edinhp@scotsman.com
Published every Thu and delivered free to most homes in. Cinema listings and details of local arts and community events, sales, fêtes etc. Large 'For Sale' columns. If given sufficient notice, usually at least two weeks, the Herald and Post can publish details of your playgroup fair or other fundraising activities free. A different edition is printed for West Lothian, Tel: 01506 503400 for enquiries or editorial.

The List

14 High St EH1 1TE
Tel: 550 3070
Fax: 557 8500
Email: editor@list.co.uk
Web: www.list.co.uk
Published fortnightly and includes a small section 'Kid's List' which provides information about events in and around Edinburgh and Glasgow. It's worthwhile checking with the specific venues regarding times etc, as information can change after the publica-

tion has gone to press. Available at newsagents.

Radio Forth
Forth House, Forth St
Tel: 556 9255
Web: www.forth1.com
Web: www.forth2.com
Daily 'What's On' slot in the morning show on Forth 1, with information on forthcoming local events. Events page on the websites.

GUIDES TO EDINBURGH

Council libraries have books, files and on-line information for reference purposes.
These include:

Capital Information Point (CAPINFO)
Web: www.edinburgh.gov.uk
CAPINFO is a free council-run information service, which provides information about your local community and council departments: education, children, young people and families, leisure and health care. You can access Capinfo on the internet, on the above address at home or in libraries throughout Edinburgh.

Citizens' Advice
published by Citizens Advice Bureau.
Web: www.adviceguide.org.uk
Edinburgh Information Pack including information on childcare, nursery education, local and regional councillors, local churches, etc.

List of local clubs and organisations.

Reference books about Edinburgh.

A-Z guide produced by City Of Edinburgh Council, listing contacts, community updates, council lists, and general information regarding the city.

SUPPORT GROUPS

This section contains listings for organisations and voluntary groups who offer support and assistance on a wide range of issues.

For more comprehensive information on Women's Groups, contact the City of Edinburgh Council Equality Unit, 12 St Giles St, Tel: 469 3603. Your local Community Education Centre and some of the Community High Schools also arrange Parents' Groups with crèche facilities; see Community Education Centres in *Activities for Parents*.

AFASIC
Tel: 0845 3555577 (helpline)
Web: www.afasic.org.uk
also: www.talkingpoint.org.uk
UK charity supporting children and young adults with speech, language or communication impairments and their parents/carers.

AFASIC Edinburgh
Contact tel: 220 3122
Local support group.

British Allergy Foundation
30 Bellegrove Rd
Welling
Kent DA16 3PY
Tel: 020 8303 8583 (helpline)
Web: www.allergyfoundation.com
An independent UK charity providing information on all aspects of allergy.

Capability Scotland Advice Service (ASCS)
11 Ellersly Rd EH12 6HY
Tel: 313 5510
Text phone: 346 2529
Fax: 346 1681
Email: ascs@capability-scotland.org.uk
Web: www.capability-scotland.org.uk
Provides information and advice on any disability matter. Services include education and therapy.

The Compassionate Friends
Tel: 657 2106
Contact: Margaret
Web:www.tcf.org.uk
A self-help group for parents and their families who have suffered the loss of a child of any age through any cause. Lending library and link scheme available.

Contact a Family Scotland
Norton Park
57 Albion Rd EH5 7QY
Tel: 475 2608
Fax: 475 2609
Email: Scotland@cafamily.org.uk
Web: www.cafamily.org.uk

Opening times: Mon-Fri 10.00-16.00

Introduces and links families whose children have special needs through local mutual support and self-help groups. Offers nationwide support and links individual parents of children with very rare disorders.

Couple Counselling Lothian

9a Dundas St
Tel: 556 1527
Email: cclothian@btopenworld.com

Opening times: Mon-Thu 9.00-21.00; Fri 9.00-16.00; Sat 10.00-13.00

Confidential counselling service for those who are experiencing disharmony and tension in their marriage or personal relationships.

Cruse Bereavement Care

3 Rutland Sq EH1 2AS
Tel: 229 6275

In addition to counselling, advisory services and friendship groups for adults and offers bereavement counselling to children.

Dosti Muslim Groups

172 Leith Walk EH6 5EA
Contact: Audrey Peacock/ Wendy Spencer
Tel: 553 2189

Opening hours: Mon-Fri 9.30-17.00

Provides: support groups for Muslim women and children; information service to Muslim families and also the wider community. Muslim mothers with pre-school children can access childcare training (with crèche), plus family activities and events. Premises have nappy changing facilities (M&F).

Down's Syndrome Scotland

158-160 Balgreen Rd EH11 3AU
Tel: 313 4225
Fax: 313 4285
Email: info@dsscotland.org.uk
Web: www.dsscotland.org.uk

Aims to provide support and information to parents of children with Down's Syndrome. Local branch activities include parent and toddler groups, music and drama workshops, computer club and outings.

The Edinburgh Miscarriage Support Group

Tel: 657 5377
Contact: Sue

The group provides emotional support for anyone suffering the effects of miscarriage and pregnancy loss. Meetings held second Wednesday of every month 19.30-21.00 at Craiglockhart Sports Centre 177 Colinton Rd.

(see also the Miscarriage Association, page 104)

Edinburgh Women's Rape and Sexual Abuse Centre

Po Box 120
Brunswick Rd EH7 5WX
Tel: 556 9437 (answerphone out of office hours)
Email: ewrasac@aol.com

Information, practical and emotional support for women who have been raped or sexually assaulted at any time in their lives. Run by women for women.

Enlighten Action for Epilepsy

5 Coates Pl EH3 7AA
Tel: 226 5458
Email: info@enlighten.org.uk
Web: www.enlighten.org.uk

Offers information, advice, support and counselling to parents of children with epilepsy and parents with epilepsy who have young children.

ERIC – Enuresis Resource and Information Centre

34 Old School House
Britannia Road
Kingswood
Bristol BS15 8DB
Tel: 0117 960 3060 (helpline, Mon-Fri 10.00-16.00)
Email: info@eric.org.uk
Web: www.eric.org.uk

ERIC provides advice and information to children, young people, parents and professionals on bedwetting, day-time wetting and soiling. Can advise you on the location of your local enuresis clinic. The charity also stocks washable duvet and mattress protectors.

Family Care – Birthlink Adoption Counselling Service

21 Castle St, EH2 3DN
Tel: 225 6441

The adoption contact register for Scotland. Counselling, support and advice for adopted people, birth parents and adoptive parents.

Family Care Social Services

Family Support Service
Temporarily based at 21 Castle St
Contact: Sally Lynch, Social Worker
Tel: 225 6441

Community based project, aimed at families, providing individual support, advice and counselling. Limited childcare for appointments.

Family Mediation Lothian

37 George St EH2 2HN
Tel: 226 4507
Email: Lothian@familymediation.freeserve.co.uk

Helps separating and divorced parents to make arrangements for the future care of their children. Also runs several 'Contact Centres' where children can spend time with the parent and other relatives with whom they do not live or see regularly. Also provides support for older children.

First Hand (formerly known as Edinburgh Sitters)

39 Broughton Place
Tel: 557 3121

This project aims to provide a regular reliable sitter service to lone parents and carers of children and young adults with disabilities in Edinburgh and to promote, provide and support volunteering opportunities. A Saturday group for children of lone parents and befriending for young adults with disabilities. This is a valuable service for those who really need it and volunteers are always needed.

First Step Community Project

37 Galt Ave
Musselburgh EH21 8HU
Tel: 665 0848

Project for families with young children offering many services for parents as well as the children. Services include home visiting, play visiting, confidential counselling, classes and groups for adults and information library. Has a special needs playgroup. Also runs a group for teenagers with babies.

Homelink

Unit 5 Abbeymount Techbase
2 Easter Rd, EH7 5AN
Tel: 661 0890
Email: homelink@tinyworld.co.uk

Provides emotional and practical support to young families, using trained befrienders. Operates in South East and South West Edinburgh and in Mayfield, Midlothian.

Homestart Leith and North East Edinburgh

172 Leith Walk EH6 5EA
Tel/Fax: 553 7819
Email: homestartleith@btconnect.com

Homestart Edinburgh South Central

35 Guthrie St EH1 1JG
Tel: 226 1331
Email: info@homestart.freewire.co.uk

Volunteers offer regular support and practical help in the home to young families who have at least one child under 5.

Humanist Society of Scotland

26 Inverleith Row EH5 5QH
Contact: Ivan Middleton
Tel: 0701 071 4778
Email:ivan@humanism-scotland.org.uk

Information about non-religious ceremonies including baby naming ceremonies

Hyperactive Children's Support Group

71 Whyke Lane
Chichester, West Sussex PO19 2LD
Contact: Sally Bunday
Tel: 01243 551313
Fax: 01243 552019
Web: www.hacsg.org.uk

The HACSG considers non-drug therapies especially important for under 6s. Provides information for parents and professionals.

Independent Special Education Advice (ISEA) Scotland

164 High St
Dalkeith EH22 1AY
Tel: 454 0082
Fax: 454 0096
Email: iseascotland@whsmithnet.co.uk

Provides support to parents in Scotland who have a child with special educational needs. Provides free independent advice on the child's legal rights to an adequate and efficient education. This includes a telephone helpline and advocacy support.

LIBRA

4 Norton Pk EH7 5RS
Tel: 661 0111

LIBRA provides free counselling and support to women who are concerned about their own or someone else's drinking.

Lochend YWCA

198 Restalrig Rd S EH7 6DZ
Tel: 554 3400

Community café; children welcomed and catered for. Full access for prams and pushchairs; nappy-changing facility; bottles can be warmed on request.

Lothian Autistic Society

5 Coates Pl
Tel: 554 9362

Runs a monthly under 5s support meeting.

Lothian Racial Equality Council

14 Forth St
Tel: 556 0441
Email: elrec@lrec.demon.co.uk

Aims to work towards the elimination of racial discrimination, to promote racial equality and equal opportunities for all and promote good race relations.

MAMA - Meet a Mum Association

77 West Bruy
Peasedown
St John
Bath BA2 8TZ
Tel: 01761 433 598
Tel: 020 876 80123 (evening helpline Mon-Fri 19.00-22.00)
Email: meet-a-mum.assoc@blueyonder.co.uk

Friendship and support to mothers and mothers-to-be through local groups or individual contacts. Support and information on postnatal illness. Send SAE for details of local contacts.

The Miscarriage Association

c/o Clayton Hospital
Northgate
Wakefield W Yorks
Tel: 01924 200799 see page 102103

Muscular Dystrophy Group

Princes House
Shandwick Pl EH2 4RG
Tel: 229 8632

National Asthma Campaign Scotland

2a North Charlotte St EH2 4HR
Tel: 226 2544
Tel: 08457 010203 (helpline Mon-Fri 9.00-17.00)
Email: enquiries@asthma.org.uk

An independent UK charity, based in London and Edinburgh, which works to conquer asthma. It works in partnership with people with asthma and all who share their concern, through a combination of research, information, support and campaigning.

National Childbirth Trust

NCT Centre – Edinburgh
University Health Service
5th floor
6 Bristo Square EH8 9AL
Tel: 668 3257
Tel: 0870 444 0907 (NCT breastfeeding line 8.00-22.00)

Provides classes, groups and counselling services, offering parents information and support during pregnancy and the early years of parenthood.

National Eczema Society

Hill House, Highgate Hill, London N19 5NA
Tel: 0870 241 3604 (information line)
Web: www.eczema.org

An independent UK charity which runs a helpline and produces a quarterly journal keeping members up-to-date with the management and treatment of eczema.

One Parent Families Scotland

13 Gayfield Sq EHI 3NX
Tel: 556 3899/4563
Email: info@opfs org.uk
Web: www.opfs.org.uk

Information and help for lone parents. Publishes newsletter, a 'Rights Guide' and factsheets including 'Reflections of a Changing World: a list of children's books portraying different families.' Free publications list and membership details. Child-friendly office.

Overload

58/1 North Fort St EH6 4HN
Contact: Gerry Corbett or Janis Hill
Tel: 555 4967

A parents group in Edinburgh for ADHD and children with behaviour problems.

Parentline Scotland

Tel: 0808 800 2222 (free helpline no.)
Web: www.children1st.org.uk/parentline

Information, advice, or someone to listen to you on the telephone.

The PF Counselling Service

Eric Liddle Centre
15 Morningside Rd EH10 4DP
Tel: 447 0876
Email: info@pfcounselling.org.uk

Counselling is available for individuals and couples (over 16 yrs) on a wide range of problems and difficulties. Open to all, on an ability-to-pay basis.

Positive Help

13a Great King St
Contact: Gareth Jenkins
Tel: 558 1122

Voluntary organisation for families and children affected/ living with HIV. Provides driving service, decorating, gardening, childcare and children befriending service.

Prison Advice and Care Trust Family Support Service

254 Caledonian Rd
London N1 ONG
Tel: 0207 2783981
Email: familysupport@pact.uk.net

Advice, information and support for the families of those in prison. Overnight accommodation for those travelling long distances to visit London prisons. Very close to Pentonville and Holloway Prisons.

Roundabout Centre (YWCA Scotland)

4b Gayfield Pl
Contact: Emma Crawshaw
Tel: 556 1168/557 4695
Email: roundaboutywca@care4free.net

Runs a multicultural crèche for 2-5 yrs (Tue-Thu 9.30-12.00, 12.30-15.30). Various classes. Volunteer training and opportunities in anti-discrimanatory campaigning and multicultural crèche and summer play scheme. Fortnightly meeting of group for parents of children of dual heritage. Resource and information library.

Saheliya

10 Union St EH1 3LU
Tel: 556 9302
Contact: Joette Thomas and Samina Digpal
Email: saheliya@connectfree.co.uk

Opening times; Mon-Fri 9.00-17.00
Well-being and mental health project for black and minority ethnic women.
Provides counselling, couples counselling, complimentary therapies and befriending. Languages spoken: Arabic, Punjabi, Singhalese, Bengali, Cantonese, Urdu. Accepts self-referrals and also referrals from other organisations and professionals.

Scottish Cot Death Trust

Royal Hospital for Sick Children
Yorkhill, Glasgow
Tel: 0141 357 3946

Gives personal support to bereaved families by letter, telephone and leaflets and puts parents in touch with other bereaved parents.

Scottish National Federation for the Welfare of the Blind

5 Balmashanner Rise,
Forfar, Angus DD8 1PD
Contact: Hon. Treasurer Mr Duncan
Tel: 01307 463099

Co-ordinates organisations working for blind people in Scotland.

Scottish Society for Autism

Chief Executive: Donald J Liddell
Hilton House
Alloa Business Centre
The Whins
Alloa FK10 3SA
Tel: 01259 720 044
Email: autism@autism-in-scotland.org.uk
Web: www.autism-in-scotland.org.uk

Seeks to ensure the provision of the best possible education, care, support and opportunities for people of all ages with autism in Scotland.

Scottish Spina Bifida Association

190 Queensferry Rd
Tel: 332 0743 (national office)
Tel: 08459 111112 (family support service – phone for local contacts).

Sexual Health Information Line

Tel: 0800 567 123

Shakti Women's Aid

Norton Park
57 Albion Rd EH7 5QY
Tel: 475 2399
Fax: 475 2301
Email: shaktiedinburgh@rapidial.co.uk

Offers information, practical and emotional support and safe, temporary accommodation to all black and ethnic minority women and their children who are being abused either physically or mentally by their partners, husbands or families.

Simpson House Drugs Counselling and Related Services

52 Queen St EH2 3NS
Tel: 225 1054/6028

Opening times: Mon-Fri 9.30-16.30

Free and confidential counselling service to drug users, friends and families. Crèche available. Runs a family support group (6 wk block). Drugs education. Sunflower Garden Project for children affected by family drug use offers play therapy, infant massage, storytelling, home visits, children's groups, parent and grandparent counselling.

Sleep Scotland

Tel: 651 1392
Email: sleepscotland@btinternet.com
Web: www.sleepscotland.org

Provides support to families of children with special needs and severe sleep problems.

Smokeline

Tel: 0800 848484 (7 days 12.00-24.00)

Freephone number offering help and support from trained counsellors. Leaflet available.

Special Needs Information Point (SNIP)

Royal Hospital for Sick Children
14 Rillbank Ter EH9 1LN
Tel/Fax: 536 0583
Email: snip@btinternet.com
Web: www.snipinfo.org

Provides information and support to parents/carers of children with special needs about the services available to them. This can be about benefits, equipment, play and leisure activities, education, respite care etc.

Monthly newsletter and regularly updated web. Fully accessible office.

Stepfamily Scotland

Tel: 225 5800
Email: info@stepfamilyscotland.org.uk
Web: www.stepfamilyscotland.org.uk

Opening times: Mon, Tue, Wed 11.00-15.00; Thu 13.00-19.00

Offers support to all members of stepfamilies and those working with them.

Stepping Stones

10 Wardieburn Rd EH5 1LY
Tel: 551 1632

Opening times: Mon-Fri 9.00-16.00

A chance for young parents who live in the Greater Pilton area to meet together and participate in various activities. Large well-staffed and equipped playroom for under 5s.

Counselling, home visits, welfare advice and support.

TAMBA Twinline

Tel: 0800 138 0509 (helpline)

A confidential listening support and information service run by trained volunteers all of whom are parents of twins or triplets. Provides information and support for parents of twins, triplets and more – and the professionals involved with their care.

Edinburgh Twins Club

Tel: 01506 411881
Contact: Sandra Cook

Support group for families with twins, triplets etc, providing help, advice and friendship. Bumps and babies, babies and toddler groups, soft play sessions, informal evening meetings, regular newsletters, discounts and library of twin related publications. Meetings in Edinburgh, East Lothian and West Lothian.

Wellspring

13 Smith's Pl
Tel: 553 6660

Provides psychotherapy and counselling service. Fees payable on sliding scale according to circumstances.

Libraries & Toy Libraries

WHAT TO EXPECT

People who live, work or study in Edinburgh full time can have free membership of 26 libraries and access to mobile facilities. To join you will need to fill in a membership application form and show two forms of identification. One should be proof of your name and address e.g. a phone or electricity bill. The other should show your signature, so something like a driving licence or child benefit book is suitable. Membership forms can be downloaded from www.edinburgh.gov.uk/libraries. Children receive their own library card and can borrow up to 6 books, including books on tape, from any city library. The parent is responsible for their children's borrowed books and for handing them back in good condition and on time, although there no fines on overdue books issued on a child's card. Children may reserve books free of charge.

Access and Toilets

Standards of access vary a great deal; the new purpose-built libraries usually have excellent all-round facilities. All of the libraries, apart from the Music Library, have wheelchair access, but not all libraries have toilets for the disabled and a few do not have public toilet facilities at all. The library staff will allow use of staff toilets if possible. Many have nappy change units and these are listed in the entries.

Activities

For information about activities such as story-telling sessions, author visits and craft events look out for leaflets and posters in the library. During the school holidays special events are organised.

Categories

In all libraries children's books are arranged by subject, interest and reading level. Shelves are clearly marked and there is a leaflet available explaining the system. All libraries have children's books on tape.

Children's Multilingual Picture Book Collections

Dual-language picture books are available in Arabic, Bengali, Chinese, Farsi, French, Gaelic, Gujarati, Hindi, Italian, Punjabi, Spanish, and Urdu. A booklet listing holdings of dual-language picture books is available in all libraries. Single language books are available in Arabic, Bengali, Chinese, Gujarati, Hindi, Japanese, Punjabi and Urdu. The Ethnic Services Library at McDonald Rd Library has extensive collections. Smaller collections are available at some community libraries. For further information, contact the Ethnic Library, Tel: 529 5643.

Information

Library public notice boards can be a great source of useful information both of local and more general interest and are well worth keeping an eye on. Libraries maintain a diary of forthcoming local events, as well as lists and books of local information.

Internet Access and Personal Computers

Now available in all libraries, free of charge. Information about other council services is available via the Council's web site (www.edinburgh.gov.uk). Library staff can help you find your way around the web site if you are new to computers. You can now go online to renew your library books, pay your Council Tax or to report problems with Rd surfaces or Street lights, and the 'events' section (www.edinburgh.gov.uk/events) lets you see what's on for children and families throughout the city.

Kinderbox

All libraries, including mobile libraries, have boxes with a stock of board books and other books for babies and toddlers. Stock includes up-to-date children's fiction and a wide range of information books; poetry, arts and crafts etc. 'Noisy', 'feely', pop-up and interactive books are available to borrow or for reference.

Libraries' Audio Service

Boasts one of the largest most comprehensive collection of publicly accessible material on music and dance held anywhere in Scotland. It provides chart material, world music, jazz and classical, which can introduce your child to a whole world of music. Children who are members of the Library Service can borrow recordings for a concessionary charge of 25p per item. Up to 6 recordings can be borrowed at any one time. All stock is listed in the library catalogue and can be requested at any public library service point throughout Edinburgh.

The Audio Service is currently available in the following libraries: Balgreen, Blackhall, Central Music, Corstorphine, Craigmillar, Currie, Gilmerton, Kirkliston, Leith, McDonald Rd, Morningside, Muirhouse, Newington, Oxgangs, Piershill, Portobello, Ratho, Sighthill, South Queensferry and Wester Hailes.

Parents' Collections

Children's books dealing with 'problem areas' — topics such as the death of a parent or a grandparent, going into hospital, starting school, new baby etc are available on loan for parents to borrow to help children with areas of concern and are available at the following libraries: Blackhall, Central Children's, Corstorphine, Currie, Fountainbridge, Gilmerton, Kirkliston, Leith, Moredun, Morningside, Muirhouse, Newington, Oxgangs, Piershill, Portobello, Sighthill and Wester Hailes.

Toys
Every library has toys and nearly all have board games.

LIBRARY OPENING HOURS

Currently, Edinburgh's libraries comply with one of two opening times. At the time of writing these are as listed.

Central, Blackhall, Corstorphine, Leith, Morningside, Muirhouse, Newington, Oxgangs, Peirshill, Portobello, Wester Hailes:
Mon, Tue, Wed, Thu: 10.00-20.00: Fri: 10.00-17.00: Sat: 9.00-13.00

Balerno, Balgreen, Central Children's, Colinton, Craigmillar, Currie, Fountainbridge, Gilmerton, Granton, Kirkliston, McDonald Rd, Moredun, Ratho, Sighthill, South Queensferry, Stockbridge :
Mon, Wed: 13.00-20.00: Tue, Thu, Fri: 10.00-17.00: Sat: 9.00-13.00

CENTRAL LIBRARIES

Edinburgh Central Library
George IV Bridge EH1 1EG
Tel: 242 8000
Comprehensive public reference and information services, major collections of local history material, a large stock of adult fiction and non-fiction, and the largest local collection of books about children e.g. parenting, play, education, problems etc. Books for young children are available to borrow from kinderboxes in the general lending department. Extensive Music, Fine Art and Scottish collections. A Kurzweil reading machine, media aids and PC access software for people with disabilities are available in the Resource Centre (Tel: 242 8136).
Toilets in basement, access by lift with stairs to negotiate. If the toilets are not open, a notice is posted at the top of the stairs. A Crèche, run by the Edinburgh Crèche Co-operative, is available to library users on Tuesdays and Thursdays 10.00-12.00. Children 0-5 years are welcome. Staff are trained and qualified, and registered with Disclosure Scotland. It is situated upstairs in the Board Room.

Central Children's Library
George IV Bridge EH1 1EG
Tel: 242 8027
Situated next door to the Central Library. Level access. Compact library that is attractively decorated and laid out to appeal to young children, although if your child needs the toilet you have to leave the building and use the facilities next door in the Central Library. Collection of children's books and audio books, including dual-language picture books in Urdu, Chinese, Arabic and French, as well as books in Gaelic. There are also games, toys and colour-in sheets. There is one internet accessible 'Connect' computer with a link to Wizard Websites, a collection of child-friendly websites, as well as a selection of CD ROMs for children's use only. Free activities and story-telling sessions run during school holidays. Crèche facilities are available in the main building, please call for current details.

COMMUNITY LIBRARIES

Balerno Library
1 Main St EH14 7EQ
Tel: 529 5500
Email: balerno.library@edinburgh.gov.uk
Ramp access. Small library, part of primary School annexe. Good selection of children's books and story tapes. Drawing table and small selection of toys available. Photocopier, PC, internet access and Cap Info. No public toilets.

Balgreen Library
173 Balgreen Rd EH11 3AT
Tel: 529 5585
Email: balgreen.library@edinburgh.gov.uk
There is ramp access to this small library. Wide range of children's books, with a selection in large print and on audio tape. Paper, crayons, toys and board games are also available. Photocopier and 2 PCs with internet access. No public toilet.

Blackhall Library
56 Hillhouse Rd EH4 5EG
Tel: 529 5595
Email: blackhall.library@edinburgh.gov.uk
Ramp access and car park. The children's section is roomy and the under 5s' area has a nautical theme. New 'Family Collection' of books and videos to support parents and carers. Toys, games

and cd-roms for use in library. Photocopier and PCs. Regular story times for under 5s, contact library for more details. New 'book return' letterbox so you can return library items even when library is closed. Toilet facilities (including toilet for the disabled). Nappy change unit.

Colinton Library

14 Thornburn Rd EH13 0BQ
Tel: 529 5603
Email: colinton.library@edinburgh.gov.uk

Car park and access with double pushchair. Children's area with books, audio tapes, games, toys and colour-in books available. Story-telling and children's events are advertised. CAPINFO. Photocopier. 3 PCs with free internet access, e-mail, cd-roms and word processing. Staff toilet is made available for use.

Corstorphine Library

12 Kirk Loan EH12 7HD
Tel: 529 5506
Email: corstorphine.library@edinburgh.gov.uk

Ramp access. Access with single pushchair only. Wide range of children's books with a selection in large print, audio tape and audio CD. Paper, crayons, toys and board games are available. CAPINFO. Photocopier. Children's PC. Six public access computers with internet connections. There is no toilet.

Craigmillar Library

7 Niddrie Marischal Gdns EH16 4LX
Tel: 529 5597
Email: craigmillar.library@edinburgh.gov.uk
Web: www.craigmillarbooksforbabies.org.uk

External wall mural based on a 'library book' theme featuring designs by local children. Ramp access. The children's area is attractively decorated with posters and the artistic creations of local children. There is a good selection of children's books, books on tape, toys, audio cassettes and games. Coin-operated photocopier. CAPINFO. 10 PCs (and CD ROMs) with access to internet (parental supervision required). Check with the library for events such as talks, games and competitions held periodically. 'Books for Babies' a national reading initiative is based at Craigmillar Library. Toilet (key at the desk). Nappy change unit.

Currie Library

210 Lanark Rd West EH14 5NN
Tel: 529 5609
Email: currie.library@edinburgh.gov.uk

Car park and access with double pushchair. Children's area with collection of books, toys, games, colour-in books, audio CDs and books on tape. Ethnic picture book collection. Story-telling and children's events are advertised. CAPINFO. Photocopier. PC. Toilet facilities. Nappy change area.

Fountainbridge Library

137 Dundee St EH11 1BG
Tel: 529 5616
Email: fountainbridge.library@edinburgh.gov.uk

The entrance in Murdoch Terrace has ramp access. Large selection of children's books, toys, games (ask at the counter). Community Room available. Photocopier. CAPINFO. PCs with free internet access in the Connect Learning Centre. 'Rhyme and Tickle' sessions for under 3s, ask library for details. Toilets for the disabled (key at the desk). Nappy change unit.

Gilmerton Library

13 Newtoft St EH17 8RG
Tel: 529 5628
Email: gilmerton.library@edinburgh.gov.uk

Ramp access and car park at rear of the building. Small but bright library with a pleasant children's area, toys plus books on tape. Games are available at the desk. Community Room and an Open Learning Centre. Photocopier. CAPINFO. Free internet access. Children's events in the library ask for details. Toilets. Nappy change unit.

Granton Library

Wardieburn Ter EH5 1DD
Tel: 529 5630
Email: granton.library@edinburgh.gov.uk

Open again after refurbishment. Access for double pushchairs. Collection of books, toys, colour-in books, audio tapes/books, ethnic picture books. Story-telling. 'Bookstart' promotions for under-3s – contact the library for details. CAPINFO. Photocopier. PC. Toilet facilities.

Kirkliston Library

Station Rd
Kirkliston EH29 9BE
Tel: 529 5510
Email: kirkliston.library@edinburgh.gov.uk

Access with double pushchair. Collection of books, toys, colour-in books, audio tapes/books. Story-telling. CAPINFO. Photocopier. 5 PCs with internet access. Toilet facilities and nappy change area.

Leith Library

28–30 Ferry Rd EH6 4AE
Tel: 529 5517
Email: leith.library@edinburgh.gov.uk

Accessible with double pushchair. Small car park at rear of building. Children's section with comfortable seating. Books, toys, colour-in sheets, audio tapes/books available. Story-telling as part of planned seasonal programme of children's activities – contact library for details. CAPINFO. Photocopier. PC designated for children only/with parent. Learning Centre with free access to internet and email. Toilet available for under 5s; ask librarian.

McDonald Rd Library

2 McDonald Rd EH7 4LU
Tel: 529 5636
Email: mcdonaldrd.library@edinburgh.gov.uk

After being closed for a year for refurbishment McDonald Rd Library is due to open again in the Autumn 2003. It will be completely redesigned internally to include the following features: ramp access; lift access to all 3 levels; and large collection of children's books including ethnic and dual-language titles. Coin-operated photocopier. CAPINFO. Public access PCs including free internet access and community language software. Public toilets including nappy changing facilities.

Mobile Library Service

Service based at:
Access Services HQ
343 Oxgangs Rd EH13 9LT
Tel: 529 5683
Email: access services@edinburgh.gov.uk

The Mobile Library Service visits about 60 locations in the Edinburgh area ranging from small villages such as Dalmeny, to large urban locations such as Wester Hailes. Other stops include East Craigs, Inch, Barnton, Juniper Green, Buckstone, Cramond, Clermiston, Prestonfield, Liberton and Gracemount. A wide variety of books are available, including an ever-changing selection of children's books. Most vehicles have powered ramps for easier access.

Moredun Library

92 Moredun Park Rd EH17 7HL
Tel: 529 5652
Email: moredun.library@edinburgh.gov.uk

Ramp access. Small friendly library with bright children's area. Lots of board games available. Photocopier (pay at the counter). Connect PC with internet access. CAPINFO. Toilets for the disabled (key at the desk). Nappy change unit.

Morningside Library

184 Morningside Rd EH10 4PU
Tel: 529 5654
Email: morningside.library@edinburgh.gov.uk

Ramp access. There is a large separate children's section with a wide range of books and large print books. Stories on tape and CD are available for loan as well. Also available are colouring-in sheets, toys, board games, and cd-roms for use in the library. Free internet and PlayStation 2 access. CAPINFO. Photocopying. No public toilet facilities yet (anticipated 2005/6)

Muirhouse Library

15 Pennywell Crt EH4 4TZ
Tel: 529 5528
Email: muirhouse.library@edinburgh.gov.uk

New library designed to be fully accessible. There is a specially designated area for under 5s with toys and soft seating. Games available for use in the library. Videos, cds and books on tape available on loan. Community Room. Learning Centre and pcs with access to the internet. Photocopier. CAPINFO. Toilet for the disabled and nappy changing facilities.

Newington Library

17–21 Fountainhall Rd EH9 2LN
Tel: 529 5536
Email: newington.library@edinburgh.gov.uk

Spacious and attractively decorated, with a large collection of picture books, fiction and non-fiction. Weekly storytelling sessions for pre-school children (Wednesday afternoons). Events and activities for children often organised, see notice board for details. Car park. Photocopier. CAPINFO. Toilets for the disabled. Nappy change unit.

Oxgangs Library

343 Oxgangs Rd EH13 9NY
Tel: 529 5549
Email: oxgangs.library@edinburgh.gov.uk

Modern library with excellent facilities and level access, but be aware of children escaping as they could get straight out into the car park. Story-telling sessions run during school holidays. Toys, games, colour-in sheets and crayons are available on request. Carpeted Community Room with kitchen facilities available. Photocopier and Fax available. pcs with internet access for both adults and children. Toilets (including disabled). Nappy change unit.

Piershill Library

30 Piersfield Ter EH8 7BQ
Tel: 529 5685
Email: piershill.library@edinburgh.gov.uk

Level access and excellent facilities. Bright children's area with extensive range of books and tapes. Children's events and story times. Toys and board games. pcs and photocopying. Toilet and nappy change unit.

Portobello Library

14 Rosefield Ave EH15 1AU
Tel: 529 5558
Email: portobello.library@edinburgh.gov.uk

Bright library with ramp access and two parking spaces for the disabled. Large children's and teenage sections with study tables. Toys and games are available in the children's area. Story-telling sessions for nursery groups can be arranged, apply to the library. Children's computers for games and word-processing – free 1 hr bookings. Playstation 2 games available. Coin-operated photocopier. CAPINFO. Toilet and nappy change unit available on request. These facilities are upstairs and require a member of staff to unlock the door. Library fabric to be upgraded shortly (during 2003-2005). See also Toy Libraries in this chapter.

Ratho Library

6 School Wynd EH28 8TT
Tel: 333 5297
Email: ratho.library@edinburgh.gov.uk

Access with single pushchair. Visitors car park. Collection of books, audio books/tapes, toys and colour-in books. Story-telling. CAPINFO. Photocopier. pcs with internet access. Toilet facilities and nappy change area available.

Sighthill Library

6 Sighthill Wynd EH11 4BL
Tel: 529 5569
Email: sighthill.library@edinburgh.gov.uk

Exceptionally spacious library with level access and automatic doors. Good stock of children's books, supplemented by books on tapes, comics, toys, and games. 'Bookstart 0–3' project based at the library. Runs stories, songs and rhyme events for parents and children (0-3). Family collection of books, videos, leaflets and magazines. Photocopier. Sega and 2 Playstation2s. CAPINFO. pcs and new Learning Centre offering free internet access for parents and children. Toilets (key at the desk). Nappy change unit available.

South Queensferry Library

9 Shore Rd EH30 9RD
Tel: 529 5576
Email: southqueensferry.library@edinburgh.gov.uk

Local community library with level access. Bright children's area with picture books and board books, toys, colour-in books, audio tapes/books. Fortnightly story telling on Tuesday mornings. Photocopier. CAPINFO. PCs with internet access. Use of toilet for young children at the discretion of the Librarian.

Stockbridge Library

Hamilton Pl EH3 5BA
Tel: 529 5665
Email: stockbridge.library@edinburgh.gov.uk

Access by ramped entrance. Bright and friendly children's area with toys and comfortable seats for adults. Large selection of children's books, audio books, comics and games. Monthly story-telling for the under fives. Check with the library for children's activities during school holidays. Community hall available for hire. Photocopier. CAPINFO. PCs with free internet access and Open Learning Centre. Toilet and Nappy change unit.

Wester Hailes Library

1 West Side Plaza EH14 2ST
Tel: 529 5667
Email: westerhailes.library@edinburgh.gov.uk

Access with double pushchair. Collection of children's books including ethnic picture books. Toys and colour-in sheets available. Community room available on first floor (access by lift). Story-telling. Bookstart Rhyme Times: Tuesdays 10:30-11:30am. Internet access and Connect Learning Centre. CAPINFO. Photocopier. Toilet. Nappy change unit.

TOY LIBRARIES

As their name suggests, toy libraries are centres for lending toys to families, carers and to children with special needs. They are mostly drop-in centres, and guidance can be given on the toys best suited to your child. There is generally a joining fee and depending on the toy library, toys can be borrowed for little or no charge. It is wise to check with each individual project. Opening times usually mirror school terms, but some do stay open during school holidays.

The two main contacts are: Edinburgh Toy Library Group, which supports toy libraries formerly run by WRVS (Tel: 441 1925) and the National Association of Toy and Leisure Libraries, Gilmerton Community Centre, 4 Drum St (Tel: 664 2746).

SPECIAL NEEDS TOY LIBRARIES

Barrie House Toy Library

Barrie House
Canaan Lane
Tel: 446 3136

Opening times:Fri 10.00-12.00, but available other times: phone for information.

A division of the Royal Blind School and, as such, the toy library is primarily for parents of children who attend the playgroup there. However, the library welcomes other enquiries.

St Bernard's Special Needs Toy Library

St.Bernard's Education Centre
Dean Park St EH4 1JS
Contact: Dr. Doreen Dinwoodie
Tel: 311 5600

Opening times:Thu 13.45-15.45

Large range of toys and equipment available for any child with special needs. Open to parents, groups, professionals and therapists citwidey. A catalogue is available to buy.

SPLATT Toy Library – Special Needs

Keycomm
St Giles Centre
40 Broomhouse Cres
Tel: 443 6775

Opening times: Mon-Fri 10.00-16.30

Switch Play, learning and technology for parents and professionals.

TOY LIBRARIES

Dalkeith Toy Library

Woodburn Community Centre
6 Woodburn Rd
Dalkeith
Contact: Kerry Brady
Tel: 663 3958

Opening times: Wed 9.30-11.15

Gorgie/Dalry Toy Library

A new toy library is forthcoming in 2004. For information, please phone:

Homestart
Contact: Val Goodwin
Tel: 226 1331

Pilton Toy Library

Under 5s Unit
Craigroyston High School
Pennywell Rd
Tel: 477 7801

Opening times: Mon-Fri 9.00-13.00

Available to parents or carers who use the Under 5s Unit and crèche.

Play Plus Toy Library

Inch House Community Centre
225 Gilmerton Rd
Contact: Helen Anderson
Tel: 657 2380

Opening times: Tue 9.30-12.30

Play sessions, quality toys for families, groups, carers etc., including toys for children with special needs. Nappy-changing facilities. Breastfeeding welcome. Audio books and ethnic picture book collection. Accessible to double pushchairs.

Portobello Toy Library

Portobello Community Library (upstairs)
Rosefield Ave EH15 1AU
Contact: Carol Strang
Tel: 529 5558

Opening times: Wed 10.00-11.00 during term time.

Available for children from 1-5 yrs.

St Bernard's Toy Library

St Bernard's Education Centre
Dean Park St EH4 1JS
Contact: Gladys Hart
Tel: 311 5600

Opening times: Thu 13.45-15.45

Open to local parents and professionals working with children, e.g. toddler groups, playgroups, nurseries etc. These groups pay a membership fee and can borrow toys for a longer period.

South Queensferry Toy Library

South Queensferry Youth and Community Centre
South Queensferry Primary School
Kirkliston Rd
Tel: 331 2113

Opening times: Fri 10.00-11.30

Springwell House Toy Library

Springwell House
Ardmillan Ter EH11 2JL
Contact: Teresa Carr
Tel: 537 7530

Opening times: Fri 9.30-11.15

SPECIALIST LIBRARIES

Scottish Poetry Library

5 Crichton's Close
Canongate EH8 8DT
Tel: 557 2876

Opening times: Mon-Fri: 11.00-18.00; Sat: 12.00-16.00
Attractive new building with ramp access from Crichton's Close. Lift to Children's section on first floor mezzanine. Bright children's area with some toys available on open carpeted area. Open stairs at far end of section, so keep an eye on adventurous toddlers. Children's poetry books and picture books for all ages, available to borrow on completion of an application form. Out of hours return facility. Toilet and nappy change available in basement accessible by lift

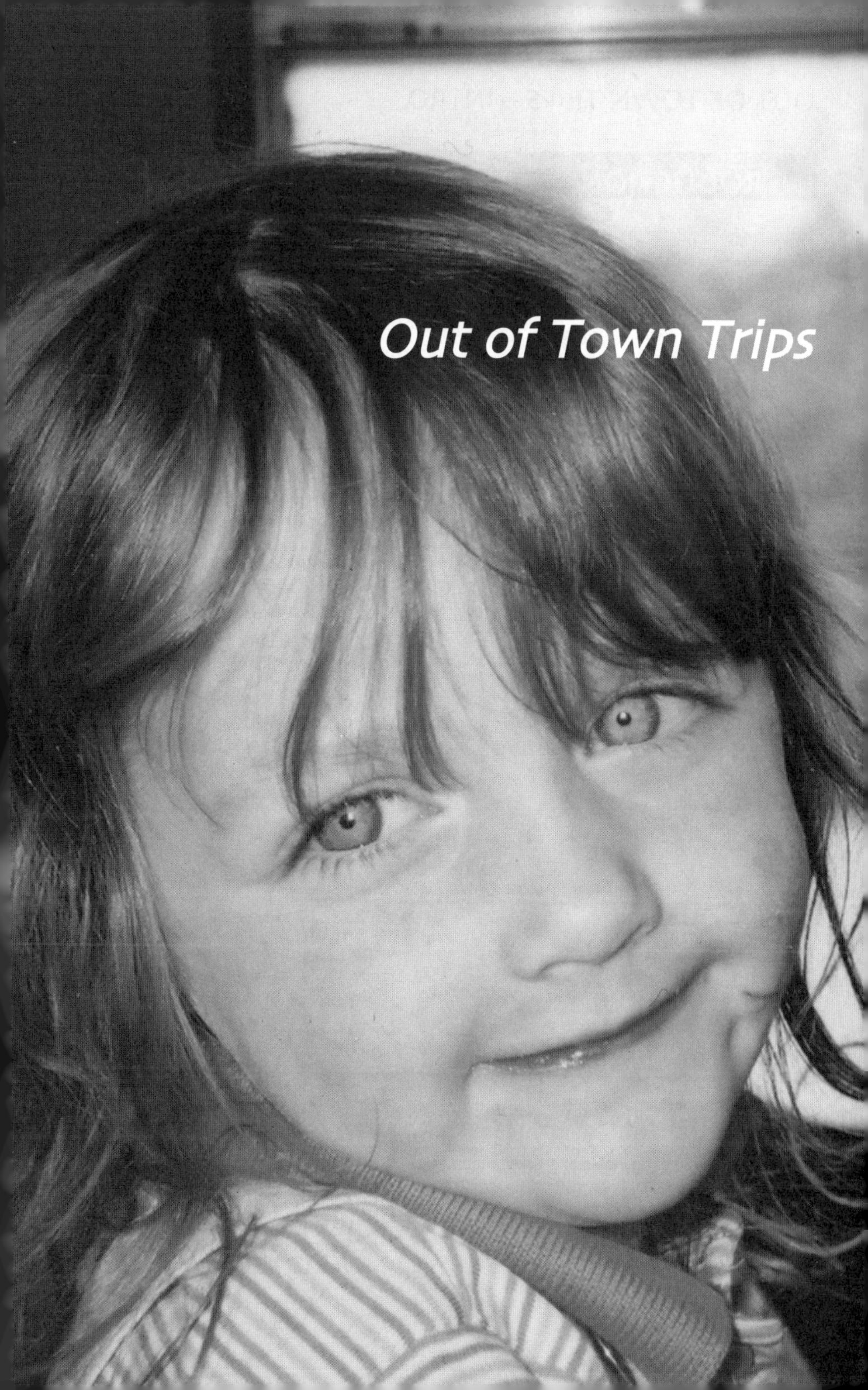
Out of Town Trips

INTRODUCTION

Edinburgh is full of places to go and things to see, but it's always nice to take a trip out of the local area. Many of our entries are within an hour's car drive of Edinburgh, whether you take motorway links or the scenic routes. We have included all sorts of visits from stately houses and country parks, to working museums and leisure centres. Hopefully, there is something to take your interest – and your children's! And remember, you don't have to be out all day if that is too tiring. For example, if you have a car, you could drive to Dalmeny station, park and take the train across the River Forth to North Queensferry and back again: a great railway adventure if you're under 5!
To turn to the practicalities, it's always wise to plan ahead. Sort out nappies, waterproofs etc, the night before, otherwise you may feel that you are never going to get away. Have an alternative visit planned in case the weather lets you down, or your first choice is too busy for you or your children. Check for possible delays, such as road works, opening times for your destination and public transport if necessary: early morning radio shows have frequent updates, as do Teletext, Ceefax etc.

Some useful travel contacts are:

All Methods of Travel

Traveline Scotland:
Tel: 0870 608 2 608

By Train

National Rail Enquiry Service
Tel: 0845 748 4950

Disabled Travel Helpline:
Tel: 0845 605 7021

By Bus

E&M Horsburgh (bus services within West Lothian)
Tel: 01506 432251
Web: www.horsburghcoaches.com

First Bus Customer Service
Tel: 08708 72 72 71 (timetable and ticket enquiries Mon-Fri 08:30 - 17:00)
Web: www.firstgroup.com

Lothian Buses
Tel: 0131 555 6363
Web: www.lothianbuses.co.uk

Scottish Citylink
Tel: 0870 550 5050
Web: www.citylink.co.uk

Stagecoach Fife Bus Information
Tel: 01592 261461

Stirling Bus Station Timetable Information
Tel: 01786 446 474

Midland Bluebird (travel info within the Stirling area)
Tel: 01324 613777

We have tried to give relevant travel information throughout the section where possible. Please remember, though, that companies can alter routes, timetables etc at the drop of a hat, so please do check before setting off on a trip.

We have listed tourist information numbers within the sections. For guides to the beaches, try the Sea-front Award and Blue Flag Office of the Tidy Britain Group, Tel: 01603 766076. Alternatively, check www.blueflag.org or www.sepa.org.uk, which provide information regarding the current cleanliness of beaches.

For guides and other countryside properties not listed here try Historic Scotland, Tel: 668 8800 or the National Trust for Scotland, Tel: 226 5922. The National Trust for Scotland produces a highly informative guide specifically for disabled visitors to their properties, noting ease of access to toilets (if any), gradients and ease of access of grounds – this is also helpful if you are taking a pushchair! It should also be noted that it is National Trust for Scotland policy not to admit pushchairs or backpacks into their houses: slings and papooses are fine. Both the National Trust for Scotland and Historic Scotland have family membership schemes.
Properties owned by these organisations have been highlighted in the text by the use of the following keys: (HS) for Historic Scotland and (NTS) for the National Trust for Scotland.
Entries in this section are listed alphabetically by geographic area, then town. This includes trips to the following areas:

- **Borders, Dumfries and Galloway**
- **East Lothian**
- **Fife**
- **Lanarkshire**
- **Midlothian**
- **Perthshire**
- **Stirling and Falkirk**
- **West Lothian**

THE BORDERS

FORTIFIED CASTLES AND TOWERS

For any child interested in castles, daring deeds and days of old, there are some fine examples of Border keeps and castles scattered over the country, many of which date from the time of the Border Reivers. While many of the buildings are in ruins, some are still fantastic to visit, and more than a few are well-preserved. Some notable examples are:

Hermitage Castle (HS)

Tel: 01387 376222
Web: www.historic-scotland.gov.uk
5 1/2 miles NE of Newcastleton, take the B6399, and watch out for the signs
Opening times: summer only (Apr-Sep), 9.30-18.30
Admission: adult £2.20; child 75p; concession £1.60. Under 5s free

A looming, eerie fortress set deep in the Borders and scene of many dark deeds – it is said that one of its first owners, William de Soules, was boiled alive in his own cauldron! Open in the summer only – and even then it might be wise to throw the wellies in the back of the car! If you have a child who's into battles and castles, this is a great example. From the outside, it's just about everything you'd want from a castle. Inside there's a covered well, a view down into the prison pit and good views out into the bleak countryside. It can be viewed externally in the 'closed' season. The terrain around is uneven and banked, so perhaps best viewed with active children rather than toddlers or babies – this also stands for the interior. There's a ruined chapel and graveyard if you turn left once you have crossed the access bridge rather than right towards the castle. There's a giant's grave outwith the chapel's walls; he was called the Cout o Kielder and owned magic chainmail – ideal story-fodder for children! When at the Hermitage or the chapel, watch out for the river. No toilets.

Smailholm Tower (HS)

Tel: 01573 460365
Web: www.historic-scotland.gov.uk
Near Smailholm village, 6m W of Kelso on the B6937, then turn on to the B6404
Opening times: all summer (Apr-Sep) 9.30-18.30 and weekends in winter (Oct-Mar)
Admission: adult £2.20; child 75p; concession £1.60. Under 5s **free**.

Smailholm Tower sits high on a rocky outcrop with a safety rail for safer viewing of the outlying land. It is a typical example of the 'bastles' that once stood all around the country. Inside there is an exhibition of tapestries and costume dolls. Open all summer and at the weekends in the winter. If you visit Kelso, it might be worth the detour just for the look. No toilets.

Threave Castle - Dumfries and Galloway (HS)

Tel: 07711 2231017
Web: www.historic-scotland.gov.uk
3m W of Castle Douglas on the A75
Opening times: summer only (Apr-Sep), 9.30-18.30
Admission: adult £2.20; child; 75p; concession £1.60.
Under 5s free

This is one straight out of days of old when knights were bold. The castle itself stands on an island in the River Dee. To access it, you ring a bell and a steward will come to ferry you over. There's a picnic area, toilets and toilets for the disabled. The last boat leaves the island at 18.00.

COUNTRY HOUSES

There are numerous old houses and of interest in this area, all of which are easily found on maps. Most have extensive gardens for walks, games or picnics, as well as a tea room or a restaurant. However, the architecture and art of the interiors will probably hold minimal interest for the young. Opening times tend to vary between houses and seasons, so it would be advisable to telephone first. Some notable examples are:

Abbotsford House

Nr Melrose TD6 9BQ
Tel: 01896 752043
On the A68, take the A6091 Melrose Bypass, heading north towards Galashiels. Turn left at the second roundabout onto the B6360.
Opening times: Mon-Sat 17 Mar-31 Oct 9.30-17.30. Sundays Mar-May, Oct 14.00-17.30; Jun-Sep 9.30-17.30
Admission: adult £4.50; child £2.25

Home of Sir Walter Scott. A beautiful example of Scots Baronial architecture. While there's little to hold much interest of under 5s, parents with babies (and an interest in literature, Scott or history) might find some of the memorabilia interesting.

Floors Castle

Nr Kelso
Roxburghshire
Tel: 01573 223 333

Well signposted from Kelso.
Opening times: 10.00-16.00 Easter-end Oct. Closed Nov-Mar.
Admission; adult £5.75; concession £4.75; child (5-15) £3.25. Under 5s **free**.

Beautiful castle, built in 1721, and set in stunning grounds. This was the castle used in the film 'Greystoke', and is the largest inhabited castle in Scotland. State rooms with priceless works of art open to public. Woodland and river walks. Toilets, nappy-changing facilities. Gift shop.
Restaurant:
Self service, licensed, breastfeeding welcome.
Open 10-16.00 (16.30 on Sun).
Coffee Shop:
breastfeeding welcome.
Open 10.00-17.00.
There is also a garden centre within the castle grounds, complete with a children's playground.

Mellerstain

Nr Melrose
Tel: 01573 881292
Web: www.mellerstain.com

Opening times: daily, 1May-30Sep, 12.30-17.00, except Sats. Also Easter weekend (4 days). Open weekends in Oct

An elegant, Adam-designed, grand house: one of the first ever built on the scale in Scotland. The Italian terraced gardens are impressive and lovely for a walk round – but there is a lake. Inside the house, there's little for the average under 5.

Paxton House

Berwick upon Tweed TD15 1SZ
Tel: 01289 386291
Email: info@paxtonhouse.com
Web: www.paxtonhouse.com

54 miles from Edinburgh. Signposted 3 miles from the A1 Berwick upon Tweed bypass on B6461
Trains to Berwick hourly am then bus no. 32 from Berwick daily except Sun
Opening times: daily from 1 Apr-31 Oct, 10.00-17.50
Gardens open 10.00-sunset
Admission to house and gardens: adult £6; child £3; family ticket £16
Admission to gardens only: adult £3; child £1.50; family ticket £8

The house is in the 18th century Palladian style, with interiors by Robert Adam. It houses the largest collection of Chippendale furniture in Scotland. Guided tour only – with 'Teddy Bear' trail for children. Lift to 1st floor only. Not suitable for toddlers or pushchairs.
There are 80 acres of woodland, parkland and gardens. Nature detective trails for children, lasting approx. 1/2 hour (costs 50p incl. crayon and sheet), and 1 mile of riverside walks accessible by pushchair if dry. Ponies and Highland cattle. Adventure playground, croquet (small charge) and red squirrel hide. There's usually a teddy bears' picnic in July for children, hosted by Paxton Ted, the house's children's mascot.
Café:
£, highchairs (2), licensed.
Serves home-cooked light meals/snacks. Secluded area for breastfeeding. Toilets. Nappy-changing facility (M&F). Gift shop.
Various annual activities and events – phone for details. Winner of various awards.

Thirlestane Castle

Lauder
Tel: 01578 722430

Follow the Lauder Road out of Edinburgh (the A68). Castle lies off the A68 and is signposted
Opening times: 1 Apr-10 Oct 10.30-17.00 (last admission 15.30pm). Closed Sat
Admission to castle and grounds: adult £5.50, family ticket £15. Under 5s are free. Admission to grounds only: £2

Pushchairs are allowed in the castle but there are many stairs to negotiate, so it's easier without. Excellent children's display in nursery with dressing up costumes for children and dungeon display. Adventure play area suitable for under 5s and older children. Plenty of picnic tables and shady areas to sit.
Tearoom:
highchair (1), breastfeeding welcomed, will warm bottles.
Child friendly menu. If you don't want to eat in, picnics are available to buy . Nappy-changing facilities at bottom of stairs in main house. Shop selling replica old toys at reasonable prices.

Traquair House

Innerleithen
Tel: 01896 830323
Email: enquiries@traquair.co.uk
Web:www.traquair.co.uk

On the B709. First bus service no. 62 from Edinburgh

Opening times: Easter-31 Oct 12.00-17.00. Jun, Jul, Aug 10.30-17.30. Opening times may vary slightly. Please phone for current information
Admission: adult £5.70; child £2.90; family ticket £16. Under 5s free

Oldest inhabited fortified house in Scotland, set in picturesque grounds. Look out for the gates which were locked in 1745 – and are not to be opened until a Stewart returns to the throne. No pushchairs inside as there are many stairs to negotiate, including the secret priest's stairs. Excellent maze in which you can lose your children for some time and pleasant children's play area. Shop selling 'pocket-money' trinkets for children.
Café:
£-££, highchairs (2), breastfeeding welcomed.
Serves children's lunch-boxes. Nappy-changing facilities in porta loos.

TOWNS AND ATTRACTIONS

Jedburgh

Historic town, set in the heart of the Borders.
Take the A68 from Edinburgh. Munro's operate the no. 29 bus from Edinburgh to Jedburgh – journey time approx 2hrs.

Jedburgh Abbey (HS)

Tel: 01835 863925
Web: www.historic-scotland.gov.uk
Open all year.
Admission: adult £3.50; child £1.20; concession £2.50. Under 5s free
Impressive building, founded in 1138. Visitor centre which houses many priceless artefacts found during excavations at the site. Cloister and herb garden.
Car park. Toilets. Shop. Reasonable access with pushchair. Picnic area.

Jedforest Deer and Farm Park

Tel: 01835 840364
Email: mervinslaw@ecosse.net
Website: www.aboutscotland.com/jedburgh
Follow A68 south, 5 miles from Jedburgh, signposted on main road, turn off right and travel mile to 1st farm you come to.
Opening times: May-Aug 10.00-17.30; Sep-Oct 11.00-16.30
Admission: adult £4; child £2.50; family ticket £12. Under 5s free.

Birds of prey demonstrations and displays each day. Chance for children to handle the tiny barn owl. Farm also includes deer and many rare varieties of most farm animals. There is a 'clapping' area where children can touch and sometimes help to bottle feed animals. Walks in wooded area following colour-coded signs lasting 1/2 - 1 1/2 hrs.
Large and small adventure playgrounds. Ranger Activities available according to season: mini-beast hunts, tree safari, pond dipping, crafts. Barbecues for hire, picnic area, cafe with high chair and shop.
Café:
£-££, high chair , no smoking, 1/2 portions available for children, seats 40 inside, more outside.
The café is self-service and provides sandwiches, soup and cakes. Breastfeeding friendly. M&F nappy changing facilities, child friendly, play areas include indoor tractors. Prams and pushchairs can be parked inside the premises. All facilities on ground floor. Children's parties hosted, includes owl treasure hunt.
See also *Birthdays and Celebrations*.

Melrose

A lovely spot to break off a longer journey, or for a day trip. Melrose nestles below the Eildon Hills – fairy hills or the resting place of King Arthur and his Knights, if you believe the tales. Ideal for a gentle stroll along the streets – though the town sits on a rise. Robert the Bruce's heart is allegedly buried in the Abbey grounds – a recent plaque marks the spot. Plenty signed parking areas. Cafés, baker shops etc. Some rather nice ice cream shops too! Public toilets nr the Abbey.
Take the A7 or A68 from Edinburgh. First Bus services cover this – no. 62 is an hourly service from 8.25-19.25 Mon-Sat, very irregular on Sundays. National Cycle Route 1.

Melrose Abbey (HS)

Tel: 01896 822562
Opening times: daily, 9.30-18.30
Admission: adult £3.30; child £1.20; concession £2.50. Under 5s free

Majestic ruins – you can see them along an ajoining path, rather than going in, if you prefer, as there is little really to interest under 5s.

Priorwood Garden and Dried Flower Shop (NTS)

Tel: 01896 822 493
Located nr the Abbey
Opening times: 1 Apr-24 Dec. Times vary with season. Phone for current opening info.

Admission: adult £2.50, concession £1.90, child £1. Under 5s free

Specialist garden, where the flowers grown are all ideal for drying. You can enjoy a walk through the orchard – and take a picnic here in the summer. Gift shop sells large range of NTS merchandise as well as dried flower gifts.

If you leave Melrose and head out towards Dryburgh Abbey on the B6404, then the B6356, then you'll see a sign for the Wallace's statue – but keep your eyes peeled. Park in the little car park and walk along the pathway. Keep walking, you turn a corner and you come across a huge statue of William Wallace (dressed in Greco-Roman finery!), staring out across the landscape toward the border with England. Certainly not worth the trip in itself, but if you're passing the area anyway, it's an odd thing that children remember seeing.

Peebles

Busy market town with museum, cafés and some interesting shops. Market day is Thursday. Walks and playground by the River Tweed.
First Bus operate no. 62 from Edinburgh. This is an hourly service from 9.00-19.25 Mon-Sat, very irregular on Sundays (approx. 1hr 10 mins).

Tourist Information

23 High St
Tel: 01721 720138

Gytes Leisure Centre

Walkershaugh
Tel: 01721 723688
Soft play area. Opening times vary and the soft play can sometimes be closed for private parties. It is best to telephone in advance. No cafe, but café area with vending machines.

Hay Lodge Park

Follow the path beyond the swimming pool along the river's edge to this large play park, 2 small flights of steps along path.

Kailzie Gardens

Tel: 01721 720007
Tel: 01721 722807 (Restaurant)

2 1/2 miles from Peebles on B7062

Opening times: daily 11.00-17.30
Admission: adult £3; child (5-14 yrs) £1; under 5s free. Honesty box mid-Oct to mid-March.

Pretty gardens with small river running through and walled garden. Picnics can only be eaten outside gardens – watch out for hungry ducks.!
Nappy changing mat in restaurant toilet. Restaurant can be busy in summer months so may be worth booking. Children will need close supervision at play area, especially on slide/climbing frame. Small gift shop.

Peebles Swimming Pool

Port Brae
Tel: 01721 720779
Opening times vary, so best to phone and check.
Main pool and toddler pool. Cafe area with vending machines.

Stobo

Dawyck Botanic Gardens

Tel: 01721 760254
B712, 8 miles SW of Peebles. Signposted from A721
Opening times: 14 Feb-mid Nov; groups by arrangement in winter
Admission: adult £3.50; concession £3; child £1, Family ticket £8. Under 5s free
Gardens are lovely for children to run about in. Picnics are a good idea as the tea-room is very small. There's pushchair access and breastfeeding welcomed, but no nappy changing area. Small gift shop. Toilet.

FIFE

POINTS OF INTEREST

Cycling in Fife

There are over 300 miles of well-signposted cycleways, following quiet roads, disused railway tracks and public rights of way. Occasionally these are a bit bumpy for smaller bike passengers, but only for short distances. Maps of the cycle-ways can be purchased from St Andrews Tourist Information Centre (Tel: 01334 472021). www.fife-cycleways.co.uk gives details of businesses in Fife which welcome cyclists.

Walking – Fife Coastal Route

The Fife Coastal Route is very well signposted. It is great if your children like walking, or you have a papoose, but generally unsuitable for pushchairs and prams.

BEACHES IN FIFE

Fife is wonderful for the bucket-and-spade brigade. Great sandy beaches include:

Aberdour

There are two lovely beaches – the **Silver Sands** (café, toilets and a car park) and the **Black Sands** (limited parking, no amenities, but really nice all the same, and it's a winner of the Seaside award from Tidy Britain Group.

Kinghorn beach

(Pettycur Bay)

Safe, sandy bay with two ice-cream shops /cafés on the front. Recent winner of seaside award from Tidy Britain Group . Fife Council Enviromental Health Department gave it a good/excellent rating for its water quality .

St Andrews

East and West Sands Beaches

Two lovely large sandy beaches. Clean – and the water status is checked regularly. West Sands continues to hold a Blue Flag award.

Tentsmuir

(near Leuchars)

A huge sandy beach, with inquisitive seals lurking offshore watching the human wildlife. There are no shops or cafés, and the rip tides are strong. Parking. Toilets. Picnic benches.

Elie Harbour Beach

Large, sandy, blue-flag beach with a café at the harbour, and also a pub (The Ship Inn) which has a beer garden, BBQs every Sunday May-Aug and overlooks the beach where the local team play cricket on Sundays. Elie Watersports (Tel: 01333 330962) at the harbour hire out pedaloes, inflatable rides, canoes, dinghies, windsurfers, etc.

TOWNS & ATTRACTIONS

Aberdour

Aberdour lies about 5 miles east of the Forth Bridges on the A921. Stagecoach buses to Kirkcaldy stop at Aberdour. Most trains to Kirkcaldy stop at Aberdour station (for train info, tel: 01592 416060).

Aberdour Castle (HS)

Tel: 01383 860519

Web: www.historic-scotland.gov.uk

Next to Aberdour railway station, and near a bus stop

Opening times: summer (Apr-Sep) daily 9.30-18.30. Winter: 9.30-16.30 closed Thu afternoons, Fri and Sun mornings
Admission: adult £2.20; child £0.75; concession £1.60. Under 5s free (Friends of HS free)

Built in the 13th Century, this partially ruinous step-gabled castle is brilliant for children – especially those interested in knights and castles. The winding stairs are fascinating for older toddlers and children, but are obviously no use for a pushchair! The interior is furnished and accessible. The bread ovens were a big hit with our three year old researcher. The banqueting hall and lawn are a popular wedding location.
Tearoom:
£-££, high chair (1).
Open during peak hours, Jun-Sept. There's also a shop with reasonably priced themed toys for children's role play (knights' helmets etc).
We incorporated this visit with a trip to one of the 2 beautiful Aberdour beaches (see above) and had a wonderful day out.

Anstruther

Take the A917, once you've crossed the Forth and are in the East Neuk of Fife.
Anstruther is the largest of the East Neuk fishing villages, which are lined out along the coast. It's a typical village of the area, with many of the shops overlooking the harbour. Look out for Buckie House, which is covered in shells.

The Anstruther Fish Bar

Tel: 01333 310518

This fish bar (£) is a frequent winner of the 'Best Fish & Chips' award. It serves take-away and eat-in meals. Provides high chairs (3) but there is no nappy changing. The freshly cooked fish and chips are great, as is the Brattisani's ice cream. But the queues can be pretty long. There is a take-away (in a trailer) opposite the Fish Bar which sells excellent home-made soup if the queue for the Fish Bar is too long.

Burntisland

Take J1 off the M90 and drive along the A921. Most trains to Kirkcaldy stop in Burntisland.
A town situated on the Fife coast. Swings, mini-golf, trampolines, paddling pool, lovely beach (Blue Flag), and fun fair in summer. Free Edwardian Fair Museum open all year, with reproduction Edwardian Fairground displays.

Beacon Leisure Centre

Lammerlaws Rd
Burntisland
Tel: 01592 872211
Web: www.thebeaconfife.com

Opening times: Mon 8.00-16.00 & 18.00-21.30; Tue 7.00-16.00; Wed 8.00-21.30; Thus 8.00-19.30; Fri 8.00-21.30; Sat 8.00-20.00 (closed 17.00-18.00); Sun 8.00-18.00
Admission: adult £2.40; child £1.40; family (2 A + 2 C) £6.90. Under 5s swim free.

Leisure centre on the beachfront of Burntisland. Swimming pool with 2 flumes & wave machine. Separate toddlers' area. Pool discos, children's activities, swimming lessons and crash courses available. Café overlooking the pool.

Collessie

Fife Animal Park

Tel: 01337 831830

By Binnie Loch. On B937 half a mile S of A91 Milnathort to St Andrews road
Opening times: Apr-Jun; Fri, Sat, Sun 11:00-17:00; Jun-Aug daily 10:00-18:00; closed for winter from end Sep
Admission: By donation or use of the restaurant

All types of birds and animals. See ostrich eggs, rabbits and newly hatched chicks. Exhibition and information area, as well as other attractions such as trampolines and pony rides, and an outdoor trail. All facilities fully accessible with pushchairs, and play areas fully enclosed.
Restaurant with high chairs and children's menu. Breastfeeding welcomed. Free parking.

Cupar

Town lies on the A91. Stagecoach operates buses from Edinburgh, St Andrew's Square bus terminus to Cupar and past the Deer Centre.

Hill of Tarvit (NTS)

Tel: 01334 653127
Web: www.nts.org.uk

The mansion house is on A916 nr Cupar. Well-signposted from A91 and A92
Opening times:
House: 1 Apr-30 Sep and Oct w/ends 13.00-17.00. Last admission 16.45
Grounds: all-year round 9.30-sunset
Admission: adult £5.00; child/concession £3.75, Family (2 A and up to 6 C) £13.50. NTS members free. Under 5s free.
The house could be a bit worrying for parents whose children are into everything. Outside is much less stressful, and there's a nice walk up to the monument. Garden has picnic tables.
Tearoom:
£-££, high chair (1), breastfeeding welcomed.
Opens 12:00-17:00 (last orders 16:30). Pleasant tearoom selling light lunches and home-baking, where staff are friendly and accommodating. . Nappy disposal unit, but no changing area.

The Scottish Deer Centre

Tel: 01337 810391

On A91, 4 miles before Cupar
Opening times:
Park: Apr-Oct 10.00-18.00; Oct-Apr 10.00-17.00.
Shop: Apr-Oct 10.00-17.30; Oct-Apr 10.00-16.30
Admission: adult £4.50; child £3.00; concession £3.50. Various family tickets also available

There's a deer farm walk to meet the deer, nature trail, picnic area, animal pens, aerial walkway. etc. There are also falconry displays three times a day, and trailer rides in Summer. Covered all-weather adventure barn. Superb outdoor adventure playground. Restaurant and snack kiosk. Coffee shop. Shops. Breastfeeding welcomed .

Dunfermline

Off the M90. Trains run hourly from Waverley. Stagecoach operate bus services to the town. Historic town from early times. King Robert Bruce is buried in Dunfermline Abbey church – though his embalmed heart lies in the grounds of Melrose Abbey.

Tourist Information Centre

1 High Street
Dunfermline KY12 7DL
Tel: 01383 720999

Abbot House Heritage Centre

Maygate
Tel: 01383 733266

Opening times: daily all year 10.00-17.00
Admission: adult £3.00; concession £2.00. Accompanied children under 14 free

Lovely old building: 'The People's Tardis'. Permanent displays of Dunfermline/Scottish life from the Picts to the 1960s and of famous people, such as Andrew Carnegie. Also hosts exhibitions and craft fairs. Upper floors unsuitable for pushchairs. However, the café with highchairs and the shop on the ground floor are accessible. Café has a 'sitooterie' with a view of the Abbey. Under 5s can play in the gardens and in the adjoining Abbey grounds, but beware of attractive hazards such as the fountain. M&F nappy changing facilities. Breastfeeding welcomed. If you are lucky, you might see a 'royal' procession to the Abbey, as school parties can hire royal/court costumes. £1/child for school tour, plus £1/costume to fit age 9-10.

Carnegie Leisure Centre

Pilmuir St
Tel: 01383 314200
Opening times: Mon 7.00-22.00; Tue-Fri 7.00-21.00; Sat, Sun 8.00-17.00
Admission : adult £2.20; child £1.40. Under 5s free

Leisure centre with swimming pool, separate toddlers' pool and fitness suite. Extensive range of swimming, fitness and gymnastics classes for both adults and children from 9 mths old. Health suite with sauna, aerotone baths and old-fashioned Turkish bath which is still in the décor of the 1900s. Expert and quality school holiday programmes and school camps age 7 plus .Well-equipped and efficiently-run crèche caters for children from 6 wks-8 yrs, open to those using the centre and to shoppers. Max 3 hr stay. Café:
breastfeeding welcomed.

Pittencrieff Park

Lovely park close to Dunfermline Abbey, with wooded glen, wide open areas and play park. Animal houses, glasshouses, and pavilion selling coffee, ice cream etc. Free entry to park. Small museum in Pittencrieff House in centre of Park.

The Butterchurn

Cocklaw Mains Farm
Tel: 01383 830169
web: www.butterchurn.co.uk
On B914 Dollar Rd, 100m from M90, J4
Open all year 9.00-21.00, except 25, 26 Dec and 1, 2 Jan

££, high chairs, breastfeeding selcomed, no-smoking area.
Country restaurant serving good food and home baking with a Scottish emphasis (Taste of Scotland award). Has a children's menu. Meals served all day including vegetarian dishes, also light snacks. Nappy changing facilities. Panoramic views over Fife. Outdoor play area. Pet farm animals. Centre of Excellence for Scottish Food and Crafts centre opposite, open 7 days, offering exhibitions, cookery and craft demonstrations, also sells children's clothing, books and educational toys.

Falkland

Falkland Palace (NTS)

Falkland
Cupar
Tel: 01337 857397
Web: www.nts.org.uk
A912, 10 miles from M90. Take J8, 11 miles N of Kirkcaldy. On National Cycle Route 1. Stagecoach bus stops in High Street
Opening times:
Palace: 1 Apr-31May and 1 Sep-31 Oct, Mon-Sat 11.00-17.30, Sun 13.30-17.30; 1 Jun-31 Aug, Mon-Sat 10.00-17.30, Sun 13.30-17:.0. Last admission 16.30
Admission – palace & garden: adult £5; child/concession £4; family (2 A and up to 6 C) £14. Under 5s free. NTS members free

Garden only: Adult £2.50; concession £1.70; child £1; family (2 A and up to 6 C) £7. Under 5s free. NTS members free
Scots Guards and members of the Scots Guards Association, wearing badges, free.

A palace straight out of a fairy tale, built by Stewart monarchs as a country residence/ hunting lodge. Pleasant gardens, with viewing access to the oldest 'royal tennis' court in Britain – built in 1539 and still in use. Partly roofed, the palace itself would have less than minimal interest for under 5s. Fully furnished rooms from all eras of the palace's use – best to give it a bye unless you are interested in the historic aspects (and have a baby in a papoose or sling) .

Kingskettle

Stagecoach express service from Edinburgh to St Andrews stops here.

The Singing Kettle Shop

Post House
26 Main Street
Kingskettle KY15 7PN
Tel: 01337 831121
Email: info@singingkettle.com
Website: www.singingkettle.com
Opening times: Mon-Fri 9.00-17.00; Sat/Sun 11.00-16.00

Shop selling full range of Singing Kettle merchandise for young fans. Small playroom with kettle theme. Toilet. Mail order facility.

Leven

Stagecoach Express operates from Edinburgh to Leven.

Lochleven Castle (HS)

Tel: 07778 040483
www.historic-scotland.gov.uk
Situated on an island in Loch Leven, reached by ferry from Kinross, off the M90
Opening times: daily, Apr-Sept 9.30-17.15 (last outward sailing)
Admission charges: adult £3.50; child £1.20; concession £2.50. Under 5s **free** . (HS members **free**). Ferry included in admission price

Plenty of room on the island for some exploration around the ruins – but watch out, the midgies can be murderous! This castle imprisoned Mary, Queen of Scots, before her dramatic escape in 1568. The ferry journey to and from the island could make this a great pocket-sized adventure. Not really suitable for babies or young toddlers, more for adventurous/active under 5s.

Vane Farm Nature Reserve

By Loch Leven
Tel: 01577 862355
On B9097, S of shore of Lochleven, 1 mile E of M90, J5
Centre open daily 10 :00- 17:00. Closed 25,26 Dec, 1,2 Jan. Reserve open at all times
Admission: adult £3; Concession £2; child 50p. Family (2A & 6C) £6. Under 5s free. RSPB members free. Free entry to visitor centre, observation area and shop
NB. No dogs allowed on RSBP reserves.

RSPB reserve with bright and cheerful observation area/visitor centre with binoculars and telescopes set up, display touch and sound boxes for children, shop and toilets (M/F nappy changing). Two nature trails: one climbing through birch woodland to the top of Vane Hill and one a grassy wetland walk, so not suitable for pushchairs and – stout footwear is essential! The wetland trail is on a reasonably robust path suitable for toddlers upwards. There are 3 hides – the Gilman hide is a large wooden hut with great colourful wooden birds for children to look at and feel and worth the walk along the trail – good for a rainy day. Nest boxes have been put up to encourage birds to nest. The geese that overwinter on Loch Leven can be observed from a hide. There are other hides for serious birdwatchers. View of loch and picnic area.
The reserve has 10 'explorer rucksacs' to loan, containing all kinds of examination devices, such as bug boxes, binoculars, tape measures, magnifying glasses and blindfolds so you can identify things by feel!
Café:
£-££, highchairs (2)
Situated in observation area. has lchildrens books for reading, and the friendly staff and volunteers serve warming fare such as soup and baked potatoes, as well as rolls and afternoon teas. Limited children's menu.

Vane Farm hosts the Scottish Wildlife & Countryside Fair in September. Free car parking at this fair.
Hot and cold snacks – no dogs as it's on RSPB land.

Kirkcaldy

Trains from Edinburgh Waverley , Haymarket and South Gyle stations.(Traveline 0870 6082608) Stagecoach Express operates services from St Andrew's Square.

Tourist Information Centre

19 Whytes Causeway
Tel: 01592 267775
Web: www.standrews.com/fife
Closed on Sundays

Kirkcaldy Museum and Art Gallery

War Memorial Gardens
Tel: 01592 412860
5 mins from Kirkcaldy railway station
Opening times: Mon-Sat 10.30-17.00; Sun 14.00-17.00. **Free**

This museum is lively, friendly and fully accessible to pushchairs and to disabled visitors with ramped access to main entrance and a lift to the first floor galleries. There is a local history display with some 'please touch' sections, galleries with temporary exhibitions and an outstanding collection of 18th century Scottish paintings. Gift shop. For further information, contact the Outreach Officer.
Café:
high chairs, breastfeeding welcomed. Nappy changing facility.

Lochore

Lochore Meadows Country Park

Tel: 01592 414300
Cross Forth Road Bridge and follow M90. At J2A, take Kirkcaldy turn off. Follow Lochgelly exit from this road, then the B920 to Crosshill. Park is signposted on the left
Opening times: buildings open 9.00-17.00 daily, park open 24

hours. Admission **free**

Park offers a multitude of activities including canoeing, hillwalking, sailing, horse riding, golf/putting, and a woodland trail. Award winning facility in 1988, but would now benefit from some maintainance. The park also has an adventure playground/beach/BBQ picnic areas . Lovely safe enclosed toddler play park but wood bark on ground wearing thin. Toilets, nappy changing room (needed some attention on day of our visit – staff happily addressed issue when raised) . Building all on one level.
Cafe:
highchairs (2), breastfeeding welcomed.

North Queensferry

Train-obsessed toddlers could spend the day watching trains going back and forth across the Forth, from North Queensferry to Dalmeny, or going on the Maid of the Forth from here to Inchcolm. The Ferry Boat Inn (££) can provide dinner at the end of the day (or lunch if you feed your picnic to the seagulls). See S Queensferry (West Lothian).

Deep Sea World

Battery Quarry
North Queensferry KY11 1JR
Tel: 01383 411411
Email: info@deepseaworld.com
Web: www.deepseaworld.com

Close to the north side of the Forth Road Rail Bridge, the road is very winding, but follow the signs and you'll get there!
Nearest station: North Queensferry. The road down to the aquarium is very steep
Opening times: Apr-Oct daily 10.00-18.00, Nov-March daily 10.00-17.00. Closed 25 Dec, 1 Jan.
Admission: adult £7.95; child (3-15) £5.75; concession £4.50; families – prices vary by family size. Under 3s free.
Annual adult ticket £21.95, Annual family ticket £44.95
Swim with the sharks £50

This award-winning aquarium offers a spectacular fishes'-eye view of the marine environment. It's divided into various areas, including 'Krakatoa', with deadly species from around the Indo-Pacific; Amazonia which has the ever popular pirhanas; and the Underwater Safari. This is fascinating, as you stand on a moving walkway to observe the fish which swim all around the tunnel you're in. The downside is that pushchairs and prams are not allowed here, due to the walkway.
There's an opportunity to see sharks in close-up, via a high-tech exhibition. Equipped with a video camera, visitors can sit in a purpose built control capsule situated in the main exhibition area and drive a ROV (Remotely Operated Vehicle), whilst watching the live footage of the sharks on the TV screens.
The touch pools, Ray pool and Dogfish pool are particularly good for Under 5s, as you can see the creatures in very close proximity. The dogfish are great fun when they are fed, as they jump out of the water. The rays like to be tickled on their backs. Free face painting, behind the scenes tours, animal handling sessions and family talks and activity sessions. Large car park.
Café:
£-££, high chairs, breastfeeding welcome.
Bright, spacious café, which serves a range of snacks, teas, coffees and lots of fizzy drinks. Nappy changing facilities, ramp access except for the Under Sea section. Birthday parties by arrangement. Shop sells a wide range of toys and marine-theme merchandise.

St Andrews

Take M90 to J8, then A91 East. Stagecoach operates services from Edinburgh.
Historic market town, famous for being the 'home of golf' and its university. Innovative Park'n'Ride runs in the summer. Free bus service running round town from well-signposted car park on outskirts.

Tourist Information Centre

70 Market Street
Tel: 01334 472021
www.standrews.com/fife

Craigtoun Country Park

Tel: 01334 473666

3 miles SW of St Andrews on B939
Opening times: Mar/Apr w/ends, May-Aug every day, Sep w/ends 10.45-17.30 (last ticket 16.30)
Admission: child (0-3) free ;(3-5) £1; (6-15) £3; 16-adult £4; OAP £2 ; disabled visitor £1 + 1 carer free; family (2A +2C over 6) £12; family (2A +3C over 6) £15. All facilities are free after payment of entry fee

Plenty to do for all the family including: Rio Grande Railway, trampolines, two bouncy castles, boating, putting, crazy golf, adventure play park, toddler play area, Countryside Centre and lots of parkland to roam. Calender of events throughout the year. Indoor picnic hut available if raining – booking recommended (especially by large parties) . Most attractions are outside so unsuitable if raining.

Tearoom:
Highchairs(3), breastfeeding welcomed.
NB. Tearoom has (distracting) stands selling plastic footballs and toys.
Toilets at various points of the park. Nappy changing facilities (clean) in toilets for the disabled. . Park appeared to be well kept and was undergoing some ground and building maintainance on the day of our visit.

East Sands Leisure Centre

Tel: 01334 476506

Opening times: Mon-Fri , 09.00-22.00 Sat, Sun 09.00-16.30
Admission: adult £2.30; child £1.75. Under 5s free. Lovely warm toddler pool with toys. Nappy changing tables and playpens in special area in mixed changing rooms.

St Andrews Aquarium

The Scores
Tel: 01334-474786
Web: www.standrewsaquarium.co.uk

Opening times: summer, daily 10.00-18.00, phone for current winter times
Re-entry all-day ticket: adult £5.50; child £3.75; concession £4.50; family £17.00/£14.00

The St Andrews Aquarium (formerly the Sea Life Centre) is under new ownership. Special feature exhibitions include tropical fish and touch pools. The centre also rehabilitates seals for release into the wild. Access to the actual aquarium area from the pay desk is down a set of stairs, but if you have a pushchair etc, access to the lower level of the aquarium can be obtained via an external ramp.
Café with children's menu and bar open to all. Gift shop.

St Andrews Museum

Kinburn Park
Doubledykes Road, St. Andrews
01334 412690 412690

Opening times: Apr-Sep 10.00-17.00 daily; Oct- daily 10:30-16:00
Free entry

Small local museum in a park about 1/2 mile from the town centre. Previous researchers have described this as 'a great bolt-hole for a rainy day' – we arrived on a dreich day and would thoroughly agree! The exhibits are not wildly exciting for under 5s, but there is a basic activity room, for school parties (on 1st floor, lift available) which provided paper and crayons for under 5s to draw. Friendly and welcoming staff were another bonus to this visit. There is easy parking, a café in the museum, plus the surrounding parkland has putting in summer months, all-year tennis, and space to run about. The museum is totally accessible to prams & pushchairs: entry was via a ramp for the disabled located at the side of the building (you need to ask staff to open the side door). Nappy changing facilities and potties in both male & female toilets.

Café in the Park (within St Andrews Museum)
£, high chairs (2), breastfeeding welcome, non-smoking, children's menu & half portions available, provided with baby plates cutlery/cups; baby food/ bottles heated on request, unlicensed.
Ever-friendly staff in café serving very reasonably priced, wholesome, savoury food (dish of the day, light snacks, baked potatoes, vegetarian dishes) and cakes. Whilst you are unlikely to spot royalty, the carrot cake alone is worth the trek.

EAST LOTHIAN

The Lothians all have something a little bit different to offer, without the hassle of long journeys to get there.

BEACHES IN EAST LOTHIAN

Gullane

Easy-to-find beach 40 minutes from Edinburgh. From A1, take A198 towards North Berwick. In the village, follow sign to the left into a paying car park (£1.40 Easter-Sep). Pleasant beach with grassy area in front. Play area with toilets nearby.

Seacliff Beach

East of North Berwick on A198
Private beach. You'll need correct money for unmanned barrier – 2x£1 coins per car. Beautiful bay, cleaned regularly. Tiny harbour. Car park. Toilets.

Yellowcraig Beach

Drive through Dirleton and turn left just before you leave the village.
Paying car park (Easter-Sep). Beautiful beach and nature trail through the woods. Difficult with a pushchair. Take a sling or backpack.

TOWNS & ATTRACTIONS

Aberlady

Take A1 to Haddington then A6137 towards Aberlady.

Green Craigs Hotel

Aberlady EH32 0PY
Tel: 01875 870301

££, high chairs (3), breastfeeding welcome (private area available), bottles heated, nappy changing area (room 6), licensed, seats 45 in each dining room.

Bar lunches: Mon-Sat 12.00-14.00, Sun 12.00-14.30
Restaurant/Bistro: 18.30-21.00 (21.30 in summer)
Open daily for refreshments from 07.30 till late

This beautifully positioned country house hotel is located one mile west of Aberlady on the coast road (A198) from Longniddry to North Berwick. With an enviable setting, surrounded by woodland and beach, this family orientated 'restaurant with rooms' has a mountain of stuffed toys and a menagerie of animals to keep children amused. Very accommodating, helpful staff.

Myreton Motor Museum

Aberlady EH32 0PZ
Tel 01875 870288

Opening times: 10.30-16.30 April-Sep. Closed over Xmas and New Year
Admission: adult £4; child £1. Under 5s free.

An interesting collection of cars, motor cycles, and World War II military vehicles, among others. Also has displays of posters and toy cars. Toilet, but no nappy changing facilities. Breastfeeding welcome. Accessible to single but not to double pushchairs.

Dirleton

Take A1 then A198 coastal trail towards N Berwick.

Dirleton Castle and Gardens (HS)

Tel: 01620 850330
Web: www.historic-scotland.gov.uk

In Dirleton, 3m W of North Berwick
Open all year
Admission: adult £2.80; child £1.00; reduced £2.00. Under 5s free.

Castle built in the 12th century. Famous gardens include and Arts and Crafts herbaceous border – the longest one in the world according to the Guinness Book of Records. Car park & picnic area.

If you wish to visit the castle, and your child isn't so keen, why not compromise and afterwards go to the play park next to the castle. This has 2 bucket swings, roundabout, slide etc and picnic table.

See also **Yellowcraig Beach**, above.

Dunbar

On A1, 25 miles from Edinburgh. First Edinburgh service no. 106 every 20 mins from Haymarket (1hr 30 mins). X6 service also goes to Dunbar – check current timetables. Trains 2 hourly from Waverley.

Tourist Information Centre

143 High Street
Tel: 01368 863353

Dunbar Splash Leisure Pool

Castlepark
Dunbar EH42 1EU
Tel: 01368 865456

Opposite end of main street from station. Special features include a gently sloping beach area where the water starts at about an inch deep and gradually gets deeper (perfect for non-swimmers, as they can stand in the water at whatever depth they prefer). Also bubble bed, flume slide and geyser sprays, as well as a wave machine which operates once or twice an hour. Brand new 'Underwater Adventure' soft play area (separate charge). Health suite with sauna, steamroom, and new Bodyworks gym. Café/spectator area is on poolside. Crèche, nappy changing and dressing facilities for mothers with children.

John Muir Country Park

Contact: Bobby Anderson, Snr Countryside Ranger
Tel: 01620 827318

Take A1 towards Dunbar, turn along A1087 for 1 mile, and turn left into Linkfield car park. For Shore Rd, continue further 1/2 mile into West Barns. 1 1/2 mile walk from bus station, or take local bus to West Barns, Shore Rd.

Large country park with a lovely beach, clifftop trail, and woodland walks. Awarded Tidy Britain Group Seaside Award in 2001 for the 8th consecutive year. Not always suitable for a pushchair – take a sling or backpack. Picnic sites at Linkfield car park and Shore Rd car park. Recently opened adventure playground on grass with bark chips at Linkfield car park. Barbecues for hire. Toilets with disabled units served by radar key.

East Fortune

From A1, take B1347 towards North Berwick. Close to the Museum of Flight.

East Fortune Market

Opening times: Sun 10.00-16.00

Similar to Ingliston Market nr Edinburgh Airport, but smaller. Wide variety of low-priced merchandise, including: clothes for babies, children and adults; toys; household goods; fresh meat, fruit and vegetables, and baked goods. Stall which sells adult and children's seconds and Clark's shoes, often at half price.

Museum of Flight

East Fortune Airfield EH39 5LF
Tel: 01620 880 308
Web: www.nms.ac.uk/flight
or www.scotwings.co.uk

Signposted off A1 on B1347 to North Berwick
Opening times: daily, all year 10.30-17.00 (18.00 July and August)
Admission: adult £3; concessions £1.50. Children (under 16s) free. Admission free with National Museums of Scotland membership scheme card.

Fascinating collection of aircraft, engines and rockets etc. Children can sit in the cockpit of a trainer aeroplane. Watch out! – guard rails are low. Shop. The friendly Parachute Café, which has a menu which changes daily.. . Toilets. It's worthwhile checking the websites for information of one-off events and tie-ins with festivals etc.
A full programme of events throughout the year, including the annual Festival of Flight in mid-July. See *Annual Events*.

Gifford

Attractive village with central square and grassy park with play equipment, toilets.
On B6369 from Haddington or B6355 from Pencaitland.

Goblin Ha' Hotel

Main Street, Gifford
Tel: 01620 810244

Opening times: Mon-Fri 12.30-14.00, 18.30-21.00; Sat-Sun 12.30-14.00, 17.00-20.00
££, high chairs (4), clip on seats (1), booster seats (2), breastfeeding permitted, nappy changing surface, licensed, seats 120.

Traditional country hotel. Staff sympathetic to needs of young children. Table service. À la Carte menu with dish of the day, light snacks, children's menu, half portions of full menu. Colouring sheets and crayons provided. Beer garden with outdoor play area and pet rabbits.

North Berwick

From A1 take A198 coastal route. Train service from Waverley Station (30 mins). Charming seaside resort with beach, harbour, parks and paddling pool. First Edinburgh service no. 124 (1hr 15 mins).

Tourist Information Centre

1 Quality St
Tel: 01620 892197

Lodge Grounds, Logan Park

Near Main Street

Interesting public park with gardens, aviary, adventure-style playground, crazy golf, skittles and trampolines (various charges apply).
Open Easter-end Sep.
Car parking nearby and nappy changing facilities in close to award-winning family toilets. Toilets open 9.00-21.00 in summer months, closed in winter.

Millers Bistro

15 Market Place
Tel: 01620 890437

Child friendly bistro/café with highchairs.

Nether Abbey Hotel

Dirleton Avenue EH39 4BQ
Tel: 01620 892802
Website: www.netherabbey.co.uk

Welcome environment for families, staff sympathetic to the needs of young children. Highchairs, nappy changing facilities, kids menu, outdoor seating area under a canopy. Children's play area with chipped bark at the side of the hotel.

North Berwick Sports Centre

Grange Rd EH39 4QS
Tel: 01620 893454

Includes swimming pool – floating floor raises to create shallow end at weekends and various other times. 6 floor-level trampolines, soft play room. Family changing cubicles, group changing rooms, nappy changing facilities. Birthday parties catered for.

Scottish Seabird Centre

The Harbour
North Berwick EH39 4SS
Tel: 01620 890202
Website: www.seabird.org
Opening times: 10.00-18.00 every day except Christmas

The Scottish Seabird Centre is an exciting Millennium Project attraction overlooking the islands of the Firth of Forth. Displays include a short film about the seabirds found in Scotland, and interactive live cameras that allow visitors to watch gannets and puffins and other nesting seabirds on the Bass Rock and Fidra. Seals and dolphins can sometimes be seen from the observation deck. A camera allows visitors to see close-ups of newborn seals on the Isle of May. Gift shop and licensed café with indoor and outdoor seating. Accessible to pushchairs. Toilets with changing facilities.

See also **Seacliff Beach**, above

Stenton

Take A1 to East Linton then right onto B6370 to Stenton.

Stenton Fruit Farm

Ruchlaw Produce Ltd
Ruchlaw Mains
Stenton EH42 1TD
Tel: 01368 850321
Take A1 to East Linton, stay on bypass, then 2nd right on to B6370 to Stenton, and follow fruit signs.
Opening times: daily, 10.00-21.00 Jul and Aug

Pick your own fruit. Ring for crop availability. Play area with chute, climbing apparatus, trampolines and table tennis. Ducks and picnic area. Refreshments – ice cream, lemonade and tea/coffee machine. Toilets. Access for single and double pushchairs. Breastfeeding friendly.

Whitecraig

On A6094. Take A1 from Edinburgh, exit at Dalkeith/Wallyford. Follow signs for Dalkeith. First village after leaving A1.

Dolphin Inn

10 Whitecraig Rd
Musselburgh EH21 8PG
Tel: 665 3354
Opening times: Mon-Fri 12.00-14.30, 18.00-19.30; Sat 12.00-19.30; Sun 12.30-19.30

£, high chairs (2), bottles heated, free baby food, feeding cups, breastfeeding welcomed, nappy change surface (M&F), licensed, seats 50

Popular family restaurant. Table service. Good quality, value for money food. Child friendly attitude towards families. Fixed menu with dish of the day, snacks, vegetarian dishes. children's menu, half portions of full menu. Equipped play area outdoors, Lego table indoors. Crayons, paper and toys also available. No-smoking area in restaurant.

LANARKSHIRE

Lanarkshire and the Clyde Valley is an often forgotten part of Scotland, but has some fantastic days out, particularly to one of its many country parks or market towns. Further information can be accessed via www.glasgowguide.co.uk or using the tourist information sites listed below.

TOWNS & ATTRACTIONS

Biggar

Biggar is a historic market town, and has many pleasant streets and shops. Centrally, along either side of the river, is a new and well maintained play area. This is not fenced, and children may require close supervision.

Tourist Information Centre

155 High St
Biggar ML12 6DL
Tel: 01899 221066
Open Easter-Oct

Biggar Museums Trust

Biggar has seven museums, which have together formed the Biggar Museum Trust. These are generally small traditional museums, with limited appeal to children. Gladstone Court is the exception to this, and offers a combined ticket to also visit Moat Park Heritage Centre. Moat Park has some interesting displays, but has no lift to its upper level, and primarily will appeal to older children and adults.

Gladstone Court Museum

North Back Rd
Biggar ML12 6DT
Tel: 01899 221050
Go through the gate near the Christmas Shop and follow signs

Opening times: Easter-mid Oct, Mon-Sat 11.00-16.30; Sun 14.00-16.30
Admission; adult £2; child £1. Under 5s free

This museum features a reconstruction of a Victorian Street, with a number of small shops which children can run into and explore. There are a number of interactive features. Accessible to single pushchairs. Breastfeeding is welcomed.

Biggar Puppet Theatre

Broughton Rd
Tel: 01899 220631
Fax: 01899 220750
Email: admin@purvespuppets.com
Web: www.purvespuppets.com
Take A702 to Biggar. Theatre is signposted
Opening times: backstage/museum, daily Tue-Fri 10.00-17.00 except 10 Jan-10 Mar (Theatre closed, but some shows may run); Easter-Aug, Sat 10.00-16.30
Show times vary, advised to phone ahead.
Admission, show: adult/child £5.00. Concessions for groups of 5 and over. Backstage tour: Adults and children £2.50. Special rates for nurseries and similar groups.

Victorian-style theatre seating 100. Puppet performances for family audiences with large-scale puppets, and special shows/workshops for younger children. Audience participation encouraged. Guided tours backstage and of puppet museum. Birthday parties hosted, min 10 including adults, please book.
Attractive grounds with picnic area and playground. Conservatory tearoom, breastfeeding welcome. Toilets, nappy changing area (M&F). Souvenir shop. Car park. Access for single and double pushchairs; wheelchair users please phone ahead.

Coatbridge

Summerlee Heritage Park

Heritage Way
Coatbridge ML5 1QD
Tel: 01236 431261
Opening times: daily, all year 10.00-17.00 (16.00 Nov-Mar). closed 25, 26 Dec and 1, 2 Jan.
Free entry
Tram ride: adult 80; child 45p

No direct public transport from Edinburgh. Take train to Motherwell or Cumbernauld and change for Coatbridge Central; or take train to Glasgow Queen St and change for Coatbridge Sunnyside. Park 5 mins walk from Central and 10 from Sunnyside. Signposted from A8/M8, J8 Coatbridge Town Centre.
Winner of 'Best Working Attraction' award. Huge undercover exhibition hall with olden-days room settings, heritage artefacts and working machinery. Outside is Scotland's only working electric tramway, a row of miners' cottages and a re-created underground mine. Mine not suitable for pushchairs or toddlers.
Special events held throughout the year with puppet or magic shows, face painting and story telling. Phone for details or copy of latest 'What's On' programme.
Children's play area and tables for picnics.
Café:
£-££, breastfeeding welcome.
Half portions and take away service available. Toilets, nappy changing room.

Drumpellier Country Park

Townhead Rd, Coatbridge
ML5 IRQ
Tel: 01236 422257
By rail: the park is close to the main Glasgow/ Airdrie line at Blairhill Station
By car: take M8 to J8 (Coatbridge) and follow brown signs.
Opening times: daily, all year from 10.30 (except 25, 26 Dec and 1-3 Jan). Jun/Jul /Aug closes 19.30. Apr/May/Sep closes 17.00. Oct-Mar closes 16.00
Admission free.

Country park with excellent adventure playground, formal garden, road train, picnic sites and ranger service. Attractive loch side walk suitable for pushchairs and ideal for toddlers on tricycles/bicycles (1.1 miles). May be very busy in good weather.
Train ride lasts 40 mins. Costs £1.20. Open Jun-Aug. During June weekends only, but during school holidays open daily. Boats available daily during school holidays.
Café: *high chairs, breastfeeding welcomed.*
Located in visitor centre. Open all year. The café has a snack menu and is not no-smoking. Nappy changing in the toilet for the disabled.

Cumbernauld

Palacerigg Country Park

Tel: 01236 720047
2 miles south of Cumbernauld. Leave M8 for Airdrie A73, then head for Cumbernauld on the B8039 and follow signs

This is a country park with a tidy playground with traditional equipment and also a bouncy castle and small fairground rides.

There is an animal collection, some nature trails, a treetop walk, and a ranger service with a strong emphasis on conservation. The millennium log houses are the base for displays of traditional crafts. The visitor centre has an interesting exhibition of creepy crawlies which is well presented, educational and fun. Breastfeeding welcome. Nappy changing facilities available to both mums and dads. There is a café (11.00-16.00) with high chairs, and a snack type menu.

East Kilbride

Calderglen Country Park

Strathaven Rd
East Kilbride G75 0QZ
Tel: 01355 236 644

By car take M8 to J8. Take M73 then follow M74 to J5. Take A725 to East Kilbride until brown sign for Calderglen
Park open all year
Free entry
Visitor centre open: summer Mon-Fri 10.30-17.00, Sat/Sun /Public holidays 11.30-18.30; winter Mon-Sun 11.30-16.00
Courtyard café opening times: summer 10.00-18.00; winter 10.00-16.00
Lovely country park with many attractions. Large adventure playground suitable for all ages, but also smaller play area specifically for younger children. Small sized children's zoo, with new meerkat exhibit, ornamental garden and conservatory with varied collection of animals and plants from around the world. Of special interest to younger children in the conservatory is the interactive tree which brings the sounds and smells of the rainforest.
Café:
Highchairs., breastfeeding welcome.
The menu at the courtyard café is excellent and does include a good choice for children. The café is accessible to pushchairs at the lower end. Nappy changing in the toilet for the disabled.

Caper House Play Barn

Macneish Way
Stewartfield
East Kilbride G74 4TT
Tel: 01355 579 836

Take M8 to J8, then M73. Take M74 to J5. Follow A725 to East Kilbride
Follow signs for Rutherglen and Glasgow (A749). At roundabout turn right, then at the next roundabout take left filter (Kingsgate roundabout) onto Stewartfield Way. Continue along Stewartfield Way, and at second roundabout (at Safeway store), take the second exit on left. Caper House Play Barn is on the left
Opening times: 7 days/wk 10.00–18.00
Admission: Mon-Fri; £2.60 for one hour, £3.10 for 1 1/2 hrs; £3.60 for 2 hours
Public holidays and Sat/Sun; £3.60 for 1 1/2 hrs
Special rates for groups (10-40); £3.00 for 2 hours (juice included). Please phone to book in advance.

Large children's soft play area. There is a central area for babies and younger children, with older children able to explore higher areas. Clean, with a large number of helpful staff. Often very busy, so wise to phone ahead.
Café:
highchairs, breastfeeding welcome.
Serves children's menu and snacks. . Nappy changing room.
Birthday parties for children 4ft 6 and under: £7.50/child (min of 10 at weekends if possible).

James Hamilton Heritage Park

Stewartfield
East Kilbride G74 5LB
Tel: 01355 276611

Take M8 to J8, then M73. Take M74 to J5, then A725 to East Kilbride. Follow signs to Rutherglen and Glasgow (A749). At roundabout turn right then at the next roundabout take left filter (Kingsgate Roundabout) onto Stewartfield Way. Take a right turn at the next roundabout.
Opening times: park is open 7 days a week, watersports centre between spring and autumn, phone to check times.

This attractive park features a 16 acre loch, a watersports centre, a nature sanctuary, a loch side walk, picnic areas and well maintained play areas, one of which is tailored to the under fives. The boats are good value for money, and small size life jackets are available. A full range of watersports are offered, but bumper boats, pedaloes, and rowers are most suitable for the younger family. Overall, well worth a visit.
Café:
£-££, highchairs, breastfeeding is welcomed.
Offers hot and cold snacks, home baking, and kids' lunch boxes. Has good pushchair access. There is a nappy changing area.

Hamilton

Hamilton Tourist Information Services

Road Chef Services
M74 Northbound
Hamilton ML3 6JW
Tel: 01698 285590
Web; www.hamilton@seeglasgow.com
Open Jan-Dec

Chatelherault Country Park

Carlisle Rd
Ferniegair
Hamilton ML3 7UE
Tel: 01698 426 213
Take M8 to J8, then M73. Take M74 to J6. Follow brown signs
Park open all year. Entry free
Visitor centre opening times: Mon-Sat 10.00-17.00, Sun 12.00-17.00
Courtyard café opening times: Mon-Fri 10.30-16.00, Sat 10.00-17.00, Sun 12.00-17.00
Country park with visitor centre, exhibition galleries, historic house, gift shop and adventure playground. Beautiful woodland trails with variety of terrain and distance. Some of the trails are unsuitable for pushchairs and toddlers on foot (deep gorge in places). Excellent 'trails' leaflet and map at reception and staff will also advise.
Café:
£, highchairs available, breastfeeding welcome.
Provides basic light menu. Nappy changing in the toilet for the disabled. Access for pushchairs.

Lanark

Lanark is a pleasant market town. Lanark Loch is situated on the left, just before the town on the A71 and has boating, attractive walks, and an imaginative loch side playground.

Tourist Information Centre

Horsemarket
Ladyacre Rd
Lanark ML11 7LQ
Tel: 01555 661661
Web: www.lanark@seeglasgow.com
Open Jan-Dec

New Lanark Visitor Centre

New Lanark Mills
Lanark ML11 9DB
Tel: 01555 661 345
Web: www.newlanark.org
Trains run hourly from Glasgow and Motherwell to Lanark station, local buses or taxis run from there. By car M8 to J5, Centre is sign-posted; or take A70 Lanark Rd from Edinburgh to Lanark. There is a steep walk down from the upper car park- parking is also available down near the exhibits for those that would find this difficult
Opening times: 11.00-17.00
Admission: adult £5.95; child £3.95; family (2A+2C) £16.95; family (2A+4C) £19.95

Award-winning Visitor Centre in famous 18th century cotton mill village, now a World Heritage Site. Ride on the new 'Millennium Experience' and see the new show, the 'Annie McLeod Story'. The visitor centre is totally accessible to prams and wheelchairs, with ramped access. There is an excellent interactive soft play zone that will amuse even the youngest children. There are games and special features for children, an adventure playground and picnic area.
Café:
high chairs, breastfeeding is welcome no smoking area, seats 1209.
Serves a healthy range of meals and snacks which are very well presented, with half portions for children and special lunch boxes available. Children's parties are hosted. Toilets and nappy changing available (M&F).
There are attractive walks in the Falls of Clyde Wildlife Reserve. Not suitable for pushchairs – the paths can be wet and muddy. Best option may be to use a backpack. Take care on the steep paths near the waterfalls.

Motherwell

Strathclyde Country Park

366 Hamilton Rd
Motherwell ML13ED
Tel: 01698 266155
Take M8 to J8, then M74 to J5. Signposted off roundabout
Open 9-5 all year, evenings during summer
Entry to the park is free, additional charges for some activities.

Strathclyde Park has 1100 acres of countryside which surround Strathclyde Loch. There are a wide variety of activities in the park for under fives including playgrounds, sandy beaches, footpaths, nature trails and exploring the park visitor centre. There are also watersports and land sports available.

M&Ds Leisure Park

Strathclyde Country Park
Tel: 01698 333999
Web: www.scotlandsthemepark.com

Opening times vary, phone before visiting.
Admission to park free. Unlimited ride wristband: over 1.35m tall £12.50; under 1.35m tall £ 8.50; family ticket £37.00. Tokens can also be purchased for the rides.

Indoor and outdoor attractions. In the Family Entertainment Centre there is there is a large soft play area which operates a strict over 2s policy only, with a charge of £2. Immediately adjacent to the soft play area is an amusement arcade, rides and video games. Guiseppe's coffee shop is nearby, selling a range of snacks. There are some of the outdoor rides which would appeal to under fives, the majority being more suitable for older children. There are a number of restaurants and bars as well as ten-pin bowling and pool.

Strathclyde Park Inn

Strathclyde Country Park
Tel: 01698 854715

Opening times: Mon-Sat 12.00-2200, Sun 12.00-21.00

A family restaurant with indoor soft play (charge £1) and outdoor play area. Children's menu available. Pleasant and helpful staff. Breastfeeding welcome.

Strathaven

Strathaven Park

Threestanes Rd
Strathaven
Tel: 01357 521995 (ticket office)

Organised groups with large numbers should phone ahead to the management office on: 01355 233451
By car, take M8 to J8, then M73. Take M74 to J8, then follow A71 to Strathaven
Park open all year. Facilities open Easter Fri-Sep holiday weekend.

Traditional Edwardian park with adventure playground. Putting, tennis and bowling open 12.00-20.30 daily during school term time (11.00-20.30 school holidays). Boats and canoes on boating pond, open daily 14.00-20.30 term time (11.00-20.30 school holidays).
Bouncy castle and café (snack menu) available at weekends during school holidays only. This may vary as it's run by private franchise – if in doubt phone ticket office.

Youngsters may like the miniature railway. Adults 50p; 40p. Runs weekends only and bank holidays Apr-Sep 1. 17.00. Breastfeeding welcome.

MIDLOTHIAN

TOWNS & ATTRACTIONS

Dalkeith

Take A68 out of Edinburgh. Bus 86, 79 and 80 to Dalkeith (First Edinburgh), 3 and 3a (LRT)

Dalkeith Country Park

Tel: 654 1666 (ranger's office)
Tel: 663 5684
Web: www.dalkeithcountrypark.com

The park is a few hundred yards away from the town centre.
Opening times: Apr-end Sep 10.00-17.30
Admission: adult/child £2; family ticket (2A&2C) £7. Under 5s free. Group rates also available

Entrance near St Mary's Church. Nature trails, woodland walks, picnic benches and large children's adventure playground with supervisor. Take care with small children on the river paths and in the riverbank tunnels.
Café:
£-££, high chairs (1), toilets, nappy-changing facility (M&F) available, seats 60.
Small space for prams and pushchairs. Children's menu. No smoking. All facilities on ground floor. Parties hosted.

Gorebridge

Take A68 to Dalkeith, then A7 . LRT service 3a goes through Gorebridge. The service runs every 30 mins (55 mins journey).

Arniston House

Gorebridge
Tel: 01875 830 515
Web: www.arniston-house.co.uk

Approx 40 mins from central Edinburgh, from A7 turn right on to B6372, signposted as Penicuik and Temple, turn right after about a mile.
Opening times: Apr-June, Tue and Wed (guided tours at 14.00 and 15.30); July-mid Sep, Mon-Fri and Sun. Guided tours 14.00 and 15.30
Admission – house: adult £5, child £2 concession £4. Under 5s free.

… lovely, well maintained grounds …airs. Toilets. No nappy-changing facil- …access.

Arniston House is lovely, but while the guided tour may be of interest to parents, there's little to interest children under 5. The tour involves a fair amount of stairs – not suitable for a pushchair, but if you have, say, a baby in a papoose, the tour is worthwhile.

Lasswade

Dobbies Butterfly and Insect World, Bird of Prey Centre, Garden Centre and Tearoom.

See *Places to Visit.*

Newtongrange

10 miles S of Edinburgh on A7. From the eastern end of City Bypass, at Sherriffhall Roundabout follow signs for Newtongrange – approx 3 miles
LRT bus no. 30, every 1/2 hr (45 mins)

Scottish Mining Museum

Lady Victoria Colliery
Newtongrange EH22 4QN
Tel: 663 7519
Email: enquiries@scottishminingmuseum.org
Web: www.scottishminingmuseum.com

Opening times: daily, 10.00-17.00 Last entry for tour 15.30
Admission: adult £4, child/ concession £2.20; family ticket £10. Under 5s free

This purpose-built visitor centre has two floors of exhibitions, interactives, displays, buttons to press and magic helmets, so while young children might not understand the exhibition, there's a good chance that they'll still enjoy it. Families can enjoy Scotland's biggest steam engine and a simulated coalface, plus an Operations Centre full of activities.

Airy café is equipped with high chairs, and serves hot and cold meals throughout the day.

Children's outdoor play centre with Victorian toys (e.g. skittles). Gift shop. Toilets with nappy changing facilities (M&F), breastfeeding welcome. Pushchair access to all areas. Free car parking.

Pathhead

The Stair Arms Hotel

Pathhead
Tel: 01875 320 277

On the A68, on the left just before Pathhead Lies on the A68
Restaurant opening times: Sun-Thu 12.00-21.00; Fri, Sat 12.00-21.30. Seasonal variation Sun-Thu 12.00-21.30; Fri, Sat 12.00-22.00

£££, high chairs (5), cushions on request, breastfeeding welcome, nappy-changing facilities – male on request, licensed, seats 75.

Friendly restaurant with waiter service and reasonable prices. Children's menu, plus half portions from adult menu. Will warm milk and baby food. Pens and paper on request. Outdoor play area, extensive grounds. On certain occasions, such as Christmas Day and Easter, there are special events, such as a magician, tractor rides, and a bouncy castle. All facilities on ground level with room to park prams and pushchairs. Hosts children's parties.

Penicuik

Take A701 out of central Edinburgh, or come off the Bypass at the Straiton Junction and continue along the A701. Penicuik lies on the road. By bus, LRT services 37, 37a go to Penicuik (20 mins).

The Happy Castle

Bankmill
Valleyfield Rd
Penicuik EH26 8LW
Tel: 01968 675638

On entering town centre, follow one way system along Bridge St, left along Valleyfield Rd, first right and right again under bridge and into car park.
Opening times: daily 10.00-18.00
Admission: £3.50/1 hr (1-12 yrs)

Specially designed and equipped children's indoor soft play centre. Separate areas for 0-3 yrs to ensure safety of younger children. Ball pools, scramble nets, snake slides, free-fall slide, biff bags, aerial slides, rope bridges and soft toys.

Café:

£, breastfeeding welcomed.

Situated within play hall, serving tea/coffee, soft drinks and hot and cold food all day. Toilets. Nappy-changing facility (M&F). Access for single and double pushchairs. Breastfeeding welcomed. Birthday parties hosted.

Vogrie Estate and Country Park

Tel: 01875 821990

Nr Gorebridge, 12 miles South of Edinburgh
Signposted from Gorebridge (A7) and Dalkeith (A68)
Open all year.
Admission free. Car park £1

This country park has a garden centre, barbecue sites, a 9-hole golf course, woodland walks, grassy areas suitable for games, and a tree trail.

There's a toddlers' playground situated next to car park for easy access. There's also an adventure playground mainly suitable for children aged 7+, with some equipment suitable for younger children. All equipment is on bark chips, so wellies are a good idea if it's been raining heavily!

Vogrie House has a visitor centre, displays, tearoom with children's menu and highchair, nappy changing facilities and toilets. Space to park pushchairs inside. Children's parties also hosted. Tearoom open during the summer months only. Please Tel: 561 5263 (contact: Norman Catto) for opening times.

PERTHSHIRE

It may not take long to travel there, and but Perthshire has a completely different landscape to the Lothians. There are plenty of places for day trips: we've listed just some of them.

TOWNS & ATTRACTIONS

Auchingarrich Wildlife Centre

Comrie, Perthshire
Tel: 01764 679 469

Easy to find. Take M9 past Stirling to A9. From A9, take A822 towards Crieff, then 2nd turn off on to B827, then follow signs to Wildlife Centre.
Opening times: daily, 10.00-dusk. Coffee shop closes at 17.00
Admission: adult £4.75; child £3.75; under 3s free; family £16

Wildlife centre set in the beautiful Perthshire hills. There's a fantastic range of animals to be seen, from Highland cattle to meerkats and maras! All the main attractions are under cover and linked by tarmaced pathways. There are some areas specifically for under 5s, where they can meet and touch friendly animals. There's also an indoor playbarn with picnic tables, which has a separate area for under 5s – ideal for rainy days. Outdoor playpark comes complete with sandpit, buckets and spades. The Pine Lodge coffee shop serves snacks, breastfeeding welcomed.

Beatrix Potter Exhibition

Birnam Institute
Station Rd
Birnam, by Dunkeld PH8 0DS
Tel: 01350 727674

Opening times: daily, 10.00-17.00
Admission: free
Just off the A9, 15 miles North of Perth

Birnam can prove a handy-time-out' stop when you're driving through Perthshire – or if you're travelling further North. Housed inside the Birnam Institute building, the exhibition charting Beatrix Potter's career and her local connections will be of interest to anyone interested in the author's creations, although you might find that the Beatrix Potter garden is more attractive to wee visitors. There's also a café and a gift shop, stacked with Peter Rabbits, Benjamin Bunnies etc

Dunkeld

A pleasant, historic town, situated a hop and a skip away from Birnam. There's a pay and display car park at the North End of the town. We've always found it best to park here and wander back along the main street, or go round the back of Stanley Hill and take the scenic route. If you make your way along the High Street, you'll come to the town's historic town square, and the road up to the cathedral. If you walk up towards the cathedral, then cut down towards the river, you'll find a picnic spot and a playbark. The park has a climbing frame, two wobble-boards (which prove a hoot to toddlers!), two bucket swings, two swings and a chute (quite high), all set on bark or rubber matting. The river's quite close-by though, so keep an eye on any adventurous children. There are also usually a few ducks waddling about in Spring and Summer. There are quite a few cafés and restaurants strung out along the High Street, should you want to pop in for a snack, but there's always the option of a picnic at the back of Stanley Hill (local legend claims that it's a fairy hill!). There are picnic benches, but there's also plenty of room to spread out a rug. There are public loos quite nearby, just through the gateway that leads on to the square. There are others in the car park, but they're pretty basic.

Drummond Trout Farm and Fishery

Comrie, Perthshire PH6 2LD
Tel: 01764 670500
Web: www.drummondtroutfarm.co.uk

1 mile w of Comrie, off A85. Look for signpost. Trout farm is at the end of a very narrow lane that should be negotiated with

care.
Opening times: 10.00-17.00 (Sep-May); 10.00-22.00 (Jun-Aug)
Admission: Adult £2.00; child £1.00; under 5s free. Price includes a bag of food (pellets) to give to the fish. Angling costs extra. Rods available for hire

Commercial fish farm that also offers angling for beginners upwards. Several lochans and pools to view, as well as nursery tanks filled with 1000s of very small trout. Careful supervision of children obviously required. There is an underwater viewing camera. Picnic tables dotted around the site. A small shop sells freshly caught trout. Nappy-changing facilities (M&F) in disabled toilet. Breastfeeding welcome. Nice weather really needed at this venue – there is very little shelter and not much to see inside.

Perth

There are pleasant riverside walks in the town centre, although the flood precautions have obscured the once-clear views. However, there are ornate gates to look through, down on to the river. As you come into Perth, on the left there's the South Inch. This is a large grassy area with paved footpaths and, during the summer months, a paddling pool, bouncy castle and a boating pond. There's also a large playground with an area suitable for younger children.
Scotrail services run from Edinburgh, as do Scottish Citylink, National Express and Megabus coaches.

Tourist Information

4 Westmill St
Perth PH1 5QP
Tel: 01738 450 600

Noah's Ark

Old Gallows Rd
Western Edge, Perth
Tel: 01738 445568
Email: info@noahs-ark.co.uk
Web: www.noahs-ark.co.uk
Opening times: daily, 10.30-18.30
Admission: adults free; child 5-12yrs £4.25; under 5s £3.75

This is a bit awkward to find, as it's situated in a residential housing area on the outskirts of Perth. From M90, follow the signs for Inverness, to a large roundabout outside the city boundary – the Broxden Roundabout. Take 3rd exit for Perth, and 500 yds ahead there is a small roundabout, McDonalds on the right. Look out for a brown tourist sign which says Noah's Ark and golf range. Follow signs through housing estate for 1 mile.

A soft play barn for the under 12s, with 3 separate areas, for 0-3, 3-5 yrs and 5+ yrs. Under 3s area is a haven for tinies. Under 5s area is an adventure for 18+ mths, with their parents' help. Outdoor picnic area (summer only), quiet lounge for frazzled fathers or mothers!
Café:
£, highchairs (tree-trunk style), breastfeeding welcomed, seats 150.
Open all day, snacks, home baking etc, .

A very imaginative softplay centre, well worth the drive for a rainy day out. It is always worth phoning in advance to find a quiet time to visit, due to large groups and buses.
There's also an indoor karting track on the same site. Costs extra. Children 3+ yrs can ride in a twin seater kart with an adult driver over 18. Great fun – not just for the child! Sessions last about 5 mins. There are also single seat karts suitable for all – minimum height 4' 4". Opening times for karts: Sat-Sun 10.30-21.00; Mon-Fri seasonal – phone for details.
Recently introduced activities at Noah's Ark are 10 pin bowling, trampolines, and a ceramic studio. Phone for further details.

Perth Leisure Pool

Glasgow Road
Perth PH2 0HZ
Tel: 01738 492410/635454
Opening times: daily, 10.00-22.00
Easy to find. Leave M90 following signs to Perth, look out for the left turn with sign to leisure pool.
Admission: adult swim £4.20; child £2.30; under 5s free. Family ticket £10.70. Group rates also available.

Large, exciting complex which combines a state-of-the-art leisure pool with a 25m swimming pool and training pool. Leisure pool has lagoon, flumes, wild water, whirl pools, and toddler area. There's also a separate children's 'Monkey Jungle' activity pool. Baby and parent and toddler classes.
Family changing cubicles with nappy changing shelf. Picnic area. Crèche. Café for meals, breastfeeding permitted. The café tends to be very warm, so make sure you have t-shirts for your children. There's a useful enclosed section in the café with toddler sized tables and chairs, as well as some adult tables. This enables small children to wander round safely in an enclosed space – the glass walls overlooking the pool should entertain them while you rest. Interactive playpark in grounds of the pool complex is a welcome stop on the way back to the car park.

Scone Palace

Perth PH2 6BD
Tel: 01738 552300
Email: visits@scone-palace.co.uk
Web: www.scone-palace.co.uk

Opening times – Palace: 1 Apr-31 Oct, 9.30-17.30
Grounds 9.30-17.45. Winter hours (1 Nov-31 Mar): Friday 10.00-16.00
Admission: adult £6.35; child 5-16 yrs £3.75; concession £5.50. Under 5s free
Admission to grounds only: adult £3.25; child 5-16yrs £1.80

3 miles North of Perth on A93, on the Braemar Road. Ancient crowning place of the Kings of Scotland. Impressive stately home, with plenty of interesting items. The grounds may be of more interest to small children. They are well kept and extensive (over 100 acres). Picnic area, ball games allowed. Adventure playground with children's playhut, swings etc. There's also the Murray Star Maze. Gift shop. Tea/snack room with high chairs.

STIRLING & FALKIRK DISTRICT

There is a wide range of things to see in these areas, some historic and some more contemporary. Although it might seem more direct to get on to the M9 and drive direct to Stirling from Edinburgh, a trip along the 'old road', past towns such as Bo'ness, Grangemouth and Airth can provide the stimulus for an interesting journey for youngsters – even the strange structures of Grangemouth's petro-chemical plants can fascinate children, no matter what the adults' views on them may be!

TOWNS & ATTRACTIONS

Bo'ness

Bo'ness & Kinneil Railway

Bo'ness Station
Union St
Bo'ness
Tel: 01506 822298 (Talking Timetables)
Tel: 01506 825855 (Office)
Web: www.srps.org.uk

Take M9 out of Edinburgh. Come off at J5 and follow the signs to Bo'ness on the A904. Alternatively, take A90 out of Edinburgh, then follow the A904 out through Newton to Champany Corner on the A904. Turn right and follow the road to Bo'ness. The railway is situated near the shore of the River Forth, in the town centre and is signposted. Nearest train station is Linlithgow – you can catch a bus to Bo'ness from the High St. and Bo'ness bus terminal is very close to the railway.
Opening times: Apr-Oct only Sat and Sun; July & August, daily except Mon
Return rail travel: adult £4.50; concession £3.50; child £2.00. Under 5s free. Family ticket (2 A & 2 C) £11.00. 10% discount for groups of 12 or more paying passengers.
Steam train trips. A very pleasant outing for both children & parents. Breastfeeding welcome. Special events are very popular e.g. Easter Egg Specials; Days Out with Thomas w/ends in May & August; Santa train trips in Dec. Special timetable and fares apply for special events. Details from Scottish Railway Preservation Society on the numbers above.
Fares are available which include Caverns of Birkhill Mine (great visit, but is a very long way back up carrying your kids). The Scottish Railway Exhibition at Bo'ness station has an interesting collection of locos, rolling stock etc. with a Scottish connection. Admission: adults £1.00; children free.

Falkirk

From M9, J5, turn left along the Laurieston Bypass. Follow signs into town. There are numerous car parks around Falkirk, with reasonable charges, and there are plenty of disabled parking bays on main streets. By train, the Dunblane service from Edinburgh stops at Falkirk Grahamston every 1/2 hr. From there, it's a short walk up to the High St and the main shopping area.

Tourist Information

2-4 Glebe Street
Falkirk FK1 1HV
Tel: 01324 620244

Falkirk has two fairly new shopping centres on the High Street and a retail park on Graham Rd, within walking distance (just!) of the High Street. Callendar Square, at the east end of the High Street has Calley's Crèche on the top floor (there are lifts and ramps) and a BhS with nappy changing. Mothercare at the west end has a mother-and-baby room, as does Boots in the Howgate Centre, in the middle of the High St. M&S also has customer toilets (nappy changing unit in toilet for the disabled). The High Street is pedestrianised, with history plaques on some walls and it is worth looking at King's Court, next to no. 129, where street names have been hand-carved into the flagstones. There are various eateries scattered round Falkirk, from Italian fish and chip bars to bistro cafés and the ubiquitous McDonalds.

Callendar House

Callendar Park
Falkirk FK1 1YR
Tel: 01324 503770
Web: www.falkirkmuseums.gov.uk

From M9, J5, turn left along the Laurieston Bypass. At the end, turn left, then right. Pass the grassy banking of the Antonine Wall and the park entrance is on your left, signposted, at a roundabout. For the House and Stables Tearoom, take 1st left past the high flats.

Opening times: Mon-Sat from 10.00, Sun (Apr-Sep) from 14.00. Last admissions 16.00

Admission: adult £3.00; OAP £1.50; child (5-16 yrs) £1.00; under 5s free; family ticket (2A + 2C) £7.00

Callendar House, the town's museum, is well worth a visit. Falkirk's location means that all sorts of Royal intrigues and battles took place here. The house is set in extensive grounds with play park and woodland trails. Inside the house are four 'interpretative areas' with costumed guides: the 1828 kitchen, the General Store, the Clockmaker's Workshop and the Printer's Workshop. You get to eat things in the kitchen and the general store and the staff are nice to everybody, including children who interrupt. There are also temporary exhibitions of art and history, as well as permanent displays . Shop selling handmade preserves and sweets and traditionally-made replicas of products from the famous Carron Ironworks. Toilets, including adapted ones suitable for disabled visitors, nappy changing unit.

Callendar Park

Directions as for Callendar House, above.

Large park with crazy golf, putting, bouncy castle, electric cars (all Apr-Sep), woodland walks and Castle Callendar – an enclosed, dog-proof play park for children of all ages and abilities, which features an irresistible spiral slide and a big sand-pit. The boating pond is inhabited by many greedy birds. Kiosk selling ice-lollies, burgers, etc. For historical interest, you can run up and down the Antonine Wall, built by the Romans, which defines the park's northern boundary.

Stables Tearoom:

In Callendar Park, near Callendar House, by east car park

high chairs, breastfeeding welcome, nappy-changing facilities (M&F.

The tearoom is small and friendly and serves children's portions of most dishes. Unfortunately, it can't cope with prams. Sit outdoors in the herb garden in summer and watch the swallows as they fly around the picturesque ruined tower. A pleasant place to spend time.

Next to the tearoom is the Park Gallery, a small contemporary art gallery (admission free) featuring temporary exhibitions and an art activity box to create your own artwork.

Cheeky Monkeys (formerly KC Kangaroo's Kids' Club)

93-97 High Street
Falkirk FK1 2ED
Tel: 01324 636660

Up the close to the left of the Howgate Centre's High Street Entrance, upstairs, but help is provided for prams and pushchairs.

Opening times: Mon-Fri, 09.30-18.00 (£2.25/ 90 mins); Sat, 09.30-18.00 (£3.00/90 mins); Sun, 10.00-18.00 (£3.00/90 mins). Last admission 16.30 to ensure 90 mins play session

A soft play which includes large ball pool, slides, and climbing. Height restriction 4'6". Separate soft play area with bricks of various shapes and sizes for babies and toddlers. Party meals held in special party house. Book in advance.

Café:

Breastfeeding welcome. Nappy changing facilities (M&F). No Smoking. Seats 45.

Self-service for meals & snacks.

Falkirk Wheel

Lime Rd
Tamfourhill
Falkirk FK1 4RS
Tel: 01324 619888
Tel: 08700 500 208 (booking line)
Web: www.thefalkirkwheel.co.uk

From Edinburgh take the M9 W for Stirling. Follow brown tourist signs for The Falkirk Wheel.

Open 7 days. Apr-Nov visitor centre opens 09.00. First boat leaves 09.30. Boats every 30 mins until 17.00. Shorter hours Nov-Mar

Admission: adult £8; concession £6; child 5-15 yrs £4. Under 5s free. Tickets can be booked by phone up to 24 hrs in advance, although there is always an allocation of tickets left to be sold on the day.

Admission to visitor centre only free. Pushchairs are not allowed on the boat, nor is there a secure place to leave them in the visitor centre. The advice is leave pushchairs in the car if possible.

The Falkirk Wheel claims to be the world's first and only rotating boat lift. Built as part of the Millennium Link, the canal restoration project that reunited the historic link between

Edinburgh and Glasgow. The trip on the Wheel is made on a pleasure cruiser that departs from in front of the visitor centre. Once on board small children should sit where they can get a good view over the side of the boat as it moves upwards on the lift. At the top of the lift the boat crosses a short aqueduct before passing through a tunnel that is partially illuminated. The boat then turns round and goes back the way it came. The round trip takes about 45 mins.

In the visitor centre there are several interactive displays. Younger children may need the help of an adult to work these properly. Also a café (with high chairs) that sells sandwiches, home baking etc, and a gift shop.

Nappy changing facility in the disabled toilet. Breastfeeding welcome, although no private area available.

Mariner Leisure Centre

Glasgow Road
Camelon FK1 4HJ
Tel: 01324 503750

Signposted from A803 on west side of town

Pool opening times: Mon 09.00-17.00; Tue-Sat 09.00-21.30

Admission: adult £1.30 off-peak, £2.00 peak; child 80p and £1.20. 10p deposit for entry band. Lockers – 20p coin

Modern Leisure centre with fun pool, including wave machine, fountain, and frog chute; toddler's chutes in shallow end; baby pool with walrus chute. Soft play area for 7s and under (85p for 45mins plus 50p deposit), games hall, squash courts, fitness room, sauna. Classes include parent & toddler swimming, pre-school swimming & pre-school gymnastics. Creche – contact centre for details.

Cafeteria:

High chairs, nappy changing area (M&F). Breastfeeding welcome, privacy available.

Open 10.00-22.00. Children's play area,. Accessible to disabled visitors. Parties hosted.

Muiravonside Country Park

Tel: 01506 845311

Take the A801 from J4 (Lathallan Roundabout), then follow the B825 towards Linlithgow and Whitecross. Country Park is signposted

Set in 170 acres of the former Muiravonside Estate. The mansion house of the estate is long-gone, but there's a stepped garden on its site, with picnic benches and a barked children's play area, complete with a large spider-web climbing structure. While the chute is very high, and the swaying log-walk are too advanced for most under 5s, the toddler playpark next to the barked area is much more accessible. There are swings (bucket-swings), a couple of animal-shaped buckabouts and a see-saw.

The main car park is sited next to Newparks Farm, where children can see an array of animals, including friendly Clydesdales, guinea pigs and rabbits in abundance, sheep and goats, Tamworth pigs and a Highland bull. There are toilets at the farm site.

There are industrial relics of the estate's past scattered here and there, so don't be surprised if you come across rusting skeletal tractors.

This is a lovely place for a stroll. However, the River Avon (said as to rhyme with Gavin) flows alongside some of the paths – and there is a weir and a mill lade, so keep a close eye on children if you take a walk along the lower paths.

There's a visitor centre: park in the small overflow carpark and walk along the road – there are a couple of parking bays for disabled drivers next to the visitor centre , which is in the old farm buildings of the estate. There are toilets (clean but basic and including those for disabled visitors) next to the centre, and there's a café on the opposite side of the courtyard (teas, coffees, juice, burgers, chips etc). If you make the visitor centre your first port of call, you can pick up a really clear map of the entire estate. Contact the Ranger Service on the number above for information and updates.

Stirling

Just off the M9, Stirling has many tourist attractions, some at which are in joint discount schemes, so hold on to your tickets. From the railway station, you can walk up through the huge Thistle Shopping Centre and its extension The Marches, across the pedestrian precinct and up into the beautiful Old Town. Scotrail Intercity, hourly service. Scottish Citylink buses also run to Stirling.

From the bus and rail stations, (or nine other stops) you can tour in an open-topped bus in the summer. Buses run half-hourly between 10.00 and 17.55 and you can get on and off as often as you wish.

Tourist Information Centres

The Royal Burgh of Stirling Visitor Centre
(At Stirling Castle)
Tel: 01786 479901
and:
41 Dumbarton Road FK8 2QQ
Tel: 01786 475019

Bannockburn Heritage Centre (NTS)

Glasgow Road
Stirling FK7 OLJ
Tel: 01786 812664

Leave M9 at J9 services and take A872 Stirling, Bannockburn HC, N for 1 mile
Opening times: Mar-Oct 10.00-17.30; Nov-23 Dec 10.30-16.00.
Admission: adult £3.50; child/concession £2.60; family ticket £9.50. National Trust for Scotland Members free. Under 5s free

This heritage centre is built near to the site of the Battle of Bannockburn, when a Scottish army led by Robert the Bruce defeated the English host and drove them out of Scotland. Displays, tableaux, model soldier layouts, and audio-visual presentation (lasts about 15 mins) of the build-up to the famous battle and the battle itself. Some gory bits! On certain days during term time there is an actor for added enjoyment. Nappy changing facility in disabled toilet. Pushchair access and facilities for disabled people. Gift shop and small café with high chairs. Breastfeeding welcome.
The heritage centre is surrounded by grassy parkland that is ideal for children to run about on.

Beechwood Bike Park

St Ninian's Road
Stirling
Tel: 01786 448308

Opening times: Easter holidays, summer 10.00-18.00. Possibly non-holiday w/ends, weather permitting. Phone first. When visited one Saturday in June we found it closed.
Charge: £1.05/hr.

Bikes of all sizes for children to hire and ride around the enclosed traffic system. Opens at 10.00 for groups by arrangement. Separate adventure playground for small children, that is in the form of an obstacle coarse.

Blairdrummond Safari Park & Adventure Park

Blairdrummond
By Stirling FK9 4UR
Tel: 01786 841456

Leave M9 at J10 and take A84 for about 3 miles
Opening times: Apr-Oct 10.00-17.30. Last admission 16.30
Admission: adult £9.00; OAP/child £5.00. Under 3s free
Prices include most attractions.

Wild animals – lions, tigers, elephants, rhinos etc. Drive through park takes $^{1}/2$hr, this may be uncomfortable on a hot day with the windows closed. Farm animals in field through which you can walk and touch animals e.g. goats, pigs, llamas. Facilities for washing hands afterwards are provided. The performing sea lion show is a must – very entertaining.
Adventure playground is suitable for toddlers and older children. Includes sand area with buckets and spades. Amusement park (extra charges apply). Also 5-seater pedal boats and 'flying fox' (no extra charge).
Restaurant, high chairs, picnic and DIY barbecue area. Private area available for breastfeeding. M&F nappy changing. Park closes 1st Oct each year.

Corrieri's Café

7/9 Alloa Road
Causewayhead

Stirling FK9 5LH
Tel: 01786 472089

Opening times: 10.00 - 21.30
£-££, high chairs (4), large no-smoking area, breastfeeding welcome, M&F changing facilities

A family run and family orientated café/restaurant beside the roundabout on the way to the University/the Wallace Monument. Italian food (pizza, pasta) but also great Scottish breakfasts, snacks and vegetarian food throughout the day. Very friendly & fun place to eat with small portions for children. Ground floor access with plenty of room for pushchairs. On-road parking along Alloa Rd. Wide range of ice creams. Very busy at weekends!

If you just fancy an ice cream – why not buy one and go to the playpark just along the road. There's a tyre swing, a tyre-balance, and a multi-level sandpit cum climbing frame. There are bucket swings (1 broken on last visit) and a double covered tube slide. Next to the playpark is a basketball/football court. Plenty of grass to run about on too.

Royal Burgh of Stirling Visitor Centre

Castle Esplanade FK8 1JE
Tel: 01786 479901

Opening times: Apr-Jun, Sept 9.30-17.00; Jul, Aug 9.00-18.30; Oct-Mar 9.30-18.00
Admission: free
Tourist Information Centre/shop with protruding windows high above the street for toddlers to stand in and listen to commentary. Impressive, audio-visual information displays enhance the walls on the way to the film theatre for an 11 min free film, 'The Story of Stirling'.

Stirling Castle (HS)

Stirling FK8 1EJ
Tel: 01786 450000
Web: www.historic-scotland.gov.uk

At the top of the Old Town, thoroughly signposted.
Opening times: Apr-Sept 9.30-18.00, Oct-Mar 9.30-17.00
Admission: adult £7.50; OAP/ concession £5.50; child £2.00. Under 5s free
Parking at Castle Esplanade £2/car

One of Scotland's most impressive castles and superb for energetic toddlers and adults, even on (very!) rainy days.
Audio-visual exhibits in the kitchens and palace, interactive displays, gargoyles on the walls, and odd, secluded corners where there are probably ghosties! Take care if you decide to walk around castle walls. Grassy gardens and stunning views, shop and restaurant. The restored Great Hall is swagged with heavy drapes, has a stunning beamed roof, but for young children, it's main attraction is as a running space. However, the military museum holds little to interest young children and is up some narrow stairs.
Café:
£-££, highchairs (2), breastfeeding welcome, seats c. 130.
A Costa Café concession, which offers a range of sandwiches, panini, as well as a range of pasta dishes. Also a range of coffees (fair trade available).
Castle has various toilets here and there, with various facilities, but there's a good one hidden away within the Great Hall, complete with a nappy-change unit.

If you are going home from Stirling by the 'low road' (the A905) through Fallin, Throsk etc, look out for the signs to the Pineapple before you get to Airth. Follow the narrow road and park up in the small car park. Through the gateway in the wall, you'll enter what was a large orchard and set in the midst is The Pineapple – a 45ft (14m) high building built in the shape of, you've guessed it, a pineapple. Built in 1761, it is now holiday properties, so you can't get inside, but it makes a quirky quick stop-off point.
The Pineapple (NTS maintain gardens, building leased to the Landmark Trust).
7m E of Stirling, off A905, then off B9124. 1m W of Airth.
Open all year, daily: 9.30-sunset. No toilets.

WEST LOTHIAN

TOWNS & ATTRACTIONS

Broxburn

Take the A89 from Newbridge Roundabout, and then follow A899 on to Broxburn Main St. First Bus buses to Livingston go via Broxburn, including 27 & 28 (from Waverley Steps).

Almondell and Calderwood Country Park

Tel: 01506 882254 (visitor centre)

Almondell North car park is nearest to the Visitor Centre and closes at sunset. Signposted off A89, the entrance is 2 miles south of Broxburn. People with walking difficulties can park next to Visitor Centre.

Country park in the grounds of an old estate. Picnic tables and barbecue site (book in advance). Walks along the River Almond. Visitor Centre Sat-Thus; closed 12.00-13.00. Has an aquarium, displays and seasonal exhibitions. One is upstairs, but the rest are fully accessible. Refreshments available; hot drinks and sweets. Enclosed 'tea garden' behind the Centre with plenty of seating. Paths are suitable for both pushchairs and wheelchairs. There are

also wilder tracks to explore.
The Rangers organise family events throughout the year (Adults £1.50, children £1) and host playgroup visits. Breastfeeding welcome.
Calderwood – it is possible to walk from Almondell to Calderwood along the River Almond, though this involves passing the Mid Calder sewage works; by road from East Calder follow B7015 for a further mile and then turn on to B8046 Pumpherston/Uphall Road. Car park is 200 yds along the right.
Calderwood has been left as a natural area to encourage wildlife. The paths are rough tracks and there are facilities. A new area called Oakbank also connects with Calderwood. This is an old shale mining area, which has been planted with nitrogen-fixing plants to restore it to nature. Access off A71, 2 miles before Livingston.

Broxburn Swimming Pool

104 East Main St
Broxburn
Tel: 01506 775680

Easy to locate on the town's main street.
Opening times: Mon-Fri 08.30-21.00; Sat 09.00- 16.00; Sun 09.00-16.15
Admission: Adults £2, juvenile £1, under 5s free, 60+ free. Soft play £1.50. Lockers use 50p coin
Warm baby pool; too deep for toddlers to stand in. Family changing cubicles, playpens, changing tables are available. The shallow pool is used for lessons, so check up before you go. Breastfeeding welcome, privacy available. Vending machines supply drinks, crisps etc.
Classes include antenatal and aquafit. There's also an after school 'happy hour' for older children. Segregated sessions for sauna steam room. 'Ladies' Time Out' evenings available.
'Pirates' Cove' soft play caters for 18mths-8 yrs.
Facilities accessible to disabled users. Children's parties hosted – soft play or swimming available. Phone for information.

Linlithgow

Linlithgow Railway Station is on the main Edinburgh-Glasgow line. The Scotrail express stops here twice-hourly and the 'slow' Dunblane trains also stop here. By car, leave the M9 at junction 3 and go West along the A803. First Edinburgh buses also serve Linlithgow, including the 38 (from Charlotte Square).

Lothians Tourist Board

Burgh Halls, The Cross
Linlithgow EH49 7EJ
Tel: 01506 844600

Opening times: Mon-Sun 10.00-17.00

This is an historic Royal Burgh. Mary, Queen of Scots was born in Linlithgow Palace, which is very picturesque, but it's best visited with older children. The large grassy, banked area by the Palace, known as the Peel, is great for picnics and is of much more interest to Under 5s, including the small playpark with a chute, two buckabouts and swings for toddlers and older children. It's near to the loch and there's no fence, so some caution is required if you have a boisterous or adventurous little one. There's a loch with ducks, geese and swans, accessed from various roads off the High Street. If you've the time and energy, you can walk right round it – stop on the footbridge at the western end and see if you can see any fish swimming below. At the west end of the High Street, behind the health centre, there's a car park and another playground with modern equipment and bark chips. Public toilets, with an attendant, are towards the centre of the town near the library. There's a small charge for all users. Nappy-changing facilities are available.
There are various special events in Linlithgow throughout the year, such as jousting tournaments on the Peel, street fairs, a Gala Day and the Riding of the Marches. There is also a Festival Link with Edinburgh's International Festival.

Linlithgow Palace (HS)

Tel: 01506 842896

Situated in the centre of the town. Best to park your car and walk up to it.
Opening times: Mon-Sat all year 9.30-18.30 (16.30 in winter). Sun: Summer 9.30-18.30, Winter 14.00-16.30
Admission; adult £3.00; child £1.00; concession £2.30. Under 5s free.

Built as a pleasure palace by various Stuart monarchs, Linlithgow was acknowledged as one of the most beautiful palaces in Europe. Now roofless and partially ruined. Full of nooks and crannies, turnpike staircases and the like, which make it unsuitable for pushchairs. Probably best visited with tiny babies in a papoose, or with older children. Information boards in key rooms in various languages. There's a huge fireplace in the Great Hall – stand inside and look up! Look out for a skittles slab, the Presence Chamber with its unique floor patterning and the charmingly named 'vomitorium'!

Beecraigs Country Park

Tel: 01506 844516
Fax: 01506 846256
Email: mail@beecraigs.com
Web: www. beecraigs.com

2 miles South of Linlithgow. Drive through the town centre, turn up Preston Rd and keep going, past all the houses and on up the road. Signposted. Ist junction leads you to deer park etc. Alternatively, keep on and next turn-off takes you into Balvormie area.
Entry free. Please telephone Park Centre for other charges.

Woodland walks, deer farm, trout farm (you can feed the fish for a small charge), fishing reservoir, outdoor pursuit activities, caravan and camping site. Park Centre for information, refreshments, craft sales, farm shop, pony route, all-terrain bicycle trail, and Countryside Ranger Service. Restaurant within the Park environs. Great atmosphere on a sunny day. Breastfeeding welcome. Toilets, ramped access where needed. In the Balvormie area there's a lovely playpark with giant 'spiderweb' climbing frame. The barbecue area is nearby – bring your own charcoal, fee; £17.60 per session. Check out the website for more information.

Linlithgow Leisure Centre

McGinley Way
Linlithgow
Tel: 01506 775440

Through Linlithgow on A803, then follow A706 for Lanark and the Centre is at the 1st roundabout.
Admission: Adult £1.75. Under 5s swim free. Lockers use 20p coin
Please phone centre for current opening hours

The Centre has a pool, 5-a-side hall, dance studio, a supervised soft play area in the mornings, 0.3m deep kiddies' pool. Accessible to pushchairs. Private area for breastfeeding, which is the preferred option. Mixed changing room and nappy changing facilities. Café with children's menu. Sports play/soft play/ bouncy castle parties hosted.

Linlithgow Union Canal Society

The Basin, Manse Rd, Linlithgow
Tel: 01506 671215
Email: info@lucs.org.uk
Web: www.lucs.org.uk

Signposted from A803, sharp right turn at first railway bridge, then up and over canal bridge. The Basin is on the right.
Opening times: Easter-1st weekend Oct: Sat&Sun 14.00-17.00. Also Jul & Aug weekdays, 14.00-17.00
Trips over the Avon Aqueduct on St Magdalene (40 seater canal boat) 14.00-16.30
Charges: adult £6.00; concession/student or child £3.00; family ticket (2 adults and 2 children) £15.00. The price includes tea or coffee and biscuits
Trips on Victoria (12 seater canal boat). Depart every half-hour from 14.00. Last trip 16.30. 20 minute trip
Charges: adult £2.50; concession or child £1.50.

Boat trips on the Union Canal. There is also a museum with audio-visual presentation (perhaps more for interested parents than under 5s). The tearoom serves drinks and home-baking. The area is accessible to pushchairs and also wheelchairs. There are toilets, but there are no nappy changing facilities. It's an enjoyable outing for under 5s.
When Santa visits the Basin at Christmas, (usually on the 2 weekends prior to Christmas) there are barge trips and a gift for children (with accompanying adults going free)– contact the Society for more details.

Looking towards the town from the Canal Society, there's an old doocot with tended gardens in front of it – nice for a sit down or a picnic. If you walk further along the canal path to the West, you can cut off the path. Go up and over the canal bridge, then walk down the first roadway lined with houses on your left. This will take you into the large Rosemount park – perfect for a run around! Keep away from the canal end – there's no fencing. There are no toilets here, but you're about 10 mins walk from Linlithgow High Street and those at the Vennel.

Livingston

By car: go via M8, come off on J3 or 3a, ando come on to A899. Follow signs from there. Major attractions such as the outlet centres and the heritage centre are clearly signposted.
By train: catch trains from Waverley and Haymarket to Livingston.
First Bus buses go to Livingston, including 27 & 28 (from Waverley Steps).

For Tourist Information refer to:

Edinburgh and Lothians Tourist Board Information Desk

McArthur Glen Designer Outlet
Almondvale Ave

Livingston EH54 6QX
Tel: 01506 418 416
Opening times: Thu 10.00-20.00; Fri-Sun 10.00-17.00
At other times, nearest Tourist Information is in Linlithgow.

Almond Valley Heritage Centre

Livingston Village
Tel: 01506 414957
First Edinburgh operates 27 bus from central Edinburgh. Livingston North rail station is a mile away.
By car, take J3 off M8 and follow A899 towards Livingston, following 'Heritage Centre' signs. Take A705 to Mill roundabout then 1st left B7015, 1st right to centre.
Opening times: all year, 10.00-17.00, except 25th/26th Dec & 1st/2nd Jan.
Admission: Adult £3.00; child £2.00; family ticket (2A & 4C) £10.00. Under 3s free. Children must be accompanied by an adult. Discounts available for advance group bookings.
Tea room open 10.00-16.30 Apr-Oct and weekends. 11.00-15.30 Nov-Mar weekdays.

A restored 18th century water mill and farm. Range of farm animals, including Clydesdale horses, cattle, sheep, goats, donkeys and a range of ducks, geese and chickens. Milking demonstrations twice daily and, in Spring, baby animals to feed. Tractor-drawn trailer rides around the farm operating throughout summer.
A play tractor course exclusively for the under 5s, a new indoor soft play area on a farmyard theme, complete with ball pit. The 'Oilshale Adventure Zone' provides imaginative indoor adventure playground for the 4-12 year olds. Countryside walks and nature trails. Picnic tables and play area with bark chips. Train rides operational during summer. In the Shale Oil Museum, walk through an oil worker's home and a laboratory. In the children's discovery area, there are interactive games, including 'horseshoes'. Manoeuvre a roof-top camera from within the museum to the farm. In the recently extended museum, there are tunnels to crawl through, secret works to explore and even a pod to go back in time in. There's also agift shop.
Café:
£, high chairs (2), Breastfeeding welcomed.
Serves light snacks. Space for pushchairs. Nappy-changing unit in Ladies' toilet and toilet for the disabled. Children's parties arranged.

Bubbles Leisure Pool

Almondvale Boulevard
Livingston
Tel: 01506 777870
Opening times (for children):
Mon, Tue, Thu: 9.00-20.00. Wed: 9.00-17.00. Fri: 9.00-20.00 (except last Fri of the month 9.00-18.00). Sat 9.00-17.00. Sun: 10.00-17.00
Please note that parts of the pool may be closed to the general public for classes. Soft play may be closed for parties.
Pool admission: adult £2.20; juveniles £1. Under 5s free; 60+ free
Soft Play admission: £2/hour unsupervised. £2.20/hour supervised (see below)

Modern leisure swimming pool with fitness suite, dance studio and McArthur Glen designer outlet shopping centre. Situated adjacent to the Almondvale Shopping Centre, behind Safeway, in the centre of Livingston. Buses from Edinburgh stop at the bus station on Almondvale Rd, at other side of shopping centre. Livingston South railway station is a mile away. There is a cycle rack outside Bubbles. By car: take M8 to J3 and follow the A899 to centre of Livingston. The leisure pool is sign-posted.
Leisure pool, soft play area, health suite and fitness centre. All areas linked by walkways. Pool features bubble bed, great for toddlers, fountains, river run, slides – min. height 1.2m and spa (remove armbands please). Floats available. Armbands can be purchased. Children under 8 yrs must be accompanied by and adult at all times. Adults can be responsible for no more than 2 children of 7 years and under. Mixed changing area adjacent to pool. Changing tables in larger family cubicles. Playpen next to showers. Different sizes of lockers, 50p charge, refundable. Hairdryers, 10p.
Soft play area has a Space Bugs theme, and is for 6mths-7yrs. It has chutes, ropes, ball pits and a climbing frame. Supervised soft play is available (for children of adults using other leisure facilities) Mon, Wed 9.00-16.00; Tue-Thu 9.00-21.00; Fri 9.00-13.00, Membership available for fitness centre (induction is required), which offers technogym equipment and 50+ fitness classes each week. Pay as you go and family membership options also available.
Soft play parties available with catering – see *Birthdays & Celebrations*.

South Queensferry

This is an ancient Royal Burgh, with harbours, boat trips, an 11th century priory church, a beach (although it's stony), and great views of the two Forth bridges. You can walk from S Queensferry through Dalmeny Estate. The annual Ferry Fair is on the first Saturday in August, with a carnival on the 'prom', and the focus on the Burry Man – it's good luck if he gives you a kiss! Buses from George St in Edinburgh run to S Queensferry police station: 3 per hr Mon-Sat, 2 per hr on Sun. Last bus 23.37 Mon-Sat: 22.58 Sun. The journey takes about 1/2 hour.

Scotrail services run to Dalmeny Station: there's a short walk down into the town

Boat Trips to Inchcolm Island

Maid of the Forth
Tel: 331 4857 24 hr (sailings enquiry service)

Sailings on Maid of the Forth from Hawes Pier, 15 mins from police station and opposite Hawes Inn
Charges: adult £11.00; child £4.50; family ticket (2 A+2 C) £27.000. Under 5s free
Cruises at various times through the day. Phone for current sailing times.

Cruise under the Forth Rail Bridge to Inchcolm Island, seeing wildlife, seabirds and seals on the way. Boat seats 225. Snack bar and fully -stocked licensed bar on board. Sailing time 45 mins each way, with 1 1/2 hr ashore to explore the 12th century abbey, sandy beach and wartime gun emplacements. Beware of dangerous drops in the ruins and on the hill. Picnic area and visitors centre. Toilets on boat and island.

Hopetoun House

South Queensferry
W Lothian EH30 9SL
Tel: 331 2451
Fax: 319 1885
Web: www.hopetounhouse.com

12 miles from Edinburgh, join the A904 from the A90 via the slip road. Take the left turning. Approximately half a mile along this road turn right into South Queensferry. Directly under the road bridge there is a sign to Hopetoun House.
Opening times: daily end Mar- end Sep from 10.00. Last admission 16.30
House and grounds admission: adults £6.00; child £3.00; family ticket (2A and up to 4 C) £16.00. Under 5s free
Grounds only: reduced prices available: contact Hopetoun House for details.

The House is described as 'Scotland's finest stately home' and approaching it via the sweeping drive, the house certainly creates quite an impact . Inside, there is a magnificent art collection throughout the impressive rooms – but there isn't much inside that will catch the attention of a mobile under 5. However, the gardens are extensive, with plenty of room for exploring (watch out for ha-has though (ditches cut into the ground to keep animals in fields without spoiling the view with fences – there's one to the left of the main drive). Picnic area, nature trails, deer enclosure, exhibitions in the stable block include 'Horse and Man in Lowland Scotland' and 'The Building of Hopetoun'. Self-service restaurant and gift shop. Toilets with nappy-changing surface. Hopetoun host various events throughout the year: go online, or see *Annual Events* for those most suited to children under 5.

West Calder

Freeport Designer Outlet and Leisure Village

5 Sisters, Westwood, Nr W Calder
Tel: 01501 763488
Web: www.freeportplc.com

J4 off M8, and follow brown tourist signs for Freeport Leisure Village, or take A71 to W Calder and pick up the brown tourist signs from W Calder.

Freeport has a wide range of discount in an outdoor village style complex, is pleasant to shop in and is child friendly. The complex has a good mix of High Street names and designer brand outlets, many of which stock children's ranges.
There are 3 restaurants, all with children's menus and facilities. All have large no-smoking areas, high chairs available and space to leave pushchairs. Breastfeeding welcomed in all restaurants; food and bottles can be heated on request. All external toilets at Freeport have separate nappy changing rooms. Free car park
'Cheeky Chimps' indoor play area. Separate areas for 2-4 yrs and 4+ yrs (height limit of 150cm/4' 9"). The over 4 section contains a steep slide, ball pit and climbing ladders to different levels. Parents can sit just outside the area to supervise; tables, chairs and vending/drinks machines provided. Small toilets and nappy-changing area within soft play. There are 2 prices, one for under 4s, one for 4+yrs: phone for current prices. Birthday parties hosted (see *Birthdays & Celebrations*).
On Mon, Wed, and Fri am during school term time, there are parent and toddler mornings. 10.00-12.00: check for current prices. Parents can relax over a free tea or coffee while the children can join in with arts and crafts, watch videos or enjoy other activities.
The complex also has the 'Tropical Rainforest World', which

houses snakes, bats, crocodiles, cayman and other exotic animals. Open Apr-Nov. Family ticket available, phone for current prices.

Polkemmet Country Park

Whitburn
Tel: 01501 743905
No public transport from Edinburgh. By car take M8, J4 then A89 to Whitburn and B7066 towards Harthill
Open all year, Entry free.

Polkemmet offers a variety of facilities, including riverside walks, picnic areas, golf course, driving range and a barbecue area which can be hired by groups for £17.60; remember to bring your own charcoal. Nearby is Fantasy Forest, a well thought-out, enclosed, dog-free play area, including a separate part for young children. This sandy area contains swing, rocking animals and a climbing frame with scoops on a chain to haul up sand! Another area for older children contains enclosed slides and larger climbing frames. Equipment very tactile and colourful. Some pieces designed especially for children with disabilities. Bark chips and rubber matting throughout. Picnic tables within fenced area. Toilets in nearby stable block, nappy changing bench in Ladies'. Block also houses a Countryside Ranger's information centre and shop in the courtyard where sweets, ice cream and drinks are sold. Accessible to pushchairs. Tables outside in courtyard.

Places to Visit

INTRODUCTION

We are extremely lucky to have a wealth of historic buildings, museums and art galleries to access in Edinburgh. However, many of these are unsuitable for young children, due to their content or physical structures. We have concentrated on those places that most children should enjoy and which could be visited comfortably by parents with young babies. We have tried to ensure that our entries will appeal to different age groups and interests. While children are welcome at all these venues, parents should be considerate to other visitors.

Information, leaflets etc, can be obtained from Edinburgh Information Centre, Princes Street (above Princes Mall), Tel: 473 3800. Libraries are also a good source of information.

For further information or ideas for trips further afield, see the Directory and Out of Town Trips. For information regarding Lothian Buses, Tel: 555 6363 or visit www.lothianbuses.co.uk. For First Bus information, Tel: 08708 72 72 71 (8.30-17.00) or visit www.firstgroup.com and choose the appropriate area. Alternatively, visit www.travelinescotland.com or phone 0870 608 2 608.

Many of the places to visit are managed by Historic Scotland (HS), Tel: 668 8600 and the National Trust for Scotland (NTS), Tel: 243 9300. Contact them for further information on membership and discounts. Please note that the National Trust for Scotland does not permit pushchairs or backpacks into some of its stately homes for safety reasons regarding your children and their property – babies in a papoose are permitted.

ART GALLERIES

Children of any age can be fascinated by paintings and sculpture and Edinburgh offers a wide variety of opportunities to expose the young enquiring mind to art. Holding young children up to see properly and giving constant reminders not to touch can be tiring but well worth the effort. Sometimes a gallery may just be a different place to go with a baby and meet friends, maybe over a cup of coffee too! There are also some great examples of art in the environment throughout Edinburgh – the best central location is probably Princes St Gardens – and here you can look and touch!

There are four National Galleries of Scotland, all of which have the same opening times, telephone number and website. You can travel free between the four National Galleries using the hourly visitor bus.

The Dean Gallery

Belford Rd
Tel: 624 6200
Tel: 332 2266 (recorded information)
Web: www.nationalgalleries.org

Opening times: Sun-Wed, Fri-Sat 10.00-17.00; Thu 10.00-19.00
Extended hours during Festival
Admission: free – occasional charges for special exhibitions

The Gallery opened in March 1999 in parkland opposite the Scottish National Gallery of Modern Art. Its setting is lovely, with an expanse of grass lawn to the front – ideal for youngsters on a warm day. It is dedicated to 20th century art – including Dada and Surrealist collections. The imposing grade A listed building has been transformed by architects, with great features for the under 5s such as a see through floor and porthole type windows to fire the imagination. Good pushchair access. Shop. Lift to brightly tiled toilets in basement where nappies can be changed. No strict policy on breastfeeding in public areas. Ground floor café – see *Eating Out*.

National Gallery of Scotland

The Mound
Tel: 624 6200
Tel: 332 2266 (recorded information)
Web: www.nationalgalleries.org

Opening times: Mon-Sun 10.00-17.00; Thu 10.00-19.00
Extended hours during the Festival
Admission: free – occasional charges for special exhibitions
Good pushchair access to most of the building via lift at the rear and ramp down into the Scottish wing. Stairs only to Early Northern and Italian Art room A1

An outstanding collection of paintings, drawings and prints by the greatest artists from Renaissance to Post-Impressionism, including Velázquez, El Greco, Rembrandt, Vermeer, Turner, Constable, Monet and Van Gogh. Also holds the national collection of Scottish Art. Welcomes parties of nursery-aged children, though prior to bringing groups, please phone the Education Department to discuss requirements, Tel: 624 6410.

There are nappy changing facilities in the toilet for the disabled. There is no designated area for private breastfeeding at present, though a room could be made available if required. This is not ideal, but the National Gallery and Royal Scottish Academy are soon to open a new revamped and extended subterranean 'link', which, we have been informed, will provide state of the art facilities for mothers and babies. This is due to open in 2004/5.

Scottish National Gallery of Modern Art

Tel: 624 6200
Tel: 332 2266 (recorded information)
Web: www.nationalgalleries.org

Opening times: Mon-Sun 10.00-17.00; Thu 10.00-19.00
Extended hours during Festival
Admission: free – occasional charges for special exhibitions.
Bus: LRT 13. Can be accessed from the river Leith, lovely walk from Stockbridge through Dean village. Gallery car park is free. Ramped entrance and pushchair access to all floors via the lift to the right of the main entrance hall. Further lift in room 21 for access to top mezzanine floor.

Scotland's finest collection of 20th century paintings, sculpture and graphic art. Includes works by Picasso, Matisse, Moore, Hockney, Davie, Campbell and Wiszniewski. The front garden has been landscaped in a Japanese design with steep, curved banks and ponds. This is fun for children to walk on but due caution is necessary as the banks are very steep in places. Walled sculpture garden to the rear. Welcomes parties of nursery-aged children. Phone the Gallery's Education Department at the number above.
Nappy changing facilities in toilets near café.
Café can be busy at lunchtimes, but there are tables outside – nice when it's warm – and a garden for children to play in: see *Eating Out*.

Scottish National Portrait Gallery

Queen St
Tel: 624 6200
Tel: 332 2266 (recorded information)
Web: www.nationalgalleries.org

Opening times: Mon-Sun 10.00-17.00; Thu 10.00-19.00
Admission: free – occasional charges for special exhibitions.
Ramped entrance to the right of the main door (West entrance), otherwise a few steps up into building via the front door. Pushchair access to all floors via the lift to the left-hand side of the main entrance hall. You may find that the gilded frieze and the large murals in the entrance hall result in an extended stay there!

Portraits in all media of people who have played a significant role in Scottish history from the 16th century to the present day, including Mary Queen of Scots; Robert Burns; Sean Connery and the Queen Mother. Also houses the National Photograph Collection with regular photography exhibitions. Welcomes parties of nursery-aged children. Phone the Gallery/Education Department at the number above.

Nappy changing facilities are being upgraded, as new toilets are being put in at time of writing. Ground floor café serving everything from home baking to salads and hot lunches. High chairs provided.

OTHER GALLERIES

The City Art Centre

2 Market St
Tel: 529 3993

Opening times: Mon-Sat 10.00-17.00; Sunday opening for special exhibitions
Admission: free, except for special exhibitions

Temporary exhibitions, often with a very broad appeal, and Scottish Art work. Some exhibitions are aimed at children with workshops for under 5s. Access to all floors by lift and escalator. Toilets for the disabled on the ground floor have nappy change facilities. Pleasant café adjacent to the centre - see *Eating Out*.

Fruitmarket Gallery

Market St
Tel: 225 2383
Email: bookshop@fruitmarket.co.uk
Web: www.fruitmarket.co.uk

Opening times: Mon-Sat 11.00-18.00; Sun 12.00-17.00. During Edinburgh International festival open daily 10.00-21.30
Admission: free
Contemporary art gallery showcasing the work of international artists and emerging talent. Pram and wheelchair accessible, with lift to upper floor. Ground floor café, contemporary culture bookshop and toilet for the disabled.

MUSEUMS & HISTORIC PLACES

Despite changes in legislation regarding access to buildings, you should remember that in the case of historic buildings, some areas of these houses, castles and even museums may be hard to access, due to the age of the building and the nature of the architecture. Slings/ papooses are recommended for very young children.

Brass Rubbing Centre

Trinity Apse, Chalmer's Close
81 High St
Tel: 556 4364

Opening times: Mon-Sat 10.00-17.00; during the Festival open Sun 12.00-17.00
Admission: free, but there is a charge for the brass rubbing

Tucked away in an old church building, between High St and Jeffrey St, the Centre is bright, warm and welcoming inside. Contains a collection of replicas moulded from ancient Pictish stones, rare Scottish brasses and Mediaeval church brasses. Of more interest to the over 5s, but a mature 4 yr old might enjoy producing a small rubbing. Materials are provided. Stop rubbings at 15.45.

Calton Hill Park

Regent Rd

Parking at top of hill, free for 30 mins
Admission to park:: free

A good place for a run around, though caution is needed near road and car park. A grassy hill (355 ft) with many monuments, including the National Monument – based on the Parthenon – which was started in 1822 but never finished due to lack of funds. Fabulous panoramic views cross the city. Popular kite flying spot. A large brass cannon provides enjoyable climbing for children as well as rocks to climb on and jump off. In the summer, an ice-cream van operates from the car park. Not recommended after dusk, despite the floodlit city panoramas, as the social dynamics completely change once evening falls.

There are two attractions to visit on Calton Hill, The City Observatory (Tel: 556 4365, open Easter-end Oct) and Nelson's Monument (Tel: 556 2716) though neither is really suitable for under fives.

Camera Obscura

Castle Hill
Tel: 226 3709

Opening times: daily, 9.30-19.00 (British Summertime); 10.00-17.00 (end Oct-Mid Mar). Also dependent on weather and daylight
Admission: adult £5.75; child £3.70. Under 5s free. Group concessions also available - 10+ children cost £2.95/child, with one leader entering free. Group visits must be booked in advance

This is the oldest purpose-built visitor attraction in Edinburgh, and adults and children alike still find it fascinating. Over 3s would probably get a lot from a visit. Under 3s usually enjoy the hologram exhibition on level 3 (though they may have to be lifted up to appreciate the effects) and the view from the rooftop terrace on level 5 more than the camera. It has to be very dark in the camera room, so if your child is nervous of this, be aware although the sight of the streets below may take up their attention! Has a very narrow staircase, which is unsuitable for prams and pushchairs. These may be left in the shop. No specific facilities for babies or young children, but there is a public toilet directly across the road. Choose a bright day to visit!

Craigmillar Castle (HS)

Craigmillar Castle Rd
Tel: 661 445
Web: www.historic-scotland.gov.uk

Opening times: Apr-1st Oct: Mon-Sun 9.30-18.30. Oct-Mar: Mon-Wed 9.30-16.30; Thu 9.30-12.30; Sun 14.00-16.30
Closed Thu afternoons and all day Fri in Winter
Admission: adult £2.20; concession £1.60; child 75p. Under 5s free
$2^{1/2}$ miles SE of Edinburgh off the A7. LRT bus services 24, 32, 33,38, 49 serve this

Handsome castle, dating from the 14th century. Its fortifications are pretty impressive – it certainly has the air of what a castle 'should be' like, especially from the Under 5 viewpoint. It was once a favourite residence of Mary, Queen of Scots. There are attractive gardens at either side of the castle and it is possible to hold a children's birthday party on the green.
Young children need to be closely supervised inside, as there are dark staircases, uneven floors and sharp drops from low open windows. Pushchairs and wheelchairs are restricted to ground floor level only. Toilet for the disabled may double as a nappy changing room. No private breastfeeding area, but breastfeeding is welcomed. Friendly custodian. Shop and visitor centre, serving tea and coffee.

Edinburgh Castle (HS)

Tel: 225 9846
Web: www.historic-scotland.gov.uk

Opening times: daily, 9.30-18.00 Apr-Sept; Oct-Mar 9.30-17.00. Last ticket sold 45 mins before closing. Closed Christmas Day and Boxing Day
Admission: adult £8.50; child £2 (children under 16 must be accompanied by an adult); concession £6.25. Under 5s free

If you choose a clear day to visit, you can enjoy stunning views over Edinburgh and across to Fife from the Castle Esplanade. You can also see the soldiers on guard outside this famous castle. Within the castle walls are attractions such as St Margaret's Chapel, the Honours of Scotland, the Stone of Destiny and the famous cannon Mons Meg. There are also tableaux of

Napoleonic prisoners. Guided tours and CD-ROM audio tours available. There's also the One O'clock Gun and a related exhibition. However, there isn't an awful lot to take younger children's interest – there are also some steep cobbled paths which are not ideal for toddlers or pushchairs. Over 3s might enjoy a short visit – or they might be happy with a walk round the esplanade! There is also a café (which can be extremely busy during the summer) and a well stocked shop with many items suitable for children. The castle has toilet facilities, a feeding and changing room, and also toilets for the disabled. A courtesy vehicle for disabled visitors is also available.

The Castle also houses the National War Memorial. Visitors going only to this can enter free, ask at the ticket office. Obviously, this right should not be abused.

Greyfriars Tolbooth and Highland Kirk

Greyfriars Pl, Top of Candlemaker Row
Tel: 225 1900
Tel: 226 5429 (Visitors Officer)

Sun services 11.00, Gaelic service 12.30. Kirkyard open 8.00-22.00 daily
Kirk visitor centre open Easter-Oct Mon-Fri 10.30-16.30, Sat 8.00-16.00 (Due to re-open for visitors Easter 2004)

Edinburgh's first reformed church built in 1620. Fine 17th century monuments in kirkyard. Many Covenanters are buried here. A secluded and peaceful stop in the city centre, much used for picnics at lunchtime as there are sandwich bars in the vicinity. Several park benches are located at the George Heriot School side of the kirkyard.
A statue dedicated to Greyfriars Bobby is situated opposite the kirk gates, at the junction of Candlemaker Row and George IV Bridge. The story of the faithful dog is always popular. His master is buried in the churchyard, as is Bobby himself.
Information, souvenirs and audio-visual programme available in kirk visitor centre.

John Knox House

The Netherbow
43 High St

John Knox House is closed until 2005 due to extensive renovations of the Netherbow Theatre.

Lauriston Castle

2a Cramond Rd S
Tel: 336 2060

Opening times: April-October Sat-Thu 11.00-13.00 and 14.00-17.00. Nov-Mar Sat/Sun 14.00-16.00.
Grounds opening times: 9.00-dusk.

Admission: adult £4.50; £3 concession/ children over 6. Appointments required for groups.
Access to the grounds: free
Bus no. 40 from The Mound/George St. There is parking, if you take your car.

The house has remained unchanged since 1926. It has a secret room – as any respectable castle has – and a notable collection of Blue John ware. Guided tours only, lasting about 40 mins and not really suitable for young children as once inside the castle you cannot leave until the tour is finished.
There are pleasant walks, suitable with a pushchair, in the peaceful and extensively wooded grounds with fine views over the Forth estuary to Fife. They are particularly lovely in the spring when the daffodils are out and the pond is full of tadpoles. There are often ponies in the fields. Activities are frequently organised in the house and gardens to coincide with school holidays. Ball games may not be played in the glade. There is a picnic area with tables and arrangements can be made for large parties – apply to the custodian. Toilet facilities, with a bench which is convenient for changing. There is also a toilet for the disabled.

Military Tattoo

See *Annual Events*

Museum of Childhood

42 High St
Royal Mile
Tel: 529 4142

Opening times: Mon-Sat 10.00-17.00, Sun 12.00-17.00 during July and August
Admission: free

The first museum of its kind devoted to the history of childhood. A wonderful collection of trains, boats, planes, dolls, teddy bears and many, many more playthings of the past are displayed in 5 galleries. Hands-on exhibits and activities have recently been added to give children more things to do in the museum. Gallery 1 has a few coin-operated working models including a nickelodeon. Gallery 2 has a rocking horse and hands-on puppets, trains and optical toys for children to use. Gallery 3 has dolls and teddy bears on display with feely boxes, games, a doll's house and family activity sheet. Gallery 4 has board games, a reading corner and a Lego wall for children to use. Gallery 5 has several period room sets with sound effects and a dressing up box. The museum also has different temporary exhibitions running throughout the year.

It is encouraging to see some of the displays at low level, suitable for viewing by small children. In spite of the recent additions mentioned small children may get bored. The museum is partly suitable for pushchairs but there are many steps and it can become very congested. It is requested that pushchairs are left downstairs at the owner's own risk. There is a lift between galleries 1, 2 and 3, ramps to gallery 3; public toilets are in gallery 4. There is a good shop at the entrance, which sells 'old fashioned' small toys/gifts; wooden, tin, paper, posters etc. There are nappy changing facilities in the toilets for the disabled, access with a uniformed attendant by the lift to the basement.

Newhaven Heritage Museum

24 Pier Pl
Tel: 551 4165
Opening times: Mon-Sun 12.00-16.45 (last admission 16.30).
Admission: free
By bus: LRT 10,11 and 16 from Princes St, 7 from The Bridges and 32/32a on the Outer Circle.

A small museum with limited interest to under 5s. The story of Newhaven is told through reconstructed sets of fishwives and fishermen, displays of objects and photographs, written and spoken accounts. Both children and adults can dress up as fisherfolk. There are wooden cutouts of a fisherman and fishwife to stick through your head and look at yourself in the mirror opposite. Also two 'feely' boxes, one with a 'palm' used by sailmakers and one with a buoy. There is also a tray of shells which can be handled. Small shop selling sea related items, some at pocket-money prices. Friendly staff. There are no toilets and no public ones nearby, although there are catering facilities nearby. Brewsters, a few minutes walk has a soft play area.

Our Dynamic Earth

112 Holyrood Rd
Tel: 550 7800
Web: www.dynamicearth.co.uk
Opening times: Apr-Oct, Mon-Sun 10.00-18.00. Nov-Mar, Wed-Sun 10.00-17.00 – closed Mon & Tue. (Occasionally open half-term, please phone)
Closed Christmas Eve and Christmas Day
Admission: adult £8.45; child £4.95. Family tickets (2A & 2C) £22.50, (2A & 3C) £26, Under 5s free

Our Dynamic Earth is one of Edinburgh's foremost interactive tourist attractions. This is a place which under 5s are more likely to come when accompanying older children as much of the exhibition is not aimed at young children. Be prepared for the fact that they may be scared when it is dark, with the flashes of light or when the floor vibrates in the volcano experience. However many under 5s will love it! Expect to spend around 1 1/2 hrs, 'travelling' through time, though you can 'escape' earlier – but you might need to be shown a quick way by a member of staff. You can meet a life-sized pterodactyl, find out what volcanic tremors feel like and touch an iceberg. There is also a small ball-pit soft play area next to the shop, The Bone Zone, which younger children will enjoy. Everywhere is pushchair accessible, with lifts where necessary. Older children tend to crowd round interactive displays – so be prepared to get stuck in there if it's busy.
There are a variety of special events during the year, some which will be suitable for under 5s. Phone or watch press for details.
Nappy change facilities available. Chair suitable for breastfeeding in the nappy changing room.
Restaurant:
£-££, high chairs (6); Bottle heating/baby food warming available.
Open all day, serving hot meals, snacks, pastries and hot and cold drinks.

Palace of Holyroodhouse and Holyrood Abbey

Foot of Royal Mile (Canongate)
Tel: 556 7371
Tel: 556 1096 (24 hr information)
Opening times: Apr-Oct, Mon-Sun 9.30-17.15 (last admission). Nov-Mar, Mon-Sun 9.30-15.45 (last admission).
Closed occasionally at other times at short notice and also when the Queen or Her Commissioner is in residence, usually in late May and early June.
Admission: adult £7.50; child (5-16 inc) £4.00; over 60 £6.00; family (2A & 2C) £19.00. Under 5s free

The Palace is the Queen's official residence in Scotland and all State and Historical apartments are open to the public. Guided tours operate between November and March with audio tour equipment, including a special 'family' edition. A 'free flow' system is in operation from April to October. In addition to the Palace, the ruins of Holyrood Abbey, dating back to the 11th Century, can also be visited. There is a limited amount of interest to under 5s. In the Palace pushchair access is limited to the ground floor. The Queen's Gallery in the Mews area of the Palace contains exhibitions from the Royal Collection. Opening times as for the Palace. Admission: adult £4, child £2, over 60 £3. Most exhibitions may not interest the under 5 group.
Toilets are available in the Royal Mews where changing and feed-

ing facilities for babies are available. From late spring and throughout the summer further seating is provided around the forecourt and in the Mews. Staff are helpful. There is also a gift shop.

The People's Story

Canongate Tolbooth
Royal Mile
Tel: 529 4057

Opening times: Mon-Sat 10.00-17.00; Sun 14.00-17.00 during Festival.
Admission: free

A fascinating museum tracing the lives, work and pastimes of the city's ordinary people from late 1700s to present day. The displays include a series of reconstructions – a fishwife, a joiner up a ladder, a servant cleaning a grate, prisoners in a cell, a tearoom and a washhouse. These are all enhanced by smells and sounds as well as photographs and displays of everyday objects which under 5s can appreciate, though on the whole it will be better appreciated by older children.
A 22-min video complements the story line. A lift allows pushchair access to 1st floor. The next level is just a few steps further up but the video room is reached by a spiral stone staircase. Pushchairs may be left at front desk. Counter selling postcards, pencils, badges, toys etc. Roomy toilets for the disabled may be used for nappy changing.

Queensferry Museum

53 High St
South Queensferry
Tel: 331 5545

Opening times: Mon, Thu, Fri, Sat 10.00-13.00, 14.15-17.00; Sun 12.00-17.00. Last admission 30 mins before closing.
Admission: free
First Edinburgh bus no 43 from Charlotte Square will take you there. Or follow signs for South Queensferry from the A90.
The museum is dedicated to the local social history of Dalmeny and South Queensferry. There are displays on the Royal Burgh, aspects of life and leisure, the spectacular Forth Bridges and the unique local annual custom of the Burry Man. The shoreline of the Forth Estuary at South Queensferry provides a variety of wildlife, which can be explored using the museum's binoculars and the display showing the natural history of this area. There are other displays which are attractive to young children. Access is not possible with a pushchair and there are no special facilities for children or for mothers who wish to breastfeed.

Royal Museum

Chambers St
Tel: 247 4219
Web: www.nms.ac.uk

Opening times: Mon-Sat 10.00 - 17.00; Sun 12.00 - 17.00. Late opening Tue (to 20.00). Closed Dec 25
Admission: free (there may be a charge for special exhibitions, however)
Membership of NMS is available, which offers a variety of benefits, such as free entry to charging exhibitions etc. The price is around £16/adult. £24/couple, £30/family
Children's tours are on Saturdays and Sundays at 14.30

This is definitely much more than a rainy-day option! A fabulous museum with plenty to interest and amuse under 5s. This vast, awe inspiring Victorian building houses international collections of Decorative Arts, Science and Industry, Archaeology and the Natural World. In children's terms this means: loads of fantastic stuffed animals, old fashioned toys, mummies and lots more. In the main foyer, there's the Millennium Clock, which chimes every half hour. The hourly 360° automata display of figures and music is fascinating to watch, for young and old alike. There are various temporary exhibitions throughout the year. There are also two fish ponds, one with exotic goldfish, the other with catfish, which are always our first port of call. By the way, the dinosaurs are part of the evolution display. There are fossilised footprints, skeletons, models etc. There's a skeleton of a giant ground sloth and an Irish Elk – popular stops with children.

The main entrance involves a flight of steps but these can be avoided using the Tower entrance to the Museum of Scotland next door. Everywhere has pushchair access with lifts to all floors.
Toilets and nappy changing facilities (in the toilets for the disabled) are available on the ground floor. There is a dedicated parent and baby room beside the female toilets, which is clean and spacious and has chairs for breastfeeding mothers.
The museum shop has a colourful children's section. NMS members receive a 10% discount.
Café Delos in the entrance hall serves drinks, cakes and substantial snacks (10.00-16.00 Mon, Wed-Sun, -19.30 Tue). There is another café - Soupson - at the rear of the building. Go through the Modern Era room (Lothian St entrance now closed at time of writing). Soupson serves soup, baked potatoes, pasta etc, as well as sandwiches and cakes. Soft drinks such as smoothies, fruit juices and water are on offer, as well as the fizzy options; and for the jaded parent, they offer 2 strengths of coffee.

High chairs and booster seats available.

Museum of Scotland

Chambers St
Tel: 247 4422
Web: www.nms.ac.uk

Opening times: Mon-Sat 10.00-17.00, Sun 12.00-17.00
Late opening Tue (to 20.00)
Admission: free
Membership available giving a variety of benefits. (see Royal Museum's entry, above)

This modern landmark was opened in 1998. The Museum presents the history of Scotland, its land, its people and their achievements. There is masses to engage under 5s - even the entrance foyer can prove to be a major part of the visit! Of particular interest to children is the Discovery Centre on level 3 which is full of interactive displays specifically aimed at children, many of which under 5s can enjoy. During the day in school term time this is often booked out to school visits but should be available to all children out of school hours. Birthday parties can be booked in the Discovery Centre, contact the Museum for details.

In the lower ground level there is an experience which talks through the weather conditions, animals and habitat of Scotland. There are plenty of interactive displays here and throughout the museum. Level 6 is dedicated to the twentieth century which possibly has more interest to parents and grandparents, seeing things they knew as 'modern' as children being represented as history. There is an IT room, ExhibIT, which has CD-ROM packages aimed at children which allows you to 'tap in' to all the objects in the museum. Other displays which may interest the under 5s include a thatched cottage, a coin store and the Silver Gallery – an entire room devoted to silver which sparkles when you walk in! Lift to roof terrace for views of the city.

Access to the building is easy for pushchairs and there are lifts to all floors. There are purpose built nappy changing facilities on the ground floor next to the shop and all adapted toilets on each floor have a pull down changing unit. Nappies can also be bought at the shop. The Tower Restaurant is quite expensive, but there are the two cafés situated on the ground floor of the Royal Museum next door.

Royal Observatory

Blackford Hill
Tel: 668 8405

Opening times: daily, Mon-Sat 10.00-17.00; Sun 12.00-17.00
Closed 23 Dec-7 Jan inclusive
Admission: adult £3.50; concession £2; child £2.50; disabled access £1. Under 5s free. Family ticket £8

This centre houses two of Scotland's largest telescopes, several hands-on exhibitions and an interactive multimedia gallery featuring CD-ROMS about space and astronomy. Excellent views of the city from the balcony. There are many steps, so it's unsuitable for pushchairs; these can be left at the reception desk. There's a gift shop and spacious toilets.

The Royal Yacht *Britannia*

Ocean Terminal
Tel: 555 5566
Email: enquiries@tryb.co.uk

Opening times: Apr-Sep 9.30-16.30 daily. Oct-Mar 10.00-15.30 daily
Admission: adult £8; child £4; family £20. Under 5s free

The Royal Yacht *Britannia* was relocated to Ocean Terminal in October 2001. Tickets can be bought at Britannia, although advance booking is recommended in August. Parking available in Ocean Terminal. By bus: LRT 22 or part of Britannia Tour, open top bus tour.

For over 40 years the Royal Yacht *Britannia* served the royal family, travelling over 1 million miles to become the most famous ship in the world. The visitor centre provides an insight into her history. It includes a royal picture gallery and a reconstruction of the original wheelhouse.

On board ship the 5 main decks are accessed by lift. A children's version of the audio tour is most suitable for 7-11 year olds – under 5s are unlikely to enjoy the slower, detailed audio tour but there is plenty to see and talk about on a parent-guided tour. Close supervision of children is required throughout as the environment/location is inevitably not entirely child-safe.

The visitor centre and tour of Britannia is fully accessible to single pushchairs and prams. Toilets both on shore and on board. Nappy changing in toilet for the disabled. Shop with range of souvenirs.

St Giles Cathedral

High St
Tel: 225 9442 (visitor services manager)
Web: www.stgiles.net

Opening times: Summer (May-Sep) Mon–Fri 9.00-19.00pm, Sat 9.00-17.00, Sun 13.00-17.00. Winter (Oct-Apr): Mon-Sat 9.00-17.00, Sat 9.00-17.00, Sun 13.00-17.00
NB at any time access may be restricted without notice
Services: Mon-Sat at mid-day, Sun 8.00, 10.00, 11.30 and 20.00

Musical recital at 18.00.
Admission: free – suggested donation of £1 per adult visitor to Thistle Chapel

A landmark on the Royal Mile. There's over 1000 years of history in St Giles – John Knox was minister there, there have been riots, executions and demonstrations all around it (and some inside it!), but under 5s may be more interested in the coloured stained glass windows. Free tours and lunchtime concerts There's a souvenir shop, to mark your visit, and a café, The Lower Aisle, can be accessed on its Southern side – see *Eating Out*.

Geoffrey (Tailor's) Tartan Weaving Mill and Exhibition

555 Castle Hill
The Royal Mile
Tel: 226 1555
Email: castlehill@geoffreykilts.co.uk
Web: www.tartanweavingmill.co.uk
Opening times: Apr-Oct Mon - Sat 9.00-18.30, Sun 10.00-18.30.
Nov-Mar Mon - Sat 9.00-17.30, Sun 10.00-17.30.
Admission: free

This is where the whole family can experience the noise and bustle of a real working weaving mill. Probably better for older children. A colourful exhibition demonstrates how a kilt is made, and how tartan is produced. The high-speed weaving looms make tartan before your eyes. Mums and Dads can try weaving on a sixty-year-old pedal loom, great fun to watch (Mon-Fri only, charge applicable).
The mill also has Ancient Scottish Costumes for the whole family to dress up in and a digital camera so you can take away an A4 photograph (charge applicable). You can search for your family's tartan at the Clan and Tartan information centre. As well as the Traditional Highland Dress dept there is an exclusive range from 21st Century kilts available.
Lift available between floors for access to exhibition, toilets, café and shop areas. Nappy changing facilities, suitable for both male and female. Accessible to single pushchairs with some manoeuvring!

The Writers' Museum

Lady Stair's Close
Lawnmarket

Royal Mile
Tel: 529 4901
Opening times: Mon-Sat 10.00-17.00, Sun 14.00-17.00 during Festival
Admission: free

Museum contains memorabilia and manuscripts relating to three of Scotland's great literary figures – Robert Burns, Sir Walter Scott and Robert Louis Stevenson. Also regular programme of temporary exhibitions covering other Scottish writers. The Museum is housed in a 17th century building with spiral stone staircases so is tricky for pushchairs. Nappy changing table in the ladies toilet which can be used by men on request. Best visited as parents of infants (perhaps in a papoose) as there's nothing of interest for children under 5. However, the close and the court-yard outside has carved paving stones with famous lines from some of Scotland's greatest poets, and provides an interesting shortcut from the Mound on to the Royal Mile.

OUTDOOR FUN

Children love animals and things that go. The following venues are particularly suitable for children as they have either of these prerequisites (or both!) in abundance!

Butterfly & Insect World

Dobbies Gardening World
Lasswade
Midlothian
Tel: 663 4932
Email: info@edinburgh-butterfly-world.co.uk
Opening times: Apr-Oct, Mon-Sun 9.30-17.30. Nov-Mar, Mon-Sun 10.00-17.00. Closed 25, 26 Dec and 1 Jan
Admission: adult £4.50; concession £3.50; child £3.50; family ticket (2A & 4C) £14. Under 3s free
Season tickets from £14; family from £40. Group rates, guided tours ad talks available
On A7, nr Dalkeith, By bus, take LRT 3. First Edinburgh 80 80A (not Sundays)
One of Europe's largest butterfly farms. Popular attraction with a minimum of 500 free-flying butterflies on display, although the numbers can escalate to 1200 at times. The butterflies live amidst a landscape of tropical plants, little waterfalls and pools, which contain fish and terrapins. Individual displays of other creatures – bees, spiders, beetles, stick insects etc some of which you get a chance to touch! Also displays of 'life-cycles of butterflies' and 'insects and habitats'. Entrance is though the shop, where there's a good selection of books and gifts.
There's a café in the garden centre, serving meals, snacks, etc. High chairs available. Toilets and nappy changing facilities are also available (go past the pay-desk and they're on the left). Outside, there's also a play area and picnic area.

East Links Family Park and Narrow Gauge Railway

1/2 mile off A1 at Beltonford roundabout, next to West Barns Village and John Muir Country Park.
Tel: 01368 863607
Mob: 0777 571 3646
Email: grant@eastlinks.fsnet.co.uk
Web: www.eastlinks.fsnet.co.uk
Opening times: 10.00-17.00, until 18.00 during school holidays
Admission: adult £5; child £4; family (2+2) £16. Group discounts available. Entrance fee allows unlimited use of facilities during day.

Set in 20 acres of farmland this has everything for a fantastic day out for all the family, particularly the under 5s. All the activities are located close to the main entrance and include a giant sand-filled pirate ship with sand diggers, pedal tractors and roller racers, soft play and bouncy castle, giant children's rabbit warren, flying fox party barn, Go-carts, milk can skittles, horseshoe pitching and a 2 acre woodland maze. More attractions are planned for the coming years.
A lovely narrow gauge railway train takes you on a tour of the whole site.
There are lots of farm animals for the children to see, including a field of llamas. There are also lots of small animals such as rabbits and chipmunks. Pony rides cost £1 when available.
Other facilities include ample car parking, a shop, toilets including nappy change facilities. Birthday parties can be booked. It is advisable to bring your own picnic.
A restaurant and education centre is planned for 2004.
NB Bring this copy of *Edinburgh for Under Fives* on your visit and you'll receive a free bag of feed for the animals.

Edinburgh Bird of Prey Centre

Dobbies Gardening World
Lasswade
Midlothian
Tel: 654 1720
On A7, nr Dalkeith
Opening times: Mar-Oct Mon-Sun 10.30-17.00. Nov-Feb

Weekends 10.30-16.00.
Admission: adult £3; child/OAP £1.50. Under 3s free

Family ticket (2A & 2C) £7.50. Large groups only by prior arrangement

Selection of birds of prey including owls, eagles, falcons and hawks, some in avaries and some tethered. Opportunities for handling these beautiful birds safely. There is a large no-smoking café with toilets in the garden centre (see above).

Edinburgh Canal Centre

27 Baird Rd
Ratho
Midlothian
Tel: 333 1320/1251
Email: info@bridgeinn.com
Web: www.bridgeinn.com

Opening times: daily, all year round

Follow 'Edinburgh Canal Centre' signs from Newbridge Interchange. By bus, take no 65 Eastern Scottish bus from St Andrew's Sq

Sightseeing cruises are available on the 'Ratho Princess', seating 32, which lasts for about 1 $^1/_2$ hours, available from April to September departing at 14.30. Refreshments available on board. Longer trips are available on the Lunch and Dinner cruises lasting 3 hours, possible though less suitable for under 5s.

Educational trips available-contact centre for details. Canal centre also runs short trips to their haunted castle. Boats can also be hired for parties or weddings.

The tow-path makes for a good walk with pushchairs though there are obvious water safety issues for those with tearaway toddlers.

There are a variety of ducks and swans for children to look at as well as a rather old but functioning parent-powered carousel. Toilets with very good nappy changing facilities (nappies and wipes provided) available in the Bridge Inn. There are toilets on all cruising boats. Santa also visits from his magical island during the festive season – see *Annual Events*.

The Bridge Inn offers meals, while the Pop Inn serves a selection of snacks. See *Eating Out*.

Edinburgh Zoo

Corstorphine Rd
Tel: 334 9171
Web: www.edinburghzoo.org.uk

Opening times: Apr-Sep Mon-Sat 9.00-18.00, Sun 9.30-18.00. Oct, Mar Mon-Sat 9.00-17.00, Sun 9.30-17.00. Nov-Feb Mon-Sat 9.00-16.30, Sun 9.30-16.30

Admission: adult £8; child £5; family tickets from £24. Under 3s

free. 20% discount for groups booked in advance, min 10. Car park £2. Pushchairs may be hired at entrance.
Bus: Lothian 12, 26, 31 and airport bus all go past the Zoo.
If you are a regular visitor it is worth considering membership, annual or life. This entitles holders to unlimited entry to Edinburgh Zoo and the Highland Wildlife Park, nr Aviemore, free parking and the use of the Member's House

A great day out for families. Set in over 80 acres of leafy hillside, the zoo has over 1000 animals, though no elephants. Constantly upgrading and improving enclosures, the Zoo aims to provide a more natural and stimulating environment for all the animals. It is also home of the world's largest penguin enclosure, complete with underwater viewing and video surveillance of nesting sites. The famous penguin parade takes place at 14:15 from Mar-Oct and 12:40 from Nov-Mar. Even in wet weather, there is much to see in the primate and reptile houses and in the 'Magic Rainforest', a covered habitat for tiny monkeys. At various times throughout the day the animals are fed, which is always exciting for children. There are also informative talks and animal demonstrations showing natural behaviour throughout the day in the summer months with keepers on hand to answer any questions. There are a number of play areas throughout the zoo. During Easter and Summer holidays there are activities to interest older children, eg brass rubbing and animal handling sessions (min age 3). The Darwin Centre is a tortoise shaped maze and covered picnic area. Several other picnic sites, self-service restaurants and numerous kiosks, ice cream, confectionery, soft drinks, are situated throughout the Zoo. Most kiosks are closed outside of the summer months. There are two gift shops selling toys, gifts and books with an animal theme.
Access is generally good for pushchairs although the push to the top of the Zoo should be taken in easy stages. The hilltop safari, which is free though they ask for a voluntary donation, takes you to the top of the hill, allowing you to take the easy route downhill. There is a Members' entrance from the car park which can save some pushing as it is higher than the main entrance. Wrap up warm in the winter.
There are several toilets throughout the area as well as in restaurants. Nappy changing facilities available.

PLACES TO EAT

The Den
Summer only, Mon-Sun 10.30-17.45
££, High chairs, breastfeeding welcome, bottles heated, nappy changing surface, seats 200, licensed, children's menu.
Self-service snack bar. Range of light meals and snacks. May be used for picnics.

Stripes
Summer: Mon-Sun 10.30-17.45
Winter: Mon-Sun 10.30-in line with Zoo closure.
££, High chairs, bottles heated, nappy changing surface, seats 120, licensed, children's menu. Large self-service restaurant serving a variety of hot meals and snacks all day.

Members' House
Mon-Sun 10.00-17.00. Winter closing in line with Zoo closure.
£££, High chairs (6), nappy changing surface, parties hosted, licensed, children's menu and half portions, seats 90
Light meals and full luncheon facilities; tables can be reserved by phone or at reception in the Members' House. No smoking in restaurant or coffee lounge. See also Birthdays and Celebrations. Upstairs there is a coffee lounge where you can have light sandwich-type lunches. Children's menu available. Great views over the Zoo to the Pentland Hills.

Gorgie City Farm

51 Gorgie Rd
Tel: 337 4202
Email: gorgiefarm@compuserve.com
Opening times: Mon-Sun 9.30-16.30 (16.00 in winter). Closed Christmas Day and New Year's Day.
Admission: free - donation box. Guided tours can be arranged in advance for a modest charge: contact the Education Officer (Tel: 623 7031) or the Farm for details;
By bus: LRT 3, 6, 21, 22, 25, 33, 34, 35, 65. First Edinburgh C55, D26, D27, D28. By car, farm lies on Gorgie Rd, which is a busy thoroughfare. There is limited free parking, though you can also park reasonably near in adjoining roads.

Especially suitable for visits by small children, this community farm is on a one-hectare site, which used to be the main refuse collection point for the city, not far from the city centre. There is a wide range of animals including sheep, goats, a Jersey cow, Shetland ponies, pigs, ducks, hens, bantams and pheasants. Also a large organic vegetable garden, a herb garden, a wildlife garden and an Education Centre. In the Pet Lodge visitors can see a range of pets - rabbits, guinea pigs, finches, budgerigars, hamsters, fish and tortoises kept in good conditions. There is a small children's play area with adjacent picnic area and a tractor to climb on. The animals are friendly and provide an ideal opportunity for children to see farm animals at close range in a suitable environment. Special events and activities are organised at different times. All areas are accessible for pushchairs. Toilets for the dis-

abled and nappy changing facilities.
There is a café attached to the farm called Jemima's Pantry, which hosts birthday parties. See *Birthdays and Celebrations*.

Lowe's Fruit Farm

Campend, Dalkeith
City Bypass at Sherrifhall, A7 junction
Tel: 660 2128

Opening times: Late June until end of fruiting season, 7 days a week 10.00-18.00, weather permitting. Advisable to phone to check at extremes of season.
By bus: LRT 82; First 86
Lowe's is well known for strawberry and other soft fruit picking through the summer. Apples, pears and plums later in the season. Great for giving children a sense of the seasons and some knowledge of where food comes from. Toilets and a grassy car park where you can picnic. Lowe's is fun but it is a working farm and parents should ensure their children's safety at all times.

OPEN TOP BUSES

Tours depart regularly from Waverley Bridge, give 'hop off-hop on' options and 24 hour tickets. Touts can be intimidating so it may be more peaceful to gather information from the Information Centre on top of Princes Mall. While the tours are all run by the same company at present, they offer slightly different experiences, and take slightly different routes round the city.

City Sightseeing Tour (on the bright red buses) offers a taped guided tour (7 languages available). Your ticket entitles you to discounted entry into various venues, museums and attractions.

The Edinburgh Tour
This tour (on the green and cream liveried buses) offers trips round the city with a guide on-board. Again, there are discounts with the ticket.

Mac Tours offers a similar tour (with multilingual scripts in 7 languages and a live guide on-board), but this is on a vintage bus

The Britannia Tour (on the blue & gold buses) takes you as far as Ocean Terminal. While there are discounts for places and shops along the tour, at time of writing the tour does not include discounted entry on to *Britannia* herself

City Sightseeing (all tours)

Tel: 0131 220 0770
Email: info@edinburghtour.com
Web: www.edinburghtour.com

Prices: adult £8.50, concessions £6.50, child £2.50 family (2A & up to 3 C) £19.50. Under 5s free

TELLING THE TIME

Edinburgh's famous One O'clock Gun is fired every day and can be heard from a considerable distance. The Floral Clock in Princes St Gardens West, at the foot of the Mound is very popular with children, who love waiting for the bird to pop out on the hour. This is seasonal – Spring-late Autumn. At the West End, Frasers has a clock outside the building which is decorated with soldiers and a castle. The soldiers march around the clock on the hour.

TRAINSPOTTING

There is a footbridge which connects West Princes Street Gardens to the lower ramparts of Edinburgh Castle behind the Ross Bandstand. Its mostly transparent sides provide a perfect viewing point for the small train enthusiast. Indeed, many of them can be found gathered at this spot regardless of the weather! The bridge crosses the 4 main railway lines into and out of Edinburgh Waverley station. The trains are of various types and run to various destinations both near and far. Drivers tend to be friendly and will usually wave back to any children that are on the bridge. Some also blow their whistles.

THEATRES AND CINEMAS

Theatres are becoming more child friendly and there are often shows for 3+, particularly during the Children's Theatre Festival as well as the Fringe. However be aware that theatres may not be suitable for pushchairs. If a show is advertised as being for children, it's still best to check beforehand on age restrictions and the duration of the show. Refreshments may not always be suitable for children.
At the time of writing, the Lyceum Theatre has a crèche facility for the first Saturday matinee for each show – phone for details. Various theatre brochures and festival publications give information on facilities such as parking, toilets and access

THEATRES

Assembly Rooms

54 George St
Tel: 220 4348 (Admin)
Tel: 220 4349 (Box Office)

Used as Science Festival venue during Mar/Apr. Lift to 1st floor and toilets. Nappy changing facilities in toilet for the disabled in Main Foyer. Quiet area on request for breastfeeding.

Brunton Theatre

Ladywell Way, Musselburgh
Tel: 665 2240
By bus: Lothian 15, 26, 44
By car: ample free parking

Situated 4 miles from Edinburgh city centre, on the main road into Musselburgh. Ramped access to foyer, staircase and lift to main theatre. Many shows suitable for young children. Every seat has a view. Runs a pantomime season. Spacious toilets with nappy-changing facilities. Caters for disabled patrons, with facilities such as viewing gallery, toilet, lift and easy access. Café serving children's meals, bar and kiosk open during performances.

Church Hill Theatre

33a Morningside Rd
Tel: 447 7597

A mixed programme of musical, drama and dance school shows all by amateur groups. Occasional shows for children, usually during Edinburgh International Festival. Ramped main entrance. Staircase to main theatre. Parking in surrounding streets. Parking for the disabled outside theatre. Toilet for the disabled with nappy changing facilities on the ground floor. Coffee bar which also sells sweets.

Edinburgh Festival Theatre

13-29 Nicolson St
Tel: 529 6000 (Box Office)
Nearest car parking: Crichton St car park, George Square parking bays

Occasional children's shows for 3 yrs and over. Level access. The 'Café Lucia' on the ground floor is licensed for children until 20.00. Toilet with nappy-changing facilities on 1st floor (lift access). Although the façade is very modern, the actual theatre is traditional and some seats have a slightly restricted view.

George Square Theatre

George Square
Tel: 651 1930
If travelling by car, there's metered parking up to 2 hrs (free after 18.30) on George Sq itself, or Crichton St car park is close by

A venue which is used during University holidays for shows, including children's shows. However, this is a university lecture theatre and consequently there are no specific facilities for young children or babies.

King's Theatre

2 Leven St
Tel: 529 6000 (Box Office)
Nearest car parking: nearby streets in evenings

Traditional theatre. Occasional children's shows, some specifically aimed at under 5s. Some shows with special low price tickets. Book early for a good seat. Ice cream and refreshments available. Toilet with nappy-changing facilities on ground floor.

The Netherbow

43-45 High St
Tel: 556 9579
Closed until 2005 for extensive renovations.

Playhouse Theatre

18-22 Greenside Pl
Tel: 0870 606 3434 (Box Office)
A wide variety of shows including opera, musicals, ballet and rock concerts. Occasional children's shows. Toilets on ground floor. Some restricted views.

The Queen's Hall

37 Clerk St
Tel: 668 2019 (Mon-Sat 10.00-17.00)
Fax: 668 2656
Web: www.queenshalledinburgh.co.uk

Some concerts and events for children. Breastfeeding welcomed. Toilet for disabled with nappy changing area. There are some restricted view seats due to the pillars in the main performance space.

Royal Lyceum Theatre

30 Grindlay St
Box Office: 248 4848

Family show at Christmas. Has also been used as a venue for the Scottish International Children's Festival in May. Lifts to all levels. Toilets for the disabled on the ground floor. Nappy changing facilities. Traditional-style theatre – very ornate and plush inside, once you are past the modern glass façade. The Theatre is providing a crèche on the first Saturday matinee of all shows. There is a baby room and one for slightly older children.

St Bride's Centre

10 Orwell Ter
Haymarket
Tel: 346 1405

Children's shows and films, usually in school holidays. Children's (4-8yr olds) general art and crafts clubs run on Wednesdays and Thursdays, phone for up to date information. Café with large, enclosed play area. Nappy changing facilities.

Theatre Workshop

34 Hamilton Place
Stockbridge
Tel: 226 5425 (Box Office)
Web: www.theatre-workshop.com

Many shows geared for school children and occasionally under 5s. Also exhibitions, classes and workshops. Concession rates apply to children's tickets. Nappy-changing facilities. Café.

Traverse Theatre

10 Cambridge St
Tel: 228 1404 (Box Office)
Tel: 228 5383 (Bar Café)

Occasional children's shows including the Scottish International Children's Festival. Generous discounts to most performances. The Traverse Bar Café is licensed for children until 20.00. Children's portions available all day. Lift to eating area and toilet with nappy changing facilities. See *Eating Out* for more details.

CINEMAS

There's a good range of cinemas in Edinburgh, from the independently owned Dominion where the manager greets you in the foyer, or the more 'arty' Cameo and Filmhouse, to the sprawling megaplexes, which seem to be showing every film released in the past six months: take your pick. You never quite know how your child will take to their first cinema outing. Remember that the sound volume can be overwhelming, as can the dark. However, there are the chairs, big and plush to little ones, the décor, such as the planetoid carpet of Ster Century and the lure of ice cream! Some cinemas have children's film clubs – check out your local one for details.

Cameo Cinema

38 Home St
Tel: 228 4141 (box office)
Tel: 228 2800 (24 hour info line)
Web: www.picturehouses.co.uk

Admission: adult £5.50, concession £3.50 available most days. Monday is cheap day, all tickets £3.50. Wed first screening £1 to concession card holders.
Babies and children of all ages admitted at parents' discretion and subject to normal film certification. Ice cream, popcorn and a wide range of confectionery on sale in the foyer. Children allowed in the bar up until 20.00.
The Cameo holds a Saturday morning Kids Club with supervised fun and activities followed by a screening. An adult must accompany all children attending the club. Unaccompanied adults will not be admitted.

THE BIG SCREAM

The Cameo can also offers parents/carers with babes-in-arms a chance to go to the cinema without having to worry about a babysitter – Thu mornings at 10.30. The films screened are different from the general programme, so check the web (go to site, then click on to 'what's on') or phone for current info.

Dominion

18 Newbattle Ter
Tel: 447 4771
Tel: 447 2660/8450 (information line)
Tel: 447 4771 (credit card booking)

Various prices dependent on time, seat type and screen.

As visited by Maisie the Cat! A lovely, old style, privately owned cinema. Shows current releases – children's access determined by rating. Babies in arms are welcome and best seated close to an exit. Breastfeeding is welcomed. Refreshments and ice cream in sale in the foyer. Comfortable bar/café in basement, selling coffees, alcoholic drinks and chocolate cake to die for! Toilets for disabled patrons on ground floor have nappy changing facilities. Other toilets at basement level.

Filmhouse

88 Lothian Rd
Tel: 228 2688

Art house films and independent cinema releases. Must be 3+ to be admitted to cinema, although younger children are allowed in the café between 10.00 and 20.00 only, which sells snacks, meals with vegetarian options, beers coffee etc. Full facilities for disabled patrons. Nappy changing facilities. Breastfeeding welcomed in café.

Odeon Cinemas

118 Lothian Road EH3 8BG
Tel: 221 1477
Plenty of buses to Lothian Road and corner of Morisson Street. Parking – not plentiful: a choice of on-street, 'pay and display' or the car park behind the cinema in Semple Street
New cinema with four screens. Not particularly targeting children though they do show occasional children's films. Easy pushchair access and lifts. Nappy changing facilities. Comfy chairs in retail area or on concourse to screens for breastfeeding.

Westside Plaza
120 Wester Hailes Rd
Tel: 453 3332
Tel: 0870 50 50 007 (24 hr booking and information line)
Eight-cinema complex. Next to Wester Hailes station. Easy parking and access is all on one level. Ice-cream, popcorn etc. Nappy-changing facilities. Family tickets available.
Under 18 mths free if sitting on parent's knee.

Ster Century Cinema

Ocean Terminal
Tel: 553 0700
By car: Parking free in Ocean terminal car parks. By Bus: Lothian 22

Large multi-screen cinema located on the top floor of Ocean Terminal shopping centre which can be easily accessed by escalators and lifts. Toilets, including nappy changing facilities and parents' rooms, are located nearby in the main shopping centre.
There is a Kids Film Club, which puts on a suitable film for children of about an hour long at 10:00 on Saturday and Sunday as well as weekdays in the holidays. Tickets are £2 for a child but accompanying adults go free. (check the film showing – not all are ideal for under 5s).
The popcorn, nachos etc are sold on the opposite side of the foyer to the ticket sales, though the ice cream and pick'n'mix vending is on the same side, but set back from the ticket sales area, so if you're trying to negotiate your way to the screen without a tantrum over sweeties it can just about be done.

UCI Cinemas

7 Kinnaird Park, Newcraighall Rd
Tel: 669 0777
Tel: 08700 10 20 30 (information and booking line)
Admission: Adult £5.35; child £3.65

Twelve cinema complex. No babies in arms. No smoking in cinemas. Quite popular with parents for child-orientated films. If you have a younger under 5, you might find that the seats fold up even when they're sitting on them – though this might be viewed as an added bonus to the film! Ice cream is on sale in the foyer as well as the usual popcorn, tortillas and dips, hot and cold drinks etc. Child-sized portions available. No nappy changing facilities.

UGC Fountainpark

Fountainpark, Dundee St
Tel: 0870 902 0417 (24 hr information and credit card booking)
Admission: adult £4.60 before 17.00 Mon-Fri, £5.40 after 17.00; child (under 16)/ concession £3.20; family ticket £13. Also, 'early bird' price of £2.95 for showings before noon. Yearly passes also available.

Large cinema complex located in a purpose built leisure park in a central location. Underground car park; fee refunded on exit with voucher supplied by cinema or other outlets. Parties hosted in a special 'party' room. Phone for further information and booking. Can be extremely busy.

Warner Village Cinema

Greenside Place
Tel: 557 3964
Web: www.cinemaniacs.co.uk
By car: Parking behind complex, in side streets or NCP St James. None of these options are free.

Large multi-screen complex, centrally located. Accessible by escalator and lift. Toilets with nappy changing facilities. Under 3s free. Good views down on to the traffic from the huge glass-fronted façade. Snacks on sale above ticket sales, so you can get to the screens without passing by, if you take the stairs!

Playgrounds and Parks

At the time of writing, there are over 150 playgrounds in Edinburgh, ranging from small housing estate play areas to larger city park playgrounds. This section lists the city parks that have playgrounds within them and a range of playgrounds for each area, including some of the most popular playgrounds and the new and recently upgraded ones. It has not been possible to list every small playground.

The new playgrounds nearly always have brightly coloured multiplay units which incorporate a variety of activities. The council is also keen to encourage imaginative play through thematic playgrounds with multiplay units in the form of castles, trains, boats etc. The Castle at Inch Park, the Noah's Ark at Leith Links and the Juni Train at Broomiehall Park, Juniper Green are examples. Other new features are the ground level panels with bells, chimes, spinning spirals, beads and noughts and crosses. Children of all abilities can enjoy these and although there is generally no specialised equipment for children with special needs, a number of playgrounds do have low decks, ramps and handrails. Scotland Yard Adventure Centre is a notable exception to this and provides play opportunities for children and young people with a special need or disability.

Priorities for redeveloped playgrounds include: playgrounds within a fenced-off area with self-closing gates; safer surfacing under all play equipment, either wood chips, rubber tiles or sand; if a playground includes equipment for a variety of age groups then age-relevant equipment should be grouped together; and increased inspection of playgrounds by council representatives. Other improvements include putting up notices displaying the name of the playground and a contact number to report any damage to. Many of the newer playgrounds have equipment made from tough plastic designed to be hard wearing and to withstand vandalism – although sadly this can mean that the vandals become more inventive. Remember, if your local playpark is vandalised etc, contact the Council (Tel: 223 2368) – that way you know that they are aware of the damage and repair may be more quickly effected. Lack of nearby toilets are still a problem at many playgrounds and while the Recreation Department can upgrade play facilities they have no say in the allocation of public toilets.

CENTRAL EDINBURGH

Princes St Gardens

The City's most famous park runs alongside Princes St under the lee of the castle. The park is a useful rest point for weary parents, mid-shopping, as there are plenty of seats. It also provides an open space for toddlers to let off steam after the confines of the pushchair in the nearby department stores.

There are lawns, flowerbeds and many statues & sculptures – to interest both parents and children. Look out for a tree with a hole through it, near the gardener's lodge in the West Gardens. The park's patrol officers will be pleased to point this out, or help you out with any other questions or problems. The gardens are locked at sunset or 22.00 (23.00 during the festival). Please note that dogs must be kept on a lead.

The park is divided in two by the Mound. The East Gardens may be accessed from the Mound, Waverley Bridge and via gates leading from Princes St. The Scott Monument, a Victorian, high-gothic memorial to the author Sir Walter Scott – and a convenient landmark – can be climbed for an admission fee. The stairs are very steep near the top and would probably not be enjoyed by small children or mothers-to-be! A nine-hole pitch and putt golf course is open from mid-Apr to mid-Sep. Trains can be viewed from the bank beneath the National Gallery. Next to the Scott Monument is a kiosk selling sweets, ices, hot and cold drinks to take away (open spring and autumn 10.00-18.00; summer 18.00-22.00). There are plenty of pigeons, sparrows and squirrels to feed and some of the kiosks sell nuts and pigeon food.

Nearest toilets (open 8.00-22.00) are by the Mound, ladies (with nappy-changing facilities) and toilets for the disabled to the East side, gents down steps on the West side of the Mound, near the Floral Clock. The West Gardens can be accessed from the Mound, Princes St, Johnstone Ter and King's Stables Rd. The famous Floral Clock, next to the steps down to the park at the junction of Princes St and the Mound is a source of delight for both children and adults alike. The clock is composed of up to 35,000 small plants and functions from spring to late autumn. A cuckoo emerges from a wooden house every quarter hour when the clock is in operation. It was the original idea of an Edinburgh clockmaker in 1903 and there are now copies all over the world including one in Napier, New Zealand.

In summer, there is often entertainment in the Ross Bandstand, children's events during the school holidays by the Norwegian Stone (both in Princes St Gardens West), and a carousel operates near the Ross Fountain.

Over the railway, the South side of the gardens is less formal, with a steep grassy slope leading up to the castle. The slope is covered with daffodils in the spring. There is a gate into the castle esplanade via a zigzag path, but the gate can be locked at times (especially during the Edinburgh Military Tattoo). There is a level entrance to the Gardens from King's Stables Rd, opposite the multi-storey car park and a sloped entrance from Johnstone Ter, round the side of the castle. These paths join up and cross a railway footbridge into the gardens near the play park. A path also leads from the bridge, behind the railway to another bridge that brings you to the Ross Bandstand. Further along is another bridge, the path here coming out near the Gardener's lodge and leading up to the Floral Clock.

Playground

The nearest entrance is from Princes St, the second gate from the West end, as the first gate has a long flight of steps. Also level access from King's Stable Rd or through St Cuthbert's Churchyard.

Although the playground is unfenced, dogs in the gardens are supposed to be kept on leads and it is relatively clean. Plenty of seating for parents but younger children will need to be watched closely, especially when the equipment is crowded. The multiplay unit is loosely based on a castle theme, with ramps, slides and walkways suitable for toddlers, eventually leading up to a higher tower with enclosed slide, interesting for older children. There's also an octagon of low-level panels with bells, perspex drums, chimes and crazy mirrors accessed by a low ramp on wooden boards suitable for wheelchairs.

Other activities include a 'television', noughts and crosses and an abacus.

The presence of the railway line in the gardens is a bonus, especially the bridge behind the Ross Bandstand from which children can safely and easily see the trains coming and going and drivers usually oblige with a wave!

Toilets are near the playground with nappy changing facilities. The key can be obtained from the attendant on duty from 10.00-22.00 (except from 15.00-16.00 when they are closed for cleaning). Note: there is no ramp up to Princes St from these toilets. Also toilets at the Ross Bandstand (open summer only 8.00-20.00, no nappy-changing facilities).

The gardens are a good place for a picnic: some of stores on Princes St sell sandwiches, yoghurt, fruit, etc, and there are many sandwich shops on the likes of Frederick St, Hanover St and Rose St. Ice cream kiosks are dotted around the park.

Piazza Open Air Café

W Princes St Gardens
Tel: 225 5533

Opening times: 7 days, Apr-May: 11.00-18.00; June-Aug 9.30-21.30; Sep-Oct 11.00-17.00; Nov-Mar closed.

£, bottles and baby food heated, seats 160.

An outdoor café with self-service fast food, snacks, etc. Close to the playground. Children's groups can be catered for by arrangement with the management. There are no toilets, but there are toilets located in the Gardens (see above).

EDINBURGH NORTH

Beaverbank Playground

Broughton Rd

A fenced playground set directly off the main road with a ramp access. Equipment is set on rubber matting and includes a large slide, a small slide, an animal seesaw, 4 swings (set within an enclosure), 3 bucket swings and a horse buckabout. It is fairly clean and all the equipment is functional if a little older-styled, but has a certain air of neglect and this park suffers from an endemic problem of broken glass . There are, however, plans for an upgrade.

Corstorphine Hill Playpark

Craigcrook Rd

A fairly new fenced-off park, on the way up to Corstorphine Hill. There's a small multiplay with slide, climbing ropes, a low 'look-out post' and a countered area underneath; a climbing frame with a plastic-covered chain commando walkway, 3 animal rockers; and a turtle-designed 4-seater buckabout. There's also a chessboard design set into part of the ground surface, which is entirely rubberised and brightly coloured. There's seating for parents/carers, and it's usually clean. Unfortunately, this park's multiplay was recently defaced by vandals.

Craigleith Retail Park

Groathill Ave or Queensferry Rd

This small toddler playground is almost hidden from view, so many visitors to this well-established retail park will be unaware of its existence. The playground is located behind trees at the exit from Sainsburys petrol station, close to the carwash. It has a multiplay set on rubber matting. There are 2 benches, 1 of which was broken when visited. Only a very basic playground, but might be worth visiting after struggling round Sainsburys.

Cramond Walled Garden

Cramond Glebe Rd
Behind Cramond Kirk

This playground can be found by going down Cramond Glebe Rd, following the sign for the Roman Fort . If you're driving, you can park behind the church hall. If you're on foot, walk through the Roman Fort and past the back of the Kirk. The playground is just through an entrance in the high wall ahead next to the Kirk Hall, though a quick stop to admire the granite lion statue is usually a must. This quiet, secluded enclosed playground has a boat shaped multiplay unit set on wood chips, with 2 slides (one slightly steeper than the other), a steering wheel and panels with chimes, noughts and crosses, numbers, shapes, the alphabet and a mirror. In the past, this park was usually clean, although there was minimal vandalism done to the ball-tracking play feature. However, recently, the multiplay has suffered from graffiti, and the park has been littered. There is seating for parents/carers and a litter bin. The surrounding area is a popular walk for people with dogs, so keep this in mind if a run-about is in order.

Dalmeny Street Park

Dalmeny St, Iona St and Buchanan St

A park area, fenced round and set down from the road, with ramp access from Dalmeny Street. The playground equipment includes a tractor shaped multiplay with slide, a dome-shaped climbing frame, a traditional seesaw, a roundabout, 4 swings (1 of which was unusable at time of visit due to wraparound), 3 bucket swings and 2 buckabout animals. All equipment is set on rubber matting. The area also includes a hard-surfaced area with basketball hoops. The playground has some grass and trees on three sides and there was some evidence of dog fouling there. The park appeared to be in reasonable order although some of the equipment could do with a lick of paint. There is no seating for parents/carers and there are no bins – which might explain some of the litter. There's a more formal park area adjacent to the playground.

Granton Mains

Off West Granton Rd

Well appointed park which is the property of local Housing Association. The playpark contains equipment for both toddlers and older children, and there is an advisory notice stating that the maximum age for playing on the equipment is 11 years. The playpark contains: a low-level multiplay, with slide, rope ladder, climbing frames, and a clockface with a turnable shape identifier (vandalised); 2 swings; 2 bucket swings; roundabout; large multiplay with slide, climbing ropes and monkey bars; and a springy seesaw. Everything is set on rubberised surfaces. There's seating and bins all round the play area. To one side there's a basketball court. Everything was in good condition and clean at time of visiting.

Granton Crescent Park

Granton Cres

Fenced playpark set on a slope between Granton Crescent and Granton View. Access via Granton Cres. There's equipment for both toddlers and older children, all set on sections of brightly coloured rubberised surfaces. Equipment includes: multiplay with 2 slides, climbing bars and tunnel; a mini-roundabout; 4-seater buckabout; a toddler chute; a chute for older children; and boat-shaped low-level wooden multiplay. There are 2 bucket swings which are enclosed within the park itself. Everything was in pretty good order, although equipment carried graffiti. Great views too.

Henderson Gardens

Henderson St, behind Great Junction St Leith

A small fenced playground in a small park with benches and a grassed area. Equipment includes a low multiplay boat with steering wheel bridge and slide, a 4-seat rocker and a horse buckabout. This is all set on blue rubberised matting with a fish design on it. There is a bucket swing set apart from the playground at the side of the park. Seating for parents/carers. Some graffiti.

McDonald Rd

Hopetoun Street Development

Multiplay unit with slide, walkways, and climbing hoops. The unit is enclosed and is set on rubberised matting. You can access it via McDonald Rd and it's set among the Hopetoun Street development.

Inverleith Park and Playground

Entrances on Arboretum Pl, Inverleith Pl and East Fettes Ave

A large grass park (61 acres) with allotments, a rose garden and a boating lake. The boating lake is near the Edinburgh Academicals Ground on Raeburn Place, and is a good place to feed the ducks and watch remote controlled boats on Sundays. The playground is near Arboretum Place and its centrepiece is a large wooden ship called the HMS Edinburgh with two slides, fireman's poles and climbing frames within it. There are also 4 animal swings, a seesaw, a circular climbing frame, a buckabout car, and 2 bucket swings. Equipment is all on rubber safety surfaces but the playground is only fenced on one side, which means children can run on to the nearby rugby pitch / cricket crease – not ideal if there's a game on! The playground has seating and litterbins and, on the whole, is reasonably tidy,although the paintwork is looking a little tired. However, the council has plans to rebuild the park 2003/4. There's an ice-cream van just outside the park's entrance on to Arboretum Pl from late Spring into early Autumn, which sells a great range of ice creams, lollies and also offers soft drinks, teas and coffees.

Keddie Gardens Play Area

Largo Place, off Ferry Rd

Fenced playground set within a small grassed area, close to the Water of Leith Walkway. The playground has a small toddler multiplay unit (with a slide, a rope ladder, and fireman's pole), a spherical roundabout, a helter-skelter slide and 4 bucket swings all set on rubber matting. The playground was fairly clean, bar some graffiti. There's seating and litterbins inside the fenced play area. There was some dog fouling in the grass around the play park, and also on the pavement approach.

King George V Park

Eyre Place

Somewhat hidden away, with an entrance off Logan Street, this park has three playgrounds, KVG for toddlers, another one for older children, and a third for children and young people with special needs (see The Yard in Adventure Playgrounds subsection. At the time of writing, the toddler area, near the Logan Street entrance, had been recently refurbished. It now has a small multiplay incorporating a wide slide, a 'look-out post', a climbing frame and a small ramp with rock-face grips on it. There's also a hemispherical climbing frame, two bucket swings, two swings and a mini-roundabout. Everything is set on a deep covering of woodchips, with rubberised surfaces under the swings. The junior playground, in comparison, is somewhat more run-down: the woodchips are more sparse, there's evidence of graffiti, and there were more abandoned bottles and paper wrappers etc. There's a very long slide set into the hill at the back of the park, accessed by a climbing wall; a smaller slide; two climbing frame areas; and four swings. To the side of the playground, there's a basketball court, but the hoop (there was only one) was broken.

Leith Links and Playground

48 acres of grass, complete with hillocks, which are the remains of 16th century gun emplacements. There are benches and paths, which are lit in the evenings, suitable for pushchairs. The fenced playgrounds are on the North West of the park.

The toddler area has a Noah's Ark themed multiplay complete with slide, 4 bucket swings, a sit-on animal roundabout and 2 horse buckabouts, all set on rubberised surfaces. There's a picnic table and other seating for parents/carers, and also litterbins.

The junior area is set on bark chips, which seemed good and deep at the time of visiting, and has a large timber multiplay climbing frame connected with a chain scramble netting, a tyre swing and a tyre commando slide. All of this is only really suitable for older children. Again, there's seating provided.

There's a third area which has an 'Eiffel Tower' climbing net and a basic balancing frame. This area is set in sand. Again, this is only really suitable for older children. These playparks are extremely popular, and are usually in pretty good condition, but there is some graffiti here and there, and on the grass round about there's dog fouling.

Montgomery St Playground

Montgomery St

A popular fenced playground accessed directly off Montgomery Street. It has a tractor-shaped climbing frame with slide; a fort-shaped multiplay unit with slide, bridge and rings; a roundabout; a rocking rocket; a tall helter-skelter slide; and 4 swings. The toddler area is separate from the main playground and has a small multiplay area; a mini roundabout; a 'spider' climbing frame; and 3 bucket swings. All equipment is set on rubberised matting. There is hard surface area beside the playgrounds with small goal posts, as well as a basket ball court with hoops and a ball-play unit.

Muirhouse Linear Park and Playground

Nr Muirhouse Dr

A relatively new playground, set in a large grassy area near to Silverknowes Primary School with a path running through from Muirhouse Park to Muirhouse Drive. The colourful, enclosed playground contains 2 bucket swings and a quiet corner with seating and games for toddlers. There is also a 'New World' unit specifically designed for toddlers, featuring games and interactive toys. Other equipment includes a climbing frame; an elevated walkway; 4 swings, a slide and a roundabout. These are set on a rubber surface with benches at the side.

Pennywell Gardens

Muirhouse End

A fenced playground suitable for toddlers consisting of a low-level multiplay with 2 slides, 3 bucket swings and buckabouts set on rubber surface. Suffering from some graffiti.

Pennywell Rd

Pennywell Grove/Gardens

Enclosed and surrounded by houses this playground is set back from the road between Pennywell Grove and Pennywell Gardens with a colourful multiplay unit and 2 springy motorbikes.

Pilrig Park and Playgrounds

Entrances via Balfour St & Pilrig St

This is a 2 acre park with football pitches and 2 playgrounds, neither of which is fenced. The first can be found by the Balfour Street and Stanwell Street entrance on the East side of the park – near Bonnington Primary School. The playground, which is suitable for toddlers, has: a slide; roundabout; seesaw; wooden balancing bridge; and 3 bucket swings all on rubberised surfaces. Unfortunately, everything was in rather a grim condition at the time of visiting: there was broken glass, painted graffiti on the ground and play unit, and chunks out of the swings. The second playground is on Pilrig Street at the West Side of the park. It has a suspended walkway, set a little bit away from the other equipment, 2 swings, 2 bucket swings and 4 animal buckabouts. This was all functioning (though it could do with some paint etc), was set in wood chips, but could not be used (on 2 visits) due to the amount of broken glass all around. There's a little hillock nearby, which is very inviting to toddlers in terms of scrambling up but, again, it was scattered with broken glass bottles. There were 2 picnic tables and benches nearby.

Ravelston Park and Playground

Craigcrook Rd

An enclosed toddler playground next to a tennis court (currently not in use) that is surrounded by a grassy park lined with trees. The playground has 2 bucket swings, 2 swings, a roundabout, 3 springy animals and a double seesaw (a traditional styled one, not the newer springy ones), a small climbing frame and a toddler multiplay with slide. The equipment is set on rubber mats. This decent-sized playground is ideal for toddlers, and is popular with families Easy parking on Craigcrook Rd. There are plans to upgrade this park 2003/4.

Redbraes Park and Playground

Broughton Rd

An enclosed playground set in Redbraes Park near the Broughton Rd entrance. Equipment includes a multiplay climbing frame, a climbing frame/rope climb with slide, 2 bucket swings and 2 swings. The swings are sectioned off within the enclosure – helps to prevent any dash out of the play area and into the park! All equipment was in good order brightly painted and set on rubber surface with pictures on a Wild West theme.

St Mark's

Warriston Rd

An enclosed play area with a dog free picnic site set in a large open park area.
Provision for toddlers include a kiddie cabin with small low decks, small climbing challenges and a slide. A low roundabout and a dog free grass area with picnic tables. Seats and bins are also provided. All design works on the welcome entrance arch and laid into the coloured safety surface were produced by pupils of Bonnington Primary School. Unfortunately, this park, like many others, attracts loitering teenagers at night. There is also a little graffiti.

Sandport Street

Leith, off Commercial St

Small enclosed park, set back from the road. There's a timber and metal multiplay with ladders, climbing platforms and a slide (this would be far beyond the scope of toddlers). There are also 2 swings. Everything is set on thick woodchips, and in addition there are rubber mats under the swings. There's a bench set a little way back from the play area.

Victoria Park and Playgrounds

Between Newhaven Rd and Craighall Rd, Trinity

A lovely 18 acre park that has a floodlit, all-weather, five-a-side football pitch. There are cycle paths running through it and is suitable for pushchairs. The park has two excellent playgrounds. The first is near Newhaven Rd and is suitable for toddlers. This enclosed area includes; a multiplay unit with a slide, 2 bucket swings, a small hemispherical climbing frame, a 4-seat buckabout, and a roundabout – all set on rubberised surfaces. There's seating for carers/parents.
The second playground is nearer Craighall Rd and is more suitable for older children and is very popular. More experienced toddlers will enjoy some of it if closely supervised. The playground is made up of modern tough plastic equipment. It has interlinked climbing frames, bridges, walkways and slides – one with a roller surface – a small helter-skelter slide, a larger tube helter-skelter slide and a whole variety of climbing, swinging and bouncing equipment.
This is all fenced off and set in wood chips with a couple of pic-

nic tables and benches nearby. Try to avoid it at lunchtime, as pupils from nearby Trinity Academy tend to swarm all over it. Minor graffiti in both play areas.

EDINBURGH EAST

Craigmillar

Niddrie House Sq

Toddler multiplay area with ramps, steps, slides, rope bridge, cargo net and monkey rings. There are also 2 bucket swings and 2 rockers. All laid out on a rubber surface.
Unfortunately prone to litter and broken glass.

Dumbiedykes Road

Faces onto Queens Dr, Holyrood Park, near Holyrood Gate.

Due to structural damage to the steps leading down into the playground from Dumbiedykes Rd, this playground has been closed. (See *Walks and Country Places*).

Figgate Park and Playground

Portobello, entrances on Duddingston Rd and Hamilton Dr

A strip of parkland with trees and grassy slopes along the Figgate Burn. Figgate Pond is good for feeding ducks. On raised ground to the Northeast of the pond is the playground with a toddler multiplay unit and bucket swings. There is also a larger multiplay unit with a curved slide, walkways, tube and ramp. All laid out on a colourful rubber surface (See *Walks and Country Places*).

Jack Kane Toddlers

Jack Kane Sports Centre, Niddrie Mains Rd

This fenced area for toddlers is adjacent to the large play area, with 2 bucket swings, a multiplay unit with slide, a small roundabout and a 4-seater rocker. All the equipment is set on wood chips. The adjoining area is for older children and consists of a high slide, a tyre slide and various balancing, swinging and climbing adventure equipment.

Joppa Quarry Park

Off South Morton St, Portobello

This is a fenced playground adjacent to a large grassy area and football pitch where dogs are walked. The equipment suits toddler and junior children and consists of 3 bucket swings, 4 swings, an elephant shaped climbing frame, a slide and a roundabout. All laid out on rubber mats.

Lochend Park and Playground

Lochend Rd

A 23-acre park with a pond. Although the pond has a fence around it, it is still possible to feed the ducks and swans. The playground is fenced, suitable for toddlers and juniors, and consists of a modern tough plastic multiplay unit with a curved slide, low slide and 2 ladders. There is also a small roundabout and 2 bucket swings. The equipment is laid out on rubber mats and wood chips.

Magdalene Community Centre

Next to Brunstane Primary School, Magdalene Dr

This playground consists of a large multiplay unit with tube slide, rope ladder and bridge, and a low slide. There's also a smaller multiplay unit with rope ladder, slide and bridge that has a small table and seats beneath it. There is a small fenced toddlers area with a bead panel, play post office/bank counter and small seats. All the equipment is laid out on brightly coloured rubber surfacing. The playground is open to the public out of school hours during daylight hours and in school holidays, except Sundays.

Mount Lodge Park

Mount Lodge Pl, off Windsor Pl, Portobello

Enclosed playground with separate toddler area. There is a large multiplay unit consisting of a slide and walkway, and also a smaller multiplay unit with a ladder, slide, swing and seesaw. The toddler area has a multiplay unit with a slide; 4 swings; 2 bucket swings, a roundabout and 3 animal rockers.

Northfield Broadway

Next to Northfield Community Centre

This toddler playground consists of a 'Pirate Ship' multiplay unit, a helter-skelter, 3 bucket swings and 2 swings. All the equipment is laid out a rubber surface.

Prestonfield Park

Prestonfield Rd, next to the Bowling Green

This playground has a separate fenced toddler and junior areas. The toddler equipment includes 3 bucket swings and a low level multiplay unit consisting of 2 slides, curved ladder, rope ladder, tunnel, fireman's pole, an abacus and noughts and crosses panel. The Junior area has modern, tough plastic walkways, climbing structures a helter-skelter and hand slide. All the equipment is laid out on a brightly coloured rubber surface. There is also a good old-fashioned hopscotch!

Rosefield Park and Playground

Rosefield Pl, Portobello

This is a small, pretty park with a bridge over the Figgate Burn. The Playground is suitable for toddlers and juniors and consists of a large multiplay unit with a slide, cargo net, low level double slide, walkway and pole, 2 animal rockers, 2 bucket swings, 2 swings and a roundabout. All the equipment is laid out on a brightly coloured rubber surface.

Straiton Place

Portobello

This is a small toddler playground with a 'Boat' multiplay unit. Handy stop-off point on the way to the beach.

Tower Bank

Off the Promenade by Tower Bank Primary School, Portobello

This playground was designed with the children from the primary school. There is a multiplay unit with 2 slides, swings and a seesaw.

EDINBURGH SOUTH

The Meadows and Bruntsfield Links and Playgrounds

The Links border Bruntsfield Place and Whitehouse Loan, while the Meadows extend along Melville Drive from Brougham Place to Buccleuch Street.

These are open, leafy and well maintained parkland areas, often busy with people playing sport, games and picnicking. There are 3 fenced playgrounds, tennis courts, and wide safe paths suitable for inexperienced cyclists.

Meadows East

Corner of Buccleuch St and Melville Dr

This is a fenced playground with a helter-skelter slide, multiplay unit with slide, bridge, and low-level playhouse, 4 swings, roundabout and seesaw. All equipment is set on colourful rubber surfacing and there are benches and bins. This is a busy playground, popular with families, but unfortunately suffers from some litter and graffiti.

Meadows West

Corner of Leven Ter and Melville Dr

This is a compact, fenced playground for young children, with an imaginative climbing frame incorporating bridges, tunnel, fireman's pole and rope ladders. There are 2 bucket swings, a roundabout and a slide. All equipment is set on brightly coloured rubber surfacing and there are benches and litterbins provided. Clean and tidy when visited.

Meadows Toddlers

Towards East end of Melville Dr, next to the tennis courts

This fenced grassy playground is suitable for toddlers with equipment set on rubber surfacing. There are slides, a multiplay climbing frame, bucket swings, a seesaw and a roundabout. The equipment was well maintained.

Buckstone Park

Buckstone Circle

This is a fenced playground well back from the road in a large grassy area, with attractive mature woodland on either side. It has 1.8m high bucket swings (to avoid wraparound problems), 2 multiplays, a slide and a roundabout. The equipment was all set on rubber surfacing, with benches and a litterbin. The park was generally well maintained, but with some minor graffiti.

Camus Park

(also known as Fairmilehead Public Park)
Entrance from Camus Ave and Pentland View

A fenced play area set in attractive parkland with 2 bucket swings, 2 multiplay units and a roundabout. The equipment was set on rubber surfacing, with benches and litterbins. Unfortunately the park was in need of some maintenance, and small pieces of glass were present in parts of the rubber surfacing.

Colinton Mains Park

Oxgangs Rd North, nr junction with Redford Rd, behind the huts

This bright playground is surrounded on two sides by playing fields. There are 3 bucket swings, 2 multiplays, a helter-skelter, a roundabout and a four-seat rocker, all set on rubber surfacing. There are plenty of seats, a litterbin and red safety fencing separating each play area. Minor maintenance required.

Falcon Gardens

Nr St Peters School, Morningside, entrance from Falcon Rd

This park is set in a walled area, back from the road, surrounded by grass. There are 3 bucket swings, a slide, seesaw and a multiplay unit. The equipment was set on rubber matting, with benches and litterbins. Clean and well maintained.

Glenvarloch Crescent

Glenvarloch Crescent, Liberton

This bright playground is enclosed by fencing and in the centre of a grassed area with estate roads to 4 sides. There are two multiplay units. The larger one is for older children but the smaller one is suitable for under 5s. It includes a slide, a climbing frame, a bridge and scramble netting, with 2 buckabouts and a plane. All equipment is set on coloured rubber surfacing and there are benches and a litterbin.

Gracemount Leisure Centre

Captain's Rd, entrance on Grace-mount Dr, to the rear of the car park

There are: two 1.8m high bucket swings to eliminate wraparound problems; a special toddler multiplay unit featuring double width slide, rubber coated decks, games and climbing; two springers; and a roundabout. Unfortunately when visited the playground was in a poor state of repair with litter, broken glass and unpleasant graffiti.

Harrison Park

West Bryson Rd, Watson Cres

A fenced park with a tree lined walkway along the bank of the Union Canal, set near playing fields, tennis courts and a bowling green. There are 4 bucket swings, a seesaw, a slide and a small climbing frame. There are benches and a litter bin and the park had some minor graffiti.

Inch Park and Playground

Access from Glenallen Dr

The playground is set in an area of parkland in front of the Inch Community Centre. The fenced playground had a central 'castle' multiplay and also another multiplay suitable for younger children. In addition, there were 3 bucket swings, and the equipment was set on rubber surfacing. Unfortunately when visited there was evidence of recent dog fouling, a large amount of litter, and also graffiti.

Liberton Recreation Ground

Entrances from Liberton Gds and Alnwickhill Rd

The fenced play area is set in the middle of the park, well away from the road. It is difficult to access with a pushchair due to the long grass, with clear evidence of recent dog fouling. There is a bright multiplay unit with slides, scramble net, tunnel tube, ramps and two platforms with red umbrella roofs, swings, 2 bucket swings and 2 buckabouts. The equipment was set on rubber surfacing and there were benches and litterbin. Generally clean, but in need of minor maintenance.

Seven-Acre Park

Stanedykehead, Liberton

This playground was accessed down a road in a very poor state of repair, and was set in parkland that made it seem very isolated. It is however a new, rather lovely, bright and modern playground with bucket swings, and a safe roundabout for toddlers, multiplay unit with helter-skelter slide, towers and wooden climbing ramp. For older children there is basketball practice shooting ring and raised covered seating and a 'hanging' seesaw. All areas set in safe coloured rubber surfacing.

EDINBURGH WEST

Dean Park

Balerno

This compact park is situated next to Dean Park Primary School and access by car is from Dean Park Pl. It is an enclosed playground set in a large grassy area, used for ball games and cycling. It has a brightly painted toddler multiplay, which has bridges, a slide, and rope climb, and a springy motorbike and tractor. The junior area is not in great condition but has a variety of activities using slides, ropes, bridges and wooden barrels. All the equipment is set on rubber matting, which features attractive designs.

Pentland View Park

Currie

This playground is situated on the busy Lanark Rd, with parking adjacent at the Pentland View car park. It is fully fenced, and the gate does not lead directly on to Lanark Rd. It has 2 bright toddler multiplays, with bridges, rope climbs, and slides, 2 bucket swings, and 4 other swings, all set on rubber matting. There are 2 benches for adults. The playground was reasonably tidy when visited, but unfortunately had the usual graffiti.

Bloomiehall Public Park

Juniper Green

This park is situated at the end of Juniper Park Rd, and accessed from Baberton Ave, opposite the entrance to Baberton Golf Course. Pushchair access can be found on a track that goes round the edge of the park. This excellent playground has a range of equipment to suit all ages. The toddler area multiplay is based on a train theme with carriages, a station and a ticket office all on a coloured track. To the side of this there are 2 bucket swings on rubber surfacing. The section for older children is behind this and separated by red metal fencing. It has a large amount of multiplay equipment with slides, rope climbing, bridges, balancing beams and large tyre slide. For the more advanced there is a large rope pyramid structure. The park is encircled by a fence, has benches, and is generally well maintained.

Clermiston Park

Clermiston Gds

For some time this enclosed playground had been badly vandalised and virtually unusable, but it has just been completely renovated with mostly new equipment. There are 2 bucket swings, separated from the rest of the playground by a metal fence, 4 other swings, a multiplay, roundabout, seesaw, and 2 springy animals, all set on rubber matting. New benches and litter bins have been added. The surrounding park is grassy with lots of new trees. There is a hard surface area next to the playground with basketball nets.

Corstorphine Park

The Play Station, Carrick Knowe Dr

A playground based on the theme of a train station, which is now showing signs of old age and vandalism. The enclosed area has painted railway tracks with a static train and coaches. The multiplay unit has low level panels, slides, a rope ladder and walkways.

Curriemuir End Park

Off Wester Hailes Rd

This playground has to be approached by foot, using either the path that leaves Wester Hailes Rd close to the junction with Viewfield Rd, or the underpass beneath Wester Hailes Rd that links the Clovestone estate to the park. An attractive playground geared more towards older children. The equipment is mainly wooden and includes 4 swings with back supports, a tall tube slide, rope pyramid structure, flexible balancing beam, and cableway. The surrounding park is grassy and hilly, and there are several picnic tables near-by.

Fauldburn Park

East Craigs

Set in a quiet, grassy area off Fauldburn Park Rd, this enclosed playground has a multiplay with bridge, tunnel and slide for toddlers one end and activities for older children on the other. There are also 2 springy animals. All equipment is set on rubber surfacing emblazoned with City of Edinburgh Council playground symbols. There are children's goal posts on grass next to the park.

Gyle Park

Accessed from Wester Broom Pl

A redeveloped public park providing five football pitches, two rugby pitches, artificial cricket square, wheels area and roller hockey. The enclosed playground lies at the Gylemuir Primary School end of the park, and is best accessed by foot from Wester Broom Pl, along a path that runs beside Gylemuir Primary School. Equipment includes 2 bucket swings, and a special toddler zone unit with rubber decks, wide slide and game panels. For older children there are swings, an extremely imaginative multiplay, and cableway. All equipment is set on colour safety surface, which incorporates children's artwork. There is a picnic table provided on a dog-free grass area within the playground, along with cycle racks and seating for adults.

Haugh Park

Brae Park Rd, Barnton

A leafy and quiet playground located close to the River Almond Walkway. Must be one of the most beautifully situated in Edinburgh. The equipment is mostly wooden and includes a climbing frame with 2 swings and a slide, a bucket swing, another 4 swings and a wooden rope bridge. All are set on a bark chip surface. There is a car park specifically for this playground close by, as parking on Brae Park Rd can be difficult and there is a picnic table and benches. There are often ponies grazing in the paddock next to the park.

Murieston Park

Murieston Cres

An enclosed area within Murieston Park that has grass and trees and a path around the perimeter. Equipment comprises a slide, buckabouts, bouncy horse, roundabout, and a climbing frame with mirror on the deck, a slide, steps, fireman's pole and rope ladder. Equipment is all on a rubber safety surface.

Roseburn

Roseburn Cres

An enclosed playground situated in the shadow of Murrayfield stadium behind Roseburn Primary School. Parking available at the end of Roseburn Cres. The only play equipment is a long multiplay unit graded from one end for toddlers to the other for juniors. This incorporates slides, ladders, a crawl through barrel and a rope bridge as well as seating under the towers. This playground is on the edge of open playing fields with a path running through them that is popular for riding bikes on. It was fairly tidy when visited, although it certainly looks as if it needs a lick of paint.

St Margaret's Park

Costorphine High St

An attractive, clean wooded and grassy park. The enclosed toddler playground has 3 bucket swings, 4 swings, a roundabout, large slide and a multiplay unit with slide and rope ladder. Dogs are often exercised in the surrounding park.

Fort Saughton, Saughton Park

Entrances on Gorgie Rd, Balgreen Rd, Stevenson Dr

This is a 47 acre park mostly designated as football pitches and a putting green. Fort Saughton Playground, which is accessed from Balgreen Rd and has its own car park, is easily one of the best playgrounds in Edinburgh since being rebuilt in 1999. The large enclosed playground has sections that cater for all ages. The toddler play area has 4 bucket swings, a seesaw, roundabout and a great sand play area, where the children can enjoy many scooping and pouring activities around two multiplay areas and some low play tables. The rest of this extensive playground is set on wood chips and has a large multiplay with a tube slide, a hanging rope roundabout, 7 swings, a separate large slide, a large climbing net, springy animals, lots of balancing games, and a cableway. There are also several benches and 2 picnic tables.

Opposite the entrance to the playground is Saughton Gardens. These gardens have been developed especially for the blind, with an emphasis on scented plants. They are attractive and well paved. There is also the Winter Gardens, an attractive heated greenhouse with tropical plants. Opening times: Mon-Wed 10.00-16.00; Thu-Fri 10.00-15.30; Sat-Sun 12.00-16.00. The cafeteria is currently not operating. Toilets available during opening hours.

Sighthill Park

Fort Broomhouse, Broomhouse Rd

A playground with an abundance of colourful equipment that is in good working order, although slightly spoilt by the excessive amount of graffiti. In the toddler area, which is separated from the main woodchip older play area by fence panels, the equipment includes a sit-down roundabout on bright rubber surface covered in spots, and toddler zone unit with games, climbing and sliding events on rubber surface with pictures of fish. There are also 2 bucket swings on a special low swing frame to help eliminate the disappointment of swing wrap round. In the junior area, which is all surrounded with bark, there is an elevated balancing bridge, a multiplay with slide and rope climb, 8 swings, a large slide, a roundabout, and for the more advanced a giant 'Space Climbing' net. Next to the playground on the surrounding grass there are two small goal posts. On two visits, the presence in the playground of gangs of youths who looked too old to be there, and who were misusing the equipment, was slightly intimidating.

Spylaw Public Park & Playground

Spylaw St/ Gillespie Rd

This large playground can be accessed from either Spylaw St, past Spylaw House, or by turning sharp left at the bottom of Gillespie Rd. The playground is beautifully situated in a leafy green park by the Water of Leith, but can feel a bit isolated on quiet days. It is very well maintained and comprises a toddler multiplay, 2 swings, a tractor and trailer climbing frame, tyre swing, slide with platform and fireman's pole, and 4-seater buckabout. There are 2 seats and the playground is fully fenced.

Wester Hailes

This area has very few large playgrounds, but it has benefited from a programme to create a number of small play centres within individual estates for children.

White Park

Gorgie Rd

Situated opposite the Hearts Football Ground Gorgie Rd entrance, this is an interesting playground to visit as it has some unusual play activities including a spiral slide and a net climbing structure. There are 3 bucket swings and 4 other swings. The playground is enclosed by a fence with 2 gates that need careful watching due to the proximity of Gorgie Rd. Inside the enclosed space there is a grassy area with 2 picnic tables.

SOUTH QUEENSFERRY

Carlowrie Cres

Dalmeny, adjacent to primary school

This fenced playground that has a castle themed multiplay with 2 slides; 2 sets of swings (one set for babies/ toddlers, and one for older children); a small roundabout; and two animal buck-abouts, all set on rubber surfacing. This is the best park in the area, and so can be busy, particularly during school hours, as it is often used by a local nursery and in school playtimes.

Dundas Park

Dundas Ave

A fairly large play area, situated next to the recreation centre, containing a smaller section for toddlers (multiplay unit in shape of a boat, swings and chute) and an area for older children (roundabout and larger multiplay climbing frame). All set on rubber surfacing.

King George V Park

Hopetoun Rd

Recently refurbished (2002) park, this playground has swings (for toddlers and older children) a roundabout and two multiplay climbing frames, all set on rubber surfacing. Surrounded by grass, which has excessive dog fouling – be warned!

Inchcolm Terrace Park

Access via Viewforth Place (off Kirkliston Rd)

Small fenced area surrounded by grass with two multi play units and two buck abouts, set on rubber surfacing.

Echline Play Park

Echline Ave

Two small playgrounds, one walled, the other situated close by. The walled area contains a slide, and two sets of swings (one for older children and one for toddlers) also two seesaws and a small climbing frame. There is no rubber matting, only bark chipping, and as this park can be frequented by teenagers drinking, there can be broken bottles which can get 'hidden' within the chips. The second area is for older children and contains a wooden multiplay area with slide. Both play areas are in need of refurbishment, and the second site is dilapidated and has areas where equipment had been removed.

ADVENTURE PLAYGROUNDS

Adventure playgrounds are less formal than the playgrounds described above and offer greater opportunities for creative play, making them harder work for parents. Some adventure playgrounds are really only suitable for older children but Vogrie Estate and Country Park can cater for all ages. There is also an adventure playground specifically created for children with a special need or disability at the Scotland Yard Adventure Centre.

Dalkeith Country Park

Tel: 654 1666/663 5684
Web: www.dalkeithcountrypark.com
The park entrance is near St Mary's Church, a few hundred yards from the town centre
Opening times: Apr-end Sep 10.00-17.30
Admission: adult/child £2.00; family ticket (2A&2C) £7.00. Under 5s free. Group rates also available.

Nature trails, woodland walks, picnic benches and large children's adventure playground on bark chips. Small unit for toddlers, more adventurous slides and equipment for older children. Take care with small children on the river paths and in the riverbank tunnels.
Café, high chairs (1), toilets, nappy-changing facility (M&F) available, seats 60. Small space for prams and pushchairs. Children's menu. No smoking. All facilities on ground floor. Parties hosted. See *Out of Town Trips*.

Vogrie Country Park

Tel: 01875 821990
Nr Gorebridge, 12 miles South of Edinburgh
Signposted from Gorebridge (A7) and Dalkeith (A68)
Open all year.
Admission free. Car park £1.

Vogrie has a toddlers' playground situated next to car park for easy access. There's also an adventure playground mainly suitable for children aged 7+, with some equipment suitable for younger children. All equipment is on bark chips, so wellies are a good idea if it's been raining heavily! As well as the playground, the park has barbecue sites, grassy areas suitable for games, woodland walks, tea room and nature trail. See *Out of Town Trips – Midlothian* for a fuller description of the Country Park.

The Yard

70 Eyre Pl EH3 5EJ
Contact: Ivan Harper
Tel: 557 899

The Yard provides adventure play opportunities for children and young people with a special need or disability. It aims to provide exciting, challenging and adventurous play for children in a safe and supportive environment. The centre has outdoor and indoor facilities. It's wheelchair accessible, and there's space for car parking. The Centre is open to families on Thu 6.00-20.30 and Sat 10.00-15.30. While there's no fee for families (brothers, sisters and friends are also welcome), it is essential to phone The Yard before visiting.

NOTES

Pre-School Play & Education

INTRODUCTION

There are a wide range of opportunities for under 5s to meet with others in the same age range. From the outset of family life, informal groups for parents and babies/toddlers can often provide a welcome break for both from the home and usually offer a larger range of toys and space than at home. This becomes particularly valuable once you are past the baby stage and want to meet others in a similar situation.

Moving on at 2 1/2 yrs, playgroups provide a more structured environment; many are now in partnership with the City Council to provide funded places for 3 yrs. We also list private nurseries; some of these provide daycare from 3 months. Many private nurseries are also in partnership with the City Council to provide funded places for 3 yrs. For 3+ yr olds, there are details of nursery schools and classes. We have also included details of nursery provision in the independent sector. Finally, there is some brief information on starting school.

Progression is usually:

Up to age 1	Parent and Baby group
Age 1-2 1/2	Parent and Toddler group
Age 2 1/2 -5	Playgroup, Home Playgroup, Private Nursery
Age 3-5	City of Edinburgh Council Nursery, Private Nursery, Independent School Nursery
OR	
Age 0-5	Private Nursery, Independent School Nursery

If you are looking for full/part-time day care for your child, you can refer to Private Nurseries in this section and also to the Childcare section, which covers nannies and childminders.

Details of multi-lingual groups and groups for children with special needs may be obtained from the Scottish Pre-School Play Association and the Education Department.

Section Contents

- **Sources of Information**
- **Parent and Baby Groups**
- **Parent and Toddler Groups**
- **Playgroups and Home Playgroups**
- **Private Nurseries**
- **Nursery Schools**
- **Nursery Classes in Schools**
- **Independent Schools**
- **Starting Schools**

SOURCES OF INFORMATION

With regards to informal groups, information is usually posted on notice-boards in libraries, supermarkets, toy shops, church halls etc. Many groups meet in church halls; you do not need to be a member to attend. Another good place to check for information regarding local groups is health centre notice boards – or ask your health visitor.

Edinburgh Childcare Information Service

PO Box 777
Edinburgh EH4 4JY
Tel: 270 6060 (Mon-Fri 08.30-16.00)
Fax: 270 6069
Freephone: 0800 0320323
Email: childcareinformation@edinburgh.gov.uk
Web: www.childcarelink.gov.uk

For full details of the service please see under Childcare

To receive a list of registered children's centres, nurseries and childminders, contact:

The Scottish Commission for the Regulation of Care

Stuart House,
Eskmills Business Park,
Musselburgh EH21 7PB
Tel: 0131 653 4100

National Childbirth Trust

NCT Centre – Edinburgh
University Health Service
5th floor
6 Bristo Square EH8 9AL
Tel: 668 3257
Tel: 0870 444-0907 (NCT Breastfeeding Line 8.00-22.00)

Please phone for new opening times.

Pupil Support Services Group

Education Department
City of Edinburgh Council
Wellington Crt
10 Waterloo Pl EH1 3EG
Tel: 469 3000.

Scottish Pre-school Play Association (SPPA)

14 Elliot Pl Glasgow
Tel: 0141 221 4148
At time of publication, there is no Lothian/East of Scotland office.

GAELIC MEDIUM GROUPS

At the time of writing, the established nursery class in Tollcross Primary School has been joined by two Gaelic playgroups (Croileagan), one in Corstorphine and one in Leith and some parent and toddler groups (Parant is Paisde). There is no requirement for parents to have any knowledge of Gaelic. For more information, contact Norma Martin on 469 3307.

POINTS TO CONSIDER

We have compiled our lists from questionnaires sent to groups registered with the Social Work Department, those sent to groups listed in the last edition of Edinburgh for Under Fives and information supplied by the authors and members of the National Childbirth Trust.
Contacts – these have been given where possible, but please bear in mind that contacts do change frequently, especially those of mother and toddler groups.

All groups which care for children under 8 for more than 2 hours without a parent or guardian in attendance are inspected and registered by the Social Work Department. This will not apply to baby and toddler groups, so it is advisable to check personally for the atmosphere and safety standards. In particular, check large outdoor equipment – like whether a climbing frame is on a safe surface such as woodchip, rubber matting or grass.

PARENT AND BABY GROUPS

These groups cater for parents and babies, and are generally held in health centres or in someone's home. Your health visitor, clinic or the National Childbirth Trust (Tel: 260 9201, Mon, Wed, Fri 9.30-11.30, Tue, Thu 14.00-17.00) will put you in touch with other parents in your area.

PARENT & TODDLER GROUPS

These groups are generally set up by local parents and are held in church halls, community centres, or schools, and cater for babies and toddlers. However, in this section, there are a few set up by the minister of the church in which they are held.
The carer (parent, guardian, nanny or childminder) stays with the child throughout the session. Some groups separate the babies and the toddlers by age and have specific days for specific age ranges.
Facilities and standards vary, but most have a selection of toys and puzzles, books, crayons and some larger pieces of equipment, such as climbing frames, chutes, play cookers, ball pits, Wendy houses etc. Princes range from nothing to approximately £5-7/term, with a small charge for tea, coffee, juice, biscuits and so on. There's usually a rota for making tea etc, and carers help set up and tidy away the toys. Where we know that outdoor play is available, this has been mentioned.
NB If you are looking for information on supportive groups, please also refer to Activities for Parents – Community Centres.

BALERNO

Balerno Toddlers

Balerno Parish Church Hall (Opposite Scotmid)
3 Johnsburn Road, Balerno
Contact: Maureen Harmer, Tel: 476 7851
or Sally Gartside, Tel: 449 3326
Mon, Thu 9.45- 11.15 (Not last Thu of the month)

St Mungo's Minis

St Mungo's Church, Ladycroft
Balerno
Contact: Andrea Brewster
Tel: 449 7030
Tue, Wed 10-11.30.

BRUNSTANE, MAGDALENE & JOPPA

Caring for Kids

Magdalen Community Centre
106b Magdalene Dr
Contact: Jacqui Cairney
Tel: 661 3109
Thu 10.00-12.00.. Part of Magdalene Sure Start project.

St Philip's Church
Brunstane Rd N
Contact: Anne Slorance
Tel: 653 0154
Fri 10.00-11.30.

BRUNTSFIELD

Barclay Bruntsfield Church Hall
Barclay Pl
Contact: Katherine Ellis
Tel: 228 4136
Tue 10.00-12.00.

CANONMILLS

Logie Green Hall
62 Logie Green Rd
Contact: Andrea Morris
Tel: 663 9562
Tue 10.00-11.30.

CARRICK KNOWE

Carrick Knowe Church
Jubilee Hall, situated to the left of the church
Saughton Rd N
Contact Christine Stewart
Tel: 334 2592
Thu, Fri 10.00-11.30.

CLERMISTON

Parkgrove Parent & Toddler Group
The Munro Centre
Parkgrove St
Tel: 539 7179
Thu 10.00-11.30.

St Kentigern's Church
24 Parkgrove Ave
Contact: Joanne Weir
Tel: 476 2323
Tue 10.00-11.30.

COLINTON

Colinton Toddler Group
St Cuthbert's Church Hall
Westgarth Ave
Contact: Janice Love
Tel: 441 9011
Mon 9.30-11.30

Stableroom Toddler Group
Colinton Parish Church Hall
Spylaw Bank Rd
Contact: Margaret Maxwell
Tel: 477 9494
Thu 9.30-11.30.

CORSTORPHINE

Corstorphine Gaelic Medium Mother and Toddler group
Corstorphine Youth and Community Centre
Kirk Loan, Corstorphine
Contact: Norma Martin, Early Years Gaelic Development Officer
Tel: 469 3307
Email: Norma.Martin@educ.edin.gov.uk
Mon 10.00-12.00. The group is open to any to join. Parents do not need to be Gaelic speakers. There is normally a playleader in place for language input.

Gylemuir Primary School
Wester Broom Pl
Contact: venue
Tel: 334 7138
Thu 10.00-11.30, 13.00-14.30.

Jack and Jill Mother and Toddler Club
St Anne's Church Hall
Kaimes Rd
Contact: Rosie Faith-Ryan
Tel: 334 1077
Wed 10.00-11.30.

St Ninian's Church Hall
St Ninian's Rd
Tue 10.00-11.30.
Contact: Maria Walker, Tel: 334 3885
Wed 13.00-14.30.
Contact: Julia Cormack, Tel: 334 4714
Fri 10.00-11.30.
Contact: Rosie Faith-Ryan, Tel: 334 1077

St Thomas Church
79 Glasgow Rd
Contact: Shirley Scott
Tel: 334 1305
Tue 10.00-11.30.

CRAIGLOCKHART

Craiglockhart Church Hall
Craiglockhart Dr N
Contact: Shirley Scott

Tel: 334 1305
Mon 10.00-11.45.

CRAIGMOUNT

Craigmount School
Craigs Rd
Contact: Community Education Office
Tel: 339 8278
Wed 13.45-15.15
Mon 13.45-15.15 (1st time mums only)

CRAMOND

Cramond Kirk Hall
Cramond Glebe Rd W
Contact: venue
Tue 10.00-11.30.

DALKEITH

Dalkeith Toy Library
Woodburn Community Centre
6 Woodburn Rd
Contact: Terri
Tel: 663 3958
Wed 9.30-11.00. 30p/week. See also *Toy Libraries*.

DALRY/GORGIE

Gorgie Memorial Hall
Gorgie Rd
Contact: Wendy Duffy
Tel: 337 9098 (9.00-12.00)
Childminders' group Tue 9.30-11.30. Parent and Toddler group Tue & Thu 13.00-15.00.

St Bride's Centre
Orwell Ter
Tel: 346 1405.
Fri 9.30-11.30. See also *Activities for Children*.

DAVIDSON'S MAINS

Davidson's Mains Parish Church
Quality St
Contact: Julie Brodie
Tel: 336 5385
Thu 9.15-11.15.

Holycross Mother & Toddler Group
Holycross Church Hall
Davidsons Mains
Contact: Juliet Pound
Tel: 336 3642
Birth to Nursery age, Mums, Dads, Grandparents and carers welcome. Call for further details.

EAST CRAIGS

East Craigs Playgroup
East Craigs Church Centre
Bughtlin Market
Contact: venue
Tel: 339 8336
Mother and Toddler groups: Tue 10.00-11.30, Thu 10.00-11.30. Childminders group Wed 10.00-11.30.

EASTER ROAD

Calton Centre
121 Montgomery St
Contact: venue
Tel: 661 5252
Tue, Thu 10.00-12.00.

FAIRMILEHEAD

Fairmilehead Parish Church
Frogston Rd W
Contact: Lynne Flood, Tel: 445 7033 or
Jennifer Saker, Tel: 445 1787
Mon, Tue, Thu, Fri 10.00-11.30.

GILMERTON

Gilmerton Community Centre
Contact: venue
Tel: 664 2335
Mon-Fri 9.15-11.15.

Inch Community Centre
255 Gilmerton Rd
Tel: 664 4710
Mon and Thu 9.30-11.30.
Other parent/carer groups may also be running. Contact venue for current information.

INVERLEITH

Mother and Toddler Group
Inverleith Church
Ferry Road
Contact: venue
Wed 9.30-12.00. Large, informal group. Home-baking, tea, cof-

fee, soft drink or water for children.

The Acorn Club
Inverleith Church
Ferry Rd
Contact: Fiona Coleman
Tel: 552 6945
Thu 9.45-11.15. Activities for 18+ mths.

Little Stars
Inverleith Parish Church Hall
Ferry Road
Contact: Nicola
Tel: 476 3324
Fri 9.30-11.00. Support, resource and playing group for children with special needs and their families and friends - entirely parent run and free of charge.

JUNIPER GREEN

Juniper Green Community Centre
Village Hall
Juniper Park Rd
Contact: venue
Tel: 453 4427
Mon 13.00-15.00.

KIRKLISTON

Kirkliston Community Education Centre
Queensferry Rd
Contact: Simon Toyne
Tel: 332 3855
Under 3s group Mon 9.00-12.00, 13.00-15.00. Wed 9.00-12.00.

Kirkliston Under 5s
Kirkliston Community Centre
Contact: Simon Toyne
Tel: 332 3855
Supportive Mother & Toddler group.

LEITH

Parent & Toddler Group
Fort Community Wing
North Fort St
Tel: 553 1074
Wed 9.30-11.30.

Leith Gaelic medium Mother and Toddler Group
Leith Community Centre
Newkirkgate, Leith
Contact: Norma Martin, Early Years Gaelic Development Officer
Tel: 469 3307
Email: Norma.Martin@educ.edin.gov.uk
Tue mornings 9.30-12.00. The group is open to any to join. Parents do not need to be Gaelic speakers. There is normally a playleader in place for language input.

LIBERTON

Liberton Kirk
Kirk Gate
Contact: Jackie Tait
Tel: 664 4205
Mon, Thu, Fri 9.30-11.30.

LOCHEND

Lochend YWCA
198 Restalrig Rd S
contact: venue
Tel: 554 3400
Carer & Toddler group, Fri 9.30-11.30. Toy Library Wed 13.00-14.30.

Ripple Project Parent and Toddler Group
St Margaret's Church Hall
Restalrig Rd S
Contact: Ripple Project
Tel: 554 0422
Tue, Fri 9.30-11.30.

Toddle-In Group
Pilrig Child and Family Centre
102 Pilrig St
Contact: Pat Southall
Tel: 554 3040
Tue 13.00-14.30.

Piershill Under-3 Project
New Restalrig Church
Willowbrae Rd
Contact: Jacqui Cairney
Tel: 661 3109
Wed, Fri 9.45-11.30. Part of Magdalene Sure Start project.

MARCHMONT

Marchmont St Giles Parish Church
Kilgraston Rd
Contact: venue
Tel: 447 4359
Thu 10.00-12.00.

St Catherine Argyle Church
61 Grange Rd
Contact venue

Tel: 667 7220
Tue 10.00-12.00.

MEADOWBANK

Holyrood Abbey Baby and Toddler Group
Dalziel Pl, London Rd
Contact: Fiona Maxwell
Tel: 446 9350
Mon 10.00-11.30.

MERCHISTON

Next Step Parent & Toddler Group
Rudolph Steiner School
60 Spylaw Rd
Contact: Helen Newton
Tel: 01506 872433
Mon-Fri 10.15-12.30. Baking, crafts, games.

MORNINGSIDE

Morningside Parish Church
Cluny Centre
Cluny Dr
Contact: venue
Tel: 447 6745
Mon, Thu 9.30-11.30.

Greenbank Church Baby and Toddler Group
Braidburn Ter
Contact: venue
Tel: 447 9969
Thu 9.45-11.30. Mothers, fathers, grandparents and carers welcome.

Morningside Baptist Church
Morningside Rd
Contact: venue
Tel: 447 9787
Thu 10.00-12.00; Fri Mother and Baby group 10.30-12.30.

The Old Schoolhouse
140 Morningside Rd
Contact: Adele Thomson
Tel: 445 5726
Thu 9.45-11.30.

MUIRHOUSE

Craigroyston Community Centre
1a Pennywell Rd
Contact Navenka Bonnar or Kerry Cunningham
Tel: 332 7360
Mon-Fri 9.30-11.15.

NEWINGTON

Duncan Street Baptist Church
Duncan St
Contact: no co-ordinator at time of writing. Contact via Duncan St Playgroup
(Lorraine Adam, Tel: 667 8097 (pm only))
Tue 10.00-12.00. Age 0-2 1/2 yrs.

NIDDRIE

Greengables Toddler Group
8a Niddrie House Gdns
contact: Kate Frame
Tel: 669 9083
Fri 9.30-11.30 (term time). See also Nursery Schools.

OLD TOWN

High School Yards Nursery
High School Yards EH1 1LZ
Contact: venue
Tel: 556 6536
Sure Start Parent & Toddler Group on Mondays 9 - 11.30am, for families with under 3s.
Sure Start Parent & Toddler Club on Wednesdays 9 - 11.30, for families with under 3s.

St Ann's Community Centre
6 South Gray's Close
Contact: venue
Tel: 557 0469
No group running from centre at time of writing, but contact venue for current details.

St. Columba's Free Church
Johnson Ter - entrance by hall door at Victoria Ter.
Contact: Catriona Lamont
Tel: 228 3782
Tue 9.30-11.30. No charge.

OXGANGS

Edinburgh Twins' Club's Bumps & Babies/Toddlers' Group
Oxgangs Neighbourhood Centre
Firrhill Dr, off Oxgangs Cres
Contact: Sue Cook
Tel: 01506 411 881
Tue 15.00-16.30; Thu 10.00-11.30. Only open to families with twins or more.

Pentland Community Education Centre
Oxgangs Brae
Tel: 445 5559
Fri 10.00-12.00. A self-supported group of parents/carers come together for crèche and a chat while children are able to play together in a safe and secure environment.

Oxgangs Sure Start Project
Pentland Community Education Centre
Oxgangs Brae
Contact: Sue Christie, Tel: 445 7690
A community-based project offering support and guidance for families and carers with children who are aged 0-3 yrs. Session days and times may vary: phone for up-to-date information.

Children's Activity Group
Pentland Community Education Centre
Oxgangs Brae
Contact: Heather Levy
Tel: 445 5559
For children with special needs/disabilities who live in Oxgangs and surrounding areas. Meets Friday afternoons 14.00-15.50. Offers a range of activities are available in safe surroundings. Meetings during school term-time only at the moment. Contact team leader for more information. Age range is 4-14, but group will welcome younger children. There is also a group on Wed 15.30-17.00, primarily for older children.

PILTON

Forthview Primary School
West Pilton Pl
Contact: Tracey Berry
Tel: 332 2468
Tue 9.30-11.00 (term time only) Mother and Toddler group. A Parents' Group also runs – please contact venue for current details of this. Both run by Educational home visitor who is teacher trained.

POLWARTH

Polwarth Parent, Baby and Toddler Group
Polwarth church Hall
Polwarth Terrace
Tue 10.00- 12.00, contact Heather Steel, Tel: 229 2760.
Thu 14.30-16.30, contact Alice Arthur, Tel: 337 8888.

PORTOBELLO

Portobello Old Parish Church
Bellfield St
Contact: Heather Gray
Tel: 669 7512
Tue 9.15-11.15.

PRESTONFIELD

Cameron House Community Centre
Cameron House Ave EH15 5LF
Contact: Susan Ferguson at venue
Tel: 667 3762
Fri 10.30-12.30.

RATHO

Ratho Community Centre
1 School Wynd
Contact venue
Tel: 333 1055
Tue, Thu 10.00-12.00.

ST LEONARDS

St Peter's 0-5s
St Peter's Church
Lutton Pl
Contact: venue
Tel: 667 9838
Mon, Thu 10.00-11.30.

SOUTH QUEENSFERRY

South Queensferry Community Centre
Rosebery Hall site
Rosebery Hall, High St
S Queensferry
Contact: venue
Tel: 331 2113
Parent& Toddlers – Mon 9.30-11.30; Wed 9.30-11.30. Childminders' group Thu 9.30-11.30.

STENHOUSE

Carrickvale Community Education Centre
Stenhouse St W
Edinburgh EH11 3EP
contact: venue
Tel: 443 6971
Thu, Fri 9.30-11.30.

STOCKBRIDGE/COMELY BANK

Comely Bank Toddlers
St Stephen's Comely Bank Church
10 Comely Bank Rd
Contact: Helen Bennett
Tel: 343 1892
Thu 9.30-11.30. 0-3 yrs.

International Playgroup
St. Stephen's Centre
Howe St
Contact: Jessica Miller
Tel: 558 1025
Mon & Fri 10:00-11:30 for babies and toddlers until 3 yrs.

St Ninian's Church Hall
Comely Bank Rd
Contact: venue
Tel: 315 3163
Tue, Thu 9.30-11.00.

TOLLCROSS

Tollcross Gaelic Medium Mother and Toddler Group
Tollcross Community Centre
Tollcross Primary School
117 Fountainbridge, Edinburgh
Contact: Norma Martin, Early Years Gaelic Development Officer
Tel: 469 3307
Email: Norma.Martin@educ.edin.gov.uk
Wed 9.00-11.30. The group is open to any to join. Parents do not need to be Gaelic speakers. There is normally a playleader in place for language input.

TRINITY

Trinity Toddler Group
Craighall Gdns
Contact: Gill McLaughlan
Tel: 551 4041
Mon-Fri 10.00-12.00; Mon, Wed, Thu 14.30-16.30; baby group Wed 10.30-12.00.

(see also Inverleith)

WEST END

St Mary's Episcopal Cathedral
Walpole Hall
Chester Street
Contact: Jane Tupper
Tel: 667 8978
Fri 9.45-11.30.

PLAYGROUPS

Most playgroups operate during school terms only; some groups have even shorter terms. The age range is usually 2½ or 3-5. Many groups run on a part-time basis, 2 or 3 sessions per week, but most are 5 days. Some require children to be potty trained.

Playgroups should be registered with The Scottish Commission for the Regulation of Care, which can provide lists of registered groups. If we have listed a playgroup in your area, please remember that an entry is not necessarily a recommendation. Safety standards should be checked personally.

The City of Edinburgh Council offers part-time pre-school education to all children in the year before they start primary school and to all 3 year olds from the term after their 3rd birthday. This can either be in a local authority nursery or a partner provider – which is usually a private nursery or community playgroup.

You register directly with the playgroup and may put your child's name on more than one waiting list. The nursery or playgroup you choose will not affect the primary class s/he goes into. We have tried to indicate wherever possible if the playgroups listed said that they receive funding for 3-5 year olds. There is often a waiting list for playgroups and it is advisable to put your child's name down as soon as possible, usually on their 2nd birthday.

You can obtain a list of all local authority childminders, playgroups, nurseries and partner providers from The Scottish Commission for the Regulation of Care, Tel: 653 4100.

Community playgroups receive a grant each year from the Social Work Department, to cover wages, rent, insurance, and fees. Term fees vary and many groups have fundraising events, at which parents are expected to participate. Groups are usually run by a committee of parents elected each year, and parents help regularly on a rota basis. Some groups charge extra if parents are unable to undertake rota duty, but childminders, nannies etc, can take their place.

Home playgroups are small groups – of between 6 and 20 children – which usually run in a playleader's home. Costs are normally higher than community playgroups, and can be compared with private nurseries. There is not normally a parental rota, although parents may be asked to help out on occasion. Most groups run for the school term, although some have a summer scheme during the long holidays.

Private playgroups do not receive a Social Work Department grant, so fees are usually higher than community playgroups. Some are run by a parents' committee and some need a rota of parent helpers.

There is a French playgroup (West End), and a 'Montessori Nursery School' (Murrayfield).

Groups are listed by area in alphabetical order.

BALERNO

The Village Playgroup
Community Centre, Main St
Contact: Alice Anderson (owner)
Tel: 451 5756
Private playgroup. 34 places am. Mornings 8.30-12.00. Ages 2-starting primary school. Open 50 weeks/year. Spacious indoors facility Contact playgroup for current fees. Also offers a lunch club provision 12.00-12.45 for a small additional fee.

Compass Playgroup
Deanpark Primary School
31 Marchbank Gardens
Balerno EH14 7ET
Contact: Mrs Jill Moody (playleader)
Tel: 449 4530
20 places. Mon-Thu 9.00-11.45. Ages 2&3 mainly. Grassy outdoor play area. Duty rota. Contact venue for current fees.

BLACKHALL

Blackhall Nursery
18 Keith Ter
Craigcrook Rd
Contact: Tina Woolnough
Tel: 337 3486
30 places am, 30 places pm, Mon-Fri 9.00-11.30 and 12.30-15.00. 3-5 yrs. Outdoor play. Free – all places are partner provider status.

Blackhall Playgroup
St Columba's Church
Hillhouse Rd
Contact: Jennifer Miller
Tel: 336 3667
25 places. Mon, Wed, Thu 9.30-12.00; Tue 13.00-15.30. Ages 2 1/2-5 yrs.

BROOMHALL

Broomhall Playgroup
Broomhall Scout Hall
81A Broomhall Ave
Contact: Linda Aitken
Tel: 0775 3148 765 (during playgroup's hours)
28 places. Mon-Fri 9.15-11.45. 2-5 yrs. £10/week. Duty rota.

BRUNTSFIELD

Bruntsfield Playgroup
Lower playground,
Bruntsfield Primary School
Contact: Fiona Anderson
Tel: 228 1526 (9.00-12.00)
Mon-Fri 9.00-11.45. In partnership with local authority, therefore all places funded from 3rd birthday. Nominal fee up to that age. Outdoor play area.

CALTON

Calton Playgroup
Calton Centre
Contact: venue and ask for play managers
Tel: 661 5252
20 places. Mon-Fri 9.15-11.45. Ages 2 1/2 – 5. £10/week. No outdoor play area, but does organise visits to parks etc.

CHURCH HILL

Holy Corner Community Playgroup
Christ Church
6 Morningside Rd
Contact: venue
Tel: 228 2768 (between 9-11.30)
24 places, Mon-Fri 9.15-11.45. 2 1/2 -5 yrs. £4/morning: partner provider with City of Edinburgh Council. Duty rota, outdoor play area.

CLERMISTON

Parkgrove Playgroup
The Munro Centre, Parkgrove St
Contact: playleaders at venue
Tel: 539 7179
24 places. Mon, Wed, Fri 9.15-11.30. 2 1/2 -4 yrs. £2/session. Outdoor play.

COLINTON

Cranley Nursery
Paties Road Pavilion, Katesmill Rd
Contact: Mrs McLean
Tel: 441 3804
Email: enquiries@ cranleynursery.co.uk
Web: www.cranleynursery.co.uk
25 places. Mon-Fri 8.00-18.00. Ages 2-5 yrs. In partnership with City of Edinburgh Council. Large, secure outdoor play area. Contact nursery for current fees.

Stableroom Playgroup
Colinton Parish Church
Spylaw Bank Rd
Contact: venue
Tel: 477 9494
16 places/session. Mon, Wed, Fri 9.15-11.45; Mon, Wed 12.30-14.30. Ages 2 1/2 -5 . Partner provider with City of Edinburgh Council. Duty Rota.

Colinton Mains Playgroup
Colinton Mains Community Centre
Firhill Loan
Contact venue
Tel: 441 6597
Sure Start group runs from venue. Call for current details.

CORSTORPHINE

Belgrave Playgroup
Belgrave Halls
34 Belgrave Rd
Contact: Jean Adams
Tel: 337 9426
24 places. Mon-Fri 9.30-12.00. Ages 2-4. £3/morning. Outdoor play.

Craigsbank Playgroup
Craigsbank Church Hall, Craigsbank
Contact: Mrs Greig
Tel: 539 1652
24 places. Tue-Fri 9.15-11.45. 2$^1/_2$ -5 yrs. Some outdoor play. Minimal fees – contact playgroup for current fees.

East Craigs Playgroup
East Craigs Church Centre, Bughtlin Mkt
Contact: Mrs Greig
Tel: 539 1652
24 places. Tue-Fri 9.15-11.45. 2$^1/_2$ -5 yrs. Some outdoor play. Small charge – contact playgroup for current fees.

Fox Covert Nursery
Fox Covert Primary School
Clerwood Ter
Contact: the playleaders (9.00-13.00)
Tel: 467 7294
40 places. Mon-Fri 9.00-11.40. 3-5 yrs. Partner Provider with City of Edinburgh Council. Outdoor play area. Duty rota.

Corstorphine Village Playgroup
Old Parish Church Hall
Corstorphine High St
Contact: playleaders (9.00-12.00)
Tel: 334 1258
24 places. Mon-Fri 9.15-11.45. Ages 2$^1/_2$ -5. Small daily fee. Fees payable/term. Heavily subscribed. Advise that child's name is put down from 1st birthday.

CRAIGENTINNY

Craigentinny/Lochend Social Centre Playgroup
Loaning Rd
Contact: venue
Tel: 661 8188
16 places. Mon-Fri 9.10-11.30. Ages 2$^1/_2$ -5. £9/week. Outdoor play area.

CRAIGLOCKHART

Craiglockhart Playgroup
Craiglockhart Church
Craiglockhart Dr N
Contact: Jacqueline Mitchell
Tel: 443 3272
21 places. Wed-Fri 9.15-11.45. 2$^1/_2$ -4 yrs. Duty rota.

CURRIE

Jubilee Playgroup
Youth Club, 280 Lanark Rd W
Contact: Joan Baillie
Tel: 538 5347
12 places. Mon-Fri 9.30-11.45. Ages 2 -5 yrs. Outdoor play. Small numbers – may be helpful for children who do not settle in larger playgroups.

DALRY

Nari Kallyan Shangho Project
Darroch Annexe
7 Gillespie St
Contact: project
Tel: 221 1915
Email: nks@nkshealth.co.uk
full-time childcare facility. 10 places. Mon-Fri 9.00-11.45, 12.15-15.00. 2-5 yrs. £3/session or £6/day. Small outdoor area.

St Martin's Playgroup
St Martin's Church, Murieston Cres
Contact: venue
Tel: 337 9714
20 places. Mon-Fri 9.30-11.45. Ages 2-5. Duty Rota. £8/week. Partner provider with City of Edinburgh Council.

DAVIDSON'S MAINS

Panda Playgroup
Davidson's Mains Parish Church Hall
Quality St
Contact: the playleader (Tue-Fri 9.30-11.30)
Tel: 312 6282
13 places Tue-Fri 9.15-11.45. 2 $^1/_2$-4yrs.

GOLDENACRE

Edzell Nursery Class
St James Church Hall
Inverleith Row

Contact: venue
Tel: 551 2179
3 yrs. 12 places. Mon, Wed, Fri 9.00-11.45. 4 yrs. 12 places. Mon-Fri 9.00-11.45. Outdoor play. In partnership with City Council.

St Serf's Playgroup
St Serf's Church Hall, Clark Rd
Contact: the playleaders
Tel: 467 7185
25 places. Mon-Fri 9.15-11.45. Ages 2 1/2 -5. In partnership with City of Edinburgh Council. Duty rota. Outdoor play area.

GILMERTON

Gilmerton Community Centre
4 Drum St
Gilmerton
Contact: venue
Tel: 664 2335
Paygroup runs Mon-Thu: contact centre for all current details or playgroup application form.

INCH

New Life Nursery
70 Dinmont Dve
Contact: Christine McPake
Tel: 666 1826
20 places. Mon-Fri 9.30-12.00, Mon-Thu 13.15-15.15. 2 1/2 -5 yrs. £2 per session. Outdoor play.

JUNIPER GREEN

Juniper Green Nursery Playgroup
Juniper Green Community Centre
Juniper Park Rd
Contact: Mrs Espin
Tel: 453 4427 w/days am
30 places. Mon-Fri 9.15-12.00. 2-5 yrs. Group accepts children in disposable nappies. Nappy changing facilities. Outdoor play.

KIRKLISTON

Kirkstyle Playgroup
Thomas Chalmers Church Centre, The Square
Correspondence add: 28 Kirklands Park Cres
Kirkliston W Lothian EH29 9EP
Contact: Mrs Goodall
Tel: 333 3725 or venue, 333 4088

24 places. Mon, Wed, Thu, Fri 9.15-11.45. 2-5 yrs. Outdoor play. Duty rota.

LEITH

Leith Academy Crèche
Leith Academy School
20 Academy Park EH6 8JO
Contact: Louise Davie
Tel: 554 0606
Accepts children 0-5yrs. Open Mon-Fri 8.15-16.15. Can be accessed by students participating in community education classes within the school or within the local area, and also by school students, staff and working parents. Offers activities and equipment incl. water and sand play, music and movement, and arts & crafts. Breastfeeding welcome.

LIBERTON

Liberton Northfield Playgroup
Liberton Northfield Church, Gilmerton Rd
Contact: Sonya Adelman
Tel: 664 1910
24 places. Tue, Thu, Fri 9.15-12.30. 2-5 yrs. Duty rota. Outdoor play. £2.50/morning. Registered charity.

MARCHMONT

Marchmont St Giles Playgroup
Marchmont St Giles Church Hall
1A Kilgraston Rd
Contact: Julia Melton
Tel: 445 2500
24 places. Tue-Thu 9.30-12.00. Ages 2 1/4-5. £12 per wk. Duty rota. Outdoor play.

MORNINGSIDE

Greenbank Preschool Playgroup
Greenbank Church Hall, Braidburn Ter
Contact: Church Office
Tel: 447 8068
25 places. Mon-Fri 9.00-11.45. 3-5 yrs. Outdoor play.

Nile Grove Community Playgroup
Morningside Parish Church
Braid Centre
1 Nile Grove
Contact: Enrolment Secretary
Tel: 447 9430
24 places. Mon-Fri 9.15-11.45. Ages 2 1/4 -5. Duty rota Outdoor play.

MUIRHOUSE

Craigroyston Project
Craigroyston Community Centre

1a Pennywell Rd
Contact: Christine Docherty
Tel: 332 7360 (venue)
16 places. Mon-Fri 9.15-11.15. Ages 2 1/2 -5 years. Outdoor play area.

MURRAYFIELD

Montessori Nursery School
Good Shepherd Church Hall, Murrayfield Ave
Contact: Mrs Park
Tel: 346 8921
24 places. Mon-Fri 8.45-12.30. 3-5 yrs. Outdoor Play. In partnership with City of Edinburgh Council.

NEW TOWN

Doune Terrace Playgroup
9c Doune Terrace
Tel: 225 3805
Contact venue for new details (finalised details unknown at time of writing)

St Mary's Playgroup
St Mary's Primary School
63 East London St
Contact: Gail Dempster
Tel: 556 1634
21 places. Mon-Fri 9.00-11.45. 2 1/2 -5 yrs. £1.75/session. Duty rota. Outdoor play.

NEWINGTON

Duncan Street Playgroup
Baptist Church Hall, Duncan St
Contact: Lorraine Adam
Tel: 667-8097 (pm only)
18 places. Mon-Fri 9.15-11.45. Part wk places available.
Ages 2 1/2 -5. In partnership with City of Edinburgh Council. Funded places available for over 3s, otherwise £3.75/morning. Outdoor play. Duty Rota.

PILTON

Funtime Playgroup
Royston Wardieburn Community Education Centre
Pilton Dr North
Contact: Frances Wallace or Lisa Rodgers
Tel: 552 5700 (between group's hours)
20 places. Mon-Fri 9.30-12.00. Ages 2 1/2 -5 – children must be toilet-trained. Outdoor play. Duta rota. £5/week.

The Prentice Centre Playgroup
The Prentice Centre, 1 Granton Mains Ave
Contact: Elizabeth Campbell
Tel: 552 0485
2 sessions of 10 places. Mon-Thu 9.00-11.30, 12.15-15.00. Ages 2-5 yrs (must be toilet trained). £1 annual membership for child: parent must also have membership £2/year. 50p/session (includes snack). Outdoor play. . Also bookable crèche on Fri, 9.15-11.45.

POLWARTH

Harrison Playgroup & Mother and Toddler Group
Phoenix Youth Club, Harrison Gardens
Contact: Fionnuala Munro
Tel: 3378832
28 places. Mon-Fri 9.30 -11.30 (term time only). Ages 2-5 yrs. Outdoor play. Please phone for current fees.

PORTOBELLO

Portobello Toddlers Hut
28 Beach Lane
Portobello
Contact: Karen Wilson
Tel: 669 6849
24 Places. Mon-Fri 9.00-11.30. 2 1/2-5 yrs. Outdoor play area. Duty rota.

St. James's Playgroup
Parish Church Hall, Rosefield Place
Contact: Mrs Peden
Tel: 669 6277
21 places. Mon, Tue, Thu 9.00-12.10, Fri 9.00-12.00. 2 1/2-5 yrs. Outdoor play. In partnership with City of Edinburgh Council. Contact for current fees.

SAUGHTON

Balgreen Playgroup
Balgreen Bowling Club
Paney Walk, Balgreen Rd
Contact: Alison or Lorraine
Tel: 313 50970
16 places. Mon-Fri 9.00-11.30. £3.50/day. Indoor soft play room. Outdoor play area in enclosed garden.

SOUTH QUEENSFERRY

Rosebery Playgroup (private playgroup)
Rosebery Hall, High St
S Queensferry
Contact: the playleaders
Tel: 331 2113

30 places. Mon-Fri 9.15-11.45. Ages $2^1/2$ -5 yrs. Outdoor play area. In partnership with City of Edinburgh Council. Contact playgroup for current fees.

TRINITY

Trinity Nursery
Wardie Church, Primrose Bank Rd
Contact: playleaders
Tel: 551 3847
20 places. Mon-Fri 9.00-12.00. 3-5 yrs. £6/session. Outdoor play. . In partnership with City Council.

WEST END

La Petite Ecole
James Gillespie's High School
Spottiswood Rd
Contact: Brigitte Guenier (president)
Tel:447 4247
or
Nathalie Bachelet, Tel: 668 3341

Tue 16.30-18.00. 3-11yrs. Group operates akin to a club. All teachers are French. Children must come from a household where at least one parent speaks French at home.

WILLOWBRAE

Northfield Playgroup
Northfield Community Centre, Northfield Rd
Contact: Brenda Devlin
Tel: 661 5723
30 places. Mon-Fri 9.15-11.45. Duty rota. Outdoor play. Partner provider. Contact venue for current fees.

PRIVATE NURSERIES

All private nurseries should be registered with the Care Commission, who can provide a list of registered groups (Tel: 653 4100). They update the list regularly and it is worth phoning them if you cannot find a suitable nursery in the required area. The Edinburgh Childcare Information Service can also help (Tel: 0800 0320 323, Web: www.childcarelink.gov.uk). Please remember that an entry is not necessarily a recommendation; facilities, type of care and safety standards must be checked personally.

If possible, get recommendations from other parents, then in order to get a realistic picture of a nursery drop in unannounced perhaps on more than one occasion at different times of the day. Visit several alternatives and take a list of questions to ask and points to consider. Ultimately the choice is a personal one but you might like to keep the following in mind:

Activities

How is the day structured? What are the children doing during your visit? What activities are available if it is a free play period? Are there lots of books in evidence? Do children have access to a TV, is a radio on during your visit – how do you feel about this? What trips and visits are provided?

Facilities

Does the nursery seem pleasant, spacious and light? Is it brightly decorated with children's paintings? Is there room for a variety of activities? Is there a peaceful room set aside for naps? Is there a garden or safe outdoor play area?

Feedback and Communication

What sort of report do parents receive at the end of the day (nappies, sleeps, meals, activities) – is this verbal or written? Is your child assigned a key worker with whom you can discuss daily matters and general progress? What opportunities do parents have to discuss their child's needs and other matters with the nursery staff and management?

Financial

Does the weekly charge include meals, milk and nappies? Are any free settling in sessions provided? Are there any discounts available for students, families on low incomes, companies and siblings?

Practicalities

Who is in charge of the nursery – are they in evidence during your visit? Are staff/child ratios being complied with? What is the staff turnover like? How long is the waiting list if any? Will they welcome expressed milk? If meals are provided, ask to see a week's menu. What provision is made for vegetarian children, or those with allergies etc, is fruit provided at snack time? The nurseries that accept real (non disposable) nappies are indicated with RN. Do you envisage your child using the nursery aged 3? If so is it (or applying to be) a partner provider?

Timetable

Do opening times fit in with your schedule? Are pick-up times flexible? Is there an after school club for older children? Is there parking available at busy times?

SECTION INFORMATION

Nurseries are listed by area: Central, North, South, East, West and alphabetically within area. Where a range of prices is given, the higher price usually refers to under 2s where the ratio of staff to children is high.

The following are referred to in the listings:

❖ These nurseries offer places for children under the age of 2. Places for the under 2s can be hard to find so try to register with the nursery as soon as possible, even before the baby is born.

⌘ Partner pre-school providers. Please note that this list is updated regularly: if in doubt refer to the Early Years Officer, Tel: 469 3438. The City of Edinburgh Council offers funded part time pre-school education to all children in the year before they start primary school and to all 3 year olds from the term after their 3rd birthday, see Nursery Education. This can be in either a local authority nursery or a partner provider – which is usually a private nursery or community playgroup. As soon as your child is 2 yrs you can put his/her name on the waiting list for the nursery or partner provider of your choice. You register directly with the nursery and may put your child's name down on more than one waiting list. The nursery you choose will not affect the primary class your child moves on to. If you wish additional hours and any other services including outwith term time, you will be charged for these. Each nursery will have arrangements about payment and you should discuss this with them before accepting a place. Nurseries selected under this scheme must meet HMI standards, have a qualified teacher and be prepared for HMI Inspections.

RN These nurseries accept children who ear real nappies.

SINA, the Scottish Independent Nurseries Association, was set up in 1991 to provide support and information for member nurseries. It aims to introduce a Code of Conduct to ensure that its members meet high standards of care, safety and play.
For general advice on choosing childcare and on childminders and nannies, see *Childcare*.

CENTRAL EDINBURGH

❖⌘ The Birrell Collection
17 Walker St EH3 7NE
Contact: Sally Tilley
Tel: 225 8031
32 places, Mon-Fri 8.15-18.00. 16mths-5yrs. under 2s £150/wk; over 2s £133/wk.
Part time available. Snacks provided. Outdoor play.

❖⌘ Careshare - Port Hamilton Nursery
69 Morrison St EH3 8BW
Contact: Lesley Brown
Tel: 228 1221
100 places, Mon-Fri 7.45-17.45. 0-5yrs. Fees on application. Nappies, snacks, lunch, suncream, birthday cake and christmas present included in fees. Investors In People award. Music & language lessons. Outdoor play.

❖Prime Time Nurseries Ltd
29 Queen St EH2 1JX
Contact: Linda Hunter
Tel: 226 7340
Email: info@primetimenursery.com
65 places for 0-5 yrs. 15 places for after-school club for 5-8yrs. Mon-Fri 7.30-18.00, 8.00-18.00 Sat. Part-time places available. Breakfast. morning snack, lunch, afternoon snack, tea can all be provided: all food is organic. Outdoor play, with safety surfacing and soft pl;ay equipment. Staff ratios as follows. 0-18mths 1:2; 18mths-3yrs 1:3: 3-5 yrs 1:4. Contact nursery for current fees.

❖⌘RN Oranges and Lemons Nursery
4 Forres St EH3 6BJ
Contact: Susan Handy
Tel: 226 5692
35 places, Mon-Fri 8.00-18.00. 3mths-5yrs. £14.15/session. Outdoor play/activities.

❖⌘ Red Apple Nursery School
4a Rutland Sq
Contact: Shona Watters
Tel: 229 8888
Fax: 229 9503
Email: rutland@brighthorizons.com
47 places, Mon-Fri 8.00-18.00. 3mths-5yrs. Under 2s £16.16/£15.44 per am/pm session. 2-3 yrs £14.18/£13.44 per am/pm session. Over 3s £16.07 per session up to 5 sessions attended, more than 5 sessions attended £13.34 per session. Snacks provided. Music, dance & French taught. Outdoor play.

❖ Royal Mile Nursery
Stamp Office Close
215 High St
Contact: Janice Davidson
Tel: 226 6574
20 places, Mon-Fri 8.00-18.00. 3mths-5yrs. £140-145/wk. Outdoor play.

⌘ Uni-Tots Nursery
University of Edinburgh
7 George Sq
Contact: Audrey Cameron
Tel: 650 3448
24 am places, 16 pm places. Mon-Fri 8.30-17.30. 2½-5yrs, morning session £10.35; lunch (12.00-13.00) £2.95; afternoon session £13.30. Part time available. Snacks provided. Large new outdoor play area.

NORTH EDINBURGH

❖⌘ Careshare - Newhaven Nursery
Next Generation Club
Newhaven Pl EH6 4TX
Contact: Mary Hammon
Tel: 467 4647
55 places, Mon-Fri 8.00-18.00. 0-5yrs. Fees on application. Nappies, snacks, lunch, suncream, birthday cake and Christmas present included in fees. Investors In People award. Outdoor play.

❖ Claremont Nursery
18 East Claremont St
Contact: Charlie Wardill
Tel: 477 4642
36 places, Mon-Fri. 6mths-5yrs. Outdoor play.

❖RN Crewe Road Nursery
122 Crewe Road South EH 4 2NY
Contact: Lorraine Suggitt
Tel: 332 8392
Email: crewerdnursery@tiscali.co.uk
46 places (22 under 3s), Mon-Fri 8.00-17.45. 3mths-5yrs, £22 per day, £100 per week, meals and snacks not included. Waiting list. Part time available. Outdoor play.

❖ Dolls House Nursery
9 Wardie Cres EH5 1AF
Tel: 552 9001
25 places, Mon-Fri 8.15-17.45. 0-5yrs. Outdoor play.

❖ Edinburgh Nursery Crèche
13 East London St
Contact: Clare Brown
Tel: 557 9014
18 places, Mon-Fri 8.00-17.45. 3mths-2yrs, £28.50 per day, £18-16.50 per am/pm session. Investor in People. SINA quality assured. Outdoor play.

also at:
71a Broughton St
Tel: 556 3373
9 places, Mon-Fri 8.00-17.45. 3mths-18mths. Investor in People. SINA quality assured. Outdoor play.

❖ Edinburgh Nursery
3 Beaverhall Rd EH7 4JQ
Tel: 556 9252
31 places, Mon-Fri 8.00-17.45. 18mths-3yrs, under 2s £28.50 per day, £16.50-18.00 per half day. Investor in People. SINA quality assured. Home cooked lunches. All weather outdoor play.

Edinburgh Nursery School
129 Broughton Rd EH7 4JH
Tel: 557 5675
20 places, Mon-Fri 8.00-17.45. 2-5yrs £28.50 per day, £16.50 per half session. Breakfast, home cooked lunch and afternoon tea included. Investor in People. SINA quality assured. Outdoor play.

⌘ Edinburgh Telford College Nursery
Crewe Toll
Tel: 315 7476
40 places, Mon-Fri 8.30-16.30. 2-5yrs. Outdoor play.

❖⌘RN Forbes Children's Nursery
12 Claremont Park
Leith Links EH6 7PT
50 places, Mon-Fri 8.00-18.00, under 2s £141.20 per wk; over 2s £128.40 per wk; 3-5 £106.31 per wk. Discount on 2nd child on 5 sessions or more. Lunch, snacks, nappies and formula milk provided. Large outdoor play area.

❖⌘ Greater Pilton Childcare Centre
18b Ferry Rd Ave EH4 4BL
Contact: Allison McDonald
Tel: 332 8001
Mon-Fri 8.00-18.00. 0-5yrs, £90 per wk (open 50wks/yr). Part time available. Lunches and snacks provided. Outdoor play.

❖⌘ Headstart Nursery School
16 Queen Charlotte St, Leith
Contact: Chris Slater
Tel: 555 0700
59 places, Mon-Fri 8.00-18.00. 3mths-5yrs, £13.75-£15 per session; £27.50-£30 per day. Outdoor play.

❖ Heriothill Nursery
32-34 Heriothill Ter
Contact: Charlie Wardill
Tel: 557 9907
100 places, 0-5yrs. Outdoor play.

❖⌘ Inverleith Town Nursery
90 Inverleith Pl EH3 5PA
Contact: Mark Loughton
Tel: 552 4143
30 places, Mon-Fri 8.00-6.00. 0-5yrs. Outdoor play.

❖⌘ Kinderquest Victoria Quay
The Scottish Executive
Victoria Quay EH6 6QQ
Contact: Beth Pearce
Tel: 244 0782

36 places, Mon-Fri 7.30-18.30. 0-5yrs, cost on application. Scottish Executive employees only. Outdoor play, access to gym hall for pre-school room.

❖ Little VIPs
2 Windsor Pl, Portobello EH15 2AA
Tel: 669 5040
54 places, Mon-Fri 8.00-18.00. 3mths-5yrs, £13.50 per session. Outdoor play.

❖⌘RN New Town Nursery
12 Dean Ter EH4 1ND
Contact: Seona Fleming
Tel: 332 5920
55 places, Mon-Fri 8.15-17.45. 3mths-5yrs, £14-£15 per session. Fully qualified staff. Outdoor play.

St Columba's Hospice Nursery
Challenger Lodge
15 Boswall Rd EH5 3RW
Tel: 551 1381, Ext 169
Contact: Brenda Ward
10 places, Mon-Fri 8.30-15.00. 2 1/2-5yrs, £2.50 per hr. All NNEB qualified staff. Outdoor play.

❖ Summerside Kindergarden
1 Summerside St EH6 4NT
Tel: 554 6560
Contact: Carol-Anne McLeod
19 places, Mon-Fri 8.00-18.00. 0-5yrs, £130 per wk; £26 per day. Outdoor play.

❖RN Trinity Tots Crèche
15 Hawthornvale EH6 4JQ
Contact: Lynda McKenzie
Tel: 552 6152
15 places, Mon-Fri 8.00-17.45. 3mths-2yrs, £14 per session ; £140 per wk full time. Lunch provided. Outdoor play.

⌘RN Trinity Tots Nursery
9 Granton Rd EH5 5QJ
Contact: Linda Kane
Tel: 551 3020
26 places, Mon-Fri 8.00-18.00. 2-5yrs, £13 per session; £520 per mth full time. Meals provided. Outdoor play.

SOUTH EDINBURGH

⌘RN The Busy Bees Nursery
20 Valleyfield St
Tel: 229 7889
13 places, Mon-Fri 8.15-17.45. 2-5yrs, £13 per session. Bilingual nursery (French speaking staff). Part time available. Outdoor play in garden.

❖RN Child's Play
8 Falcon Road EH10 4AH
Contact: Niki Thomson
Tel: 447 0077
Email: childsplaynursery@btconnect.com
47 places, Mon-Fri 8.00-18.00. 0-5yrs. No waiting list. £15-16 per session, £26-29 per day, £130-140 per week, home cooked lunches and 2 snacks per day included. Child must be potty trained by 3 yrs. Outdoor play.

❖⌘RN The City Nursery
47 Greenbank Dr
Contact: Julie Henderson
Tel: 446 0088
55 places, Mon-Fri 7.30-18.00. 3mths-5yrs: under 2s £31.10 per day; over 2s £29.70 per day; discount on full time/2nd place taken. Lunch included with am sessions. New, purpose-built building, large outdoor play area.

❖⌘RN Colinton Private Nursery
22 Dreghorn Loan
Contact: Marion Towers
Tel: 477 7330
59 places, Mon-Fri 8.00-18.00. 3mths-5yrs, £26.50-£28.60 per day. Outdoor play.

❖⌘RN The Corner House Day Nursery
2 Spylaw Rd
Contact: Jacqueline Drinkwater
Tel: 229 1500
64 places, Mon-Fri 8.00-18.00. 3mths-5yrs, £27.50-£31.50 per day; £130.60-£149.60 per wk. Part time available. Meals provided. Outdoor play.

❖⌘RN First Class Nursery
1b Drum St EH17 8QQ
Contact: Elizabeth Coyle
Tel: 664 5376
Email: info@firstclassnurseries.com
39 places, Mon-Fri 8.00-18.00. 0-5yrs. Part time available. Snacks provided. Outdoor play.

❖⌘RN Forbes Children's Nursery
5 Forbes Rd EH10 4EF
Tel: 229 5511
25 places, Mon-Fri 8.00-18.00. 0-2s £147.20 per wk; 2-3s £136.85 per wk; 3-5s £114.67 per wk, discount on second child on 5 sessions or more. Lunch, snacks, nappies and formula milk provided. Large outdoor play area.

⌘ Grange Private Nursery
180 Grange Loan
Contact: Stacey Gilchrist
Tel: 667 9547
20 places am & pm, Mon-Fri 8.00-18.00, 2-5yrs, £12.50 per session. French spoken daily. Outdoor play.

⌘ Headstart Nursery School
64-66 Morningside Dr
Contact: Chris Slater
Tel: 447 4778
40 places, Mon-Fri 8.00-18.00. 2-5yrs, £13.75 per session; £27.50 per day.

❖⌘RN The Hermitage Day Nursery
2 Hermitage Ter
Contact: Mary Cumming
Tel: 447 5202
29 places, Mon-Fri 8.00-18.00. 0-5yrs, under 2s £13.80 per session, £27.60 per day, £127 per wk; over 2s £12 per session, £24 per day; £108 per wk. Snacks provided. Own transport. CCTV in all playrooms. Music club. Swimming lessons in term time. Outdoor play.

❖⌘RN Kath's Kindergarten
14 & 27 Angle Park Ter
Contact: Kath Stewart
Tel: 337 7793 or 337 4157
33 places, Mon-Fri 8.00-17.30. 3mths-5yrs, £125 per wk; £3.25 per hour. Outdoor play.

❖⌘RN Little Monkeys
28 Kilmaurs Road
Contact: Grace Kerr
Tel: 667 5544
Email: info@little-monkeys.net
44 places, Mon-Fri 7.00-19.00, Sat 9.00-17.00. 3mths-5yrs 0-2 £28.50 per day, 2-5 £27.50 per day. Part time available. Meals provided. Soft top playground and climbing frames.

❖⌘ Meadows Nursery
5 Millerfield Place
Contact: J Jamieson
Tel: 667 5316
35 places, Mon-Fri 8.30-17.30. 3mths-5yrs, £27 per day; £121 per wk. Part time available. Snacks provided. Outdoor play.

❖⌘RN Mother Goose Nursery
6 Ferniehill Rd EH17 7AB
Contact: Manager
Tel: 664 3276
32 places, Mon-Fri 8.00-18.00. 0-5yrs, £12-£13 per session. After school care. Part time, breakfast club and holiday care available. Drop off/collection from school. Outdoor play.

❖⌘RN Mother Goose Nursery - 2
3 Spence St, EH16 5AG
Tel: 668 2722
Contact: Manager
46 places, Mon-Fri 8.00-18.00. 0-5yrs, £12-£13 per session. After school care. Breakfast club and holiday care available. Drop off/collection from school. Outdoor play.

❖RN Playdays Kindergarten
17 East Suffolk Rd
Contact: Ashira
Tel: 662 0010
27 places, Mon-Fri 8.00-18.00. 0-5yrs, under 2 £110 per wk, over 2 £95 per wk, part time available, lunch provided for over 2s. Outdoor play. Unrestricted parking.

❖ Royal Hospital for Sick Children Nursery
11 Millerfield Pl
Tel: 536 0682
Contact: Rosie Allanson
21 places. 0-5yrs.

❖ Small World Nurseries
1 Claverhouse Dr
Contact: Patricia Stefanovic
Tel: 664 3434
40 places, Mon-Fri 8.00-18.00. 0-5yrs, under 2s £25 per day, over 2s £23 per day. Part time available.
Cooked meals provided. Outdoor play. Extra curricular classes for 2-5 yrs.

❖RN Scallywags Children's Nursery
62 Longstone Rd EH14 2BA
Contact: Rhona Adams
Tel: 443 2002
Email: rhona-adams3@hotmail.com
45 places, Mon-Fri 8.00-18.00. £26.50-£28.50 per day. Part time available. Breakfast, lunch, snacks, nappies and wipes included. Outdoor play.

❖ Stepping Stones Nursery
1 Chalmers Crescent EH9 1TW
Contact: Carolyn Bennett
Tel: 662 0364
Also:
21A Millerfield Place EH9 1LW
Tel: 668 4249
15 places, Mon-Fri 7.00-18.00. £4 per hour. Snacks provided. Outdoor play

❖RN Strawberry Hill Nursery
13 Minto St EH9 1RG
Contact: Pamela Ellis
Tel: 668 3300
59 places, 7.45-18.00. 0-2yrs £26 per day; £130 per wk; 2+ £24 per day, £120 per wk. Home made meals and snacks, milk provided. Large garden with grass and playtop rubber surfacing, climbing frame, outdoor toys. Car park.

❖RN Tick Tock Nursery
10 Lasswade Rd EH16 6R2
Contact: Barbara Lord
Tel: 658 1279
42 places, Mon-Fri, 0-5yrs.

EAST EDINBURGH

❖RN Bus Stop Nursery
17 Bridge Street
Musselburgh EH21 6AA
Contact: Catherine Malcolm
Tel: 653 2714
43 places, Mon-Fri 8.00-18.00. 0-8yrs. £3 per hour, £25 per day, £125 per week, snacks included. Outdoor play.

❖⌘RN Butterflies Nursery
11-15 Stoneybank Ter
Musselburgh
Tel: 665 5353
Contact: Jane Bergin
120 places, Mon-Fri 8.00-18.00. 0-8yrs, £22.75-£24.50 per day. Lunch provided. Outdoor play. After school club available.

❖⌘RN Elsie's Red Apple Nursery
1 Waverley Pk
Spring Gdns, Abbeyhill
Tel: 661 8551
Email: elsies@brighthorizons.com
Contact: Fiona McDonald
62 places, Mon-Fri 8.00-18.00. 0-5yrs, under 2s £12.80 per session; 2-3yrs £12.07 per session; over 3s £13.93 per session for up to 5 sessions attended, more than 5 sessions attended £12.07 per session, £130 per wk; £3.70 extra hr. Music, dance & French taught. Snacks provided. Outdoor play.

❖RN Hamilton House Nursery
7 Brunstane Road North
Portobello EH15 2DL
Contact: Jennifer
Tel: 669 1067
60 places. Mon-Fri 8.00-18.00. 0-5yrs. Waiting list. £14.25-15.25 per session, meals and snacks included. Outdoor play.

❖⌘RN Links Nursery
8 Balcarres Rd
Musselburgh
Contact: Jennifer Shearer
Tel: 665 0008
59 places, Mon-Fri 7.30-18.00. 3mths-5yrs, under 2s £29.50 per day; over 2s £27.50 per day.

❖⌘RN Little Acorns Nursery School
1c Duddingston Pk
Contact: Frances Kay
Tel: 669 0405 or 699 0706
100 places, Mon-Fri 8.00-17.30. 3mths-5yrs, £135-£140 per wk. French & music taught. Outdoor play.

⌘RN Mr Squirrel's Nursery School & Wraparound Day Care
27 Cargil Ter
Tel: 552 0499
Outdoor play.

❖⌘RN The Pelican Nursery
225/227 North High St
Musselburgh
Contact: Sharon Thomson or Jennifer Condie
Tel: 653 6882
51 places, Mon-Fri 8.00-18.00. 0-5yrs, £12.50-£13.50 per session. HMI inspected. Outdoor play.

❖⌘ Rocking Horse Nursery
60a Duddingston Rd
Contact: Fiona Schulte
Tel: 669 0819
29 places, Mon-Fri 7.45-18.00. 3mths-5yrs. After school club 5-8yrs with qualified staff. Outdoor play.

❖⌘RN Seabeach Nursery
27 Straiton Pl
Portobello
Contact: Jeanne Macmillan
Tel: 657 3249
25 places, Mon-Fri 8.00-18.00. 0-5yrs. Outdoor play.

WEST EDINBURGH

❖RN Asquith Court
c/o David Lloyd Health Club
Glasgow Road, EH12 8LH
Contact: Claire Barr
Tel: 334 8055
50 places, Mon-Fri. 3mths-5yrs. £33 per day approx. Part time places available. Morning snack, 2 course lunch and snack tea

provided. Outdoor play area with childsafe surface, climbing frame and cars/bikes.

❖⌘ Barnton Nursery
534 Queensferry Rd
Contact: Alison Bruce
Tel: 339 6340
61 places, Mon-Fri 7.30-18.30. 3mths-5yrs, £12.50 per session. Outdoor play.

Careshare - Lochside, Beechwood and Hillview Nurseries
1 Lochside Pl, Edinburgh Pk EH12 9DF
Contact: Sheila Haddow
Tel: 339 1245

❖RN Lochside
Contact: Lynsey Hutchinson
44 places. Accepts ages 0-2 yrs

Beechwood
Contact: Fiona Fairley
41 places
Accepts ages 2 1/2 -5 years

⌘Hillview
Contact: Sarah
57 places. Mon-Fri 7.45-17.45. 2 1/2 -5 years. Fees on application. Fees include nappies, snacks, lunch, suncream, birthday cake and Christmas present. Investors in People award. HMI Inspected. Music & language lessons. Outdoor play.

❖⌘RN Crewe Road Nursery
Fet-Lor Youth Centre
122 Crewe Rd
Tel: 332 8392
Contact: Lorraine Suggitt
22 places, 0-3yrs; 24 places 3-5yrs, Mon-Fri 8.00-17.45. £11 per session; £100 per wk; concessions for students and single parents. Outdoor play.

❖⌘RN Croilegan Nursery
6A Featherhall Ave
Tel: 334 2960
Contact: Christine Sinclair or Catherine Groat
15 places 0-2yrs; 40 places 2-5yrs, Mon-Fri 8.00-17.45. Full day and full time places. Qualified staff. Outdoor play area with safety matting.

❖⌘RN Darmel House Kindergarten
13 Osborne Ter EH12 5HG
Contact: Kay Brown
Tel: 337 6171
Email: kayjbrown@aol.com
49 places, Mon-Fri 8.00-18.00. 3mths-preschool. Part time available. Meals and snacks provided. Outdoor play.

❖ The Gyle Nursery
Gyle Shopping Centre
Contact: Karen Fairlamb
Tel: 539 7099
40 places, Mon-Fri 7.30-18.00. 0-5yrs, full day £28.50 or £16.50-£18 per session. Purpose built nursery. Outdoor play. SINA quality assured. Investors in People.

❖⌘RN Jigsaw Nursery
5 Main St
Balerno
Contact: Sue Ingham
Tel: 449 4516
36 places, Mon-Fri 8.00-18.00. 0-5yrs, under 2s £27 per day; over 2s £25.50 per day. All weather impact absorbing play surface.

❖RN Jigsaw Babies
32 Main St
Balerno
Contact: Sue Ingham
Tel: 624 4517 or 449 4516
12 places, Mon-Fri 8.00-18.00, 0-2yrs, £27 per day. Small homely nursery. Individual routines adhered to. Separate sleep room. Soft play room.

⌘ Juniper Green Private Nursery
8 Woodhall Dr
Contact: Moira McLean
Tel: 458 3003
30 places, Mon-Fri 8.00-18.00. 2-5yrs, £12.50 per session or £120 per wk. Outdoor play.

❖⌘ Kinderquest Nursery (East Craigs)
SASA, 78 Craigs Rd EH12 8NH
Contact: Romana Taddei
Tel: 244 8948
Email: eastcraigs@brighthorizons.com
15 places, Mon-Fri 7.30-18.30. 15wks-5yrs, cost on application. Scottish Executive employees only. Outdoor play.

❖⌘RN Little Flyers Nursery
4a Ingliston Rd
Newbridge
Contact: Karen Murray
Tel: 335 3679
21 places, Mon-Fri 8.00-18.00. 0-5yrs, under 2s £26 per day, over 2s £25 per day.

Part time available. Snacks provided. Outdoor play.

❖⌘ Murrayfield Nursery
52 Saughton Cres
Contact: Maxine
Tel: 346 4459
Mon-Fri 8.00-18.00. 6wks-5yrs. Specialise in full time care only. Home cooked lunches. Outdoor play.

❖⌘RN Nippers Nursery
Scotstoun Ave
South Queensferry
Contact: Donna Sneddon
Tel: 331 7635
42 places, Mon-Fri 7.30-17.30. 3mths-5yrs, £27.50 per day. Part time (£24.50) may be available. Lunch provided for 2yrs+. Outdoor play.

❖⌘RN Orchard Nursery
Royal Victoria Hospital
13 Craigleith Rd EH4 2DN
Tel: 343 6617
Contact: V Henderson
56 places, Mon-Fri 7.00-18.30. 3mths-5yrs, under 2s £14.00 per session/£26.50 per day/£130.50 per wk; over 2s £13 per session/£25 per day/£122.50 per wk. Snacks provided. Large garden and play area. SINA quality assured. Investors in People.

❖⌘RN Peek-a-Boo Nursery School
12 Pargrove Loan
Contact Sally-Anne Peek
Tel: 339 9161
41 places, 8.00-18.00. 3mths-5yrs, under 2s £30 per day; over 2s £28 per day. Part time available, waiting list for babies approx 6mths. Snacks provided. French, kid club, large secure garden for outdoor play.

❖RN Pinocchio's Nursery @ Heriot Watt University
Riccarton Campus EH14 4AS
Contact: Kimberley Milton
Tel: 451 5236
55 places, Mon-Fri 8.00-18.00. 3mths-5yrs, from £130.50 per wk. Part time available. All meals provided, cooked by qualified chef. Nappies, wipes cream provided. Outdoor play. Open to the public.

❖⌘RN Playhouse Nursery
20a Old Kirk Rd
Contact: Karen Brown
Tel: 334 5859
15 places, Mon-Fri 8.00-17.45. 3mths-5yrs, under 2s £138 per wk; over 2s £125 per wk.

❖⌘ Red Apple Nursery School
11 Ardmillan Terrace EH11 2JW
Contact: Debbie McKay
Tel: 337 5940
Fax: 346 4767
Email: ardmillan@brighthorizons.com
22 places, Mon-Fri 8.00-18.00. 3 mths-5 yrs. under 2s £13.10 per session. 2 - 3 years £12.07 per session. Over 3s £13.93 per session, more than 5 sessions attended £12.07 per session. Snacks provided. Music, dance & French taught. Outdoor play.

NURSERY EDUCATION IN EDINBURGH

The City of Edinburgh has 17 nursery schools, 1 under 5s centre and nursery classes based in 81 primary schools for children aged 3-5 yrs. Children are entitled to a free, part-time place, 5 mornings or afternoons during school term, in a council nursery the term after their 3rd birthday. Some schools and classes offer the option to buy additional hours while some offer wrap-around care, before and after school.

There are no catchment area restrictions for nursery schools or classes. This means you can send your child to any nursery in the city if places are available. There may be a long waiting list for your nursery of choice and you should put your child's name down as soon as possible after their 2nd birthday. At some schools you may be more likely to get a place if you require an afternoon session – check with the school when you fill in the application form. Your child does not need to subsequently attend the primary school to which the nursery school is attached. Children with special needs are integrated in all nursery classes. Parents are encouraged to participate in activities but there is no duty rota.

In addition to places in their own nursery schools and classes, there are also 112 partner provider centres which include private, workplace and community-run nurseries and playgroups, as well as independent schools. Partner providers, through the Education Department, receive Scottish Executive grants towards the cost of places for 3-5 year olds. This allows them to reduce their fees to parents. For details of these providers, see *Playgroups* and *Private Nurseries* in this section.

To find out more about the services available contact the Early Years Section of your local education department:

City of Edinburgh Council Education Department
Wellington Court
10 Waterloo Place
Edinburgh EH31 3EG
Tel: 469 3421

East Lothian Council, Education and Community Services
John Muir House
Haddington
Tel: 01620 827631

Mid Lothian Council
Education Department
Fairfield House
8 Lothian Rd
Dalkeith EH22 3ZG
Tel: 271 3703

Below is a list of nursery schools and primary schools with nursery provision.

NURSERY SCHOOLS

EAST LOTHIAN

Levenhall
Moir Pl
Musselburgh EH21 8JD
Tel: 655 7599

North Berwick
Law Rd
Tel: 01620 8930782

Prestonpans
Kirk St
Tel: 01875 811440

Tranent
Sanderson's Wynd
Tel: 01875 610 899

EDINBURGH

Balgreen
175 Balgreen Rd EH11 3AT
Tel: 337 1454

Calderglen
220 Wester Hailes Rd EH11 4NG
Tel: 453 5754

Cameron House
Cameron House Ave EH16 5LF
Tel: 667 5117

Children's House
30 Wauchope Ter EH16 4NU
Tel: 661 1401
Fax: 661 1401

Cowgate Under 5's - Centre
172 High Street
7 Assembly Close EH1 1QX
Tel: 225 7251

Grassmarket
11/15 The Vennel
Grassmarket EH1 2HU
Tel: 229 6540
Fax: 228 5129

Greengables
8a Niddrie House Gdns EH16 4UF
Tel: 669 9083
Fax: 669 0566

High School Yards
High School Yards EH1 1LZ
Tel: 556 6536
Fax: 558 8407
Full & part-time (morning) places.
Breakfast Club (8.00-9.00) and After School Club (15.00-17.30).
Holiday provision throughout school holidays & in service days. (8.00-17.30 Mon-Fri)

Hope Cottage
Cowan's Close
East Crosscauseway EH8 9HF
Tel: 667 5795

Kirkliston
Queensferry Rd Kirkliston EH29 9AQ
Tel: 333 2336

Liberton
Mount Vernon Rd EH16 6JQ
Tel: 664 3155

Lochrin
8 West Tollcross EH3 9QN
Tel: 229 7743
40 place nursery, part-time with a few full-time places. The head teacher is available on Thu from 9.00-15.30.

Princess Elizabeth
14 Clearburn Cres EH16 5ER
Tel: 667 0946

St Leonard's
North Richmond Street EH8 9SY
Tel: 667 4674
Fax: 668 1378

Stanwell
Junction Pl Leith EH6 5JA
Tel: 554 1309
Web: www.stanwell.edin.sch.uk
Part-time & full- time places.

The Spinney Lane
13a The Spinney EH17 7LD
Tel: 664 9102
Fax: 664 9102
Email: headteacher@spinneylane.edin.sch.uk

Tynecastle
15 McLeod St EH11 2NJ
Tel: 337 5461

Westfield Court
Alexander Dr EH11 2RJ
Tel: 337 4914
Mainstream nursery with provision for 8 special needs places.

NURSERY CLASSES IN PRIMARY SCHOOLS

EAST LOTHIAN

Campie
3 Stoneyhill Farm Rd
Musselburgh EH21 6QS
Tel: 665 2045

Direlton
North Berwick EH39 5HE
Tel: 01620 850 267

Dunbar
Lammermuir Cres
Dunbar EH42 1DG
Tel: 01368 863 773

East Linton
School Rd
East Linton EH40 3AJ
Tel: 01620 860 216

Elphinstone
School Sq
Elphinstone
Tranent EH33 2LX
Tel: 01875 610 358

Gullane
Muirfield Ter
Gullane EH31 2HL
Tel: 01620 843 455

Haddington
Haddington Infant
Victoria Rd
Haddington EH41 4DJ
Tel: 01620 823 271

Innerwick
Kirk Brae
Innerwick
Dunbar EH41 1SD
Tel: 01368 840 227

Longniddry
Kitchener Cres
Longniddry EH32 0LR
Tel: 01875 853 161

Loretto RC
20 Newbigging
Musselburgh EH21 7AH
Tel: 665 2572

Musselburgh
Kilwinning Pl
Musselburgh EH21 7EF
Tel: 665 3407

Ormiston
Meadowbank
Tranent EH35 5LQ
Tel: 01875 610 382

Pencaitland
The Glebe
Pencaitland
Tranent EH34 5EZ
Tel: 01875 340 260

St Martin's RC
High St
Tranent EH33 1HJ
Tel: 01875 610211

St Mary's RC
Tynebank Rd
Haddington EH41 4DN
Tel: 01620 823 298

Saltoun
East Saltoun
Pencaitland

Tranent EH34 5DY
Tel: 01875 340318

Stoneyhill
Off Clayknowes Way
Musselburgh EH21 6UL
Tel: 665 3119

Wallyford
39 Salters Rd
Wallyford
Musselburgh EH21 8LE
Tel: 665 2865

West Barns
Forth View, West Barns
Dunbar EH42 1TZ
Tel: 01368 863209

Whitecraig
44a Whitecraig Cres Whitecraig
Musselburgh EH21 8NG
Tel: 665 3278

Yester
Walden Ter
Gifford
Haddington EH41 4QP
Tel: 01620 810435

EDINBURGH

Abbeyhill
Abbey St EH7 5SJ
Tel: 661 3054
Fax: 478 7067

Bonaly
1 Bonaly Grove
Edinburgh EH13 0QD
Tel: 441 7211
Fax: 477 7046

Bonnington
139b Bonnington Rd EH6 5NQ
Tel: 554 1370
Fax: 554 6632

Broomhouse
Saughton Rd EH11 3RQ
Tel: 443 3783
Fax: 444 0446
Full-time and part-time places.

Broughton
132 Broughton Rd EH7 4LD
Tel: 556 7028
Fax: 556 7001

Brunstane
106 Magdalene Dr EH15 3BE
Tel: 669 4498
Fax: 669 7457

Buckstone
79 Buckstone Loan East EH10 6UY
Tel: 445 4545
Fax: 445 7709
Web: www.buckstone.edin.sch.uk

Burdiehouse
1 Burdiehouse Cres EH17 8EX
Tel: 664 2351

Carrick Knowe
Lampacre Rd EH12 7HU
Tel: 334 4505
Fax: 467 7923

Castleview
2D Greendykes Rd EH16 4DP
Tel: 661 6429

Clermiston
18 Parkgrove Pl EH4 7NP
Tel: 336 3361
Fax: 538 7251

Clovenstone
54 Clovenstone Pk EH14 3EY
Tel: 453 4242
Fax: 453 2598
Web: www.clovenstone.edin.sch.uk

Colinton
Redford Pl EH13 OAL
Tel: 441 1946
Fax: 441 4861
Web: www.colinton.edin.sch.uk

Corstorphine
62 Corstorphine High St EH12 7SY
Tel: 334 3865
Fax: 538 7274
Web: www.corstorphine.edin.sch.uk

Craigentinny
4 Loganlea Dr EH7 6LR
Tel: 661 2749
Fax: 467 7212

Craigour Park
Moredun Park Rd EH17 7HL

Tel: 664 7594
Fax: 672 1063

Craigroyston
Muirhouse Place West EH4 4PX
Tel: 343 6465
Fax: 343 2766

Cramond
4 Cramond Cres EH4 6PG
Tel: 312 6450
Fax: 312 8710

Curriehill
210 Lanark Rd W EH14 5NN
Tel: 449 3359
Fax: 476 7019

Dalry
Dalry Rd EH11 2JB
Tel: 337 6086
Fax: 337 3798
Morning, afternoon & full day places. A breakfast and after school club operates within the school and will accommodate pre-school children (4+ yrs) as well.

Davidson's Mains
Corbiehill Rd EH4 5DZ
Tel: 336 1184
Fax: 467 7784
Web: www.davidsonsmains.edin.sch.uk

Dean Park
31 Marchbank Gdns
Balerno EH14 7ET
Tel: 449 4529
Fax: 449 5990

Drumbrae
Ardshiel Ave EH4 7HP
Tel: 339 5071

Duddingston
70a Duddingston Rd EH15 1SW
Tel: 669 5092
Fax: 669 4224

Dumbryden
Dumbryden Gdns EH14 2NZ
Tel: 453 5686
Fax: 339 2512

East Craigs
79 Craigmount Brae EH12 8XF
Tel: 339 7115
Fax: 538 7276

Ferryhill
Groathill Rd N EH4 2SQ
Tel: 538 7382
Fax: 538 7381

Flora Stevenson
175 Comely Bank EH4 1 BG
Tel: 332 1604
Fax: 343 6310

Fort
25 North Fort St EH6 4HF
Tel: 467 7131
Fax: 467 7139

Forthview
West Pilton Pl EH4 4DF
Tel: 336 2468
Fax: 332 2201

Gracemount
Lasswade Rd EH16 6UA
Tel: 664 2331
Fax: 621 7029
30 am and 30 pm places.

Granton
55 Boswall Parkway EH5 2DA
Tel: 552 3987
Tel: 467 7045 (Direct Line)

Gylemuir
10 Wester Broom Pl EH12 7RT
Tel: 334 7138
Tel: 334 6742 (Direct Line)
Fax: 334 5148
Web: www.gylemuir.edin.sch.uk
2 rooms, dolphin & starfish, each with a morning class 9.00-11.30 and an afternoon class 12.30-15.00. The premises are new purpose-built classes which opened Easter 2000.

Hailesland
4 Hailesland Pl EH14 2SL
Tel: 442 3894
Fax: 458 5750

Hermitage Park
Hermitage Pk EH6 8HD
Tel: 554 2952
Fax: 538 7280
Web: www.hermitagepark.edin.sch.uk

Hillwood
Station Rd Ratho Station EH28 8PT
Tel: 333 1210
Fax: 333 1210

Holy Cross RC
Craighall Rd EH6 4RE
Tel: 552 1972
Fax: 478 7033

Hunter's Tryst
Oxgangs Green EH13 9JE
Tel: 445 1510
Fax: 445 7710

James Gillespie's
Whitehouse Loan EH9 1BD
Tel: 447 1014
Web: www.jamesgillespies-ps.edin.sch.uk

Juniper Green
Nursery Department
1 Woodhall Ter EH14 5BS
Tel: 467 7984
Fax: 467 7980

Leith
St Andrew's Pl EH6 7EG
Tel: 554 4844
Fax: 467 7988

Leith Walk
9 Brunswick Rd EH7 5NG
Tel: 556 3873
Fax: 556 6524

Liberton
229 Gilmerton Rd EH16 5UD
Tel: 664 2337
Fax: 666 0599
Web: www.liberton-ps.edin.sch.uk

Lismore
1 Bingham Ave EH15 3HZ
Tel: 669 4588
Fax: 6572970

Longstone
Redhall Gr EH14 2DU
Tel: 443 4743
Fax: 443 5297
Web: www.longstone.edin.sch.uk

Lorne
Lorne St EH6 8QS
Tel: 554 2308
Fax: 0131 467 7228
Web: www.lorne.edin.sch.uk

Murrayburn
Sighthill Loan EH11 4NP
Tel: 453 5339
Fax: 442 1709
Web: www.murrayburn.edin.sch.uk

Newcraighall
Whitehill St Newcraighall EH21 8QZ
Tel: 669 3598
Fax: 657 4134

Niddrie Mill
267 Niddrie Mains Rd EH15 3HG
Tel: 468 7025
Fax: 468 7027

Orwell
17 Orwell Pl EH11 2AD
Tel: 337 6181
Fax: 337 6626

Oxgangs
43 Colinton Mains Dr EH13 9AE
Tel: 441 3649
Fax: 441 9838
Web: www.oxgangs.edin.sch.uk

Parson's Green
60 Meadowfield Dr EH8 7LU
Tel: 661 4459
Fax: 661 6405

Pirniehall
West Pilton Cres EH4 4EP
Tel: 332 5256
Fax: 538 7093

Prestonfield
Peffermill Rd EH16 5LJ
Tel: 667 1336
Fax: 662 0813

Ratho
1 School Wynd
Ratho EH28 8TT
Tel: 333 1293
Fax: 333 2847

Roseburn
64 Roseburn St EH12 5PL
Tel: 337 6096
Fax: 0131 476 7810
Web: www.roseburn.edin.sch.uk

Royal High
61 Northfield Broadway EH8 7RX
Tel: 669 3200
Fax: 669 1552
Web: www.royalhigh-ps.edin.sch.uk

Royal Mile
86 Canongate EH8 8BZ
Tel: 556 3347
Fax: 557 9186
Web: www.royalmile.edin.sch.uk

Royston
123 Boswall Parkway EH5 2JH
Tel: 552 4534
Fax: 538 7321

St Catherine's RC
30 Gracemount Dr EH16 6RN
Tel: 664 4257
Fax: 672 2919

St David's RC
West Pilton Cres EH4 4EP
Tel: 332 3500
Fax: 332 6085

St Francis' RC
15 Niddrie Mains Rd EH16 4DS
Tel: 621 6600
Fax: 621 6603
Web: www.stfrancis.edin.sch.uk

St John's RC
Hamilton Ter EH15 1NB
Tel: 669 1363
Fax: 657 3122
Web: www.stjohns.edin.sch.uk

St John Vianney RC
17 Ivanhoe Cres EH16 6AU
Tel: 664 1742
Fax: 672 2854

St Joseph's RC
Saughton Road EH11 3RQ
Tel: 443 4591
Fax: 444 2802

St Mark's RC
63 Firrhill Cres EH13 9EE
Tel: 441 2948
Fax: 441 7601

St Mary's RC (Leith)
30 Links Gardens EH6 7JG
Tel: 554 7291
Fax: 554 8523

St Ninian's RC
150 Restalrig Rd S EH7 6JA
Tel: 661 3431
Fax: 652 1458

St Peter's RC
25 Falcon Gdns EH10 4AP
Tel: 447 5742
Fax: 447 8226

Sighthill
1 Calder Park EH11 4NF
Tel: 453 2464
Fax: 442 2842

South Morningside
116 Comiston Rd EH10 5QN
Tel: 447 5446
Fax: 446 9839
Web: www.southmorningside.edin.sch.uk

Stenhouse
4 Saughton Mains St EH11 3HH
Tel: 443 1255
Fax: 467 7792
Web: www.stenhouse.edin.sch.uk

Stockbridge
Hamilton Pl EH3 5BA
Tel: 332 6109
Fax: 333 6109
Web: www.stockbridge.edin.sch.uk

Tollcross
117 Fountainbridge EH3 9QG
Tel: 229 7828
Fax: 229 5838

Towerbank
Figgate Bank EH15 1HX
Tel: 669 1551
Fax: 657 3907

Westburn
55 Sighthill Rd EH11 4PB
Tel: 442 2997
Fax: 453 6859

SOUTH QUEENSFERRY

Dalmeny
Carlowrie Cres
S Queensferry EH30 9TZ
Tel: 331 1447
Fax: 331 1447
Email: admin@dalmeny.edin.sch.uk
Web: www.dalmeny.edin.sch.uk
20 am & 20 pm places. Playpark and listed nature reserve adjacent to school. Mini assault course for nursery pupils.

Echline

Bo'ness Rd
S Queensferry EH30 9XJ
Tel: 331 3397
Fax: 319 2385

Queensferry

Burgess Rd
S Queensferry EH30 9NX
Tel: 331 1349
Fax: 331 5771
Web: www.queensferry-ps.edin.sch.uk

INDEPENDENT SCHOOLS

The independent schools in Edinburgh with nursery departments are listed below with fees for 2003/04. Most offer the choice of a morning, afternoon or whole day placement. The Scottish Council of Independent Schools (SCIS) will send you a free booklet containing basic information about all the Independent Schools in Scotland. Contact them at:

Scottish Council of Independent Schools

21 Melville St
Edinburgh EH3 7PE
Tel: 220 2106
Fax: 225 8594
Web: www.scis.org.uk

Cargilfield School

37 Barnton Ave W EH4 6HU
Tel: 336 2207
Email: secretary@cargilfield.edin.sch.uk
Web: www.cargilfield.edin.sch.uk
Co-educational nursery from 3 yrs. Mornings £800/term, afternoon sessions optional. Before and after school clubs also available.

Clifton Hall School

Newbridge EH28 8LQ
Tel: 333 1359
Co-educational. Full day, 8.30-15.15, £1325 including lunch. Minimum 5 mornings £655.

The Compass School
West Rd
Haddington EH41 3RD
Tel: 01620 822642
Co-educational nursery from 3 1/2 yrs. £1005-£1375/term.

Edinburgh Academy Nursery
The Edinburgh Academy Junior School
10 Arboretum Rd EH3 5PL
Tel: 552 3690
Email: Juniorschool@j.s.edinburghacademy.org.uk
Web: www.edinburghacademy.org.uk
Co-educational nursery. £750-£1239/term. Full and Part-time places for 3-5 year olds. Part-time places for 2-3 year olds. Care available before and after nursery.

George Heriot's School
Lauriston Pl
EH3 9EQ
Tel: 229 7263
Web: www.george-heriots.com
Co-educational. £2952 (morning), £4494 (full day) annually.

George Watson's College
Colinton Rd EH10 5EG
Tel: 447 7931
Web: www.gwc.org.uk
Co-educational. £2754 (am), £2058(pm), £4818 (full day) annually.

The Mary Erskine and Stewart's Melville Junior School
Queensferry Rd EH4 3EZ
Tel: 331 1111
Fax: 331 1199
Email: jssecretary@esmgc.com
Web: www.mesmjuniorschool.edin.sch.uk
Co-educational. £4962/session or approx £3465 including local authority preschool grant.

The Edinburgh Rudolf Steiner School (Kindergarten)
60 Spylaw Rd
EH10 5BR
Tel: 337 3410
Web:www.SteinerWeb.org.uk

Co-educational. £646 per term. Afternoon care until 15.15pm Registered with local authority for Partnership Funding. Children start kindergarten at the age of 3 1/2 and stay until they are 6. The emphasis is on play and on learning by doing. The school's aim is to facilitate the development of physical, as well as social skills and to nourish a healthy emotional life and a rich imagination. Artistic and creative activities take the place of formal learning, which does not begin until the children enter the main school at the age of 6.

St George's School Early Years Department

Garscube Ter EH12 6BG

Co-educational nursery. £575-£1440 /term. Little Nursery (2-3yrs), Mon -Fri 9.00-12.00 or 13.00-15.00; Early Years (3-5 yrs), 8.30-15.00. Pre-school care 8.00-8.30; after school care until 18.00.

St Margaret's School

East Suffolk Rd EH16 5PJ
Tel: 668 1986
Web:www.stmargaretsschool.net

Care and education from 3mths-5 yrs. Early morning & after school care and holiday club available.

LOOKING FORWARD TO STARTING SCHOOL

There is only one entry date for children starting primary school in Scotland, and that is August. Children starting P1 in August must have either celebrated their 5th birthday in the preceding 6 months (from 1 March onwards) or are due to celebrate their 5th birthday in the following 6 months (birth dates up to 28 February). You should contact the Education Department if you have just arrived from England or Wales, where the admission ages differ.

Parents can choose not to send their child to primary school until the session after their child's 5th birthday. Children with birthdays in January & February have the right to deferred entry and a free pre-school education place for any extra year. Children with birthdays after the start of the autumn term to 31st December also have the right to delay the start to school but the allocation of a free pre-school place is not automatic and is at the discretion of the education department. If you are concerned about your child's entry into school speak with the staff at your child's nursery in the first instance.

To enrol your child at the school in your catchment area, tele phone the Head Teacher and arrange an appointment. If you wish to send your child to a school outside your catchment area, your application will be considered, provided there is a place available. You must apply for a place at a non-district school between November and 15 March for the following August. However, registration is normally dealt with in early December. A form for this purpose may be obtained from the school or nursery or from Pupil Support Services at the education department. You must also inform the Head Teacher of your catchment school that you have applied to a school outwith their area.

A list of all primary schools may be obtained by contacting Pupil Support Services at the education department. A prospectus should be available from the school.

If you feel that your child may benefit from attending a special school contact Pupil Support Services.

For details of school uniform stockists, see *Shopping – Children's Clothes*.

Rainy Days

The saying 'always put something by for a rainy day' suddenly takes on a whole new meaning when you have to entertain boisterous or restive youngsters. We've included some ideas which might help fill 10 mins here or 40 mins there – or hopefully even more.

Why not start a collection of toilet roll/ kitchen roll tubes, yoghurt pots, shiny paper (sweet wrappers, gift wrap etc), lolly sticks (cleaned up or bought from craft sections of larger stationers or art shops), cereal boxes and so on? You can make trains, robots, rockets, monsters, fairy tale castles – anything your under 5 wants to!

MESSY STUFF

Make a Snowman

Snowmen are popular in our house all year round. You need a toilet roll tube (or a cut-to-size kitchen roll tube), cotton wool balls, glue and some other oddments. Cover the tube with the cotton wool balls, then decorate it. Either use sticky label dots for eyes, buttons etc, or use some dots made from card or paper and a paper-punch. Decorating a colourful paper scarf with crayons, stars etc extends this pastime.

Pasta

I'm still trying to work out whether pasta is more popular as a play thing or a food stuff with my daughter. You can stick it down in collages or string it to make necklaces. Under 5s don't seem to care about painting it but if you do have tricolore and don't mind sacrificing it, you can have instant colour.

Play Dough Recipe

1 cup flour
1/2 cup salt
2 teaspoons cream of tartar
1 cup water
2 teaspoons of oil

Heat the oil in a saucepan. Add other ingredients and cook for 3 minutes stirring constantly. Drop the ball of dough in waxed paper till cool
enough to handle. Knead the dough, separate into portions and add food colouring if desired. Will stay soft if kept in fridge in a polythene
bag.

Tray/Table Art

Shaving foam (as cheap as you like)
In homage to Tony Hart – or if you're too young to remember him, Art Attack. Spray the foam over a melamine or plastic tray or over a table top and make messy patterns. If you cover the top with cling film first, there should be less mess!

Printing

Potatoes, carrots, onions, old sponges etc etc
Paper
Paints
You'll need something to squeeze the paint on to or into – paper plates, empty margarine tubs etc. Cut the stampers into shapes (they don't have to be fancy). Stand back and let your under 5 at it (cover the tables, floor etc with newspaper or splashsheet before they commence!).

FOOD

Cress Heads

(best for older under 5s)
You need cress seeds, a cleaned out egg shell, cotton wool and some water. You'll also need an egg cup and some card to go round it, or a piece of card rolled into a tube, which will hold the egg shell.
The egg shell can be decorated as a monster, person, animal – anything your under 5 wants, ditto with the card which forms the body of said character. Fill the egg shell with dampened cotton wool, place in a dark, warm place and it should sprout within 5 or 6 days. The cress then makes the 'hair' of the character drawn on the shell.
Alternatively, patterns, letters or names can be created by cress seeds on some dampened kitchen towel set on a plate or lid. Place in a dark, warm place. The cress will sprout into shapes, names etc – which you can bring out a week later when the activity has been forgotten about, cut it and eat on sandwiches

Chocolate Crispies

100g chocolate
50g butter
4 tablespoons syrup
75-100g corn flakes or crispies – you might need more dependent on the brand and type of cereal
Cake cases
Decorations – cherries, chocolate chips, angelica – anything you or your under 5 fancy or have to hand

This should be enough for about 10-12, but it all depends on the type of chocolate and cereal used.
Melt chocolate, butter and syrup in a pan on a low heat. Remove from heat and stir in the corn flakes or crispies. Children can help with this part onwards – drop some mixture into each case. Decorate any way you want. Chill in fridge. Eat.

Funky Toast
Make some toast. Cut out various shapes with cookie cutters (time is usually spent choosing the cutters). Spread with whatever you like. Eat.

Tea Biscuit Decoration
Raid the kitchen cupboards for hundreds and thousands, chocolate vermicelli, sugar flowers, sweeties etc. Make up some water icing. The biscuits get iced and then get decorated. And – perhaps – eaten.

Keeping a favourite character cake mix in the cupboard can also be popular on wet days. Bob the Builder, Tweenies etc have baking merchandise.

NOISY STUFF

Music Shakers
Put some dried pulses in a yoghurt pot or into a toilet roll tube with one end sealed with paper or card. Cover the open end. Shake vigorously (and probably repetitively). Older children might like to decorate their instrument: every little thing that adds to the experience can get your under 5 past the critical boredom threshhold and back into a better mood!

Bubblewrap
If you get a parcel etc with a sheet of the large-sized bubble wrap, keep it. Bring it out, lay it on the floor and have a manic 5-10 mins stomping about on it. The bigger the bubbles, the noisier the 'pop'. Why not play your favourite music at the same time?

GOING OUT

Soft plays are a popular choice (though bear in mind that many other parents will have the same idea), as is the Royal Museum on Chambers Street. Check the *Activities for Children* and *Places to Visit* chapters for more ideas, both indoor and outdoors.

Or get your wellies on, find the biggest puddles you can and jump right in!

NOTES

Shopping

INTRODUCTION

Shopping when pregnant or with small children requires a completely different approach from shopping you may have been used to. Browsing at leisure can become a distant memory, you have to discover good sources of maternity, baby and children's equipment and clothing, and you may also find that planning, timing, and toilet stops become of the utmost importance – for you and your child.

In this section, we've tried to give some ideas where to shop for yourself and your children's needs, plus information for planning a less stressful shopping experience (why not check out *Eating Out* too). As with any expedition, planning is the key and knowing the easiest entrance and department locations can lessen some of the hassle.

Feeding and changing rooms are now considered a standard requirement in large department stores and shopping centres. They are available to male and female carers, although if you encounter a combined feeding/changing room, and you are male, it might be prudent to ask an assistant to check the room: some breastfeeding mothers may feel uncomfortable with a male stranger sharing the facility. Some stores have anticipated this, and have secondary rooms for male carers. These rooms should be separate from customer toilets, but it is an advantage to be near toilets, especially if you have an older child with you. The standard of parent and baby rooms in the centre of Edinburgh is generally high, but should you find them lacking in facilities, or not clean, it is worth mentioning this to a manager or supervisor (some rooms have a comments book), as it is only through such information that store managers are aware of customer requirements.

Urgent toilet stops for expectant mums and young children can be a great problem when shopping. Our research is done by questionnaire, and if an entry indicates that use of a staff toilet is permitted, we have included the information – and if you find opposition, mention that fact. See also *Toilet Stops* and *Eating Out* sections.

USEFUL INFORMATION

- Most city centre shops have late night shopping on Thursday. Some stores use Tuesday and Wednesday mornings for staff training and open at 9.30.
- Tuesday or Wednesday is usually half-day closing in the outlying areas.
- Many stores open later and longer in the summer or during the Festival.
- Many city centre shops have Sunday trading hours (usually opening at 11.00 or mid-day). Sunday trading in suburban areas is almost standard practice.

SECTION CONTENTS

- Key information on chemists, crèches, department stores, malls and supermarkets.
- Clothes and shoes, baby and children's wear, make-your-own, maternity and second-hand clothes.
- Specialist shops – books, bikes, hairdressers, nursery equipment, photography and toys.
- Shopping from home, incl. nappy services
- Hiring

We have used 'baby' to describe clothes for under 2s and 'children's' for over 2s.

Where we have listed shops with several branches, the description generally refers to the flagship or main stores, and you may find that smaller branches do not have the same choice of goods: if you know what you're looking for, why not phone ahead for confirmation.

CHEMISTS WITH EXTENDED OPENING HOURS

The Lothian Health Board Primary Care Division, 555 Gorgie Rd, Tel: 537 8423, keep a list of chemists and operate a rota to provide pharmaceutical services outside normal shopping hrs. There is also an Emergency Prescription Dispensing Service. This operates through local police stations: if you have a prescription that has been marked 'Urgent' by your doctor you should call at, or phone, your local police station who will advise you how to contact a chemists participating in the scheme. With regards to holiday opening hours, it's always worthwhile checking with your local chemist if you have one. It can save time and worry to know which chemists are going to be open when.

OPEN AFTER 18.00

Boots the Chemist

Cameron Toll Centre
6 Lady Rd
Tel: 666 1111

Late closing: Thu, Fri 20.00

98 Craigentinny Rd
Tel: 661 2523
Late closing: Mon-Fri 19.00

Craigleith Retail Park
Tel: 332 6114
Mon-Fri 9.00-20.00, Sat 9.00-18.00; Sun 10.30-17.30

Gyle Shopping Centre
Tel: 317 1288
Late closing: Mon-Wed, Fri 20.00; Thu 21.00; Sat 19.00

207-209 Morningside Rd
Tel: 447 6188
Late closing: Mon-Fri 19.00

101-103 Princes St
Tel: 225 8331
Late closing: Thu 19.30

48 Shandwick Pl
Tel: 225 6757
Late closing: Mon-Fri 21.00; Sat 19.00

St James' Centre
Tel: 556 1062
Late closing: Thu 19.00

E. Moss
Asda Wal-Mart
The Jewel
Edinburgh EH15 3AR
Tel: 669 3550
Late closing: Mon-Fri 21.00; Sat 20.00

Safeway Pharmacy
1 Bughtlin Mkt
Maybury Craigs
Tel: 339 1188
Late closing: Mon-Fri 20.00

38 Comely Bank Rd
Tel: 332 5573
Late closing: Mon-Fri 20.00

Southside Pharmacy
79 Nicolson St
Tel: 667 4032
Late closing: Mon-Fri 19.00

OPEN SUNDAY

Boots the Chemist

Cameron Toll Centre
6 Lady Rd
Tel: 666 1111
Sunday opening: 11.00-17.00

Craigleith Retail Park
Tel: 332 6114
Sunday opening: 10.30-17.30

48 Shandwick Pl
Tel: 225 6757
Sunday opening: 10.00-17.00

E. Moss
Asda Wal-Mart
The Jewel
Edinburgh EH15 3AR
Tel: 669 3550
Sunday opening: 9.00-18.00

Safeway Pharmacy
1 Bughtlin Mkt
Maybury Craigs
Tel: 339 1188
Sunday opening: 9.00-18.00

38 Comely Bank Rd
Tel: 332 5573
Sunday opening: 10.00-14.00

Southside Pharmacy
79 Nicolson St
Tel: 667 4032
Sunday opening: 12.00-17.00

CRÈCHES WHILE SHOPPING

Edinburgh has an all-year-round crèche at The Gyle Shopping Centre. In addition, there are sometimes 'one-off' crèche facilities provided for particular annual events, dependent of availability of funds and an appropriate venue. These include the Edinburgh Book Festival, Edinburgh International Festival and Festival Fringe. See *Annual Events*.

The Edinburgh Crèche Co-op

297 Easter Rd EH6 8LH
Contact: Pam or Brenda
Tel: 553 2116

The Edinburgh Crèche Co-op is Lothian's leading flexible childcare provider and is a Registered Workers Co-operative, specialising in delivering flexible, professional childcare services including: setting up and running crèche facilities, training, consultancy and staff cover. Anything from weddings to after school care.

The Gyle Nursery

Gyle Avenue
South Gyle Broadway
Tel: 539 7099
Opening times: Mon-Fri 7.30-18.00

Purpose-built full day nursery within the Gyle Shopping Centre. Quality assured nursery, grant-assisted places on offer for 3 and 4 year olds.

IKEA Crèche

Straiton Rd
Loanhead, Midlothian
Opening times: Mon-Fri 9.00-20.00 (last entry 19.15); Sat-Sun 10.00-18.00 (last entry 17.15)

Located at the entrance. Available to children aged 3-7 yrs old. Parents or carers can shop for an hour (1/2 hr for last entries) while the qualified staff supervise children's play in the play area. As well as a huge ball-pool, there is a wide range of play equipment, including paint, drawing materials, musical play and a reading corner.
See under *Department Stores*, also *Nursery Equipment* and *Toys*.

DEPARTMENT STORES

Due to High St competition and legal requirements regarding access, as well as any sense of customer care, large shops are increasingly family and child friendly. Automatic doors, lifts, and in-store nappy changing facilities are just some of the things which have become of the expected contents of department stores, as has the presence of a café or restaurant which has high chairs, may offer a bottle and a baby food warming service, and recognises the requirements of people with young children.
Some other things don't change: large stores do alter their layout fairly often, so always check information against a store guide. If you have something to return, ask as soon as you enter the store for the correct procedure: you may be directed to a Customer Service Desk, which may save you a trek to the wrong department.

Aitken and Niven

77-79 George St
Tel: 225 1461
Web: www.aitken-niven.co.uk
Opening times: Mon-Sat 9.00-17.30

Access: two entrances from George St, both with a few steps up. Left to menswear, right to shoe dept.
A well-established, traditional, quality shop in a prestigious location in George St. A fitting room can be set aside for feeding and nappy changing.
Ground floor: see 'Shoes'
1st: see 'School Wear'
Toilets

Also at:
6 Falcon Rd W
Morningside
Tel: 477 3922
Opening times: Mon-Sat 9.00-17.30

Access: street-level entrance.
Shop stocks schoolwear, sportswear and children's shoes.
Nappy changing facilities. Toilet.

Argos

11-15 North Bridge EH1 1SB
Tel: 558 1474

52 Kinnaird Park
Newcraighall Rd EH15 3RD
Tel: 657 3574

Unit 7
Craigleith Retail Park
S Groathill Rd
Tel: 332 3762

Easy shopping. Stores carry a range of home goods. Stores also have clothing catalogues. All catalogues free to take away and choose purchases at leisure. Some items on display in-store.
Fill in catalogue no. on a slip and hand it to the cashier: goods are collected from the stockroom for you. You have 16 days to return goods if not satisfied. Argos also offers a ring and reserve service, if you have a catalogue at home and want to check that your store has what you want before you make the journey. Good value. Argos also has a home-shopping website,

www.argos.co.uk. See also 'Bicycles', 'Nursery Equipment' and 'Toy Shops'.

BhS

64 Princes St EH2 2DJ
Tel: 226 2621
Opening times: Mon-Wed 9.00-17.30; Thu 9.00-20.00; Fri/Sat 9.00-18.00; Sun 12.00-17.00

Access: good from Princes St, with central escalators giving access to all floors. Small lift halfway along left hand side. From Rose St through restaurant, escalator down to Ground Floor.
Basement: children's clothes – have ranges for ages 2-6 and 6-13 yrs: these tend to follow fashion colours and trends. Home department stocks special children's bedding range, with accessories in various bright colours and character ranges. Night lights too.
Rose St Restaurant - see *Eating Out*
Feeding and changing room, toilets: on 1st Floor, upstairs from restaurant. No lift access. Toilet for the disabled on restaurant level.

Also at:
Cameron Toll Shopping Centre
6 Lady Road EH16 5PB
658 1154

Ocean Terminal
Ocean Drive EH3 6DZ
Tel. 555 3284

Boots the Chemist

101 Princes St
Tel: 225 8331
Opening times: Mon-Sat 9.00-18.00; Thu 9.00-19.30; Sun 12.00-17.00

Access: two automatic doors. Public lift and escalator, both on the left hand side of the store. Staff lift available for double pushchairs.
Store has wide, clear aisles, although the ground floor can be very busy at lunchtime, due to sandwich and snack sales.
Ground floor: personal care, beauty, dispensing chemist. Mother and Baby Room at rear of floor. No access for double pushchairs. Bottle warmer, wipes, nappies etc usually available. Men are welcome to use this room, but should ask first, in case a mother is feeding.
1st floor: baby toiletries, baby food. Nappy collection service available. Babitens to hire. Baby consultant available for advice. Also stocks toys, photographic dept.
2nd floor: dentistry and chiropody.

Also at:
Gyle Shopping Centre
Tel: 317 1288
Opening times: Mon-Wed 9.00-20.00; Thu 9.00-21.00; Sat 9.00-18.00; Sun 10.00-18.00

Store all on one level. Baby equipment, located towards the back of the store, but no clothing. Demonstrations of Babitens, which are available to hire. Nappy collection service. Store is near the centre's main entrance, which provides ease of parking for large purchases i.e. bulk buying of nappies. Staff toilet is available. No nappy-changing facility in-store, but store does sponsor Gyle's Mother's Room.

Craigleith Retail Park
Tel: 332 6114
Opening times: Mon-Fri 9.00-20.00; Sat 9.00-18.00; Sun 10.30-17.30

Access: automatic doors. Parent and child parking directly outside (2 bays).
Store all on one level. Toilets with nappy changing facilities, including emergency supplies of nappies, on the left as you enter the store. Good range of baby accessories , toys and clothing are situated towards the rear of the unit. Also beauty, personal grooming, photographic developing and chemists.
NB: this store now has a dispensing pharmacy.

Fort Retail Park
Tel: 669 4428
Store all on one level. Good range of baby accessories , toys and clothing are situated towards the rear of the unit. Also beauty, personal grooming, etc

Stores (with smaller ranges of products) also at 48 Shandwick Pl, St James' Centre, North Bridge, and various suburban locations (see Phone Book). See also *Chemists with Extended Hours*.

Debenhams

109-112 Princes Street
Tel: 225 1320
Opening times: Mon-Wed, Fri 9.30-18.00; Thu 9.30-20.00; Sat 9.00-18.00; Sun 11.00-17.00. Times may extend during Festival

Access: Main access from Princes St, with lifts to left of main entrance. Escalators to all floor. Also access from Rose St, where there is access to Champion Sports, men and women's wear. There's also a lift into the main Princes St building.
Store can be rather daunting, as there are several sublevels due

to the size. If in doubt, ask!
This store operates the VIP Baby Service, which relates to their restaurant. It includes: free baby food with any adult purchase over £2 (they carry Organix range); bottle warmers; stay-warm plates; baby wipes; high chairs.
Store also has Customer Order and Home Shopping services. There's also a free Personal Shopper Service.
Basement: menswear
Lower Ground: children's wear
Ground: Beauty, perfumery, accessories, jewellery
1st floor: Casual wear, maternity wear (Dorothy Perkins), designer wear
2nd floor: Ladies' wear, including lingerie where nursing bras are sold
3rd floor: bedding and soft furnishing
4th floor: Restaurant. See *Eating Out*
Toilets: on 4th floor opposite main lift. Toilet for the disabled is small, but there is a small changing shelf.

Also at:
Ocean Terminal
Ocean Drive
Leith EH6 7DZ
Tel: 553 8100
Opening times: Mon-Fri 10.00-20.00; Sat 10.00-19.00; Sun 10.00-18.00
Store on two floors. It has a capsule selection of those ranges available at the large Prince St store. It's fairly easy to walk round, with wide walkways. Escalators are placed in the centre of the shopfloor. There are 2 lifts to access one floor from the other (lifts serve the entire centre). Store stocks various ranges of children's clothing, along with homeware, menswear and women's wear. Has a reasonable range of lingerie which includes some maternity ranges. Also has beauty, perfumery, accessories, and jewellery sections

Frasers

145 Princes St EH2 4DL
Tel: 225 2472
Opening times: Mon, Wed 9.00-17.30; Tue 9.30-17.30; Thu 9.00-18.00; Fri 9.00-17.30; Sat 9.00-18.00; Sun 9.00-17.30

Access: Two entrances from Princes St to Ground floor, one from Hope St side of building. Lift at rear, escalators on right to all departments. Ground floor is on a split level, with a few steps between. Perfumery is best accessed via Princes St, Accessories via Hope St (where the lift is).
Basement: Oasis, fashion and diffusion lines
Ground: beauty and accessories
1st floor: ladies wear
2nd floor: ladies' fashion, plus lingerie. Including maternity wear and nursing bras
3rd floor: menswear
4th floor: homeware
5th floor: restaurant
Toilets: on 5th floor, with feeding and changing room nearby.

Harvey Nichols

30-34 St Andrews Sq EH2 3AD
Tel: 524 8388
Fax: 524 8399
Web: www.harveynichols.com
Opening hours: Mon-Wed 10.00-18.00; Thu 10.00-20.00; Fri, Sat 10.00-17.00; Sun 12.00-18.00

Store on 4 floors, with stylish concession areas. Buckle My Shoe stockists. Store carries children's wear by various designers in a compact area on 3rd floor. There's a juice bar on the ground floor and The Forth Floor bar and restaurant is on the fourth floor – get the pun?. The store's very chi chi, but unfortunately it has to be said, it's probably best visited without little ones in tow. The layout on the ground floor is not given over to easy negotiation with a pushchair and it's a toddler's dream of shiny, feathery, sleek (and expensive) things to grab at.

IKEA

Straiton Mains
Straiton, Loanhead EH20 9PW
Tel: 448 0500
Web: www.ikea.com
Opening times: Mon-Fri 10.00-22.00; Sat 10.00-19.00; Sun 10.00-18.00. Bank Holiday opening 10.00-18.00
Take the Straiton exit from the bypass on to the A701 and follow the signs. Various bus stops nearby.
There are parent and child parking bays, but these can be busy: it's best to try and go at off-peak times if you want to avoid congestion in the car parks and the lifts.

Huge store on the outskirts of Edinburgh: a shopper's delight – or a nightmare if you like to just shop and go! Unsupervised play area for older toddlers outside at entrance. Crèche/ballroom inside; see *Crèches while Shopping*. Pushchairs available, as are trolleys for a toddler plus a store carry bag (£1 coin required, refundable). There are also normal single and double supermarket-style trolleys (from the first floor, take the lift or stairs down to the marketplace where trolleys are stored, then bring it back up before you begin the trip round the store). Trolleys are not allowed in the car park – cars must be brought to the pick-up point and your purchases loaded from there. Staff will 'mind' a trolley with child, or you can take your child/ren to the car and leave the trolley in one of the 4 secure lock-up point (£1 coin, refundable).

The route round the store is mapped out, staff are friendly and accommodating. Should you wish to deviate from the path, watch out for the 'shortcuts' marked throughout the store. There are excellent playhouses on the first floor in the children's furniture and toy area, and also in the café (see below). In other areas, there are little play areas for young children, with chairs and tables, bricks, bead mazes etc.

Large room on the ground floor, near the entrance for breastfeeding and changing, with comfy chairs and screen. There is also a smaller nappy-changing room. Nappies are available in vending machine in all nappy changing areas. There are also changing facilities on the first floor adjacent to the café, and also near the snack bar after the pay point on the ground floor.

Café

Opening times: Mon-Fri 9.30-19.30; Sat-Sun 9.30-17.30

£, highchairs (20), breastfeeding welcome, nappy changing facilities (M&F), licensed, seats 306.

Extensive café/restaurant with self-service and amiable staff. Unsupervised children's play area in one corner, with miniature chairs, tables, play house and selection of toys overlooking the stairs on 1st floor. Varied menu with snacks and main courses including vegetarian and Swedish options. Children's half portions, children's options and boxed meals available: at the time of writing, children's meals are supplemented by a free piece of fruit. Limited selection of organic jarred baby food. Bottle heaters and microwaves available to heat bottles and baby food. Area is mainly no-smoking: smoking area has been moved so you no longer have to walk through it to access the toilets.

Jenners

48 Princes St
Tel: 225 2442
Fax: 260 2240

Opening times: Mon, Wed, Fri, Sat 9.00-18.00; Tue 9.30-18.00; Thu 9.00-20.00; Sun 11.00-17.00

Access: Both Princes St entrances have stairs up to the doors, as does South St David St – though there are less here, and there's also a revolving door which some older toddlers might like. For easiest access, enter by Rose St next to the Barber's Shop and take the lift up.

Traditional, independently owned store with large galleried well and many different levels. Because of its design, the building can be awkward to negotiate, although there are many (small) lifts to the various floors: the largest lift is that situated towards the rear of the store – ground floor access via Men's Designer Dept.

It's worth persevering in the store, as it is very attractive, with friendly staff on the whole. There are store guides posted on the walls near the lifts, or you can request one. The store has undergone various refurbishments in recent times and there's a good mix of the traditional and the contemporary. At Christmas time a huge tree is erected in-store which can be viewed from the gallery – look out for the robin singing in the branches! Store offers a delivery service (free to EH postcodes 1-22 and 24-30; there's a small charge outwith this area), an alteration service (free to its cardholders) and a 'left shopping' service (based on level 2) so you can wander round at least unhindered by shopping bags.

Key locations are:

Basement: toys, children's books (lift behind perfume dept on ground floor). See *Toyshops*.

Lower ground: jewellery, toiletries, hair accessories, accessories

Midway/1st floor: ladies' wear, including lingerie.

1st floor: Kids at Jenners (recently refurbished).

Restaurants: Five to choose from. See *Eating Out*.

Toilets: on 3rd floor. Parent and baby rooms adjacent to ladies' toilets. Clean, comfortable and pleasant – and usually not too busy. The changing room and the feeding room are separate and have sofas and chairs.

See also *Baby and Children's' Wear* and *Nursery Equipment*.

John Lewis

St James' Centre EH1 3SP
Tel: 556 9121
Tel: 0131 556 9121 (Alison de Lorey, Nursery Advisor)
Fax: 550 3000
Email:JL_Edinburgh@johnewis.co.uk

Opening times: Mon-Wed, 9.00-18.00; Thu 9.30-20.00; Fri 9.00-20.00; Sat 9.00-18.30; Sun 11.00-17.00

Access: from Leith St, opposite Greenside Car Park which takes you into the store via the flooring department. Glass lift to other floors is hidden behind the escalators. Two entrances in the St James' Centre. Entrance into basement and Customer Collection Point from Little King St, adjacent to St James' Centre Car Park.

Large department store providing a wide range of goods and services. Store is on several levels, with roomy lifts and escalator access in the main store area. Customers can ring and reserve items, plus the store offers free delivery throughout Edinburgh

and parts of Central Scotland, Fife and Borders.
Having recently undergone extensive upgrading and refurbishment, this is a sleek, stylish store, which still has loads of room to access the various departments and concessions with pushchairs or prams.
Points of interest:
Store offers a personal fashion advisor: service is free of charge.
Extensive Nursery section. Store stocks prams, pushchairs, cots, car seats, accessories, as well as a range of babies' and children's clothing (own brand, plus branded items).
Basement (Leith St): carpets & flooring
Lower Ground: computing, hi-fis etc, kitchenware, fabrics, soft furnishings
Ground: Beauty, ladies accessories, stationery, haberdashery, accessories, toys
1st floor: women's wear, menswear, lingerie , children's wear, nursery equipment. Café nr menswear.
2nd floor: home furnishing, restaurant, see *Eating Out*
Toilets on 2nd (Changing trolley in F toilets). Refurbished Feeding and changing room. Automatic door to ease access. There are 4 nappy changing areas, 3 of which are static, 1 of which is a pull-down unit. In the toilets inside the feeding/changing area, there's a toddler height loo. The breastfeeding area has views out over N Edinburgh and over to Fife. While there's a partition wall, there isn't a screen between the entrance door and the breastfeeding area, so if you need a bit of privacy, settle yourself at the window side of the room.
See also *Toys*, *Outdoor Toys* and *Bicycle Shops*.

Marks and Spencer

91 Princes St EH2 2ER
Tel: 225 2301
Web: marksandspencer.com
Opening hours: Mon-Wed, Fri 9.00-19.00; Thu 9.00-20.00; Fri 9.00-19.00; Sat 8.30-18.00; Sun 11.00-17.00. Stores extend opening hours over the Christmas period.

Access: via Princes St: automatic door nr The Body Shop.
Extensive department store on 4 levels. Good lift access. Self-service café at the rear of the basement, see Eating Out. Toilets and nappy-changing on ground floor to the left hand side of store as you enter. There's also a mother and baby room for mothers to breastfeed in private. Space for prams and pushchairs. Toilets are in the same area - they can be very busy.
Basement: ladies' wear/lingerie, including nursing bras (M&S have a bra fitting service), maternity underwear etc: Children's wear towards rear, see also Nursery Equipment. Marks and Spencer's baby range includes toiletries, clothing, bedding and furniture. Store also offers ordering and alteration services.

54 Princes St EH2 2DQ
Tel: 225 2301
Fax: 459 7802
Opening hours: Mon-Wed, Fri 9.00-19.00; Thu 9.00-20.00; Fri 9.00-19.00; Sat 8.30-18.00; Sun 11.00-17.00. Stores extend opening hours over the Christmas period.

Access: easy access from Princes St to all floors via lift and escalators at rear of store. Two entrances from Rose St – left hand side has automatic door and level access.
Menswear, homeware and foodhall in this branch. Five levels. Escalator access to upper areas. Toilets on Rose St level. 'Collect by car' food service available from this store.

Gyle Shopping Centre
21 Gyle Avenue EH12 9JT
Tel: 317 1333
Fax: 317 1444
Opening times: Mon-Fri 9.00-22.00; Sat 8.00-20.00; Sun 9.00-18.00. Store has extended opening hours during the Christmas period

Access: from car park, where parent and child parking bays are nearby, or through the Gyle Centre.
Extremely spacious store, all on one level. Children's wear, including some nursery equipment, ladies' wear, lingerie (including underwear and nursing bras: bra fitting service in-store), men's wear and home furnishings. Cash machine in-store (nr menswear).
Two cafés, one nr the car park entrance, the other nr Children's wear. There are nappy changing facilities near both cafés, along with toilets, but the larger facilities are nearer Children's wear and also have a room for those mothers who wish to breastfeed in private.

Unit 31-33
Kinnaird Park EH15 3RD
Tel: 669 7695
Fax: 669 7893
Opening hours: Mon-Fri 9.00-21.00; Sat 9.00-19.00; Sun 10.00-18.00
Foodhall, with an in-store bakery. There's also a Café Revive, and a small range of general merchandise, including cards & wrap, hosiery, cosmetics & makeup and homeware gifts.

Ocean Terminal
Unit 3, Ocean Terminal
Ocean Drive EH6 6HW

Tel: 225 2301
Opening hours: Mon-Fri 9.00-20.00; sat 9.00-19.00; 10.00-18.00
Foodhall, with small Café Revive.

Mothercare World

Unit 6
Hermiston Gait Retail Park EH11 4DG
Tel: 4531383
Opening times: Mon-Fri 9.00-20.00; Sat 9.00-18.00; Sun 10.00-17.00

Store all on one level. Stocks clothes (Mothercare brand) and maternity wear. Also stocks a range of nursery goods & bedding (own brand), car seats, pushchairs (various brands) and toys. Convenient parking and shopping trolleys (£1 coin returnable charge). Nappy-changing facilities (M&F), toilets and private breastfeeding area available. See also Baby and Children's Clothes, Children's Shoes, Maternity Wear, Nursery Equipment, and Toyshops.

Also at:
Unit 11C The Fort Retail Park
New Craighall Road EH15 3HH
Tel: 657 4050
Opening hours: Mon, Wed, Thu, Fri 9.00-20.00; Tue 9.30-20.00; Sat 9.00-18.00; Sun 10.00-17.00
Similar layout and range as store at Hermiston Gait. The store has nappy changing facilities and toilets. There's also a public telephone located in-store.

Sainsbury's

Cameron Toll Shopping Centre
Lady Rd
Tel: 666 5200
Opening times: Mon-Fri 7.30-22.00; Sat 7.30-22.00; Sun 8.00-19.00

Good level access. Stocks Baby and children's wear. Lighting department sells dimmer switches and night-lights. Small toy, book and stationery departments and good selection of baby foods and toiletries. Novelty birthday cakes or personalised cakes from the bakery with 3-4 days notice. NO sweets at ANY checkout. Changing room at right, off clothing sales area. Ask at Customer Service Desk if you need a nappy. See Shopping Centres and Markets.

Toys'R'Us

Kinnaird Park
Newcraighall Rd
Tel: 657 4121
Opening times: Mon-Sat 9.00-22.00; Sun 10.00-18.00. Operates Bank Holiday hours.

Huge store which sells more than just toys: see various listings below. The Babies'R'Us area stocks baby food, toiletries, and nappies in bulk quantities, as well as nursery equipment. Store directory guides to different areas, and there's a pick-up point for bulky items and electrical toys. Reward card scheme.
See also *Toy Shops, Outdoor Toys, Bicycles, Children's Clothes.*

Woolworth's

170-174 Constitution St
Leith
Tel: 554 3872/0210

142 Lothian Rd
Tel: 229 4644

36-38 Raeburn Pl
Stockbridge
Tel: 332 2613
Sunday opening: 10.00-16.00

181 St John's Rd
Corstorphine
Tel: 334 6644
Sunday opening: 12.00-16.00

91-93 High Street
Musselburgh
Tel: 0131 665 2910
Fax: 0131 665 3819

At time of writing, all stores open Mon-Sat 9.00-17.30
Stores stock selection of toys, party supplies, stationery, videos, as well as pick'n'mix sweets (look out for pilfering tiny fingers!) and haberdashery. The 'Ladybird' brand is Woolworth's' See also *Baby and Children's Wear* and *Toys.*

Big W

25 Milton Link Milton Road
Tel: 0131 669 1298
Fax: 0131 669 4937

This megastore has a vast array of goods, including children's clothing, outdoor toys, toys and games.

SHOPPING CENTRES & RETAIL PARKS

If mall shopping is your thing, or you prefer having the big names all in one place, Edinburgh has a good selection of shopping centres, both in and out of town. Most of the malls offer hire of small pushchairs and toddler straps. We have listed the general opening hours of the centres: they may operate restricted hours on Bank Holidays and longer hours in the run-up to Christmas.

Almondvale Shopping Centre

87 Almondvale South
Livingston EH54 6HR
Tel: 01506 432961

Opening times: Mon, Tue, Wed, Fri, Sat 9.00-17.30, Thu 9.00-19.00, Sun 11.00-17.00. Hours vary by store – Asda Wal-mart and Safeway trade for longer hours.
Accessible from M8-A71 (parent/child parking) or by bus from St Andrews Square. NB the car parks at Safeway and Asda Walmart both have a 3-hour maximum stay policy in place.

Adams, Asda Wal-Mart, BhS, Boots, Clarks Shoes, Mackays, Mothercare, WH Smith, Superdrug Woolworth's.
Places to eat, include Bakers Oven, BhS Café, the Mall Café and Safeway Café. Mothercare have a good feeding and changing room located at the back of store (M&F). The nappy-changing area is locked (key from assistant).
The whole mall is one level so it's easy to navigate. There are two nappy changing areas, a shopper's crèche and bottle warming facilities available from the cafés and restaurants. There are also various coin-operated children's rides around the centre.

Almondvale Childcare

Tel: 01506 436474

Shopper's Crèche
Opening Times Mon-Fri 10.00-17.30; Sat 10.00-17.00; Sun 12.00-17.00. Sliding scale of charges. £1.65/1/2 hr, £3.30/hr; £4.95/ 1/2hr; £6.00/2hrs. Maximum stay is 2 hours.
There's also a nursery based at Almondvale.
Full time / part time places available between 8.00-18.00, Mon-Fri.
Call no. above for more information.

Cameron Toll Shopping Centre

Lady Rd
Tel: 666 2777

Opening times: Mon-Wed, Sat 10.00-18.00, Thu-Fri 10.00-19.00; Sat, Sun 11.0-19.00
Hours of individual shops vary but generally all open late on Thu and also on Sun afternoons.

Two large car parks serve both front and rear entrances. Can be very busy on Fri and w/ends.
Keep a tight grip on small children in car parks. Pedestrian access from Lady Rd but closely set bollards and a rollbar designed to prevent shoppers from taking trolleys out mean large prams and pushchairs need careful manoeuvering.
Self-opening doors, seats, public phones in a leafy mirrored mall. Petrol station and taxi rank. A variety of trolley designs to accommodate various ages of babies and small children. Many smaller shops do not allow trolleys inside.
A variety of shops include Adams Children's Wear, BhS, Boots, Clarks, Mackays, Ottaker's, Dorothy Perkins, Sainsbury's, Claire's Accessories, jewellers, travel agents, banks and building society – all on the main shopping floor.On the 1st floor, there's the food-court, which, at the time of writing, has a refurbishment scheduled, which should see the likes of Burger King, Café Select and Lavazza joining the existing retailers. Bottle warming facilities available
The centre usually hosts of activities for Easter, Mother's Day etc, such as puppet shows, magicians and other children's entertainers.
Toilets on ground and first floor s(lift on left outside entrance to Sainsbury's). There's a separate nappy-changing room with 2 changing units and enclosed area for feeding.

Craigleith Retail Park

South Groathill Rd

Compact shopping centre with good parking, largely catering for Edinburgh W.
Sainsbury's supermarket is open Mon-Fri 7.00-00.00; Sat 7.00-22.00; Sun 7.00-20.00.
Boots has pharmacy with pharmacist for advice, but can't accommodate prescriptions. Other shops include Mamas & Papas, Curry's, Homebase, TK Maxx, and Holiday Hypermarket. Easily accessible toilets in Sainsbury's include a toilet for the disabled – useful if taking combinations of children/babies to toilets/nappy-changing. Boots has a nappy-changing area in the ladies toilets. Separate nappy-changing. Sainsbury's in-store café, with an unsupervised play area, is another useful diversion.

Fort Kinnaird

(formerly Kinnaird Park and the Fort)
Newcraighall Rd
Tel: 669 9242
Access from A1

Around 55 outlets set around 3 large car parks. Opening hours of individual shops vary but most open late on Thu and all day Sun.
In what was Kinnaird Park, shops include Argos, Borders, Early Learning Centre, Gap, H&M, Toys 'R' Us, Curry's, Warner's and a M&S food hall. The Early Learning Playstore has plenty of options to 'try before you buy', as well as planned activities.
Also in Retail Park are the UCI 10-screen cinema and Megabowl, a 10 pin bowling alley which welcomes families.
In the area which was formerly the Fort there are more outlets, including:
Boots, Mothercare World, Laura Ashley, Dorothy Perkins, Adams, Next, Birthdays, New Look etc.
Restaurants/cafés/fast food: Chiquitos, McDonald's 'Drive Thru', Costa Coffee (in WH Smiths), Esquires Coffee House in Clinton's Cards, Starbuck's in Borders, Café Revive in M&S, Frankie & Benny's. There are bottle warming facilities in: Borders, Chiquitos, ELC, Frankie & Benny's, The management suite and McDonald's.
Toilets: Mothercare has a good feeding and changing room, Borders Books café has a changing room and Boots also has a nappy-changing room (M&F). Early Learning Playstore has an excellent baby changing facility and children's toilet facility, and a baby 'dining-room' with seats for breastfeeding and bottle warmers.

Freeport Shopping and Leisure Centre

See *Out of Town Trips – West Lothian.*

Gyle Shopping Centre

Gyle Avenue
South Gyle Broadway
Tel: 539 9000
Opening hours: Mon, Tue, Wed, Fri 9.30-20.00; Thu 9.30-21.00; Sat 9.00-18.00; Sun 10.00-18.00. Certain individual stores, such as Marks & Spencer and Safeway, have longer hours, and hours extend at Christmas.

Large colour coded car park, with parent and child parking, parking for the disabled, and special requirements parking (such as the two groups previously mentioned) to all entrances. Maximum stay is 3 hrs. Taxi rank outside main entrance. Petrol station near main entrance. There are other entrances, which give easy access to Safeway and Marks and Spencer. Single and double pushchairs and child reins available to hire free (ID required) at Customer Services Desk in mall opposite main entrance. Small outdoor play areas with climbing frames etc.
Self-opening doors, seats, public phones in a spacious well-planned centre, with around 60 shops all on one level. A variety of trolleys to accommodate various ages of small children (available at Safeway & M&S).
Lift and escalator to upper level where the 500-seater Food Court offers a range of snacks, meals and drinks. There are bottle/baby food heating facilities. Also situated on 1st floor is a fully-equipped Baby Room (M&F). Within the baby room is a small screened area for privacy while breastfeeding. There are toilets on the ground floor beside the main entrance and also on the 1st floor – both include facilities for disabled visitors. M&S and Safeway also have cafés, plus there's Starbuck's and Nardini's on the ground level.
Shops include: Accessorize, Body Shop, Boots, Clarks, Disney Store, Early Learning Centre, Gap, Mackays, Marks and Spencer, Next, Next for Children, Safeway and WH Smith. There are also jewellers, a building society, travel agents etc.
There's a Post Office in Safeway, with times: Mon-Fri 8.00-19.00; Sat 8.00-18.00; Sun 9.00-18.00.

Hermiston Gait Retail Park

Take 1st exit marked Glasgow off A720 City Bypass coming from South Gyle.
Do not follow sign to Glasgow, go straight on which will take you to traffic lights. Turn left and follow signs.
Mothercare World open Mon-Fri 9.00-20.00 Sat 9.00 18.00 Sun 10.00-1700
Opening hours of other shops vary.

Large Car Park: keep a close eye on mobile youngsters – as the car park is usually quite quiet, drivers have a tendency to cut across parking bays rather than using the road layout.
Shops include Curry's, Office World, JJB Sports, and Homebase.
Toilets: Feeding and Changing room located in Mothercare World.

McArthur Glen Designer Outlet Livingston

Almondvale Avenue
Livingston
W Lothian EH54 6QX.
Tel: 01506 423 600 (automated information line)
J3 off M8 – follow signs to Designer Outlet Centre. Regular buses from Edinburgh – bus station is directly in front of the

Centre.
There is also a taxi rank.
Centre opening times: Mon-Tue, Sat-Sun 10.00-18.00; Wed-Fri 10.00-20.00. Individual stores' opening hours may vary.
Various car parks (there's 2000 spaces in all) although easiest access seems to be Centre West.

Large shopping centre on two levels. Mixture of designer and casual clothes shops including Aquascutum, M&S Outlet, Ice Blue, Gap, Clarks, and various sports shops. Other shops include ELC, The Toyworld Store and At Home. Various cash dispensers. 8-screen Circuit Cinema located on the 1st level.
Various options for food such as: Ashoka Shak (Indian 'tapas'), McDonald's, Rollover Hotdogs, Spud-u-like and Refresh. Various coffee shops located on the ground floor.
Toilets: 2 nappy changing areas with 3 changing units in each, plus closed feeding area. One is located opposite Gap and the other one is in the Boulevard.

Meadowbank Shopping Park

Just off London Rd before Meadowbank Stadium.
Sainsbury's open Mon-Fri 8.00-22.00; Sat 07.00-22.00; Sun 9.00-19.00.
Opening hours of other shops vary.

Large Car Park with Parent Child Parking.
Shops include Sainsbury's, JJB Sports, T-K Maxx, Brunswick Warehouse, Brantano, Kingdom of Leather, Poundstretcher and Au Naturale.
Toilets and nappy changing facilities in Sainsbury's

Newkirkgate Shopping Centre

Off Great Junction St
Leith

Opening times of individual shops vary. Closed Sun. Large car park.
Some shops around open square, others in covered mall. Shops include Woolworth's, Young Days, Boots (small store), Wool Warehouse, which has a good selection of wool and patterns. Various other shops. No toilets in centre.

Ocean Terminal

Ocean Drive
Leith EH6 7DZ
Tel: 555 56
Web: www.oceanterminal.com

Opening times: Mon-Fri 10.00-20.00; Sat 9.00-19.00; Sun 11.00-18.00
Airy, modern mall on 3 levels, with wide walkways and plenty to take youngsters' attention, whether it's the huge propellers on display, or the sight of boats in the River Forth from the eateries. Lifts and escalator access to 1st floor.
Stores include: Athena, Debenhams, Baxter's, BhS, Claire's Accessories, Waterstone's, M&S Foodhall and the Bear Factory.
It also houses a tourist centre and shop for the Royal Yacht Britannia, which is moored alongside the shopping centre.
It has parenting suites on two of the 3 floors, which have baby changing facilities and seating for breastfeeding mothers.
There's a wide range of places to eat. You're not tied down to fast food style options, although some venues are much more expensive than others and do not really cater for young children:
Places to eat include: Baxter's café, Ocean Kitchen, O'Brien's sandwich bar, Terence Conran's stylish Zinc bar, Zizzi, Café Revive (in M&S) and Ma Potters.
Ster Century operates a kids club cinema screening on weekend mornings at around 10.00 am, although it can sometime screen a PG certificate film – check press for details – for the price of £2 for an adult and child (babies under 2 go free). See *Places to Visit* for more details.

Princes Mall

Corner of Princes St and Waverley Bridge
Tel: 557 3759

Opening times: Mon-Sat 8.30-18.00; Thu 8.30-19.00; Sun 11.00-17.00
Hours for individual shops vary and not all shops open on Sun.

Built on 3 levels with 6 entrances, 2 with access ramps; Waverley Bridge and Princes St, next to Waverley Steps, which leads to the small, busy lift which serves all floors.
Busy mall with Tourist Information Centre located on the rooftop (access ramp from Princes St available).
There are over 50 businesses, including New Look, Quiksilver and, for children of all ages, Junior Station. Shops for children include The Natural World and Bookworld.
Restaurants: McDonald's, KFC, Rollover, O'Brien's, Spud-u-Like, Harry Ramsden's, Café Fraiche, Coffeestop and Costa Coffee on the roof.
Toilets: Two sets both on lowest level at opposite ends. Washrooms beside the Food Court, 20p. Free nappy changing room and toilet for the disabled to the right of the washrooms (easy access with pushchair).
Toilets with a separate nappy-changing room inside the ladies' toilets through a set of doors market 'Exit' at the other end of Princes Mall.

St James' Centre

Princes St / Leith St
Tel: 557 0050
Web: www.thestjames.co.uk
Centre open Mon-Wed, Sat 7.30-18.30; Thu-Fri 7.30-20.30; Sun 10.30-17.00. Some shop hours vary

Pedestrian access from the corner of Leith St, Princes St and Elder St via The Walk, which connects St James to the Harvey Nichols complex. Vehicular entrance to St James' multi-storey car park from Leith St and Elder St (lift access to centre via this car park), a but an alternative is to park in Greenside car park, on Leith St, and enter via the main door or by John Lewis.
Large shopping centre. Numerous shops including Adams, Boots, John Lewis, Mackays, Dorothy Perkins, Thornton's etc. Cash dispensers, seats and public phones.
The eating area – Food on 1 – is on the upper floor, along with the toilets for the disabled and the nappy changing facilities (awkward to access with pushchair, though). This is accessible via a lift near the Princes St end of the mall. John Lewis has excellent changing/feeding room with a separate male changing/feeding room (on the store's 2nd floor, near to The Place to Eat). There's also cookie and juice stands. in the mall.

Westside Plaza Shopping Centre

Wester Hailes Rd
Tel: 442 3123
Opening times: Mon-Sat 8.30-18.00 (19.00 Thu and Fri). Opening hours of individual shops vary, some close Wed pm.
Large car park, plus railway station, bus terminal and taxi rank nearby.

Indoor shopping centre on 2 levels with lift and escalators. Shops include Iceland, Poundstretcher, Lloyds (chemist), Browns (opticians), Post Office and a variety of other food, gift, toy, hardware, newsagent and charity shops, plus an indoor market on the ground floor. Multiscreen cinema, library, Citizens Advice Bureau, Job Centre and City of Edinburgh Council Local Housing Office nearby. Toilets: located on ground floor – separate nappy-changing area (M&F).

FAIRS AND MARKETS

Assembly Rooms

54 George St
Tel: 220 4348
Box Office: 220 4349
Lift to all floors at rear left of main entrance

Hosts regular craft and collectors fairs – there's always a couple in the run-up to Christmas. Forthcoming events advertised in local press and windows. Christmas Charity Hypermarket held in December. Craft Fairs usually include baby and children's clothes, wooden toys, patchwork etc. Fairs tend to get very busy especially at lunchtime, which renders pushchairs and small children a liability. Occasional children's shows presented during school holidays. Toilets: back left of ground floor, down a few steps or at the right of the 1st floor (nappy changing facilities).

Christmas Village

Princes St Gdns E
A seasonal event. Stalls sell a range of goods and Christmas orientated merchandise. There's also food stalls. See *Annual Events*.

Edinburgh Farmers' Market

Castle St
1 and 3rd weekend of the month, Sat 10.00-14.00

A selection of stalls, where you can buy meat, poultry, game, fish, dairy products and more. Much of it is organic. The stall-owners, being the farmers and manufacturers, know their stuff about what they're selling. As well as the raw food stalls, there are stalls selling baking, drinks, fruit and veg, as well as some knitwear. The range seems to grow every week. As well as the samples which are on offer at many of the stalls (a good way to find out if your child likes what you're about to buy!), there are beverages and snacks along the lines of freshly cooked 'real' crisps, wild boar burgers and roast suckling pig rolls on sale. There is sometimes an entertainer, such as a juggler, clown etc.
NB. The Council would like to move this market to the Grassmarket: the majority of the stallholders are against the move, but the market may relocate in 2004.

Ingliston

Airport Rd
Tel: 333 3801 (Spook Erection, market operators)
Off A8 at Ingliston, Newbridge
Opening times; Sun 9.30-15.30

Open-air market of huge proportions with plenty free parking space and good traffic marshalling. Variety of stalls including baby and children's clothing, jeans and cheap toys: be wary of cheap toys, but there are bargains to be had. Tannoy system covers market. Toilets and feeding and changing area are well signed. Clean and functional. Lost Children's Centre at First Aid Post.
Snacks: snacks of all descriptions, such as ice-cream, fish and chips, burgers, kebabs and curry, from a variety of stalls and vans, some with tables and chairs.

SUPERMARKETS

No one would ever say that doing the weekly shop with young children is easy, but hopefully this chapter will give you an idea of the most suitable places for you and your child to shop.

Hours:
We have not listed these, as they are so varied, and in the ongoing 'supermarket wars', they change fairly regularly. Most are open Mon-Sat, from at least 9.00-19.00 or 20.00, although many of the larger stores are open to midnight, and some have 24 hr opening. Sunday hours are around 12.00-17.00, and most are open all year, only closing on Christmas and New Year's Days.

Car parks:
All stores listed have car parks and many now offer 'parent and child' spaces, usually near to those for disabled drivers. These are usually situated near to the store entrance – but don't expect other people to respect their role!

Trolleys:
We have listed the types of trolleys provided by the store. Safety instructions for each type of trolley should always be followed. These are often found on the bar or handles. Always use the restraints – and if you find the trolleys on offer do not have functioning restraints, why not report the matter to the store management. Remember, too, that once they are loaded with shopping and children, trolleys can become unwieldy, so be aware of your own physical limits! As a general guide, baby cradle types are suitable for babies up to 9kgs (20 lbs) and the toddler types are suitable up to around 3 yrs. Other trolley types (baby, double baby, baby and toddler and double toddler etc) are less common, but the larger the store, the greater the range.
While stores usually state that they allow all trolley types out of the store, you may find that, in practice, the combination trolleys are not allowed out of the store boundaries, though if the store owns the car park, this usually makes life easier. Rather than repacking your shopping into another trolley and struggling with a small baby or several children, why not ask for an escort out to your car – make the stores compete for your custom!

Carry Out Service:
Check with at the Customer Services before you start your shop whether this is available – it should be! Then, ask at the check-out if you need assistance.

Lost children:
Stores offer a lost child policy, but they tend to differ. The first rule is try not to panic, then contact a member of staff immediately you become aware of the disappearance. Describe what your child was wearing and where you last saw them. Think of anything that might have attracted them on the way round the store. Try to carry some ID that identifies you as the child's carer; a recent photograph is useful. In shopping centres, stores always contact the centre's security. If you can, try to teach your child to approach a member of staff in a shop if they become lost.
We have tried to list those aspects in the following stores which are specific to parents with young children,

Asda Wal-Mart

100 The Jewel
Brunstone EH15 3AR
Tel: 669 9151

also at:

Chesser Ave
Tel: 444 8425

Baby, double baby, baby and toddler, toddler and double toddler trolleys. Nappies, babyfood. Nappy-changing facilities (M&F). See also Baby and Children's Toys. Toyshops. Range of well-known brands and value-line foods.

Marks and Spencer

Web:www.marksandspencer.com

91 Princes St
Tel: 225 2301

54 Princes St
Tel: 225 2301
£5 home delivery of foods Mon-Sat to EH1-EH17 postcodes inclusive, from 54 Princes St. Large selection of prepared meals for adults, no babyfoods, but do have ready-made novelty birthday cakes.
M&S also stocks nursery equipment, small range of pushchairs and baby toiletries: 91 Princes St and Gyle stores stock the ranges.

Gyle Shopping Centre
Has the advantage that the store is all on one floor. Stocks children's, ladies' and men's wear. Also home furnishings, nursery accessories etc.

Safeway

Web: Safewaycollect.co.uk
Online shopping avilable via Gyle store: £3.50 delivery charge. Also have Wines Direct online - p&p payable.

38 Comely Bank St
Tel: 332 4469
Baby, toddler and baby, double toddler and toddler trolleys. Car

park entrance on Fettes Ave. 'Parent and Child' parking near lifts. Range of baby foods and accessories. Nappy changing facilities, private breastfeeding area and toilets. Take-away food facility, but no actual café: there is a lunch-bar affair, but it's not suitable for young children.

Cramond Rd S
Davidson's Mains
Tel: 336 4234
Baby, toddler and baby and toddler trolleys. Baby food, toiletries and nappies. 'Parent and Child' parking near entrance. May use staff toilets on request.

Ferry Rd
Tel: 315 4970
Large store with coffee shop and petrol station. 'Parent and Child' parking. All combinations of trolleys available. Nappy-changing facilities and toilets.

Gyle Shopping Centre
Tel: 317 1197
Large number of baby, double baby, baby and toddler, toddler and double toddler trolleys. Customer toilets, feeding and changing room to right of entrance within the centre. Post Office within store. Coffee shop with toddler seating areas plus high chairs. Bottle warming. See also *Shopping Centres and Markets*.

Bughtlin Market, Maybury Dr, East Craigs
Tel: 339 2073
Baby, double baby, baby and toddler, toddler and double toddler trolleys.

145 Morningside Rd
Tel: 447 9955
Car seat, baby, baby and toddler, toddler and double toddler trolleys.

30 New Swanston, Oxgangs
Tel: 445 5647
Baby, baby and toddler, double toddler and toddler trolleys. Free food warming in coffee shop. Free nappies and wipes in changing facilities. Private breastfeeding area.

4 Piersfield Ter
Tel: 661 5661
Baby, double baby, baby and toddler, double toddler and toddler trolleys. Coffee shop with children's play area. Breastfeeding permitted. Customer toilets and nappy-changing room in front of check-outs.

Sainsbury's

Web: Sainsburystoyou.com
Internet shopping available: £5 delivery charge. Sainsbury's have introduced novelty trolleys with toy cars on the front of them, available in some stores. Ideal for older toddlers and children – and parents with good steering capabilities!

185 Craigleith Rd
Tel: 332 0704
Full range of trolleys. Store stocks some nursery equipment, baby and toddler food, nappies, wipes etc. Also stocks range of Adams clothing and ELC toys. Customer toilets and feeding and changing room (M&F) behind check-out area. Room is pretty small – and has been unsuitable for use on several occasions – but store does provide free nappies. If there are none in the changing area, ask at Customer Services.
Café:
£-££, high chairs (3), no smoking area, breastfeeding welcome.
Range of snacks and meals. Secure trolley lock-up area at café entrance (on the left) keeps trolleys etc out of the restaurant. Unsupervised children's play area.

Meadowbank Retail Park
Tel: 656 9377
Large number of baby, double baby, baby and toddler, toddler and trolleys for children with disabilities. Full range of baby and toddler foods and nappies. Limited range of ELC toys. Nappy-changing facilities. Toilets behind checkouts.

Straiton Retail Park
Tel: 448 2181
Full range of trolleys. Large store, with Adams clothing section, ELC toys, large selection of nappies, wipes, creams and some baby equipment. Baby and toddler food. Nappy-changing facilities behind checkouts near foyer. Café, welcomes breastfeeding.

Cameron Toll Shopping Centre, Lady Rd
Tel: 666 5200
Large range of car seat, baby, double baby, baby and toddler, and toddler trolleys. Large store with clothes, toys, lighting and bakery offering personalised cakes. Two aisles of baby food and toiletries. Wide, easily accessible aisles. Store can provide customer helpers for assistance around store and/or to car park. Nappy-changing room on right, off clothing sales area. Nappies and wipes available at Customer Service desk.

Scotmid Co-operative Society

Many stores throughout the city and outlying areas, ranging from small local shops, to larger stores.

Facilities vary from store to store.

37 Boswall Parkway
Boswall
Tel: 552 2132

230 Oxgangs Rd N
Colinton Mains
Tel: 441 2915

236 Crewe Rd N
Crewe Rd
Tel: 552 4251

1 Drum Brae
Drum Brae
Tel: 317 7152

112 Easter Rd
Easter Rd
Tel: 661 5742

Superstore
236 Gorgie Rd
Gorgie
Tel: 346 7859

21 Gracemount Dr
Gracemount
Tel: 664 1663

76 Duke St
Leith
Tel: 555 4000

6 Bath St
Portobello
Tel: 657 1952

283 Calder Rd
Sighthill
Tel: 443 6139

34 Warrender Pk Rd
Warrender Park
Tel: 229 8195

Somerfield

Baby and toddler trolleys. Range of nappies, food etc.

114 Dalry Rd
Tel: 337 6376

Gorgie Pk Rd
Tel: 337 9451

Tesco

Web: www.tesco.com.

Internet shopping available: £5 delivery charge. Also catalogue shopping – pick up copies in-store.

7 Broughton Rd
Tel: 456 8400

Parent and Child parking spaces. Store refitted in July 2002, including increased number of Parent and Child spaces, which is monitored by Euro Car Parks to prevent abuse of these spaces Baby, single and double toddler trolleys. Some baby and toddler trolleys.

Range of baby food, wipes and nappies. Also carry a decent range of organic food for babies and others, from fresh fruit/veg, through tinned foods, chilled and frozen foods. Customer toilets and feeding/changing room to rear of checkouts.

14 Colinton Mains Dr
Tel: 470 7400

15 Drumbryden Rd, Wester Hailes
Tel: 465 2500

Meadow Place Rd
Tel: 470 0700

Baby, baby and toddler, double baby and double toddler trolleys. 'Parent and Child' parking.

Huge choice of nappies, including reusables, plus accessories. Calpol, karvol, teething remedies etc. Large range of baby food plus bowls, spoons, drinking cups. You could buy every party requisite here from the cake, party-bag fillers, present, wrapping paper to the party dress/outfit. Good selection of affordable clothing for babies up to teens. Help with packing and assistance to car. On-line shopping (see web site to check delivery area), for £5 fee, has the added bonus of all your purchases delivered not just to your door step but into your kitchen.

Toilets, nappy-changing room and feeding room on right behind checkouts. Café (not 24 hrs) with 5 high chairs, ample space for pushchairs or trolleys, bottles warmed, breastfeeding welcome, baby food available to buy, kids' lunch boxes.

94 Nicholson St
Tel: 456 2400

Car seat, double baby, baby and toddler and toddler trolleys. This is a 'Metro' store, so it is more compact and has less of a range than some of the larger stores.

CLOTHES SHOPPING: BABY AND CHILDREN'S CLOTHES

Most department stores, an increasing number of larger supermarkets, and some chemists stock baby and children's clothes, underwear and socks. Not all are listed here, as we have tried to include those with a good range, exciting stock, competitive prices, or those which have something special to offer.

Apart from the problems of finding the right style, fabric and colour – at the right price – there are two main bugbears when shopping for children's clothes: the lack of a standard sizing system and seasonal availability.

The large department stores and major brand names all have different sizing systems. Most are still based on the now out-of-date British Standard, with manufacturers adding their own allowances for growth, comfort etc. The age range given to sizes is therefore only a rough guide. Most shops will refund if an item is unsuitable, but always hold on to the receipts.

Some of the smaller shops in this section will make-to-measure, at little or no extra charge for children with specific needs.

Clothes for low birth weight babies (from about 3lbs) are available from some department stores or by post (see *Shopping from Home*), although more stores are now stocking such ranges.

For children's ski wear, see *Outdoor and Ski Shops*.

This section also includes details of dancewear (although many dance teachers do sell leotards, shoes etc), kilts, schoolwear and shoes.

We have tried to give exact opening hours for these stores, but it's always wise to phone ahead if you are making a special trip, as this information may change.

Adams Children's Wear

Brightly coloured clothing for girls and boys including outerwear. Also stock baby bodysuits, scratch-mitts (larger sized than most), sleepsuits, padders, hats, gloves etc. Competitively priced.

Unit 11-13
64 St James' Centre EH1 3SR
Tel: 556 0692
Opening hours: Mon-Wed, Fri-Sat 9.00-17.30; Thu 9.00-19.00; Sun 12.00-16.00

Unit 26
Cameron Toll Shopping Centre EH16 5PB
Tel: 664 0776
Opening hours: Mon-Wed, Fri-Sat 9.00-17.30; Thu 9.00-21.00; Sun 11.00-17.00

Unit 7
Fort Retail Park
Newcraighall EH15 3HS
Tel: 669 6547
Opening hours: Mon-Tue, Thu-Fri 10.00-20.00; Wed 10.00-17.30; Sat 9.00-17.30; Sun 11.00-17.00

Ocean Terminal Shopping Centre
Leith EH6 6JJ
Tel: 555 2728
Opening hours: Mon-Wed, Fri 10.00-21.00; Thu, Sat 10.00-22.00; Sun 10.00-17.00
Also in-store at the following Sainsbury's stores: Cameron Toll, Craigleith Retail Park and Straiton.

Asda Wal-Mart

100 The Jewel
Edinburgh EH15 3AR
Tel: 669 9151
Opening times: 24 hours
Attractive, reasonably priced babies and children's clothes and footwear. Bibs, padders, underwear, sleepwear, casual clothes, schoolwear and outdoorwear. Also toys and a café.

Baggins

12 Deanhaugh St
Stockbridge
Tel: 315 2011
Web: www.bagginsonline.co.uk
Opening times: Tue-Fri 10.00-17.00; Sat 10.00-14.00
Access: awkward – down a flight of steps to a basement.
A great range of dressing-up clothes and accessories like wands, wings, hats etc. Outfits include: fairies, clowns, spacemen, firemen, tigers, belly dancers, nurses, Indians etc. Personalised clothes for clubs, playgroups, nursery schools etc. Small orders welcomed. Toys for all ages. Toys for children to play with while you browse.

BhS

64 Princes St
Tel: 226 2621
Basement: good range of everyday wear for babies and children, at reasonable prices. Casual wear, outdoor wear, underwear, footwear and special occasion clothes. See *Department Stores*.

Blessings & Blossoms

132 St Johns Rd EH12 8AX
Tel: 334 8322
Web: www.blessingsandblossoms.co.uk

Opening times: Mon-Sat 09.30-17.00

This Aladdin's cave in Corstorphine stocks quality traditional and designer clothes and shoes for casual day wear or special events. Everything from flower girl, bridesmaid, party and communion dresses plus page boy outfits can be made to order by in house designer Pauline Mullanif, or you can choose from the wide range in the shop. There are also christening outfits plus wonderful ideas for baby gifts. Although the shop is small and there are a couple of steps to navigate it is well worth a visit. Breastfeeding and nappy changing, plus toilet available for emergencies. The train in the window is always an attraction plus there are toys to keep the little ones occupied while you browse.

Boots the Chemist

Web: www.boots.com

Full range of own brand (Mini Mode) baby and children's clothing, up to 6 yrs. Clothes tend to be pretty hardwearing, in bold, bright colours. Many in 100% cotton. Also do baby range for sensitive skins. Boots also stocks a range of clothing for low birth weight babies ('up to 2.3 kg' and 'up to 4.5 kg').

Available from:

101 Princes St
Tel: 225 8331

Opening times: Mon-Sat 9.00-18.00; Thu 9.00-19.30; Sun 12.00-17.00

Clothing on 1st floor

Craigleith Retail Park
Tel: 332 6114

Opening Times: Mon-Fri 9.00-20.00; Sat 9.00-18.00; Sun 10.30-17.30

The Fort
Tel: 669 4428

Opening times: Mon-Fri 9.00-20.00; Sat 9.00-18.00; Sun 10.00-17.30

Clothing also available at other selected stores, but *not* the Gyle. See also *Department Stores*

Debenhams

Wide range of clothing for babies and children (3-14 yrs), including own-brand ranges ('Trader', 'Casual Club' and 'Maine'), and designer names. Other names include Babbleboom, Tigerlilly and Jasper Conran for babies. For boys and girls, ranges include Barbie for Girls, JCB, IDX for Girls (7-14 yrs) and Red Herring, as well as those previously listed. See also Department Stores.

Available from:

109-112 Princes Street
Tel: 225 1320

Opening times: Mon-Wed, Fri 9.30-18.00; Thu 9.30-20.00; Sat 9.00-18.00; Sun 11.00-17.00. Times may extend during Festival

Children's clothing situated on lower ground floor.

Ocean Terminal
Ocean Drive
Tel: 553 8100

Opening hours: Mon-Fri 10.00-20.00; Sat 10.00-19.00; Sun 11.00-18.00

Slightly smaller range, but carries the same brands as Princes St branch.

The Disney Store

Selection of clothing for under 5s featuring Disney characters, including sleepwear. Also stock Disney character costumes and dressing up wear. See Toy Shops.

Available from:

18 Princes St
Tel: 557 2772

Opening times: Mon-Wed, Fri-Sat 9.00-18.00; Thu 9.00-19.00; Sun 11.00-17.00

Gyle Shopping Centre
Tel: 339 4944

Opening times: Mon, Tue, Wed 9.30-20.00; Thu, Fri 9.30- 21.00; Sat 9.00-18.00; Sun 10.00-18.00

Gap, Gap Kids & Baby Gap

Offers fashionable babywear 0-4yrs, with extensive newborn collection. Also stock daywear for 2-13 yrs. Range changes regularly.

Fort Kinnaird
Tel: 657 5613

Opening times: Mon-Fri: 10.00-20.00, Sat 9.30-18.00; Sun 10.30-18.00

Gyle Centre
Tel: 339 5972

Opening times: Mon-Wed 9.30-20.00; Thu, Fri 9.30-21.00; Sat 9.00-18.00; Sun 10.00-18.00

131-133 Princes St
Tel: 220 3303
Opening times: Mon-Wed, Fri, Sat 9.00-18.00;Thu 9.00-19.00; Sun 11.00-18.00
Access: direct access from Princes St. Lift, on left, at rear of shop. Nappy changing facilities.
Ocean Terminal
Tel: 553 6744
Opening times: Mon-Fri 10.00-20.00; Sat 10.00-19.00; Sun 11.00-18.00

Hand-in-Hand
Hirsel Law Schoolhouse
Nr Coldstream TD12 4HX
Tel: 01890 883496
Opening times: by appointment
Antique Christening gowns, bonnets and shawls. Period children's clothes, lace quilts, paisley shawls. Table and bed linen.

Jenners – Kids at Jenners
48 Princes St
Tel: 225 2442
Extensive range of quality and designer children's clothing, 0-8 yrs. Ranges include low birth weight baby clothing & beautiful Christening gowns. See *Department Stores*.

Laura Ashley
Carry range of co-ordinating clothing for girls (2-9 yrs). As well as traditionally styled 'little girl' smocks and dresses, and coats, there are more contemporary-styled dungarees, pinafores, t-shirts, knitwear and hats for casual and special occasions.

Available from:
51 George St
Tel: 225 1121
Opening times: Mon, Tue, Fri 9.30-17.30; Wed 10.00-17.30; Thu 9.30-19.00; Sat 9.00-17.30; Sun 12.30-16.30

Fort Retail Park
Tel: 669 2757
Opening times: Mon-Fri 10.00-20.00; Sat 9.00-18.00; Sun 10.30-17.30

Mackays
www.mackaysstores.co.uk
Good range of affordable baby and children's wear. Lots of co-ordinating outfits, sleepwear, leisure wear, underwear, padders and pram shoes, and clothes for outdoors and school. Staff tend to be friendly and helpful.

Children's wear available from:

Unit 5
Gyle Shopping Centre EH12 9JT
Tel: 538 8765
Opening times: Mon, Tue, Wed 9.30-20.00; Thu, Fri 9.30- 21.00; Sat 9.00-18.00; Sun 10.00-18.00

Mamas and Papas
Craigleith Retail Park
Tel: 0870 830 7703
Web: www.mamasandpapas.co.uk
Opening times: Mon-Fri, Sat 9.30-18.00; Thu 9.30-19.00; Sun 11.00-17.00
Stylish baby clothing, up to age 6 mths. Outfits and separates, all in subtle colours. Small range of contemporary designed maternity wear. Also stock prams and ranges of co-ordinating nursery equipment and accessories.

Marks and Spencer
Good range of durable baby and children's clothes, many in 100% cotton. Underwear, sleepwear, leisure wear, and party clothes, as well as clothes for outdoors and school. Also stock dressing up outfits, although these tend to be for over 5s, and link with seasons (such as Hallowe'en) or recent film releases (recent years' outfits have included Scooby Doo and Baloo). Range of padders, pram shoes and shoes (up to sizes 39/40). Baby range starts from newborn, with clothing for low birth weight babies.

Available from:
91 Princes St
Tel: 225 2301
Opening hours: Mon-Wed, Fri 9.00-19.00; Thu 9.00-20.00; Fri 9.00-19.00; Sat 8.30-18.00; Sun 11.00-17.00

Gyle Shopping Centre
Tel: 317 1333
Opening hours: Mon-Fri 9.00-22.00; Sat 8.00-20.00; Sun 9.00-18.00

Mothercare
Large selection of own brand clothes for children, from newborn to 10 yrs, including underwear, sleepwear (including sleep gowns), casual and fancy outfits, shoes and outerwear. Also carry a selection of low birth weight clothing. See also *Department Stores*.

Available from:

The Fort Retail Park
New Craighall Road EH15 3HH
Tel: 657 4050
Opening hours: Mon, Wed, Thu, Fri 9.00-20.00; Tue 9.30-20.00; Sat 9.00-18.00; Sun 10.00-17.00

Hermiston Gait Retail Park
Tel: 453 1383
Opening times: Mon-Fri 9.00-20.00 Sat 9.00-18.00 Sun 10.00-1700

Next

Babies (0-2 yrs), boys' and girls' clothing from 3-10 yrs. Contemporary, hard-wearing separates and casuals in vibrant colours. Underwear, footwear, outdoor wear, many in 100% cotton. Also stock party wear and some dressing up outfits. Schoolwear available via home shopping by catalogue or online. See *Shopping from Home* for details.

Available from:

107-109 Princes St
Tel: 225 9290
Opening times: Mon-Wed, Fri, Sat 9.00-18.00; Thu 9.00-19.30; Sun 11.00-18.00
Children's wear located in basement. Lift access.

Unit 8
Fort Retail Park
Tel: 657 1530
Opening times: Mon-Wed, Fri 9.30-20.00; Thu 9.30-21.00; Sat 9.00-18.00; Sun 10.00-18.00

Gyle Shopping Centre
Tel: 339 5989
Opening times: Mon-Wed, Fri 9.00-20.00; Thu 9.00-21.00; Sat 9.00-18.00; Sun 9.30-18.00

St James' Centre
Tel: 558 9590
Opening times: Mon-Wed 9.00-17.30; Thu 9.00-19.30; Fri, Sat 9.00-18.00; Sun 12.00-17.00

New and Junior Profile

88-92 Raeburn Pl
Stockbridge
Tel: 332 7928
Opening times: Mon-Sat 9.00-17.30
Children's wear, designer and casual 0-10 yrs. Good selection of wooden toys, rocking horses, dolls' prams and soft toys. Also sell lovely painted furniture.

Pine and Old Lace

46 Victoria St
Tel: 225 3287
Opening times: Mon-Sat 10.30-17.00, closed Wed
Phone to check if you are making a special trip, as this is a one-woman shop. Stock always includes antique Christening gowns. Shop not accessible to double pushchairs.

Softwear

4 Howard Street EH3 5JP
Tel/fax: 556 1242
Email: softwearscotland@aol.com
Web: www.softwearscotland.com
Small shop nr Canonmills which sells a lovely selection of clothing and accessories for babies and children, including blankets, 'buggy bags', pullovers, trousers, hats, mittens, t-shirts etc etc. There's an area to the rear of the shop where fleeces etc are made. Clothes (for both children and adults alike) are made from various fabrics, the patterns of which are just that little bit different.

The Royal Edinburgh Repository and Self Aid Society

23a Castle St
Tel: 220 1187
Opening times: Mon-Thu 9.30-17.00; Fri 9.30-16.30; Sat 9.30-16.30
The Society encourages people, particularly those in low income groups, to work in their own homes, using skills such as knitting, sewing, toy-making etc. The Edinburgh shop sells a unique collection of handmade articles, including beautiful baby and toddler hand-knitted items, handmade smock dresses etc, as well as toys. The shop also sells traditional old-fashioned items such as shawls and sleeping gowns. Special orders can be taken. All the money from the sale of goods is returned to the members direct.

DANCEWEAR

Along with the listing, some department stores also stock basic dance or keep-fit wear. It does pay to shop around. As we mentioned in the introduction to this section, some dance teachers also sell shoes and/or leotards etc.

Dancewear

182 Rose St
Tel: 226 5457

Opening times: Mon-Fri 9.30-17.15; Sat 9.00-17.00
This shop provides a patient and knowledgeable service for children of all ages. Competitive prices for shoes for ballet (satin and leather), tap, Highland, jazz and country dancing, as well as silk and satin shoes suitable for bridesmaids. Also sell leotards, tights, catsuits, ballet skirts, cross-over cardigans, tu-tus and ballet giftware. Will send out telephone orders with payment by card.

KILTS

Edinburgh has several good options when it comes to shopping for kilts. There are specialist shops, although shops such as Aitken and Niven, Jenners, Ortak, and John Lewis stock kilts, tartanwear and/or accessories.
Proper kilt pleats should fold back behind the previous pleat: this is what gives that wonderful swing, but it also makes them rather heavy and very expensive, as so much fabric is used. However, if you do choose to buy a full kilt, you will have a family heirloom, which can be handed down the generations. A reasonable alternative is a 'half kilt', in which not all the pleats are full, but it still swings well and looks good. Many shops also sell kilted skirts off the peg. Small kilts can have straps or a bodice to hold them up, and you can get jabot shirts with elastic around the waist to cover this up.
Shops which sell made-to-measure kilts usually have books of tartan (you may need to choose a tartan with a small set for a small kilt). These stores can usually help you link your surname to a specific sept or clan. They can also give the kilt a good 'wrap around' and a generous hem to let down. Some will change the wrapover side for different sexes.
You can really go overboard with the accompanying regalia, such as: jackets, shirts (with jabot or bow tie), sporran, shoes, socks, flashes – and for teenagers and adults, a sgian dubh. A kilt can also look good with a Fair Isle, Arran or Shetland jumper, or just a plain white shirt and socks. As your children get older, you may find teenagers turn to the trendy alternative look of big boots, pushed-down socks and t-shirts!
What is worn under the kilt is anyone's guess (except toddlers can't resist showing everybody!!). If you only need a kilt for your child (or other family members) for a special occasion, a good alternative is to hire one. See *Hiring*.

The following shops all stock kilts in various sizes.

Highland Laddie

6 Hutchison Ter
Tel: 455 7505
Complete outfits sold. All accessories available, jacket and shirt, brogues and shoes, ties, sporrans etc.

Hugh MacPherson Ltd

17 W Maitland St
Tel: 225 4008
Complete outfits made. Any size from a range of patterns. Also stock a selection of dresses, shorts and sweatshirts in tartan designs.

Hector Russel, Kiltmaker

Stocks full range of kilt and kilt regalia. Dress and evening accessories. Also stock tartan accessories and gimicky items.

Shops at:

95 Princes St
Tel: 225 3315

137 High St
Tel: 558 1254

MAKE YOUR OWN

Edinburgh has an excellent choice of wool and fabric shops, and you always end up with an 'exclusive' outfit. The shops listed below are those which we feel have something special to offer, and those which are more 'out of the way'.
John Lewis, The Cloth Shop and Kings Fabrics probably have the largest choice of pattern books and paper patterns. In these tomes, you'll find everything from maternity wear to pyjamas, dressing gowns and dressing up outfits. 'Teen' dolls can also have an extensive wardrobe to match your own, and there are usually popular soft toy patterns available.
There are many wool shops scattered around the suburbs and most stock baby wools. Pingouin and Rowan have children's knitting patterns in up to the minute designs and Pingouin also has a baby/toddler magazine. Paton's have a wide range of knitting patterns for small babies, starting at 14".

The Cloth Shop

169 Bonnington Rd
Tel: 554 7733
Opening times: Mon, Tue-Wed, Fri-Sat 9.30-17.00; Thu 9.30-19.00 . Sun 11.00-16.00
Large warehouse-style shop, with a fantastic selection of dress, curtain and upholstery fabric, and all the haberdashery that goes along with it. Stencil kits and cushion pads available, along with some great tulles and seasonally printed fabrics for dressing up

clothes. Small customer toilets near the children's play area. Car parking.

The Embroidery Shop

51 William St
Tel: 225 8642
Opening times: Mon-Fri 10.00-17.00; Sat 10.00-16.00
Embroidery supplies, birth sampler kits, lace and tapestry supplies. Also stock patchwork and quilting fabrics, patterns and notions. Specialist shop which also runs classes.

The Finishing Touch

17 St Patrick Sq
Tel: 667 0914
Opening times: Mon-Sat 10.00-17.30
Huge range of buttons in all shapes, sizes and colours. Novelty greetings cards, wrapping paper and ribbons. Every imaginable utensil and ingredient for cake decorating. Lots of helpful hints and advice. See also *Birthdays and Celebrations* and *Hiring*.

Helios Fountain

7 Grassmarket
Tel: 229 7884
Selection of craft materials, huge range of beads. Good selection of both wooden and cuddly toys, plus children's books.

Jenners

48 Princes St
Tel: 225 2442
4th floor: extensive range of haberdashery, knitting wools and patterns, and needlework kits. Also have a good range of stencil kits and accessories. Exhibition of needlework and kits in the spring. See *Department Stores*.

John Lewis

St James' Centre
Tel: 556 9121
Fabric & Haberdashery: wide choice of fabrics, from cheap and cheerful prints to sumptuous velvets. Stock sheeting, quilted fabrics, braiding, ribbons, buttons, motifs, lace etc. Craft materials such as beads, felt, fur fabric, tapestry and embroidery yarns, craft and needlework kits including samplers. Dolls' house kits, knitting wools and patterns, sewing and knitting machines and craft books.
Soft furnishings: Some great children's patterns, plus 'blackout' curtain lining, blinds. Also wipe-clean fabric for e.g. tablecovers.

Kings Fabrics

88 Newington Rd
Tel: 667 7210
Opening times: Mon-Sat 9.00-17.30; Sun 12.00-17.00
Large selection of fabrics, from cheap and cheerful cottons to fine silks. Also stocks a range of sheeting, fur fabric, felt, quilting, cords and wools — and of course, paper patterns. Lots of trimmings and motifs. There is also a range of curtain fabric and accessories.

MATERNITY CLOTHING & GOODS

More and more stores are offering maternity clothing which can reflect your usual dress-sense: no longer are mums-to-be forced to wear white-collared tent dresses. You can have anything from sleek suits to leopard print trousers, and all points in between. Maternity clothes now tend to be comfortable, fashionable and even flattering. See also *Make Your Own, Shopping from Home, Hiring* and *Baby and Children's Clothes*.
It's sensible to take time to pamper yourself, especially when pregnant. It keeps your own sense of identity and it's a great excuse for some 'you' time! We've tried to include some ideas of how and where you can get some pampering.
Remember though, don't use essential oils while pregnant, and it's recommended to keep away from nut oil bases, if you're thinking about massage oils etc. This also goes for baby massage/pampering products – you'd be surprised how many have almond oil bases, and how many assistants don't recognise that as a nut! In general, the only 'safe' essential oils to use with young children are lavender and chammomile; if in doubt, seek professional advice.

The Body Shop

Body Shop range includes all kinds of lotions, gels and pampering items for mums and mums-to-be, including cooling leg gel, massagers, and moisture-rich body creams, which intensify your skin's moisture content (might reduce stretch marks!!) As well as their tried and tested cocoa butter stick, the African Spa range is rich in cocoa butter and has no essential oils in it.
Selection changes throughout the year – there's usually special offers around holiday times.

Gyle Centre
Tel: 538 3333
Opening times: Mon, Tue, Wed 9.30-20.00; Thu, Fri 9.30- 21.00; Sat 9.00-18.00; Sun 10.00-18.00

Ocean Terminal
Tel: 555 4523
Opening times: Mon-Fri 10.00-20.00; Sat 10.00-19.00; Sun 11.00-18.00

Princes Mall
Tel: 556 2641
Opening hours: Mon-Wed, Fri, Sat 9.00-18.00; Thu 9.00-19.00; Sun 11.00-17.00

90a Princes St
Tel: 220 6330
Opening times: Mon-Sat 9.00-18.00; Thu 9.00-20.00; Sun 11.00-17.30

Boots the Chemist

Web: www.boots.com
Stocks a range of maternity accessories, nursing equipment, including washable breast pads. Babitens available to hire.

Craigleith Retail Park
Tel: 332 6114
Opening times: Mon-Fri 9.00-20.00; Sat 9.00-18.00; Sun 10.30-17.30

The Fort
Tel: 669 4428
Opening times: Mon-Fri 9.00-20.00; Sat 9.00-18.00; Sun 10.00-17.30

Gyle Shopping Centre
Tel: 317 1288
Opening times: Mon, Tue, Wed 9.30-20.00; Thu, Fri 9.30- 21.00; Sat 9.00-18.00; Sun 10.00-18.00

101 Princes St
Tel: 225 8331
Opening times: Mon-Sat 9.00-18.00; Thu 9.00-19.30; Sun 12.00-17.00
Also stocks some maternity bras.

Crabtree and Evelyn (London) Ltd

4 Hanover St
Tel: 226 2478
Opening times: Mon-Sat 10.00-18.00 (Thu 10.00-19.00 May-Xmas); Sun 12.00-17.00
Stepping into the shop, you're greeted by the sweet aroma of soaps, shampoos, bath gels and oils for mums in the tub. Creams, lotions, brushes and combs for after. The range includes traditional fragrances as well as more contemporary blends. There's also a range for dads. Small selection of Beatrix Potter soaps, bubble bath, lotions and creams for children. Also sells room fragrance products.

Dorothy Perkins

Web: www.dorothyperkins.co.uk
Range of co-ordinated maternity separates for both formal and casualwear. Selection of dresses also available.
Available from:

Unit 24
Cameron Toll Shopping Centre
Lady Road EH16 5PB
Tel: 664 7279

Debenhams
109-112 Princes Street
Tel: 225 1320
Opening times: Mon-Wed, Fri 9.30-18.00; Thu 9.30-20.00; Sat 9.00-18.00; Sun 11.00-17.00. Times may extend during Festival. Concession on 1st floor.

Unit 4a
Fort Retail Park
Lawhouse Toll EH15 3RH
Tel: 657 4351
Opening times: Mon-Fri 10.00-20.00; Sat 9.00-18.00; Sun 10.00-18.00

Unit 17
Gyle Shopping Centre EH12 9JR
Tel: 317 1693
Opening times: Mon, Tue, Wed 9.30-20.00; Thu, Fri 9.30- 21.00; Sat 9.00-18.00; Sun 10.00-18.00

Unit 34-36
St James' Centre EH1 3SL
Tel: 556 5076

Formes

4 Howe Street
Tel : 0131 225 9777
Web: www.formes.com
Opening hours: Mon-Wed, Fri-Sat 10.00-18.00; Thu 10.00-19.00
A new location for this company in Edinburgh. Emphasis on contemporary styling – so plenty of strong lines. Pricing towards the upper end of high street prices.

Frasers

145 Princes St
Tel: 225 2472
2nd floor: maternity and nursing bras. Bra fitting service. See *Department Stores*.

John Lewis

St James' Centre
Tel: 556 9121
Ground floor: maternity tights
1st: casual co-ordinated separates and some more formal suits and dresses. Good range of swimsuits and maternity bras. Helpful, trained staff. See *Department Stores*.

Mamas and Papas

Craigleith Retail Park
Tel: 0870 830 7703
Web: www.mamasandpapas.co.uk
Opening times: Mon-Fri 9.00-20.00; Sat 9.00-18.00; Sun 10.00-17.00
Capsule range of contemporary designed maternity wear. Also nursery accessories and baby clothing up to 6 mths.

Marks and Spencer

Stock maternity underwear and hosiery. Nursing bras also available in the lingerie departments: bra fitting service available. Available at:

91 Princes St
Tel: 225 2301

Gyle Shopping Centre
Tel: 317 1333
Opening hours: Mon-Fri 9.00-22.00; Sat 8.00-20.00; Sun 9.00-18.00

Mothercare

Selection of Mothercare branded clothes for both everyday wear and special occasions. Swimwear, nightwear and maternity/nursing bras, plus accessories, such as breast pumps and breast pads. See Department Stores.

Available at:
Fort Retail Park
Tel: 657 4050
Opening times: Mon, Wed-Fri 9.00-20.00; Tue 9.30-20.00; Sat 9.00-18.00; Sun 10.00-17.00

Mothercare World
Hermiston Gait Retail Park
Tel: 453 1383
Opening times: Mon-Fri 9.00-20.00; Sat 9.00-18.00; Sun 10.00-17.00

SCHOOL UNIFORMS

Many shops and stores stock a selection of shorts, trousers, pinafores, skirts, shirts, blazers and socks in traditional school colours. Their stock is most extensive in Jul and Aug, but most have a small stock tucked away somewhere throughout the year. These include:
Asda, BhS, Frasers, John Lewis, Marks and Spencer, Next, Sainsbury's, Woolworth's, although there are many more.

Aitken and Niven

77-79 George St
Tel: 225 1461
Web: www.aitken-niven.co.uk
Opening times: Mon-Sat 9.00-17.30
Access: two entrances from George St both with a few steps up.
Ground floor: see Children's Shoes
School wear dept is situated on 1st floor.

And:
6 Falcon Rd W
Morningside
Tel: 477 3922
Opening times: Mon-Sat 9.00-17.30
Access: street-level entrance. Shop stocks schoolwear, sportswear and children's shoes.
Nappy changing facilities.
See also *Department Stores*.

Clan House

117 Grove St
Tel: 229 6857

9 S Clerk St
Tel: 667 4282

Shops stock blazers in traditional colours, and most Edinburgh school badges to sew on. Also stock Edinburgh school ties. Good stockist for independent schools.

SECOND-HAND GOODS

Charity shops throughout the city, such as Oxfam, Cancer Research, Shelter, The Bethany Trust and so on, are worth keeping an eye on for children's clothes. As some areas of the city offer much richer pickings than others, it's sometimes worthwhile going further afield than your local shops. See under 'Charitable and Benevolent Organisations' in the Yellow Pages for addresses of their shops. Most are staffed by volunteers, so

opening times can be short, with lunchtime closing.
You could also look through the small ads in local newspapers and publications, notices in supermarkets, health centres, newsagents etc. Jumble sales, NCT sales, YWCA Toy Fairs are also good sources.

Hand-in-Hand

Hirsel Law Schoolhouse
R Coldstream TD12 4HX
Tel: 01890 883496
Opening times: by appointment
Antique Christening gowns, bonnets and shawls. Period children's clothes, lace quilts, paisley shawls.

National Childbirth Trust Sales

NCT Centre
University Health Service
5th floor
5 Bristo Square EH8 9AL
Tel: 668 3257
Please phone for current opening times.
Spring and Autumn sees NCT Nearly New Sales held in local venues in the city. Baby and children's clothes, equipment, toys and maternity wear. Percentage of selling price goes to NCT funds. Check press or contact centre for details.

Pine and Old Lace

46 Victoria St
Tel: 225 3287
Opening times: Mon-Sat 10.30-17.00, closed Wed.
Phone to check if you are making a special trip, as this is a one-woman shop. Stock always includes antique Christening gowns. Shop not accessible to double pushchairs.

St Fillan's 'Nearly New' Children's Clothes Shop

St Fillan's Church Hall
8 Buckstone Dr
Contact: Sharon Hunter
Tel: 445 3078 (16.00-20.00)
Opening times: 1st Mon 19.00-21.00 and 1st Tue 9.30-12.00 of each month during term time.
Good quality, reasonably priced clothes for babies-teens, including school, dance, organisation and sports wear.

SHOES

Many mothers think that retailers put children's shoe departments in basements or on 1st floors simply to irritate them and to add to the overall hassle of the shoe-buying trip. In fact, it is for safety – to ensure that junior does not take a trip straight out the door into the street when asked to take a few steps to see if the shoes fit!
Many stores now operate a ticketing system: it's best to take a ticket before looking around. Try to avoid Saturdays and school holidays if possible, as these departments tend to be particularly busy.
The shops below with an asterisk mark (*) after their name are listed in the Children's Foot Health Register, whose aims are endorsed by the British Medical Association, and other health, shoes and chiropody associations. The CFHR lists shops which promise to: stock children's shoes in full and half length sizes from infants size 3 to size 5 1/2 for boys and girls; stock 4 width fittings; employ trained staff to measure both feet and carefully fit shoes at time of sale.
This list is updated annually and is available from: The Children's Foot Health Register, PO Box 249, London W4 5EX, enclosing a 9"x6" SAE. Some libraries keep a copy for reference. It also lists the full aims of the register, useful information on foot care and lists footwear retailers throughout Britain, who promise to abide by the register's aims.
Don't be shy where your child's feet are concerned. If you don't think a shoe fits, ask to have it checked by another fitter. Complain to management if you feel standards in a shop have slipped. Several shops which sell nursery equipment also sell soft shoes for babies and toddlers.

The following shops sell good quality 'good brand' names in width fittings.

Aitken and Niven*

77-79 George St
Tel: 225 1461
Medium-sized ground floor dept. Start-rite shoes and slippers.

Clarks Shoe Shop*

79 Princes St
Tel: 220 1261
Opening times: Mon-Wed, Fri 9.30-17.30; Thu 9.30-19.30; Sat 9.00-18.00; Sun 11.00-17.00
Children's department downstairs. Pushchairs can be left with staff on ground floor. Good selection. A range of pre-walking

shoes, available in sizes 3-4½ and width fittings E-H. As in all Clarks Shops, the Toddler Team Club is available for first shoe customers. A picture is taken of the child in their first 'new shoes', a fitting record is also provided, a competition entry and a booklet outlining general foot care.
Also has an 'odd shoe service'. Once your child's foot has been accurately measured, you select a suitable shoe (most styles are available). This information is then sent to head Office and a pair is sent to the shop in approx 3 weeks. These shoes cost 25% more than a standard pair. For entertainment, there's wall Lego, books and car rides (profits from which go to charity). Children may use staff toilet if accompanied by a parent and a member of staff.

Also at:
Cameron Toll Shopping Centre*
Tel: 664 9111
Opening hours: Mon-Wed, Fri: 9.00-19.00; Thu 9.00-20.00; Sat 9.00-18.00; Sun 10.00-17.00

Gyle Shopping Centre*
Tel: 317 1456
Mon-Wed, Fri: 9.30-20.00; Thu 9.30-21.00; Sat 9.00-18.00; Sun 10.00-18.00

John Lewis
St James' Centre
Tel: 556 9121
Dept on 2nd floor which offers a timed appointment service during peak times. Stocks Start-rite, Clarks, Buckle My Shoe, and various continental and designer brands, such as Elefantin and Timberland. Offers a full range of shoes, slippers, dance shoes, wellies and sandals.

Russell and Bromley Ltd
106 Princes St EH2 3AA
Tel: 225 7444
Opening times: Mon-Wed, Fri, Sat 9.30-18.00; Thu 9.30-19.30; Sun 11.00-17.00
Extensive range of children's shoes. Staff are fully trained in fitting. Children's dept is on the 1st floor. Stock Clark's, Start-rite, Kickers and many more makes of shoe. If required, assistance is given by staff to access it with, for example, a pram. Children may use the staff toilet in an emergency. Accessible by double pushchairs. Also stock wellies and slippers. The colourful carousel horses always attract under 5s attention!
If special help is required when making purchases, the store advises that 'back to school' periods are best avoided, as it's an extremely busy time: otherwise, please phone branch in advance.

Shoos
8 Teviot Pl
Tel: 220 4626
Opening times: Mon-Sat 9.30-17.30
Access: direct from street
Start-rite main stockist with a comprehensive range of shoes and boots in up to 6 width fittings, starting from baby size 2. Also stock slippers, wellies, sandals, canvas shoes and leather trainers in width fittings. Fully trained staff, with a member of the Society of Shoefitters usually present. All on ground level with toilet facilities. Start-rite odd shoe service.

BICYCLES

See *Travel & Transport: Cycling* for general information on cycling with children.

Child Seats and Equipment

Most shops will fit a child seat for nothing, or for a minimal charge if you have purchased it at their store. Do not lose any of the nuts and bolts, as some are unique and irreplaceable.
The addition of a child seat will obviously affect the handling and stability of your bike, as well as placing a greater strain on it, so keep it well maintained, especially the brakes and the wheels.

Rear Child Seats
The best rear child seats are made from high-impact, rigid moulded plastic, with headrests to support a child who has fallen asleep. They should also have the following items: a safety harness, footguards and straps to prevent feet getting caught in the rear wheel. If you have a sprung saddle, it makes sense to either cover or replace it, so that little fingers do not get caught. Suitable for children from around the age at which they are able to sit unsupported (usually 6/7 mths) until they get too heavy for the seat. This aspect varies with manufacturer recommendation, but it's usually 22kg approx. up to age 3-4.

Front Child Seats
These are not recommended. The child feels colder than would be the case in a rear-mounted seat, shielded by your body. Also, if a child falls asleep in a front mounted seat, you must use one arm to support the child and ride one-handed, which is unsafe.

Child Trailers
These are two wheeled pushchairs that attach to the rear fork of adult bike. The fixing device allows the adult bike to be laid on

its side without tipping the trailer up. Most can carry two children from 9 mths- 5/6 yrs, with the limiting factor being the weight of the children – the maximum combined weight is usually 50 kg. A very young child can also be carried when strapped into a child seat, although this will leave no room for a second child. Most trailers also have a luggage space at the back. Trailers usually come with a rain-and-sun cover and a visibility flag. The best also have quick release wheels and can be folded down for easy carriage in trains, buses and cars. They are fairly expensive, but they do tend to have a high resale value. They also make useful luggage or shopping carriers, long after families have grown up. Makes include: Adams, Burley, Bike Trax.

Compared with a child seat, the child misses the view, feels the bumps more and is right at exhaust height on any road. However, a single adult can take two young children at once, the balance of the adult bicycle is less affected and the trailer may stay upright if the adult bicycle falls over.

Trailercycles

These consist of a special frame, without front wheels and with forks, which attach to an adult bike (or tandem), either at the seat post or rear rack. The child can help with the pedalling, but braking and steering are left to the adult. They are excellent for taking children out cycling in situations where either it would not be safe to let a child cycle independently, or where a child wouldn't be able to cope with the distance or hills. It's also a great way for a child to learn about observing traffic, signalling and road positioning while being safely in the control of an experienced adult. Some models have gears so children can learn how to change gear without having to worry about steering at the same time. The great advantage of trailercycles is their versatility. You can buy a 'seconds' tow hitch, which allows the trailercycle to be quickly swapped between adult bikes. A trailercycle can also be carried easily on trains by simply detaching and storing alongside the adult bike in the cycle storage area. Trailer bikes are suitable for children from 3 or 4 yrs up to around age 9 yrs. Makes include: Bike Trax, Adams, Ally Cat.

You can get conversion kits to alter a regular child's bike to a trailercycle. Obviously, they are much cheaper, but they do not really give satisfactory results.

Tandems

There are several options:

'Junior back' style tandem. These have a frame designed for an adult 'pilot' at the front and a child 'stoker' at the back. A potentially good solution if you are to do a lot of cycling, but they're not very versatile. Makes include: Dawes, Orbit, Thorn, Swallow.

Ordinary tandem fitted with 'kiddy cranks' or crank shorteners. More versatile than a junior back tandem, as it can easily be converted back to an ordinary tandem again.

The advantage of a tandem over a trailercycle is that a few of them can also be fitted with a rear child seat to carry a very young child, in addition to the older child that is pedalling. The disadvantage is that they are not easy to store or to carry on trains.

Tricycles

A tricycle fitted with one or two child seats at the back can also be a good way of getting the family on the move. Suitable for children from 12 mths to 5 yrs.

Helmets

Though not legally compulsory, a helmet should be an essential piece of equipment for all cyclists. It is important to take your child to the shop to have them fitted properly so they don't wobble. Look for one which has a European or American standard, preferably both as these standards have superseded the British one. To make them more acceptable for children, go for the coolest looking one you can afford! Children who are putting a lot of effort into pedalling will also appreciate one with plenty of ventilation. Makes include: Met, Hamax, Cateye, Specialized, Giro, Bell. Helmets are all 'first impact', so after a serious bash, in an accident or in play, they are damaged and should be replaced.

General Safety

Under no circumstances should you cycle with a baby in a backpack or sling.

Keep children's shoelaces short and tucked away. The same applies to scarves and other loose clothing. Dress children in brightly coloured clothing, so that they are visible to motorists. Think twice before carrying a very restless child. Beware of very cold and wet weather. Make sure that the adult bike is kept in good mechanical order. Especially ensure that the brakes are always working well to cope with the additional weight that the bike will be carrying.

A Good Tip!

It's a good idea to try out some of the more expensive items like trailers or trailercycles before you buy, to make sure that you are happy with the handling and that it's the right bit of gear for you. Try and borrow from another family, or consider hiring for a weekend – you could save yourself an expensive mistake!

Go to a bike shop specialising in trailer bikes or tandems for advice on the best and most suitable equipment to buy.

BICYCLE SHOPS

Alexander Paterson Bicycle Repairs

Unit 3
37 Roseburn St
Tel: 538 7329

Opening times: Mon-Fri 10.00-18.00; Sat 10.30-12.30; Sun closed.

Specialises in all aspects of cycle repairs and building cycles to customers' specifications. Does have access to cycles for retail selling but does not stock them. Also sells trailer bikes, child trailers and tandems. Repairs take 24-48 hours. Sells and fits child seats.

Alpine Bikes

48 Hamilton Pl
Tel: 225 3286
Web: www.alpinebikes.co.uk

Opening times: Mon-Wed, Fri, Sat 9.00-18.00; Thu 9.00-19.00; Sun 12.00-17.00

Adult and child bikes, child seats and helmets, trailer bikes and child trailers. Also Gore bikewear, Altura clothing and panniers. Bike spares and repair service with 24 hour turn around. Hires out trailer bikes, child trailers and mountain bikes.

B.G. Cycles and Blades

48 Portobello High St
Tel: 657 5832
Web: www.bgcycles.co.uk

Opening times: Mon-Fri 9.00-18.30; Sat 9.00-18.00; Sun 10.00-17.00

Adult and child bikes, trailer bikes, child seats and helmets. Also in-line skates. Also repairs and spares – can uplift and deliver bikes for repair or service within a 15-mile radius for a small charge. Hires out mountain bikes (adult only) and skates.

Bain's Bicycles

21 Newhaven Main St
Tel: 551 2839

Opening times: Tue-Sat 16.00-20.00

Mainly a repair and wheel building shop, though some spares are sold. Does not sell bikes or child seats.

The Bicycle Repair Man

111 Newington Rd
Tel: 667 5959

Opening times: Mon-Sat 9.00-17.30; Sun 11.00-17.00

Adult and child bikes, child seats and helmets, trailer bikes and child trailers. Bike spares and same day repair service.

The Bicycleworks

29-30 Argyle Pl
Tel: 228 8820

Opening times: Mon-Fri 8.00-20.00; Sat & Sun 10.00-18.00

A repair and wheel building shop with a wide range of spares and accessories. Also sells child seats. Instant puncture repairs or tyre replacement. Fast turn around on all other repairs/servicing.

Also at:

3 High St, Peebles
Tel: 01721 723423

Bike Trax

11 Lochrin Pl
Tel: 228 6633
Web: www.biketrax.co.uk

Opening times: Mon-Sat 9.30 -18.00; Sun 12.00-17.00

Adult and child bikes, child seats and helmets, trailer bikes, child trailers, tandems and folding bikes. DAWES, Ridgeback, Giant, Brompton etc. Free after sales service. Bike repair shop will repair any make of bike, including children's bikes. 24 hr turn around where possible – miracles take longer. Free estimates. Free advice on cycle matters, local cycle routes, etc. Also hires out bikes and equipment. Hire before you buy, hire charge deducted from purchase price.

Blackhall Cycles

15 Marischal Pl
Tel: 538 8580
Web: www.blackhallcycles.co.uk

Opening times: Mon-Sat 9.00-18.00 (closed for lunch 13.00-14.00). Closed Sun.

Adult and child bikes, trailer bikes, child trailers, child seats and helmets and bike spares. Free fitting of child seats if seat bought at shop. Same day repairs and servicing.

City Cycles – The Roof Rack Shop

30 Rodney St
Tel: 557 2801
Web: www.roofrackshop.co.uk

Opening times: Mon-Sat 9.00-17.30; Sun 12.00-16.00

Specialists in children's cycle helmets, child seats, cycle clothing, spares and safety accessories. Comprehensive range of quality bicycles for 2+ yrs up at competitive prices. Free after sales safety check on all new cycles and fast repair service on any make of cycle. Massive range of car roof and boot racks in stock to transport bikes for all the family.

Cycles
12 West Preston St
Tel: 667 6239
Opening times: Mon-Sat 9.00-17.00 (early closing Wed – 14.00). Closed Sun
Bikes for adults and children over 5 years. Child seats, repairs and spares. BMX specialist.

Dave's Bicycle Store
39 Argyle Pl
Tel: 229 8528
Opening times: Mon-Sat 10.00-18.00. Closed Sun
Used bikes for adults and children. Trade-ins welcome.

Edinburgh Bicycle Co-operative
5-9 Alvanley Ter
Whitehouse Loan
Tel: 228 1368
Web: www. edinburgh-bicycle.com
Opening times:
Summer hours – April-Sept: Mon-Fri 10.00-19.00; Sat & Sun 10.00-18.00. Winter hours – Oct-March: Mon-Wed, Fri 10.00-18.00; Thu 10.00-19.00; Sat & Sun 10.00-18.00.
Large selection of approved children's helmets. Child seats from America that can be detachable or permanently fitted to your cycle. Children are welcome and there are toys to keep them amused while you shop. Free customer newsletters and mail order catalogue available.

Edinburgh Cycle Hire & Cycle Safaris
29 Blackfriars St
Tel: 556 5560
Web: www.cyclescotland.co.uk
Opening times:
Summer: daily, 9.00-21.00. Winter: Usually daily, 10.00-18.00 (but please phone before setting off).
Sells adult and child bikes, child seats, trailer bikes, child trailers, tandems. Repairs and servicing. Also hires out large selection of adult and child bikes, tandem, trailer bikes, child trailer, child seats etc. Also organises cycle tours, holidays and days out.

Freewheelin'
91 Slateford Rd
Tel: 337 2351
Opening times: Mon-Fri 9.30-17.30; Sat 9.30-17.00; Sun 11.00-17.00 (Closed on Sun in Jan-Mar).
Adult and children's bikes, child seats and helmets. Can also order trailer bikes, child trailers and tandems. Spares and repair service with same/next day turn around.

Great Bikes No Bull
276 Leith Walk
Tel: 467 7775
Opening times: Mon-Wed, Fri, Sat 9.00-17.30; Thu 9.00-17.30. Closed Sun
Adult and children's bikes. Full range of safety accessories including child seats and helmets. Christmas Club. Hire before you buy, hire charge deducted from purchase price. In basement, Recycling (Tel: 553 1130) offers reconditioned adult and child bikes guaranteed for 3 months.

Halfords Superstore
Seafield Rd, Leith
Tel: 554 4140

11 Straiton Mains, Straiton
Tel: 448 2248
Opening times: Mon-Fri 8.00-20.00; Sat 8.00-18.00; Sun 9.00-17.00
Good selection of children's sit-and-ride toys, trikes, pedal cars and bikes - Apollo and Raleigh. Child seats, spare parts and accessories. Christmas club. Free after sales service. Usually repair bikes bought here, but may occasionally do small outside repairs. Major repairs in-store. Free fitting of child seat if bike bought at Halfords.

JRS Cycles
46-48 Silverknowes Rd
Tel: 312 6046
Opening times: Mon-Sat 9.00-17.00; Sun 11.00-16.00
Adult and children's bikes, child seats and helmets. Spares and repair service with same/next day turn around.

McDonald Cycles
26-28 Morrison St
Tel: 229 8473
Opening times: Mon-Sat 9.30-18.00; Sun 11.00-17.00
Good selection of children's trikes and bikes – Raleigh, DiamondBack, Giant and Dawes. Cycle parts (amongst others), child seats, children's helmets, children's cycle capes, spare parts and safety accessories. Christmas club. Free after sales service. Will repair any bike, if parts available. Usually 24-hr turn-around, sometimes quicker for own customers. Will fit child seat free if both bike and seat are bought here, otherwise £8.

Also at:

35 High St, Musselburgh
Tel: 665 1777
Opening times: Mon-Tue & Thu-Sat 9.00-17.30. Closed Wed & Sun

118 Dalry Rd
Tel: 346 0191
Opening times: Mon-Sat 9.00-1730; Sun 11.00-17.00
Both the Musselburgh and Dalry shops have free parking nearby.

Sandy Gilchrist Cycles
1 Cadzow Pl, Abbeyhill
Tel: 652 1760
Opening times: Mon-Wed, Fri 9.30-18.00; Thu 9.30-19.00; Sat 9.00-17.30; Closed Sun
Children's trikes and bikes – Giant, Peugeot, Universal and Muddy Fox. Wide selection on view. Several types of child seats, both high back and low back. Children's helmets, spares and safety accessories. ACT member. Christmas club. Repairs done on any make of bike, 24-hr turn-around when possible. Free estimates. Charge approx. £7 to fit child seats.

Velo Ecosse
25-27 Bruntsfield Pl
Tel: 477 2557
Email: veloecosse@freeuk.com
Opening times: Mon-Wed, Fri 9.30-18.30; Thu 9.30-19.30; Sat/Sun 10.00-18.00
Children's and adult bikes, child seats and helmets. Trailercycles and trailers and large range of cycle clothing. Spares and accessories. Repairs and servicing done within 24-48 hours.

BOOKS

Even in these days of Amazon.com etc, there is nothing quite like looking around a real bookshop. No matter whether you are looking for new, second-hand, or trying to track down a title from your childhood, Edinburgh is well-provided by bookshops. Admittedly, conditions are not always ideal: small spaces, crammed with bookshelves which seem so appealing when you are childless, suddenly become more of an obstacle course when you are pregnant or have children. However, on the whole booksellers try to accommodate children – and those shops with trained (or willing!) staff will always be prepared to fetch a title for you, if they know where it is.
Most shops now have some sort of distraction for toddlers and young children, such as boxes of toys, tables and chairs, or reading-books. Better stores have staff who are well-trained, specialise in children's books and can give invaluable advice and recommendations.
If you cannot find the book you require, most bookshops will be happy to order it for you. You may find that the smaller stores can order it in for you just as quickly as the larger chains: In addition to books and audio books, you can also order large print books and books in other than English via bookshops, should you require them.

Despite television and videos, books are still extremely popular with under 5s. Books can be introduced at the baby stage, where the focus is on bold pictures and robust pages. By 9 mths, most babies will be happy to sit on your knee and look at a book, for at least a few moments. The bedtime story for a toddler is an ideal way to wind down after a hectic day, and to spend 10 mins or so talking with the child. Books introduce children to words and language they would not normally hear in normal conversation (or on television!) and greatly increase language development. They can also help introduce children to concepts, ideas and situations out of their normal, everyday life, so helping to stimulate their imagination. There are also titles which can help young children to come to terms with some of the more traumatic aspects of growing up, such as the loss of a grandparent. If you are looking for such titles, ask in your bookshop – the education dept can be helpful if it has one.
There is a tremendous choice for under 5s, superbly illustrated in many different styles, which are entertaining for parent and child alike – though be prepared for the 'favourite' book, you may find yourself reading it at least twice everyday: our family's record is eight times in a row!

We have tried to list the best stocked and most friendly bookshops. Children's books are also sold in supermarkets, department stores, toy shops, some stationers and also via mail order (see *Shopping from Home*).
New books may seem expensive, but they compare very well with the price of toys and videos, and they offer excellent value for money; well-loved books can be handed down through families as well as toys etc. You could also ask for Book Tokens for gifts for your children at Christmas or birthday time: ask for National Book Tokens, which can be used in most UK bookshops, rather than shop-specific ones. From the age of around 3+, a child will enjoy choosing their very own book!
Look out also for charity shops, church book sales, second-hand and jumble sales. Libraries also host sales, and sometimes you can pick great bargains, such as '10 for the price of 1'!

Library tickets are available for children from birth (see Libraries) and regular library visits help to expand the choice of books available to your child. Some toy libraries also lend books and cassettes. Also, look out for any storytelling or author sessions during holidays in your local library or bookshop.

The Edinburgh Book Festival is an annual event, held in Charlotte Square Gardens, which has storytelling and author events specifically for children, usually from around 3 yrs+. In addition, there is always a children's book marquee, which has a great range of titles, and often has some available in advance of their actual general publication date or at special prices.

A few children's books have an Edinburgh theme. There are many on the subject of Greyfriar's Bobby, and there is also the famous 'Maisie' series. While they have good illustrations, many of them are unfortunately rather too text-heavy for small children. That said, they are often popular choices for gifts: note that some of the 'Maisie' series are also available in Gaelic.
As a child Robert Louis Stevenson lived in Heriot Row, in Edinburgh, and in his 'A Child's Garden of Verse', the poem 'The Lamplighter' is about the man who lit the lamp outside his home – the lamp is still there, though it's electric now. And for older children's interest, JK Rowling wrote the first Harry Potter novel in Edinburgh.

Out of Print Books

Some bookshops offer a free search service for out of print titles. Others may be able to guide you towards companies which specialise in searching and locating out of print titles – it's always worth asking! Alternatively, start trawling the second-hand bookshops, where you can still find hidden jewels.

Bauermeister Booksellers

19 George IV Bridge
Tel: 226 5561
Email: orders@bauermeister.co.uk
Web: www.bauermeister.co.uk
Opening times: Mon-Fri 9.00-20.00; Sat 9.00-17.30; Sun 12.00-17.00

Popular general and academic bookshop with recently expanded stationery department downstairs. The children's section is on the ground floor, next to the stairs to the lower ground floor. Books and cassette sets (including Scottish titles) in the children's department. Greetings cards are on the ground floor, all other stationery is on the lower ground from where staff will be happy to bring it, should this be necessary. Friendly staff will advise on titles, and can order any book in print in the UK. Will allow the use of staff toilet for children.

Blackwell's: Thin's Bookshop South Bridge

53-62 South Bridge,
Edinburgh, EH1 1YS
Tel: 0131 622 8222
Fax: 0131 557 8149
Email: Edinburgh@blackwell.co.uk
Opening hours: Mon, Wed-Fri 9:00-20:00;Tue 9:30-20:00; Sat 9:00 - 18:00; Sun 11:00 to 17:00

The Book Swop

28 Bruntsfield Pl EH10 4HJ
Tel: 229 9451
Email: jim@thistledhu.co.uk
Opening times: Mon-Sat 10.00-17.00; closed Sun

Another way to expand on your reading selection. You trade in your unwanted books and, if they are suitable, you receive a credit voucher, valid for 1 year, which can be used to purchase titles from the other pre-owned books. The shop usually has several hundred second-hand children's titles in good condition! There are also second-hand titles for cash sale only. You can also return a used book bought from this shop and use it as part exchange for another (a third of the price you pay towards another book).
Also stocks discount and full-price new books, as well as atlases and maps.

Borders

Unit 26
Fort Kinnaird Retail Park EH15 3RD
Tel: 657 4041
Opening hours: Mon-Sat 9.00-22.00; Sun 10.00-20.00
Car parking: parent & child parking spaces located near to store.

Bright, airy store on one floor. With a lovely children's area, complete with scatter cushions, towards the rear of the store. Good range of titles, including touchy-feely books, gift boxes with books & related soft toys etc. for younger children. Usually have a range of books with tapes. Store also carries a pretty good range of graphic novels, comics, magazines and journals from around the world. Hosts a storytime every Sat and Sun at noon. During school holidays, there are daily art events (starts at 14.00). Check the events board in-store for current details, or phone.
Breastfeeding welcomed, and there's a private area, should a mother prefer privacy. Nappy-changing area (M&F).

Ottakar's

57 George St
Tel: 225 4495
Opening hours: Mon-Wed, Fri-Sat 9.00-19.00; Thu 9.00-20.00; Sun 11.30-17.00

Excellent children's department with a large selection of books and tapes, along with a wide range of games and educational toys, for all ages, up a ramp at the middle (left) of the ground floor. Spacious, with plenty of room for pushchairs. At the time of writing, there's a wooden rocking horse for children to have a ride on in the dept: this certainly lengthens our stays! Able to order most UK books if not in stock. Toilet facilities are situated upstairs beside the café – see *Eating Out*.

Stockbridge Bookshop

26 North West Circus Place
Tel: 225 5355
Fax: 220 5323
Email: sbridge@flatman.co.uk
Opening times: Mon-Wed, Fri 8.30-20.00; Thu 8.30-21.00; Sat 8.30-20.00; Sun 11.00-19.00

Bright, colourful children's section up 2 steps at back of shop, marked by a colourful sign above the entrance. Good selection of board books, paperbacks, bargain books and gift books. Some book and tape sets. Range expanded at Christmas. Good general range of hardback, paperback and discounted titles.
Birthday cards and gift wrap paper. Selection of cut-price cds. Table and chairs for browsing.
There is also an extremely well-stocked schools showroom in basement, which has a large selection of non-fiction titles. Happy to donate posters and publicity material to teachers. If you can't find what you're looking for, they are usually happy to check if relevant titles are downstairs, although it's not always possible for them to do so at the weekend. Can produce a computerised list on specific topics requested. Will reserve books, and can also offer a 48 hr order service for general in-print titles: while more obscure titles may take longer, they can often get your order in within 24 hrs. Friendly staff will allow use of the staff toilet for young children, and can find space for breastfeeding.

Waterstone's Bookshop

13/14 Princes St (East End)
Tel: 556 3034
Mon-Fri 9.00-21.00; Sat 9.00-19.30; Sun 10.30-19.00

Well-designed children's section at back of ground floor. Bold colour scheme, lowered ceiling, shelves that children can reach, and seating. Books are classified in age groups. Excellent selection of hardback and paperback titles. Regular activities for children – ask to be put on the children's mailing list. Happy to donate posters and publicity material to teachers. Staff toilet is available in emergencies; it's in the basement, so you have to escorted by a member of staff. There is a lift which can be used for prams and pushchairs, but again ask for assistance.

Also at:

128 Princes St (West End)
Tel: 226 2666
Mon-Sat 8.30-20.00; Sun 10.30-19.00
Lift to children's dept on 1st floor. Good range of books, cushions to sit on. Toilet for the disabled in the basement and a baby room for feeding and changing at front of basement up a few steps. Starbuck's Coffee Shop on 2nd floor.

83 George St
Tel: 225 3436
Mon-Fri 9.30-21.00; Sat 9.30-20.00; Sun 11.00-18.00
A large shop on 2 floors and a mezzanine with a vast range of books for both adults and children. Its emphasis is on 'fun for all the family' with events and long opening hours. The shop is packed with books, but has been made more pushchair friendly. The children's department is on the ground floor. Brightly decorated with unusual kites. Huge selection of titles – and staff are always ready to help. Baby room and public toilet adjacent to the children's section. Baby room has complimentary wipes and cream.

The following stores also stock children's books

Bargain Books

100A Princes St
Stocks some very cheap picture books and activity books. Some very low cost children's board and picture books – great for party bags etc. Frequent offers include the like of '5 for £5'. Also stocks cut price gift wrap and Christmas paper.

Bookworld

63 Princes St
Princes Mall

Popular children's paperbacks and some very low-priced picture and storybooks, some as low as 30p-50p; great for party prizes and stocking fillers.

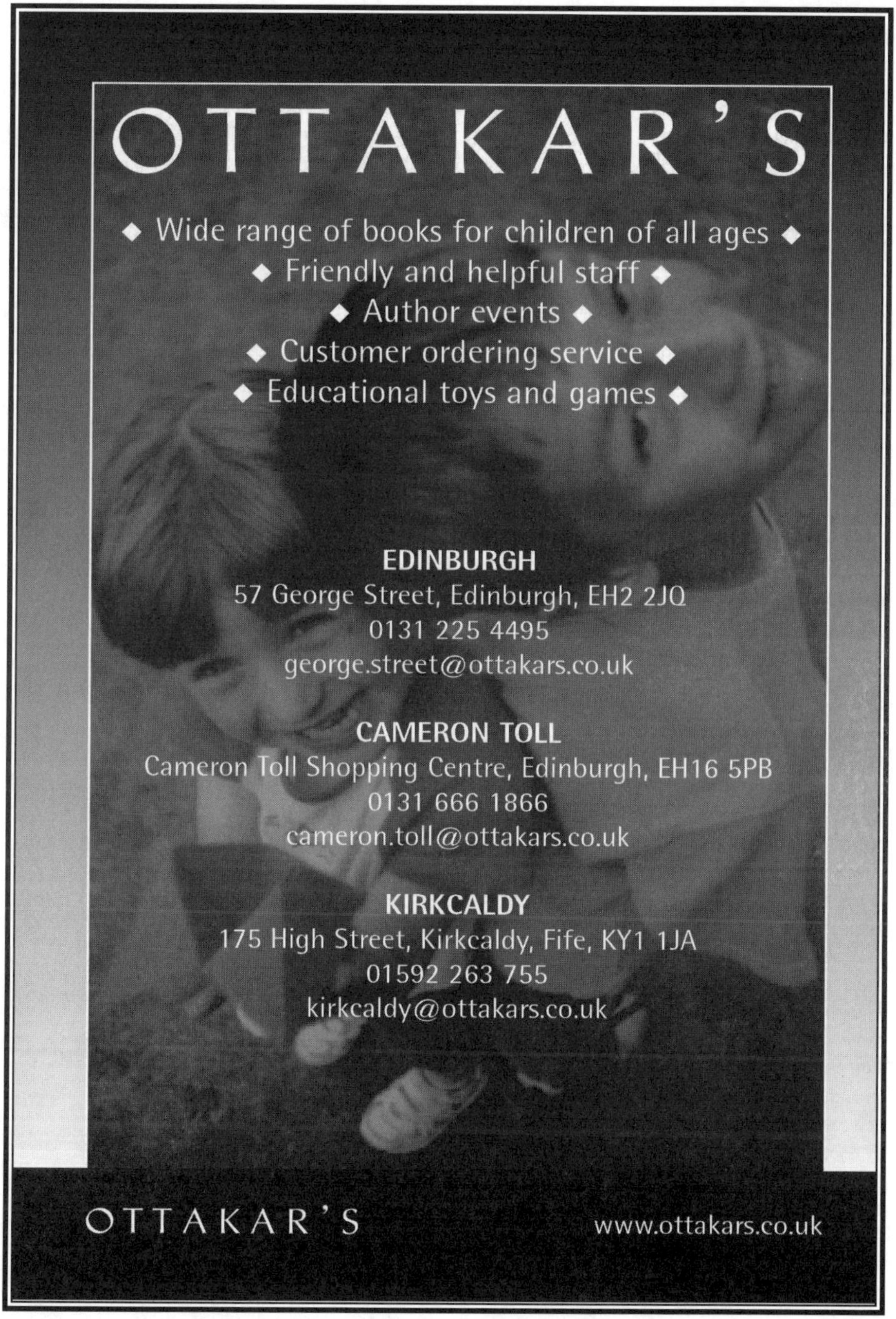
OTTAKAR'S
◆ Wide range of books for children of all ages ◆
◆ Friendly and helpful staff ◆
◆ Author events ◆
◆ Customer ordering service ◆
◆ Educational toys and games ◆
EDINBURGH
57 George Street, Edinburgh, EH2 2JQ
0131 225 4495
george.street@ottakars.co.uk
CAMERON TOLL
Cameron Toll Shopping Centre, Edinburgh, EH16 5PB
0131 666 1866
cameron.toll@ottakars.co.uk
KIRKCALDY
175 High Street, Kirkcaldy, Fife, KY1 1JA
01592 263 755
kirkcaldy@ottakars.co.uk
OTTAKAR'S
www.ottakars.co.uk

Early Learning Centre
St James' Centre'

Shandwick Pl

Gyle Shopping Centre

Good selection, though limited range. See *Toy Shops* for full details.

Jenners
Good selection of popular authors and publishers. Children's books in basement, next to the toy department. See *Department Stores*.

John Lewis
Stock a range of board, picture and storybooks. Also have musical/noise books. Any book which is in print can be ordered, some within 24 hrs. See *Department Stores*.

Royal Museum of Scotland Shop
Selection of children's reference books, special emphasis on natural history and activity books.

HAIRDRESSERS

Having a haircut can be traumatic for a young child. Some love it – enjoying the attention – while others need a little more persuasion. If you already use a hairdresser regularly, it is worth asking if they would cut your child's hair, and how much they would charge, although what suits you might not be the best for your child. You need someone who is relaxed with children and has a calm approach to them. Many hairdressers have special seats so that children can sit at the right height, and have books and toys to keep them amused while they are waiting. A few even have videos to show, which is one way of getting your child to keep his or her head still. If your child is shy, it might be worth asking if s/he can sit on your knee while her/his hair is being cut.
Timing of the haircut can be critical, both for your child and the hairdresser. Choose a time when your child is usually on good form, perhaps early in the morning or after a nap. If it's possible, try to choose a quiet period at the hairdressers; there's likely to be a quieter atmosphere, as well as a shorter waiting time.
If it is your child's first visit to a salon, you will probably find it better to make the appointment in person, giving your child the chance to see where s/he is going and what it will be like. It may also help to take your child along if you are having a haircut yourself – though this plan is best put into action only if you have someone who can take your child away for a little while, as an adult cut can change from fascination to boredom pretty quickly!
If you are looking for a new hairdresser for your whole family, why not have a haircut first yourself. It will give you the opportunity to chat to the stylist and find out how keen s/he is to cut your child's hair, or if one of the salon's stylists specialises in children's cuts. Some salons offer reduced rates for children when a parent has a haircut too. Check out local salons – there may be no need to trail across the city with your toddler for a good cut. Another option if you find it difficult to get out, or you find that your child is intimidated by the surroundings of a salon, would be to have a hairdresser come to your home. Check out Yellow Pages or local press – or why not ask around at any group you attend. You may find that haircuts at home are a practical solution for your family, and an exciting afternoon for your small child!

The Edge
94 Marchmont Rd
Tel: 447 2222
Opening times: Mon-Wed 9.00-18.00; Thu, Fri 9.00-19.00; Sat 9.00-17.00
Mon-Wed - concession for children

Welcomes children of all ages. £5.00 for under 5s. Appointment recommended. Special seats and children's books available.

Angus Gordon
3 Seaforth Ter
Blackhall
Tel: 332 2833
Opening times: Tue, Fri 9.00-18.00; Wed, Thu 9.00-21.00; Sat 9.00-15.30

Children of all ages welcome. Salon has a sliding scale for children's haircuts:
0-2 yrs £6.00; 3-6 yrs £7.50-£8.00; 7-9 yrs £9.00-£11.00; 10-15 yrs £11.00-£14.00. Shampoo £2 extra. Shampoo and blow-dry £5.00 extra.
Has books, teddies and special seats. Appointments essential.

Hair by Patricia Charles
7 Western Corner
Saughtonhall Drive
Tel: 313 1212
Opening times: Tue, Wed, Fri, Sat 9.30-17.30; Thu 9.30-19.00

Children under 5 get a free haircut if mum or dad have a cut and blow-dry. Various toys and books available, and a special racing car seat to make visit enjoyable. Sweetie jar for after (or sometimes during!) haircut. Double doors for pushchairs. Appointment recommended.

Kids' Stop

36 Morningside Rd
Tel: 446 0123
Opening times: Mon-Fri 9.00-18.00; Sat 09.00-16.00. Closed Sun

Extremely child-friendly salon, which also welcomes adults! Special children's seat provided (horse, rabbit, bike), video while having a haircut, play area with toys, video and books.First cut (up to 2 yrs) £6.90. Boys' cuts from 3yrs £8.90; full head with clipper £5. Girls' cuts: 3-5 yrs £8.90; 6-9 yrs £12.50; 10-12 yrs £15.90; 13-15 18.50. Fringe trim £4.00.
Toilet and nappy changing facilities available. Appointments not always necessary. Make-over parties also available – please call salon for more information.

Medusa

6-7 Teviot Pl
Tel: 225 6627
Opening times: Mon- Fri 9.00-18.00; Sat 9.00-16.00

Salon has special seats, children's books and toy box. Changing mat available in toilet. Children's TV/ video and lollipops provided.Children's prices: under 12s – 50% off list price. Under 12-16s – 25% off list price. Valid Mon-Thu.

Also at:
26 Bread St
Tel: 622 7277

115 High St
Musselburgh
Tel: 665 1199

Raymond

11 Comiston Rd
Tel: 447 3177

79 Saughton Rd N
Tel: 334 7942
Opening times: Mon, Tue, Thu 9.00-18.00; Wed 9.00-21.00; Fri 9.00-19.00; Sat 9.00-17.00

Welcomes children of all ages. Toys and books available. Appointments required.

Special Effects

210a Newhaven Rd
Tel: 552 2899
Opening times: Tue, Wed, Thu, Fri 9.00-18.00 (closed 13.00-14.00); Sat 9.00-14.00

Welcomes children of all ages. Salon has a sliding scale of prices for children's haircuts: Up to 2 yrs £6.00; pre-school children (3-5) £7.50; children (5-12) £8.50; school children (13 upwards) £10.50. Sorry, no children on Sat. Appointments not always necessary. Special seats, toy box and children's books available.

Gordon Wilson Hairdressing

9-13 Salisbury Pl
Tel: 667 2692
Opening times: Mon, Sat 8.45-17.00; Tue, Wed, Fri 8.45-18.00; Thu 8.45-19.30.
Welcomes children of all ages. Prices from £3.50. First cut free if adult is having a haircut. Appointment not always necessary. Videos, toy box, books, plus drawing books and coloured pens to entertain children. Varied refreshments and nibbles are also supplied free of charge.

Zoots Hair

41 Broughton Rd
Tel: 557 5831
Opening times: Tue, Wed 9.00-18.00; Thu 9.00-19.00; Fri, Sat 9.00-18.00
Salon welcomes children from first cut onwards. Children under 5 £3. Appointments not always necessary. Toilet is available. Space for pushchairs. Special wooden horse seat, plus books and toys provided

NURSERY EQUIPMENT AND REPAIRS

Many shops in Edinburgh sell well-known brand name equipment. If you decide to buy second-hand or an uncommon make, you must satisfy yourself as to its safety. Second-hand equipment can be in very good condition, but it may not conform to current safety standards. When it comes to cot/Moses basket mattresses, these should always be bought new: never buy a second-hand one. The same applies to car seats: you can't be sure if the seat has been in a traffic accident – there may be stress damage that you can't see, but which could endanger your child.
After sales service should be an important consideration when making your choice of equipment; ask about servicing and repairs before you buy. Most of the outlets that we have listed will do both to the brands they sell, and most will consider lending you a temporary replacement if the repair will take some time. It is a good idea to retain your receipt for a long time, as

this is usually required as proof of purchase before repairs will be undertaken. Talk to friends before you buy – you only discover the pros and cons of equipment once you have lived with it for a while.

Shops usually keep one demonstration pram in stock. Ordering your style and colour can usually take from 6 to 20 weeks! No shop will make you buy a pram if you discover you do not need it (if you discover you're having twins, for example) and most will store it until you need it. All other equipment is usually held in stock.

Which? Magazine and *Practical Parenting* often have reports on nursery equipment and it is worth checking back numbers in the library, even if it's just to see what to look out for. See also *Hiring*.

Argos

Moderate selection of equipment, though individual brand choice may be limited. One year guarantee on pushchairs:

catalogue features Graco brand. Superstore in Kinnaird Park has a larger selection than most stores displayed in nursery dept. Argos offers a 16 day money back guarantee – see instore or catalogue for details specific to pushchairs. See *Department Stores*.

Corstorphine Pram Centre

115-117 St John's Rd
Tel: 334 6216

Wide selection of prams, pushchairs, cots, travel cots, backpacks, car seats and other equipment required for baby. Also a large selection of nursery décor ranges and furniture.

The Foam Centre

176 Causewayside, Newington
Tel: 667 1247

Opening times: Mon-Sat 9.30-17.30. Later at Christmas

Different foams cut to any size and shape. Can be made to fit cots, Moses baskets (also in stock), bumpers, booster seats etc. 'Beans' to top up or to make your own beanbags. Maternity wedges, lumbar supports also supplied.

IKEA

Straiton Mains
Tel: 448 0500

Located on the 1st floor, along with the toys and to the right of the café. Range of cots, changing tables, beds, chairs, tables, high-chairs and various storage options etc, the majority of which are flatpacked and reasonably priced. Co-ordinated bedding ranges available. Children's cutlery, crockery and starter packs including training cups also to hand. See *Department Stores, Toys* and *Crèches while Shopping*.

John Lewis

St James' Centre

Good selection of equipment, including pushchairs, prams, high-chairs, cots, nursing chairs etc. Ranges include Mamas and Papas, Cossatto, McLaren. Also stocks range of soft furnishings, including own brand options. Larger items of furniture also available. Free delivery within city boundaries and a little beyond. See *Department Stores*.

Mamas and Papas

Craigleith Retail Park
Tel: 0870 830 7703
Web: mamasandpapas.co.uk

Selection of own-brand prams, travel systems, car seats, cots and other nursery equipment. Also stock ranges of décor and co-ordinating bedding and trims etc.

Musselburgh Pram Centre

35 High St, Musselburgh
Tel: 665 2530
Web: www.pramcentre.co.uk

Opening times: Mon-Tue & Thu-Sat 9.00-17.30; Closed Wed & Sun

Wide selection of nursery equipment including prams, pushchairs, all-terrain strollers, cots, travel systems, backpacks and car seats. Also wide selection of nursery toys and large selection of nursery décor ranges and furniture. Free parking nearby.

Also at:

118 Dalry Rd Tel: 346 2011

Opening times: Mon-Sat 9.00 - 17.30; Sun 11.00 - 17.00

Mothercare

Fort Kinnaird Retail Park

Mothercare World

Hermiston Gait Retail Park

Stock large selection of Mothercare, Britax, McLaren, Mamas and Papas, Bébécar, Cossatto etc baby/nursery equipment, including car seats, cots and prams. Baby toiletries, nappies and baby food also available. See *Department Stores*.

National Childbirth Trust

NCT Centre
University Health Service
5th floor
5 Bristo Square EH8 9AL
Tel: 668-3257

Please phone for current opening times.

The 'Boom' catalogue features baby equipment, as well as books and leaflets on many aspects of pregnancy, birth and parenthood. Phone office for details. See *Health Care*.

Graham Tiso

115/123 Rose St
Tel: 225 9486
Email: edinburgh@tiso.com
Web: www.tiso.com

Opening times: Mon-Tue, Fri-Sat 9.30-17.30, Wed 10.00-17.30; Thu 9.30-19.30 Sun 12.00 -17.00

Stocks baby carriers, small toddler- and child-sized rucsacs, nappy bags and pushchairs.

Graham Tiso: Edinburgh Outdoor Experience

41 Commercial St
Leith
Tel: 554 0804
Email: edinburgh_oe@tiso.com
Web: www.tiso.com

Opening times: Mon-Tue, Fri-Sat 9.30-17.30, Wed 10.00-18.00; Thu 9.30-19.30 Sun 11.00-17.00

Stocks Karrimor and Wild Rover baby carriers. Will help to fit. Toddler-sized rucsacs also available. Very helpful staff. See also Outdoor and Ski Shops.

Toys'R'Us

Kinnaird Retail Park

Wide range of pushchairs, car seats, cots and highchairs by McLaren Cindico, Britax and Mamas and Papas. One year guarantee on items, but must retain receipt. Car and home safety equipment also stocked. See *Department Stores*.

OUTDOOR AND SKI SHOPS

For those parents wishing to take their children outdoors in Britain, our weather can always prove problematic. Keeping the small members of the family warm and dry is essential to everyone's enjoyment of an outing. There's a good selection of dedicated outdoor shops in Edinburgh, and many offer clothing and equipment for under 5s.

Babycarriers (or backpacks) allow you to go off the beaten track with your child safely away from mud, wet grass, sheep droppings, and all the other delights a small child can find in the countryside. These carriers can be equally useful in town, allowing negotiation of busy streets without many of the problems associated with pushchairs, such as other people (!), getting through doors and using escalators. The big drawback is the potential strain on your back – so the adage 'try before you buy' is essential, as with any piece of outdoor clothing. Remember, you and your partner may be carrying the pack considerable distances. Also, think about your intended use: if you want something for walking in the country, you'll probably want something which is reasonably rugged as well as comfortable. However, if the pack is more for 'urban' use, take this into account.

As with most things, with outdoor equipment and clothing, you get what you pay for. So, keep your primary usage in mind, and keep comfort as a priority.

Blacks Outdoor Leisure Ltd

13/14 Elm Row
Tel: 556 3491
Opening times: Mon-Sat 9.00-17.30; Sun 12.00-1600

Store stocks Vango babycarriers, plus children's boots and socks. There is a small step into the wide doors, also an interior staircase to 1st floor, the tent and sleeping bag sales area.

24 Frederick St
Tel: 225 8686
Opening times: Mon-Sat 9.00-18.00; Thu 9.00-19.00; Sun 12.00-17.00
Similar stocks as above in a more crowded sales area.

Nevisport

81 Shandwick Pl
Tel: 229 1197
Opening times: Mon-Tue, Fri-Sat 9.00-17.30; Wed 10.00-17.30; Thu 9.00-18.30; Sun 11.00-15.45

Stocks Macpac babycarriers for babies from 6mths. Also carries a range of waterproof clothing for toddlers upwards, fleeces and lightweight boots. For skiers there is a range of clothes and equipment for children. Skis from 70cm up, boots from size 16' (mondopoint sizing). Access good, doorway big enough for tandem pushchair, ask for help to basement sales area. Staff toilet available for emergencies.

Snowlines

14/15 Bruntsfield Pl
Tel: 229 2402
Web: www.snowlines.co.uk
Opening times: Mon-Fri 9.30-18.00; Sat 9.00-17.30; Sun 11.00-17.00

Stocks specialist clothing and footwear for running, skiing/ snowboarding and outdoor pursuits. Offers a free instore video gait analysis. Operates an instore discount scheme, details of which can be checked out on the website – see cartblanche cards. Skis for hire.

Sports Warehouse

24-26 Coburg St
Tel: 553 6003
Opening times: Mon-Sat 9.00-17.00 Sun 11.00-16.00

This sports and outdoor supplier has the Karrimor and Vango babycarriers. Pentland cagoules and trousers suitable for 3+ yrs. Also stock boots from size 12, junior sleeping bags and swimming aids. Car parking. Staff toilet is available for use in emergencies.

Graham Tiso

115/123 Rose St
Tel: 225 9486
Email: edinburgh@tiso.com
Web: www.tiso.com
Opening times: Mon-Tue, Fri-Sat 9.30-17.30; Wed 10.00-17.30; Thu 9.30-19.30 Sun 12.00-17.00

This store is located on 4 floors and caters for children from 6 mths to 16 yrs. Clothing includes range of fleeces and waterproof jackets, suits and over trousers, including Wild Rover (own brand), Helly Hansen, Trespass, and Lego. Wellingtons, leather and lightweight boots from size 10. Selection of babycarriers, including Wild Rover and Macpac suitable for 3 mths - 4 yrs as well as pushchairs by Pegasus. Ski goggles, hats and gloves etc are also available in winter months. Customer toilets available.

Graham Tiso: Edinburgh Outdoor Experience

41 Commercial St
Leith
Tel: 554 0804
Email: edinburgh_oe@tiso.com
Web: www.tiso.com
Opening times: Mon-Tue, Fri-Sat 9.30-17.30, Wed 10.00-18.00; Thu 9.30-19.30 Sun 11.00 -17.00

This store – the largest of its kind this side of the country – is situated on one level with a car park available. 'Outdoor Experience' on ground floor is an interactive shop with everything from a 'shower tower' to an ice-wall. – as well as a large range of equipment and clothing.
Comfy sofas are available to rest your feet and there's car parking for 60 cars.

PHOTOGRAPHY AND ART

Whether it's putting an announcement in the paper or having a family portrait taken for posterity, most families find recording the event comes into their lives with the arrival of a baby.
A birth announcement can be placed in the Scotsman or the Evening News (see *Help & Information*). Unlike death notices, no proof is required to place your announcement and they can be made in person at the Scotsman Offices or by phone with a

credit card. Payment is required at time of order.
Department stores such as Boots and Debenhams and shopping centres such as Cameron Toll or The Gyle Centre often have visiting companies which specialise in photographing young children. Look out in the Herald and Post for details of these companies. The Herald and Post also has details of firms which are willing to video or photograph your party or Christening. The following companies specialise in working with under 5s.

Dimple Photos

100 Northfield Cres
Willowbrae Rd EH8 7QB
Tel: 661 5031
Mob: 07946 518 244
Email: Portraits@dimple-photos.co.uk

Established in 1985, servicing maternity hospitals. Photographs of new borns. Specialists in baby portrait packs

David Johnston LMPA

31 Bridgeside Ave
Whitburn, W Lothian
Tel: 01501 742710

Children's portraits, babies, Christenings, family groups etc. Relaxed, informal photography in studio or on location.

Máté Gibb Photography LBIPP

Tel: 477 1477
www.mategibb.co.uk

Contemporary lifestyle photographers. Specialises in creative portraits. Family and children's portraits taken in your home or on location.

Photo Express

7 Melville Ter EH9 1ND
Tel: 667 2164
Email: info@photo-express-edinburgh.co.uk
Opening times: Mon-Fri 9.00-17.00; Sat 9.00-12.00
Specialises in children and family groups. Portraits taken in-studio. Breastfeeding welcome. Toilet facilities available.

Genuine European Portraits

Freepost SCO3533
EH10 0BR
Tel: 229 7556
Web: www.portraits.org
Specialises in hand drawn portraits on a sale or return basis for nurseries, playgroups, toddler groups etc, which receive commission for each portrait, so it's a good fundraiser. Individual drawings from photos can be ordered through the website.

TOY SHOPS

This section includes doll repair, special gifts and outdoor toys. Make sure you always satisfy yourself as to the safety of toys – particularly if you are buying from an unorthodox source. When buying for playgroups etc it is always worth asking whether discounts are available. Many shops and department stores expand their range and extend their opening hours before Christmas. See also *Department Stores*, *Supermarkets*, the specialist party shops in *Birthdays and Celebrations*, and *Bicycle Shops* for full shop details, where limited information is given here.

Argos

A wide range of popular toys, including up and coming trends. Superstore has most products. See *Department Stores*.

Arkadia

Edinburgh Zoo
Corstorphine Rd
Tel: 334 9171
Opening times: Mon-Sun 9.00-17.00

Run by the zoo, but with a separate entrance, so you don't have to go into the zoo itself. A real treasure trove, full of animal- and bird-related toys, games, books, clothes, and gifts – including pocket-money toys.

Asda Wal-Mart

Selection of big name toys, including Duplo, Lego, stationery etc. See also *Baby and Children's Clothes* and *Supermarkets*.

Baloo

117 Bruntsfield Pl
Tel: 229 4006
Opening times: Mon-Sat 09.30-17.30

Sells a wide range of toys and books, including Brio, Galt and Lego. There is a play area at the rear of the shop.

BhS

Small selection within children's clothes dept, including baby and pre-school toys. Range tends to expand slightly at Christmas. See *Department Stores*.

Digger

35 W Nicolson St
Tel: 668 1802
Opening times: Mon-Sat 10.00-18.00

Small shop up 3 steps. An Aladdin's cave of handmade and traditional wooden toys. Dolls' house furniture, wooden framed mirrors, bookends, clocks decorated with teddies, stocking fillers and party goods.

The Disney Store

18 Princes St
Tel: 557 2772
Opening times: Mon-Wed, Fri-Sat 9.00-18.00; Thu 9.00-19.00; Sun 11.00-17.00

Gyle Shopping Centre
Tel: 339 4944
Mon-Wed 9.30-20.00; Thu, Fri 9.30-21.00; Sat 9.00-18.00; Sun 10.00-18.00

Colourful stores which sell everything in the Disney theme, including collectables and animation art. Both stores have lively laser screen video entertainment for children. Both stores are on one floor, which makes for easy access for pushchairs. Friendly 'cast members'. See also *Baby and Children's Clothes*.

Early Learning Centre

67-83 Shandwick Pl
Tel: 228 3244
Opening times: Mon-Sat 9.00-17.30; Sun in Dec

Unit 11
Gyle Shopping Centre
Tel: 538 7172
Opening times: Mon-Wed 9.00-19.30; Thu-Fri 9.00-20.00; Sat 9.00-18.00; Sun 10.00-17.00

61 St James' Centre
Tel: 558 1330
Opening times: Mon-Sat 9.00-17.30; Sun in Dec 12.00-16.00

Chain which sells toys that are educational, safe and robust, with a focus on younger children. Laid out in the shops under sections such as 'First Years', 'Pretend Play', 'Finding Out', 'Sound and Music' and so on. Also stock a range of outdoor toys including climbing frames, slides, swings, sandpits and trampolines. St James' Centre store is the largest and therefore carries an extended range. Toilet for the disabled and well equipped mother and baby room in St James' Centre store. Sainsbury's also carries a range of the smaller ELC toys. See also *Shopping from Home*.

Early Learning Playstore

Fort Kinnaird
Tel: 669 9513
Opening times: Mon-Fri 9.00-20.00; Sat 9.00-18.00; Sun 10.00-18.00

Part of the Early Learning Centre chain, this superstore has a huge play area which allows children to "try before you buy". There are also activities every day, including face painting, messy time, etc at either 10.00 or 14.00 so it's best phone beforehand to find out so that you don't miss out. In the back of the store, there is a baby changing room and a separate baby dining room, which includes bottle warmers, table and chairs, and a chair for breast feeding mothers.

Geraldine's of Edinburgh and Dolls' Hospital

35a Dundas St
Tel: 556 4295
Opening times: Mon-Fri 9.00-17.00; Sat 9.00-13.00, Closed Wed

Family-run store. Sells teddies, dolls, and toys for any occasion. The unique aspect of this shop is Ward 10, where dolls and soft toys can await repair to injuries caused by the ravages of time or over exuberant play. And once your child's (or your) beloved toy is back to full 'health' or complement of limbs etc, this shop also stocks a range of accessories such as dresses, shoes etc to complete the picture - some from as little as 25p.

Harburn Hobbies Ltd

67 Elm Row, Leith Walk
Tel: 556 3233
Mon-Sat 9.30-18.00

Specialises in model railways and die cast road vehicles. Hornby railways collector centre, plus other makes, with Scottish trains commissioned exclusively for the shop. Scalextric car racing and Corgi collectors' centre. Toy range includes Thomas the Tank Engine, Bob the Builder, and Britain's farm animals and tractors range as well as a range of the French company Papo's knights and romans. Also has a stock of colourful wooden dolls houses and furniture including the Swedish Lundby dolls house range.

IKEA

Straiton Mains
Straiton, Loanhead
Tel: 448 0500

Located on the first floor (lift access) near to the café. Good selection of wooden and soft toys, musical instruments, crafts, and learning games. There are also pocket-money soft toys. There are well-equipped play-houses, so your child can try some of the toys first – and you can work out how noisy they could be! See *Department Stores, Nursery Equipment, Crèches while Shopping.*

Jenners

48 Princes Street
Tel: 225 2301
Located in the basement - access by lift from the ground floor. Excellent, enormous and competitively priced toy department. If you can drag yourself away from a walk down memory lane, there is everything from pocket-money toys to rocking horses, train sets, small bikes – they also stock Steiff bears, if you are looking for that extra-special gift.
Other brands stocked include Brio, Duplo, Galt, Lego and Playmobil, although there are many others. There is also a good book, tape and video section. There are TV screens set in the wall at one side to keep young one's attention. Special events held periodically. See also *Department Stores.*

John Lewis

St James' Centre

Nursery toys such as teddies, rattles, bath toys etc on the first floor (lift access). Wide selection including most big name brands. Also stocks pocket-money toys.
Ordering service for a range of climbing frames, swings, slides, bikes, sandpits and other outdoor toys. These can be delivered, often free of charge (dependent on location). Samples usually on display in the summer months, however, the full range can be viewed via a catalogue. See *Department Stores.*

JRS Cycles

46 Silverknowes Rd
Tel: 312 6046
Opening times: Mon-Tue, Fri-Sat 9.00-17.00; Wed 11.00-1700

Small, friendly shop with selection of toys, puzzles and games, including pocket-money toys. Easy parking.

Mothercare

Fort Kinnaird Retail Park
Tel: 657 4050

Mothercare World

Hermiston Gait Retail Park
Tel: 453 1383

Toy department within stores. Includes own-brand toys from small bikes, sit-and-ride cars etc to pencil cases and rattles. Also stock 'famous names' brands. See *Department Stores.*

Mr Macawz

10 Roseneath St, Marchmont
Tel: 228 3327
Opening times: Mon-Sat 10.00-18.00

Small gift shop with a nature theme. Extensive range of cuddly toys, puzzles, cards, badges, brightly coloured mobiles etc. Shop has a low price policy. Party bag fillers a speciality.

The Mulberry Bush

77 Morningside Rd
Tel: 447 5145
Opening times: Mon, Wed-Sat 9.30-17.00; Tue 9.30-15.45 (closed 12.30-13.30)

Garvald's Centre's craft shop. Beautifully made wooden toys – rocking horses, puppet theatres, dolls' prams, houses and furniture. Also stocks musical instruments, such as wooden drums, xylophones, lyres etc., handicraft materials and books. Order dolls' houses by early Oct for Christmas.

The Natural World

Unit U3
Princes Mall
Tel: 556 3659

Toys such as kites, stuffed animals, puppets, educational games, music and sounds of nature CDs.

The Owl and the Pussycat

166 Bruntsfield Pl
Tel: 228 4441
Opening times: Mon-Sat 9.30-18.00

Wide selection of teddies and other soft toys, stylish cards and gifts. Local artist Alison has a range of teddy drawings and prints.

Poundstretcher

Budget/value stores. A selection of inexpensive toys, including some educational toys, small bikes and stationery.

42 Shandwick Pl
Tel: 225 1611
Opening times: Mon-Wed 9.00-17.30; Thu-Sat 9.00-18.00; Sun 11.00-16.30

10 West Harbour Rd
Tel: 552 0213

Opening times: Mon-Fri 10.00-17.30; Sat 9.00-17.30; Sun 12.00-16.30

4/6 Brunswick Pl
Tel: 557 0693

Kirkgate Shopping Centre
Tel: 555 5344

100/106 South Bridge
Tel: 225 8540

Fort Kinnard, Newcraighall Rd
Tel: 657 4244
Opening times: Mon-Fri 10.00-20.00; Sat 9.00-18.00; Sun 10.00-17.00

Gorgie Rd
Tel: 346 7741

Unit 1 Meadowbank Shopping Park
Tel: 652 6005

Unit 36 West Side Plaza, Westerhailes
Tel: 458 4553

Sainsbury's

Cameron Toll Shopping Centre

Craigleith Retail Park

Straiton Retail Park

Small selection of toys, including Duplo, Lego and own brand stationery. Also stocks ELC toy ranges, as well as own-brand 'learning through play' toys. The stores' general ranges expand at Christmas. See *Supermarkets* for more information.

Studio One

10-14 Stafford St
Tel: 226 5812
Opening times: Mon-Fri 9.30-18.00; Thu 9.30-19.00; Sat 9.30-17.30; Sun 12.00-17.00

Down steps to basement shop full of pocket-money toys, stocking fillers, novelties, Christmas decorations, wooden toys, colourful rugs, cushions and bedspreads.

Toys Galore

193 Morningside Rd
Tel: 447 1006
Opening times: Mon-Sat 9.30-17.30, Open Sun in November and December 9.30-17.00.

Good choice of toys for all ages with some to try out while you browse. Most major brands stocked and many others from pocket-money range upwards. 10% discount to playgroups. Difficult to manoeuvre pushchairs, but they can be left supervised at the front of the shop. Goods can only be returned if faulty.

Toys'R'Us

Kinnaird Park
Newcraighall Rd
Tel: 657 4121
Opening times: Mon-Sat 9.00-22.00; Sun 10.00-18.00. Operates Bank Holiday hours.

Huge range of pre-school toys, soft toys, dolls, games, Lego, Playmobil, outdoor toys and so on. A store directory points to the different areas and there is a pick-up point for bulky items and electrical toys. Climbing frames, chutes, swings, sandpits and Wendy houses available with samples on display.
There is no play area and as such a vast array of toys may prove tempting, parents may find it easier to shop without their offspring. Toilets. See *Department Stores*.

Wind Things

11 Cowgatehead
Tel: 622 7032
Opening times: Mon-Sat 10.00-17.30; Sun 12.00-17.00

Scotland's premier kite shop. Sells selection of kites, from stunt kites to pocket-kites.

Wonderland

97-101 Lothian Rd
Opening times: phone for current times.

Specialises in radio controlled cars, boats, planes and helicopters, as well as in model-making kits and railway sets. Stocks Scalextric. Good range of die-cast cars, buses and trucks. Dolls' houses kits or ready assembled, plus accessories. Will order in specific models for customers. Easy access for all pushchairs. Also stock fantasy/graphic novel figures - good for dads etc too.

Woolworth's

Selection of big-name toys, Lego, Duplo etc. Tapes, CDs, videos, stationery. Wide range of pocket-money toys. Range will vary dependent on store size. see also *Department Stores*.

OUTDOOR TOYS

For bikes and sit-and-ride toys, see *Bicycle Shops*.

Sand for sand pits is often available from builders' yards and increasingly so from garden centres, but make sure you buy washed or silver sand, as orange sand stains clothes. Washed sand is sometimes sold in bags in the spring and summer by shops selling sand pits. If you are buying or making a sandpit, make sure that you can secure a lid over it: wet sand is no fun – and any sand can prove irresistible to local cats!

Early Learning Centre

Climbing frames, slides, swings, sand pits, sand, trampolines. See above in *Toy Shops*.

John Lewis

Extensive range of climbing frames, swings, slides, bikes and other outdoor toys. Choose from 'top activity sports' brochure, delivered to your door. Store occasionally has some display samples, especially in the summer months. See *Department Stores*.

Toys 'R' Us

Climbing frames, slides, swings, sandpits and Wendy houses, with samples on display. See *Department Stores* and above in *Toy Shops*.

HIRING

The main thing to remember is to phone in advance to make sure that what you require is available and, particularly when the business is run from home, that someone will be available to help you.

BICYCLES

Alpine Bikes

48 Hamilton Place
Tel: 225 3286
Web: www.alpinebikes.co.uk
Opening times: Mon-Wed, Fri-Sat 9.00-18.00; Thu 9.00-19.00; Sun 12.00-17.00
See *Shopping - Bicycles*.

B.G. Cycles and Blades

48 Portobello High St
Tel: 657 5832
Web: www.bgcycles.co.uk
Opening times: Mon-Fri 9.00-18.30; Sat 9.00-18.00; Sun 10.00-17.00
See *Shopping - Bicycles*.

Bike Trax

11 Lochrin Pl
Tel: 228 6633
Web: www.biketrax.co.uk
Opening times: Mon-Sat 9.30-18.00; Sun 12.00-17.00
See *Shopping - Bicycles*.

Edinburgh Cycle Hire & Cycle Safaris

29 Blackfriars St
Tel: 556 5560
Web: www.cyclescotland.co.uk
Opening times: Summer: 9.00-21.00 (7 days/wk); Winter: Usually 10.00-18.00 (but please phone before setting off).
See *Shopping - Bicycles*.

Great Bikes No Bull

276 Leith Walk
Tel: 467 7775
Opening times: Mon-Wed, Fri-Sat 9.00-17.30; Thu 9.00-17.30. Closed Sun.
See *Shopping - Bicycles*.

CAKE TINS

The Finishing Touch

17 St Patrick's Square
Tel: 667 0914
Refundable deposit, £1/night. Over 40 novelty tins to hire, plus numbers, letters, squares, hexagons etc. Most with instructions and/or pictures.
See *Birthdays and Celebrations*.

Studio One

71 Morningside Rd
Tel: 447 0452
Opening times: Mon-Fri 9.00-18.00 Sat 9.00-17.30 Sun !2.00-16.00

£5 deposit, £1.95/night. Letters, numbers, hearts, squares.

CLOTHES

Davison Menswear

Dress Hire Shop
31-33 Bruntsfield Pl
Tel: 229 0266
Web: www.davison-dresshire.co.uk
Email info@davison-dresshire.co.uk
Opening times: contact shop for current opening hours.

Hire of Highland outfits, morning suits(with tails) and top hats from age 2 yrs-adult.

Highland Laddie

6 Hutchison Ter
Tel: 455 7505
Kilt hire available. See also *Kilts*

NURSERY EQUIPMENT

Baby Baby Equipment Hire

45 Glendevon Pl
Tel: 337 7016

Run from the proprietor's own home and can supply all baby needs, from car seats, backpacks, playpens to cots, travel cots and pushchairs. All equipment regularly checked, cleaned and serviced. Hire from one day to 3mths. Delivery available. Member of the Baby Equipment Hirers Assoc.

National Childbirth Trust

NCT Centre
University Health Service
5th floor
5 Bristo Square EH8 9AL
Tel: 668 3257
Please phone for current opening times.

Hire of Egnell breast pumps £1/day. Person will require package of beakers to fit these pumps which cost £8.50. Contact the centre for your local agent.

INFLATABLES

AD Hire and DIY Garden Centre

9 Featherhall Ave, Corstorphine
Tel: 334 2348
Opening times: Mon-Fri 9.00-17.00, Sat-Sun 10.00-13.00

Small bouncy castles for home indoor/outdoor use: phone for current prices.

Bennets Hire Centre

9 Meadowplace Rd
Tel: 334 4545

Bouncy castles in various sizes. One ideal for young children (8'x8') suitable for garden or indoor use, cost £45. Full delivery and set-up service.

Monkey Business

167 Morrison St
Tel: 228 6636
Web: www.smiffys.com
Opening times: Mon-Wed, Fri-Sat 9.30-17.00; Thu 9.30-18.30; Sun 12.00-16.00

Castle mini-bouncer and ball pond for hire, suitable for indoor or outdoor use. Full size bouncers also available. Sells a large range of party goods and hires out an automatic helium balloon pump. See also *Birthdays and Celebrations*.

SKIS

Snowlines

14/15 Bruntsfield Pl
Tel: 229 2402
Opening times: Mon-Fri 9.30-18.00; Sat 9.00- 17.30 Sun 11.00-17.00
Skis for hire. See also *Shopping – Outdoor and Ski Shops*.

NAPPIES

Modern cloth nappies are not only a la mode, they're easy to use too: no pins, no boiling, no complicated folds and - if you use the local nappy laundry - no washing either. Cloth nappies are effective, comfortable and convenient. They can save you money and they're good for the environment too – did you know that all the disposable nappies used by one baby in one year would fill 40 black plastic bin bags?. That's a real waste. Cloth nappies, on the other hand, can be used again and again, and if you have another baby you could make even greater savings.

The Edinburgh Real Nappy Network (ERNN) provides unbiased information about cloth nappies. Their website is full of information about why and how to use cloth. ERNN runs monthly nappy chats, where parents and carers can see our 'nappy library', ask questions and find out more about which type of cloth nappy would suit them and their child. You can also arrange to see the nappy library at other times. For more information, see:

ERNN

Tel: 0870 9913 236
Email: info@ernn.org.uk
Web: www.ernn.org.uk

LOCAL SUPPLIERS

Boots the Chemist

102 Princes Street
Tel: 225 8331

Own brand terries and plastic pants. Own brand all-in-one, with booster pads.

Eco-Babes Ltd

Birthbase
The Rondo Guest House
62 Queen Street
Dumfries DG1 2JP
Contact: Angela Green (Agent)
Tel: 01387 265501

Advice and trial nappy kits available, newborn to toddler. Also ecotoiletries for mothers & babies.

Earth Matters

67 High Street
North Berwick
East Lothian EH39 5NZ
Tel: 01620 895401
Web: earthmatters.co.uk

Stocks a wide range of ecofriendly baby products and clothes. Nappies include Tots Bots, Imse Vimse and Tushies.

John Lewis

See *Shopping – Department Stores.*
Stocks Nappi Nippas

Lollipop Children's Products

Contact: Morag Davidson (Local Agent)
Tel: 01506 419083
Email: morag_davidson@mac.com
Web: www.teamlollipop.co.uk

Free advice and demonstration of the different types of nappy to help you decide what's best for you and your baby.

Macdonalds Pram Centre / Musselburgh Pram Centre

See *Shopping – Nursery Equipment*

Both stock the full range of Bambino Mio nappies and accessories.

Mothercare World

See *Shopping – Department Stores.*

Own brand terries and shaped terries. Kooshies Ultras. Nappy buckets, plastic pants, pins, liners.

Natures Gate

83 Clark Street EH8 9JG
Tel: 668 2067

Stock two types of flushable nappy liner, Moltex ecofriendly disposable nappies and baby's toiletries. Items can be ordered for customers.

Nappy Days

Contact: Leslie Healy and Colette Valvona Healy
Tel: 669 8851
Email: real@nappydays.free-online.co.uk
Web: www.realnappydays.co.uk

Nappy Days delivers weekly – directly to your door – freshly laundered, 100% cotton prefold nappies. The service provides nappies, bins etc. and is convenient for parents who are interested in using real nappies, but have little time or no access to washing machines or drying areas. One month trial available.

Nippers

131 Bruntsfield Place EH10 4EB
Tel: 228 5086
Email:Nippers@btinternet.com
Web: www.nippersforkids.com

Motherease nappies and wraps and biodegradable liners

Supermarkets

Safeway and Tesco stock Kooshies Ultras. The Tesco Baby catalogue also includes the Diaper Basics range. Sainsburys stocks flushable liners.

Simply Nappies

Tel: 343 6544
Email: info@simplynappies.co.uk
Web: www.simplynappies.co.uk

Independent nappy retailer based in Edinburgh stocking a wide range of cloth nappies and accessories. Unbiased advice on choosing suitable nappies and free local demonstrations.

TotsBots

Unit 5, Green City
23 Fleming Street
Glasgow G31 1PQ
Tel: 0141-550 1514
Fax: 0141 550 1556
Email: info@totsbots.com
Web: www.totsbots.com

Totsbots are a range of shaped toweling nappies made in Scotland. Forget fiddly folds and nappy pins, cloth nappies have evolved. Voted best British nappy.

Young Days

Kirkgate shopping Centre, Leith
Tel: 554 4666

Stocks Kooshies & terry nappies and biogradable liners.

MAIL ORDER NAPPY SUPPLIERS

Listed below is a selection of mail order nappy suppliers. A more extensive list can be found on the ERNN website at www.ernn.org.uk.

Eco-Babes Ltd

17b Paradise Road
Downham Market
Norfolk PE38 9HS
Tel: 01366 38 7851
Email: Nappies@ecobabes.co.uk
Web: www.eco-babes.co.uk

Elvika Nappies

36 Kings North Road
Faversham
Kent ME13 8SB
Tel: (08456) 443490
Fax: 01233 639 915
Email: nappy@elvika-nappies.co.uk
Web: www.elvika-nappies.co.uk

Independent nappy seller selling a large selection of cloth nappies.

Greenfibres

See *Shopping from Home – Children's Clothes*

Lollipop Children's Products

Bosigran Farm
Pendeen
Penzance
Cornwall TR20 8ZZ
Tel: 01736-799512
Email: info@teamlollipop.co.uk
Web: www.teamlollipop.co.uk

Order on-line or contact your nearest agent for help and advice on buying and using real nappies and accessories.

Little Green Earthlets

See *Shopping from Home – Baby Equipment*

Sam-I-Am

Besthorpe Road
North Scarle
LINCS LN6 9EZ
Tel: 01522 778440
Email: www.sam-i-am.co.uk
Web: www.nappies.net

For a wide range of cotton washable nappies, wraps and accessories, swim pants, nursing bras and much more.

Schmidt Natural Clothing

See *Shopping from Home – Clothes*

The Nappy Lady

'Arcady'
16 Hill Brow
Bearsted
Maidstone
Kent ME14 4AW
Tel/fax: 0845 456 2441
Email: info@thenappylady.co.uk
Web: www.thenappylady.co.uk

The Natural Collection

See *Shopping from Home – Children's Clothes*

Twinkle Twinkle

Beggars Hill Road
Lands End
Twyford
Berkshire RG10 0UB
Tel: 0118 934 2120
Email: miranda@twinkleontheweb.co.uk
Web: www.twinkleontheweb.co.uk

Comprehensive selection of nappies and free advice.

SHOPPING FROM HOME

Shopping from home is much easier than struggling through crowds with a pushchair. In the last few years there has been a large increase in the number of companies with a presence on the internet, a lot of which are already familiar names, but speciality shops are also reaching a far wider audience by being available on the world wide web. Most sites these days have secure online ordering – and remember it's still more secure to enter credit card details on the web than it is to hand your credit card over to a waiter in a restaurant who takes it out of your sight! Some sites allow you to order a catalogue if you prefer to browse through that and then order. This is a quick, easy and 24-hour way to shop, and now you can also get hold of things that you maybe couldn't get locally.

The Internet is fast becoming the way of researching and buying baby and toddler clothes and equipment. There are a vast number of companies now with a presence on the Internet, and the number is increasing almost every day. The following are just a few of note, but you can find many, many more if you look at one of the Internet search engines, or one of the internet children's directories, such as www.ukchildrensdirectory.com. This section also includes mail order.

BABY EQUIPMENT

BabyCentre

Web: www.babycentre.co.uk

This is a UK version of the American sister site (www.babycenter.com) which provides a wealth of information on pregnancy and childcare for babies 0 to 3 (for older children see www.parentcentre.com).

At time of printing, BabyCentre in the UK no longer has an online shop. However, the site produces some great buying guides if you are confused about the range of different baby and toddler paraphernalia available. (www.babycentre.co.uk/buying-guides)

BabyWorld

Web: www.babyworld.co.uk

This site, like BabyCentre, offers information on pregnancy and babies. At the time of writing, BabyWorld is part of a bigger site called iCircle, a website aimed specifically at women and women's issues. You can buy various products through it from medicines to clothes to books through their various partners – John Lewis, Boots, Figleaves.com, and Interflora

BickiePegs

Tel: 01224 790626

A long-established Scottish firm (trading since 1925). Teething biscuits for babies available from Boots and all leading chemists. Small mail order brochure in pack. 'Doidy' children's training cup, finger toothbrushes, thermometers and personalised pottery.

The Great Little Trading Company

124 Walcot Street
Bath BA1 5BG
Tel: 0990 673008
Web: www.gltc.co.uk

Practical products for parents and children. Large catalogue full of helpful and interesting products. Also sells children's clothes. No quibble returns policy.

Little Green Earthlets Ltd

Units 1-3 Stream Farm
Chiddingly
East Sussex BN8 6HG
Tel: 01825 873301
Web: www.earthlets.co.uk

Washable nappies, environmentally friendly baby goods, cotton toys. Also Baby Jogger – the original 3-wheel pushchair, including double, triple, special needs – and bike convertible pushchairs.

Tesco Direct

Tel: 08457 024024
Web: www.tesco.com

Baby and toddler catalogue includes wide range of value-for-money equipment, bedding, clothes, toys etc. You can order all products available through catalogue on their online store, which is also where their online grocery shopping service can be found (see *Shopping from Home - Food*)

Babies'R'Us

Web: www.babiesrus.co.uk

Babies' equipment section of Toys'R'Us. Babies'R' Us has its own catalogue available instore, and you can order online. Very useful if Toys'R'Us are out of stock in your local store – it can be faster to order online than ask the store to reserve something for you next time it gets into stock.

CARDS & CRAFTS

Joyful Junie Stationery Co.

16 Craig-Na-Gower Avenue
Aviemore PH22 1RW
Contact: June Armstrong
Tel: 01479 811527

Offers a unique range of hand-made, personalised Birth Announcement & Thank You cards, Christening and Party invitations. The range features delightful ink and wash illustrations.

Speedy service guaranteed. Call for mail order catalogue.

Tryst Crafts

Contact: Lesley Protheroe
Tel: 445 5789

Handmade cards and gifts for any occasion. Can be personalised.

CHILDREN'S BOOKS

Amazon

Web: www.amazon.co.uk

Great for Internet shopping for books – especially if you like following other buyers' recommendations. Estimated delivery times advertised for each book. Wish lists can be set up to allow others to buy what you would prefer. Personalised recommendations based on your past purchases. Also sells large selection of children's toys.

Books For Children

4 Furzeground Way
Stockley Park
Uxbridge UB11 1DP
Tel: 08701 650299
Web: www.booksforchildren.co.uk

Fifteen catalogues per year. Editor's recommended selection for each of five specific age groups sent automatically. Covers books from 0-12 yrs.

Custom Books Ltd

61 Alpine Street
Reading
Berks RG1 2PY
Tel 0118 9622666
Web: www.custombooks.co.uk

Personalised children's books where your child becomes the star of the story. Books can also contain friends' names, home town, pet names, etc. Available in different languages.

The Red House Children's Book Club

Windrush Pk
Range Rd
Oxfordshire OX8 5YF
Tel 01993 893471
Web: www.redhouse.co.uk

Children's book club; no automatic selection/purchase commitment. Monthly magazine and selection of family/practical parenting titles. Hard back and paperback books, audiotapes, CD-Roms, videos, games and activities plus character merchandise.

Usborne Books

Contact: Nicky Sommer
Tel: 665 8628

Local distributor for this publisher. Books, games, puzzles, videos and CD-Roms. Can order direct from Nicky, or she can come to parties or playgroups.

CHILDREN'S CLOTHES

Baby Care by Dollycare

2 Winchester Avenue
Blaby Bypass
Blaby
Leics LE8 4G2
Tel: 0116 278 3336

Clothes, nappies and soothers made especially for small and premature babies from 1+lbs (500g).

Bishopston Trading Company

193 Gloucester Rd
Bishopton
Bristol BS7 8BG
Tel: 0117 924 5598
Web: www.bishopstontrading.co.uk

Clothes for adults and children from birth-14yrs. Made from natural fabrics, mostly organic cotton. The company is a workers cooperative set up to create employment in a South Indian village. Catalogue and online ordering available. They also sell their stock through One World in St John's Church on the corner of Princes St and Lothian Rd.

Blooming Marvellous, Blooming Kids

PO Box 12F
Chessington
Surrey KT9 2LS
Tel: 020 8391 0022
Orderline: 0870 751 8944
Web: www.bloomingmarvellous.co.uk

Colourful children's clothes 0-3 yrs. Mix'n'Match range. Maternity clothes, nursery goods, swimwear.
See also Mini Marvellous, below

The Children's Warehouse

Unit 4
44 Colville Rd
London W3 8BL

Tel: 020 8752 1166
Web: www.children's-warehouse.com

Comfortable logo-free clothes in mainly natural fabrics at reasonable prices. Free returns.

Cotton Moon

FREEPOST
PO Box 280
London SE3 8BR
Tel: 020 8305 0012
Web: www.cottonmoon.co.uk

100% cotton clothing and accessories for boys and girls from 6 months. Free returns.

Dancewear

182 Rose Street EH2 4BA
Tel: 226 5457
Web: www.dancewear-edinburgh.co.uk
Opening times: Mon-Fri 9.30-17.15; Sat 9.00-17.00

This shop can take phone orders, and payment made with credit/chargecard. Website for information only, no online ordering at time of writing.

Freemans

Tel: 0800 900200 for catalogue
Web: www.freemans.com

Branded children's clothing, e.g. Adams, Mothercare, Levis and Kickers amongst others. Interest-free credit subject to status.

Greenfibres

Westbourne House (EF)
Plymouth Rd
Totnes
Devon TQ9 5NB
Tel: 01803 868001
Web: www.greenfibres.com

Organic cotton and wool clothes for babies and children, washable nappies, organic cotton toys.

Hopscotch Dressing Up Clothes

61 Palace Rd
London SW2 3LB
Tel: 0208 674 9853
Web: www.hopscotchmailorder.co.uk

Dressing up outfits 18 mths-9yrs. Cloaks, clowns, princesses, animals, astronauts, etc. Website shows all costumes and you can order online.

La Redoute

PO Box 777
Wakefield WF2 8XZ
Tel: 0500 777 777
Web: www.laredoute.co.uk

Fashionable children's clothes at reasonable prices, along with teenage and adult ranges. Personal account option. Orders can be taken on website – there are often 'free p&p' options if orders are placed online. Free returns.

Mini Boden

Midland Terrace
Victoria Rd
London NW10 6DB
Tel: 020 8453 1535
Web: www.boden.co.uk

Logo-free, reasonably priced and stylish clothes for children up to the age of 12, made mostly of natural fabrics.

NCT (Maternity Sales) Ltd

239 Shawbridge Street
Glasgow
Tel: 0870 112 1120
Web: www.nctms.co.uk

The catalogue features baby clothes, accessories, gifts, books, leaflets and videos. Also stocks maternity clothing, sleepwear and a good range of MAVA bras. See Maternity, below.

The Natural Collection

Eco House

Monmouth Place
Bath BA1 2DQ
Tel: 01225 442288
Web: www.naturalcollection.com

Organic cotton clothing, bedding and washable nappies.

Next

Tel: 08456 100 510
Web: www.next.co.uk

All stock available also through their Next for Kids shops. 48 hr 'to your door' courier service. Next also offer service whereby you order your items, but pick them up from your nearest dedicated store; this way you save paying the delivery charge.

Pedlars

The Stables
Glen Dye
by Banchory AB31 6LT
Tel: 01330 850400
Web: www.pedlars.co.uk

Hard-wearing children's and adults clothes, stylish and colourful in age 2-adult. Cannot order from website, but catalogue available.

Schmidt Natural Clothing

21 Post Horn Close
Forest Row
East Sussex RH18 5DE
Tel: 01342 822169
Web: www.naturalclothing.co.uk

Organic and natural clothing for babies, children and adults, including fine wool, silk and cotton underwear. Suppliers comply with fair trade guidelines. Small charge for catalogue refundable with first order. 3 months interest-free credit option on larger orders.

Stuck for Words

Tel: 0131 332 1998
Web: www.stuckforwords.co.uk

Hand-painted children's clothes, created in Scotland
Stuck for words is a mail order company offering a range of 100% cotton clothes for children from birth to 10 years. Current products include t-shirts, sleep suits and baby vests, all of which can be decorated with one of our striking and child-orientated designs. All items are also available tie-dyed in a range of colours. As you would expect from a company run by the mother of two boys under five, all the clothes are machine washable at 60° (with whites if necessary) and can be tumble-dried.
Each item is hand-painted or dyed to order, tied with purple ribbon and despatched in an elegantly simple paper carrier, thus making our clothes an inspired gift for any child. Call for a brochure.

Tesco

Tel: 08457 024024
Web: www.tesco.com

Good value children's clothes from birth-4yrs, maternity clothes, disposable nappies, baby toys and equipment.

VertBaudet

18 Canal Rd
Bradford
PO Box 125
BD99 4XB
Tel: 0500 012345 (freephone)
Web: www.vertbaudet.co.uk

Two hundred-odd page catalogue selling babies', children's and maternity clothes and nursery goods. Also have a range of bedding and children's bedroom accessories. Personal account facility. Free returns. Also stock small range of low birth weight baby clothing.

Yahoo Auctions

Web: uk.auctions.yahoo.com/uk/ (yes - there's no 'www')

Great way of finding cheap children and baby clothes, toys or equipment. You put in your bid, what you're prepared to go up to in case someone else outbids you, and then put your feet up! If you win, you send payment to seller who sends it on to you. Works on trust, but sellers and buyers have ratings to help you. Think of it as car boot sales without the rain or sharp elbows ... (or even NCT Nearly New Sales without the queues!)

FOOD

East Coast Organic Boxes (ECOBox)

24 Boggs Holdings, Pencaitland
East Lothian EH34 5BD
Tel/Fax: 01875 340227
Mobile: 07971 209081
Email: ecobox@eastcoastorganics.freeserve.co.uk

Organic vegetable boxes as well as organic fruit, eggs and bread. Free delivery service available – phone for details. Collection points throughout Edinburgh or collect direct from farm. Fri 16.00-20.00, Sat 9.00-12.00

Ian Miller's Organic Meats

Jamesfield Farm
FREEPOST EH3582
Newburgh
Fife KY14 6BR
Tel: 01738 850498
Fax: 01738 850741

Organic meat, poultry, bacon, fish, haggis, venison, specialty sausages and stuffing.

Iceland

Tel: 0800 328 0800
Web: www.iceland-shop.co.uk

All stock available through website. Min order value £40 on the web, no min order by phone. You can order catalogue by phone no. too. You can place your order up to 4 days in advance and if you order before 15.00 Mon to Fri you can have your shopping delivered the next day. If you order after 15.00, it'll be delivered the day after that. Once you're happy with your order, you'll be offered a choice of available delivery dates and time slots.

Pillars of Hercules Organic Farm

By Falkland
Fife
Tel: 01337 857749
Web: www.pillars.co.uk

Organic vegetable boxes as well as organic fruit and eggs. Free catalogue available. Delivery to Edinburgh and Fife areas.

Sainsbury's

Web: Sainsburystoyou.com

Home grocery and delivery service. Shop for your favourites over the Internet, or browse the virtual shelves. It's all delivered to your home for a £5 delivery charge.

Simply Organic Food Company Ltd

Web: www.simplyorganic.net

Vast array of organic groceries available to order online.
Deliver anywhere on UK mainland by 12 noon on your chosen delivery day, to home or office. They need 36 hrs to put together your order.

Tesco

Web: www.tesco.com

Home grocery shopping and delivery service. You shop on the internet using your usual favourites, browsing, or even choosing recipes and the ingredients are automatically put in your order. You choose the delivery time in 2-hour slots, and off you go. £5 charge per order for this service. Great for busy parents.

V.W.Quested

Newsagent/Grocery Store
21 Strathearn Rd
Tel: 447 1361

Opening times: Mon-Fri 4.00-19.00; Sat 3.30-19.00; Sun 5.00-17.00

As well as daily newspaper delivery also does early morning milk and bread deliveries to Marchmont, Sciennes, Grange and Newington areas. Milk delivery prices compare favourably with supermarket prices. Grocery prices also very competitive and can be delivered.

MATERNITY

We have listed a few home-shopping services, both on-line and catalogues, which stock maternity wear: some have dedicated collections, the other echo the trends of their main lines.

Blooming Marvellous

PO Box 12F
Chessington
Surrey KT9 2LS
Tel: 020 8391 0022
Orderline: 0870 751 8944
Web: www.bloomingmarvellous.co.uk

Range of contemporary clothing for mothers-to-be. Casual and formal wear, plus hosiery, lingerie, sleepwear and accessories such as breast pads. See also Children's clothing, above.

Formes

Tel: 08689 2288
Email: e-shopping@formes-uk.com
Web: www.formes.co.uk

browse and buy the clothing available in the boutiques without leaving home. Offers urbanwear, leisurewear and nightwear, along with a range of often funky separates. A pretty website, but it can take ages to load,

JoJo Maman Bébé

Tel: 0870 241 0560
Web: www.jojomamanbebe.co.uk

Online ordering (or mailorder) on a range of modern-styled maternity clothing (incl. workwear, casual and evening collections), and lingerie. Also offer children's wear and home accessories.

NCT (Maternity Sales) Ltd

239 Shawbridge Street
Glasgow
Tel: 0870 112 1120
Web: www.nctms.co.uk

The catalogue features maternity wear such as swimsuits, bras and nightwear.. Mava bras with zip and drop cups designed by breastfeeding mothers and counsellors. Wide range of sizes from 32A to 46J. Some bras have a high cotton content. Mava bras are recommended by midwives. For the number of your nearest Mava fitting agent contact the NCT Edinburgh Centre on 260 9201.

Next

Tel: 08456 100 510
Web: www.next.co.uk

Catalogue stocks range of maternity wear for casual and formal wear, which echoes the trend styles of main collection. Also stocks maternity swimwear (dependent on season). Next also offer service whereby you order your items, but pick them up from your nearest dedicated store; this way you save paying the delivery charge.

VertBaudet

18 Canal Rd
Bradford
PO Box 125
BD99 4XB
Tel: 0500 012345 (freephone)
Web: www.vertbaudet.co.uk

Although primarily a children's wear catalogue, there is a maternity section. Range of mainly casual and daywear, plus some underwear and nightwear. Personal account facility. Free returns. See also *Children's Clothes*, above.

MISCELLANEOUS

Cash's Name Tapes

J&J Cash Ltd
Torrington Ave
Coventry
Tel: 01203 466466
Web: www.jjcash.co.uk

Woven name tapes available online. Also widely available from shops such as John Lewis, Clarks Shoes, Mothercare and Aitken and Niven department stores.

Golden Hands, Silver Feet

Contact: Nicky Sommer
Tel: 665 8628
Web: www.goldenhands.co.uk

Babies' hands or feet cast in bronze/aluminium as a 2D plaque or 3D replica, ideal for family presents. Will travel to your home or even hospital. Gift vouchers available.

Croft Mill

Lowther Lane
Foulridge, Colne
Lancs BB8 7NG
Tel: 01282 869625
Web: www.croftmill.co.uk

Fabric by post. Very reasonable prices. Please note that none of the fabrics are flame proofed. Website has more information only and brochure ordering service – no online ordering at time of writing.

Nature's Best Health Products Ltd

Freepost PO Box 1
Tunbridge Wells
TN2 3EQ
Tel: 01892 552117

Vitamin and health supplements including children's supplements suitable for age 4+ yrs.

Pharmacy2U

Web: www.pharmacy2u.co.uk

Offers a complete range of high street pharmacy products and services online, including an 'ask our pharmacists' service.

SHOES

If your child has very narrow or broad feet, or he/she has uneven sizes, you may need to have shoes made. This is not as expen sive as it sounds, although it does cost slightly more than high street prices. It is also worth investigating these companies if you want a particular style but can't get it in the shops.

Charles MacWatt Handmade Boots and Shoes

7 Christmas Steps
Bristol BS1 5BS
Tel: 0117 921 4247

Made to measure and to order shoes, boots and sandals for children and adults.

Soled Out

Unit 14, Forge Lane
Moorlands Industrial Estate
Saltash
Cornwall PL12 6LX
Tel: 01752 841080

Made to measure shoes and boots for children and adults in bright coloured leather with crepe soles.

Shoes made to fit each foot.

TOYS & GIFTS

There are plenty of websites available for children's toys. Below are some names of note. For a fuller list, go to a search engine such as Google.

Bright Minds

Braysdown Yard
Peasedown St John
Bath BA2 8LL
Tel: 0870 44 22 124
Web: www.brightminds.co.uk

Offer a range of learning toys, from ages 2+-adult. For pre-school children, the range include puzzles, games and interactive toys. Products for older children are divided into subject categories, such as maths, music, nature studies, chemistry and so on.

Colourworld

Regina Thorne
1 Newton Street
Chartham Hatch
Canterbury CT4 7LT
Tel: 01227 730204

Pretty coloured birch wood toys and gifts, including cookers, coat pegs, etc.

Dawson & Son

Tel: 08700 367 869
Web: www.dawson-and-son.com

Huge selection of wooden toys and games with good search engine – simply type in the age and price range for suitable options.

Early Learning Centre

Tel: 08705 352 352
Web: www.elc.co.uk

Mail order/online ordering of the high street store. Good search facility.

Frog Hollow

PO Box 550
Markyate
Hertfordshire AL3 8QP
Tel: 01582 842117

Personalised toys and gifts.

Hawkin & Co

St Margaret
Harleston
Norfolk IP20 0PJ
Tel: 01986 782536

Intriguing catalogue packed with amusing gifts, toys, novelties and gadgets. Very reasonably priced. Ideal for stocking fillers or difficult to buy for people. Please note that most toys are not suitable for under 3s.

Hopscotch Dressing Up Clothes

See under *Shopping from Home – Clothes*

Letterbox

PO Box 114
Truro
Cornwall TR2 5YR
Tel: 0870 600 7878
Web: www.letterbox.co.uk

Collection of games, gifts, wooden farms, arcs, dolls' houses,, dressing up clothes etc. Extensive range of personalised gifts, ranging from name boards, jack-in-the-boxes, to chairs and sleeping bags. Also offer bedroom accessories. Loads of stocking filler/ party bag ideas, many with age recommendations.

Mini Marvellous

www.bloomingmarvellous.co.uk

A range of toys, clothing, accessories etc for children aged 1-5: online shopping available via parent Blooming Marvellous site.

Playsongs Publications

39 Byrne Rd
London SE26 5JT
Tel: 020 8778 0708

Music for the very young. Cassette tapes of all the best songs and nursery rhymes, sung and played by professionals. Action songs, lullabies, lively time and sleepy time songs.

Super Tramp Trampolines

Langlands Business Park
Cullhampton
Devon EX15 3AA
Tel: 01884 841305
Web: www.supertramp.co.uk

Outdoor garden trampolines and wooden garden play equipment – also available from John Lewis: see Shopping – Dept Stores.

Tesco

See *Shopping from Home – Children's Clothes, Baby Equipment*

Toys 'R' Us

Web: www.toysrus.co.uk

Online ordering from the familiar toy and game warehouse.

Tridias!

124 Walcot Street
Bath BA1 5BG
Tel: 0870 2402104
Web: www.tridias.co.uk

Inventive toy and game ideas for children. Catalogue available with over 400 toys and games, or view and order online.

Toilet Stops

TOILET STOPS

The toilets listed below are maintained by City of Edinburgh Council. For any comments or nore info on them, contact:
City of Edinburgh Council
Environmental and Consumer Services
Tel: 529 3030
Email: env.con.svs@edinburgh.gov.uk.

Please note that the Council reserves the right to alter opening times etc. There are other, automated, loos (at eg. St Andrew's Sq) but you'll need to spend much more than a penny to operate them!

10.00-22.00 (* denotes open from 8.00)
Ardmillan Ter, Gorgie Rd; Bath St, Portobello; Haymarket; High St, S Queensferry; Hunter Sq *; London Rd; Mound*; Taylor Gdns, Leith; Tollcross; West End*.

10.00-20.00 (* denotes open from 8.00)
Bruntsfield; Canaan Lane, Morningside; Canonmills; Castlehill*; Castle Ter Car Park*; Hamilton Pl, Stockbridge; Middle Meadow Walk; Nicolson Sq; St James' Centre*.

10.00-18.00
Colinton Rd, Colinton; Cramond; Currie; Fairmilehead; Granton Sq, Granton; Hawes Pier, S Queensferry; Hope Park, Joppa; Juniper Green; Liberton Gdns, Liberton; Silverknowes; St John's Rd, Corstorphine; Westerhailes.

Seasonal Opened Toilets (1 May-30 Sept)

10.00-20.00
Pipe St, Portobello; Ross Bandstand*, Princes St Gdns; Pittville/Bellfield, Portobello.

Toilets with nappy changing facilities

Ardmillan Ter, Gorgie
10.00-22.00

Bath St, Portobello
10.00-22.00

Canaan Lane
10.00-20.00

Canonmills
10.00-20.00
Castle Ter Car Park
10.00-20.00

Haymarket
10.00-22.00

High St, S Queensferry
10.00-22.00

London Rd
10.00-22.00

Middle Meadow Walk
10.00-20.00

Mound
10.00-22.00

St James
10.00-20.00

Taylor Gardens, Leith
10.00-22.00

West End, Princes St Gardens
10.00-22.00

Travel & Transport

As with most things, getting out and about with small children requires a lot of energy and a certain amount of planning ahead. It needn't turn into a military operation, but being prepared is the key, although it also makes sense to be prepared for things not going according to plan! The aim of this chapter is to give you as much information as is currently available to enable you to be prepared as you get out and about in Edinburgh.

Over the years there have been proposals to upgrade the public transport system serving the city, such as the building of a new tram system linking the airport to the city. However, while the completion of the rail link to Edinburgh Park is imminent, many proposals remain in (very long!) pipelines, actual improvements are years away, and for now your options are walking, cycling, or taking a car, bus, taxi or train.

TRAVELINE & NADICS

Traveline

Tel: 0870 608 2608 (every day 8am-8pm, except 25, 26 Dec and 1 Jan: national call rates apply)
Web: www.traveline.org.uk

For information about public transport, such as timetables, details of available concessions, or details of transport for people with disabilities, contact Traveline, where you'll receive impartial advice, based on current published timetables. The website can direct you to many others, and help you plan a journey in Scotland, Wales or England.

NADICS

Web: www.nadics.org.uk

Run by the Scottish Executive, the NADICS (NAtional Driver Information and Control System) site provides up-to-date information on roadworks, delays etc, and can help when planning a journey.

AIR TRAVEL

Edinburgh Airport

Edinburgh EH12 9DN
Tel: 333 1000

The airport is located 8 miles west of Edinburgh.

GETTING THERE

The airport is easily accessible by car, just off the A8 dual carriageway to the west of the city.

PARKING

Edinburgh Airport currently has 3 short-stay car parks and 1 long stay one: work is underway on a new multi-storey car park, which will provide 2000 more spaces.

CAR PARK RATES

1 hour – £1.20/30mins; £2.20/ 1 hr
Short term – £4.00 for up to 2-4 hours or £8.00/ day. Special weekend (18:00 Friday-10: 00 Monday) rates are available if you pre-book (Tel: 0870 000 1 000)
Long term - £5.00/day (a courtesy coach to terminal building included)
Further park and ride facilities available near airport, Tel: 335 3666.

BUS LINKS

Lothian Buses operate a service called Airlink, Tel: 555 6363. The service runs to and from Waverley Bridge to the airport. The journey time is approx. 25 mins with buses leaving Waverley Bridge every 10 mins during the day. At the time of writing, the fares currently stand at £3.30 single/ £5 open return for an adult traveller, with Child fares at £2/£3. There is an option for a saver ticket which incorporates travel on the Airlink and also on regular fleet buses.

TAXIS

Black cabs and private hires can take passengers out to Edinburgh Airport (expect to pay around £14 or so), but it's a point of great contention what happens then. There are dedicated Airport Taxis (in white livery) which have an official rank, but there is an ongoing battle of wits and legalities waged by some black cab operators …

Airport taxis available for hire are saloon or estate cars. Approximate cost to the City Centre is £14-£16. Child seat belts are available in the back, if advance notice is given.

For full details of all airline numbers and website addresses please contact the Airport Switchboard on 333 1000.

THE AIRPORT TERMINAL

While Edinburgh Airport has many facilities, one thing which did succumb to the building improvements in recent years was the spectators' gallery; however, while junior plane-spotters can no longer watch the arrivals and departures from the terminal, there are several children's play areas throughout the Terminal and Departure lounges.

There are baby care rooms on both floors. They are situated

next to toilet facilities in both the UK and International arrivals halls, on the first floor departure concourse and in the departure lounge opposite gate 10 and in the toilets at gate 1c. All rooms except gate 1c are fitted with vending machines supplying nappies and have a private nursing room. They contain nappy-change surfaces, sink unit, a playpen, a comfy chair and an activity wall hanging. An en suite toilet and a small room with a chair for feeding complete the facilities. All toilet areas are facilitated with unisex and wheelchair accessible toilets. If you are travelling with a child of the opposite sex to yourself and need to use the toilets, then you can use the unisex accessible toilets.

The eating areas have been moved and now have a view of the Pentland Hills. Apart from Costa Coffee on the ground floor, the whole food court has been relocated to the east end of the first floor. Accessible by escalator, lift or stairs the food court boasts a wide selection of both snacks and full meals. There are plenty of highchairs and a selection of tinned baby food is available. Bottles can be warmed on request.

AIRPORT & TOURIST INFORMATION

The Airport & Tourist Information Desk can be found in the International Arrivals area. The staff will help you with details on airport facilities, places of interest, accommodation and car hire. Edinburgh Airport has 5 car hire firms, based within the Domestic Arrivals Hall.

SHOPPING

A number of shops selling gifts, clothes, books, magazines, confectionery, etc can be found on the first floor. All retail outlets are easily accessible for all passengers by escalator or lift.

TRAVELLING BY PLANE WITH BABIES OR TODDLERS

Always let the airline know in advance that you are travelling with a baby or toddler and check out the facilities available when booking. If you have a lively toddler, it may be worth finding out if you can use a car seat on board. You may have to pay for the seat, depending on the airline and how busy the aircraft is. Car seats can also travel in the hold – but check your baggage allowance! British Airways have recently unveiled a new airline seat for the under 2s. Initially these seats will be fitted into Boeing 747s for long-haul flights, but there are plans to extend the service. Booking is essential so check when booking flights.
Pushchairs can either be taken on as hand luggage or brought to you when you disembark. Ask when booking or checking in. Skycots are available on long-haul flights. Attached to the bulkhead, they provide respite for tired arms by holding sleepy babies.
Take tried and tested snacks and toys for in-flight entertainment. During take-off or landing, swallowing food or drinks will help prevent earache arising from changes in cabin pressure. Nappy-changing facilities vary with each aircraft; you may have to resort to your knee.
If in doubt, ask. Staff will probably be more than happy to help, particularly if the alternative is having miserable passengers on board.

TRAVELLING BY BUS

Two companies – Lothian Buses and First Bus – provide the majority of services in and around Edinburgh, although other operators provide localised transport.
Lothian Buses still have some maroon and white double deckers which have been part of Edinburgh for years, but updated livery has gold and red squares joining the maroon and white.
First Edinburgh operates fewer routes in the city centre, but has more buses which service the outlying zones of the city. First's livery is white, indigo and red for the majority of the fleet – though you also see green and gold liveried First buses, especially operating outside the city.
Both companies have introduced lower-chassied single deckers, which are easier to board than the older style buses, and which have more space for pushchairs inside.
Under 5s travel free on buses of both companies, on the understanding that they will surrender their seat for a fare paying passenger. A maximum of two under 5s may accompany one adult, and a standard child fare must be paid for further children. Both companies say they welcome breastfeeding on their services, although they recommend discretion, as, unfortunately, they cannot guarantee the response of other passengers.
Fares are similar on both services, based on a stage principal for both adults and children; there's a flat fare for concessionary travel: currently, adults can expect to pay around 60p for 1-2 stages. At the time of writing, people who have concession passes for Edinburgh, East Lothian and Midlothian can travel free after 9.30, Mon-Fri and all day Sat and Sun.

Both companies sell bargain day tickets which means you can hop on and off their buses as you require. As well as the day tickets, there's a raft of saver options available, so if you use buses frequently, it might be worth taking the time and working out what's your best option: weekly, monthly and even yearly passes are available. Lothian Buses offer a SmartCard ticket, paid by direct debit, which allows the bearer nigh-on the freedom of that network (excepting the company's tour buses).

Frequency of buses varies depends on the route. However, a 15-20 minute frequency is usual on most main routes during weekdays 7.00-19.00. Off peak bus services vary enormously, so always check a current timetable, available from the respective bus offices or websites, or phone the enquiry lines, otherwise, you could be in for a long wait. In addition, when it comes to route changes, be aware that alterations can occur with what appears to be little public notification, so, again, if in doubt, contact the companies.

CONTACT DETAILS

Lothian Buses

Lothian Buses plc
Annandale Street EH7 4AZ
Tel: 0131 554 4494
Fax: 0131 554 3942
Email: info@lothianbuses.co.uk
Web: www.lothianbuses.co.uk

Lothian Buses Travelshop

27 Hanover Street
EH2 2DL

Shandwick Pl, and

31 Waverley Bridge

Bus Times & Information
Tel: 555 6363 (24 hrs)

Lost Property
Tel: 558 8858

First Bus

Carmuirs House
300 Stirling Road
Larbert FK5 3NJ
Tel: 01324 611 111
Fax: 01324 611 287
Web: www.firstgroup.com/firstedinburgh

Edinburgh Busline enquiries
Tel: 08708 727271

General Timetable enquiries
Tel: 0870 6082608

Travelling Further Afield

Long distance buses operate out of St Andrews Square. There are services to many parts of Scotland, London and other parts of England. The main operators are Citylink, National Express and Stagecoach. Although fares tend to be cheaper than rail fares, a long distance coach trip with small children can be difficult, so the pros and cons should always be weighed up carefully.

Edinburgh has a new bus terminal, which is much sleeker – and much less draughty – than its predecessor. One thing to watch out for are the automatic doors which screen the waiting area from the bus ranks.

The following companies provide coach travel from Edinburgh to various destinations. If you're not sure which company goes where, try Traveline for information (see above).

EXPRESS COACH SERVICES WITHIN SCOTLAND:

Scottish Citylink

Buchanan Bus Station
Killermont Street
Glasgow G2 3NP
Tel: 08705 50 50 50 (Contact Centre)
Tel: 0141 332 9644 (head office)
Fax 0141 332 4488
Email: info@citylink.co.uk
Web: www.citylink.co.uk

NB: One child under five years of age not occupying a seat, and accompanied by an adult fare-paying passenger, will be carried free of charge. Any additional child or children under five years of age, accompanied by the same adult, and all children aged 5 to 15 years inclusive can get discounts of up to 30% off normal fares.

Stagecoach Buses

Stagecoach have several locally managed companies in Scotland in Glasgow, Perth and Fife. The Head Office contact address is:

Stagecoach UK Bus
10 Dunkeld Road
Perth Scotland PH1 5TW

Information regarding Stagecoach Fife is available in Travel Shops, such as:

Bus Station
Kingsgate
Dunfermline
Tel: 01383 621249

Bus Station
Church Street

Glenrothes
Tel: 01592 610686

Bus Station
Hill Street
Kirkcaldy
Tel: 01592 642394

Bus Station
City Road
St Andrews
Tel: 01334 474238

Megabus

Web: megabus.com

Stagecoach also provides the Megabus.com inter-city service. Tickets are bookable online: book online and take you booking reference when you travel.

NB: Children under 3 years of age, but they are not guaranteed a seat unless a specific seat has been purchased for them and the reference number provided. All children under 14 yrs of age must be accompanied by an adult (someone aged 16 years old or over).

EXPRESS COACH SERVICES THROUGHOUT THE UK AND IRELAND:

National Express Limited

Ensign Court
4 Vicarage Road
Edgbaston
Birmingham B15 3ES
Tel: 08705 80 80 80 (Bookings & information)
Tel: 0121 4238479 (Disabled Persons Travel Helpline)
Web: www.nationalexpress.com

CYCLING

Given the numbers of hills in and around Edinburgh, cycling may not be the first thing you think of doing with your baby or toddler, but with a wealth of off-road routes in and around the city, maybe you will be inspired! Your child will certainly be thrilled by feeling the breeze and watching people and objects speed by.

Before taking off, a few guidelines. Firstly, get your bike checked over at a specialist shop and keep it well maintained, especially the brakes and the wheels, as they will be under greater strain than normal. Next, buy the best child seat you can afford. See *Shopping - Bicycles* for details and availability. Finally, wear a helmet and ensure that your baby, toddler or child wears a helmet at all times both on road and off road.

Whether you cycle alone or with your child, dress brightly and make use of fluorescent strips to maximise visibility and if it may get dark while you are out, remember to have working front and back lights. The use of a flashing red rear light in addition to the legally required steady red light is recommended. Beware of the effect other road users' actions may have on you, such as car doors opening unexpectedly, and of the effect your actions may have on other road users, such as overtaking a stationary queue of traffic at a junction. Never jump the red lights at pedestrian crossings – if you can't obey the rules designed to protect pedestrians, why should vehicle drivers obey the rules designed to protect cyclists?

Compared with cycling alone, you will find that the bike feels heavier with a child on or attached to your bike. That's what those low gears are for. If using the more common rear-mounted child seat, it is advisable to carry any necessary luggage in front panniers to balance the weight front and back. You may find that wider handlebars give better control over the steering, but if you are using a mountain bike, change the knobbly tyres for smooth ones to reduce resistance on off-road paths and tarmac surfaces.

Although some keen cyclists have been known to tow babies as young as a few weeks old in child trailers, it is advisable not to take them cycling until the baby can support its head and sit up unassisted, usually around 6 mths. Babies and toddlers can be taken cycling in a child trailer towed behind the bike or in a rear-mounted child seat which clips into a bicycle's rear rack. There are pros and cons to both and what is most suitable for you will depend on the type of cycling you intend to do and your budget. Once the trailer or child seat have been outgrown (3-4 yrs depending on size), the choice is a trailercycle which attaches to your bike or a tandem bicycle. Again there are pros and cons to both. See *Shopping - Bicycles* for further details and for fully comprehensive information you could try a book such as *Bicycling with Children* by Trudy E. Bell.

BIKES ON TRAINS

All ScotRail trains are fitted with bike accommodation, although the space can vary from 2-6 bikes/train, depending on the service. On some services, pre-booking is required, on others it is to be recommended and on the rest it's not possible. While ScotRail no longer operate a bike charge, some other companies still do and some require bike spaces to be reserved. Note that tandems, tricycles and trailercycles are not carried on ScotRail services. Full details are on their website at www.scotrail.co.uk/cycle.

CHILD SAFETY

It is not advisable to allow children under 9 into traffic. Cycle training for primary age children (usually at Primary 6/7) should be available through schools under a scheme run by Lothian and Borders Police. If your child's school does not offer training, ask them to consider doing so. Spokes offshoot, Lothian Safe Routes, can offer advice. Basic cycle training and safety should be promoted to under 5s, in addition to making sure that all their cycles and equipment are well maintained. All cyclists should wear a helmet at all times.

CYCLING IN PREGNANCY

If you are reasonably fit and used to cycling, there is probably no reason not to keep cycling during pregnancy – but do follow your doctor's advice. Consider lower gears and inverting dropped handlebars to enable a more upright sitting position for greater comfort. Be aware that your balance may change as your bump grows.

CONTACTS

CTC

Cotterell House
69 Mead Row
Godalming, Surrey GU7 3HS
Tel: 0148 341 7217
Web: www.ctc.org.uk

The Cyclists Touring Club is Britain's largest national cycling organisation. It campaigns for all cyclists regardless of age, ability or type of bike. Members receive a range of services, including a bi-monthly magazine, touring information and technical advice, public liability cover and legal claims advice. The CTC offers a range of insurance policies designed for cyclists.

There is a local group, the CTC Lothians District Association. There are occasional rides for parents with children – on child seats, tandems, pushchairs, own bikes.

Local contact:

Mike Harrison (Secretary)
11 Stead's Pl
Edinburgh EH6 5DY
Email: secretary@ctclothians.org.uk
Web: www.ctclothians.org.uk

Spokes

St Martin's Church
232 Dalry Rd
Tel: 313 2114
Web: www.spokes.org.uk

A Lothian cycle group which campaigns for cyclists, Spokes is an entirely voluntary organisation. It produces Cycle Maps of Edinburgh, Midlothian, East Lothian and West Lothian. These detailed and easy to follow maps show alternative routes to your destination along cycle tracks made from disused railway lines, river valleys, minor roads etc, avoiding busy and cobbled roads. Steep gradients, schools and parks are clearly marked. Available from bike shops, bookshops or post-free from Spokes, £4.95 per map or all four maps for the price of three. Lothian Safe Routes is an offshoot set up to encourage and advise projects that will allow more children and families to walk, cycle or take the bus to school and improve local road conditions.

Sustrans

35 King Street
Bristol BS1 4DZ
Tel: 0117 926 8893
Web: www.sustrans.co.uk.

A charity working on sustainable transport projects, the flagship project being the National Cycle Network: a 10,000-mile network of cycle paths combining a mixture of off-road routes and traffic calmed streets. National Route 1 from Dover to John O'Groats, the Orkneys and Shetland passes through Edinburgh and Aberdeen and there are now several regional routes starting in Edinburgh. Up to date details are on the website. Sustrans maps and guides are available from bike shops, bookshops or direct. Sustrans also offers advice on Sate Routes to School projects.

TRAVEL BY CAR

There's no doubt that Edinburgh is becoming increasingly convoluted, as more roads become one way, and building programmes cause lane closures and restrictions, and with road tolling an ever-present presence on the horizon, it can seem that drivers are persona non grata. However, despite what it feels like when you're crawling along Queen Street at peak times – and despite what some of the pro-toll lobby say – the city doesn't really suffer from gridlock. Getting from a-b isn't too much of a chore, if you keep to the limits and don't have to travel at absolute peak times. However, there are more speed cameras planned, and while many are familiar landmarks to local drivers, it's worthwhile remembering that manned speed checks could be right round the next corner!

PARKING

The main headache in Edinburgh is not driving, but parking.
If you choose to visit one of the outlying shopping complexes, this problem is negated by the provision of ample and free parking at centres such as the Gyle, Fort Kinnaird, Straiton, Hermiston Gait etc. See *Shopping*, for more details.
However, sometimes parking in or near the city centre cannot be avoided. In the last few years parking restrictions have become tighter and charges have become steeper. There are 2 zones, a Central and a Peripheral one. Expect to pay no less than 30p/15 mins: in prime locations, such as George St, the current charge is 45p/15 mins.
Parking restrictions vary per zone. In the Central zone, restrictions generally apply Mon-Sat 8.30–18.30. In the Peripheral zone they run Mon-Sat 8.30–17.30, but keep your eyes peeled; some streets' restrictions only operate Mon-Fri.

The alternative is to use one of the various multi-storey or one-level car parks within the city's environs. They have a combined total of 5975 spaces, so with fingers crossed, you might just find one. The problem with the multi-storeys, such as Castle St (nr Princes St West End, is that they don't have lifts. You either have to tackle narrow stairs or ramps with cars approaching you – neither of which is really suitable for parents with children in pushchairs. Currently, one of the most pushchair friendly multi-storey car parks is at Greenside Place. New Street car park is all on one level, and isn't too much of hike with a pushchair from Princes St, if you cut along Market St and on to Waverley Bridge. Parking options in the Old Town include the Grassmarket, which is often very busy, Crichton St NCP, George Square (ticket machines), while Chalmers St NCP is also handy for the Meadows and Tollcross areas.
For more information about city parking, click on to: www.edinburgh.gov.uk/parking.

SAFETY

Safety while driving with small children is a priority. Accidents can be easily caused by unrestrained children, often with dreadful results. Since Sept 1989, if seat belts or child restraints are fitted in the rear of a car, it is the driver's responsibility to ensure that children under 14 use them – no matter how short the journey is. Further information on child car safety and the seatbelt laws can be obtained from The Scottish Executive, Victoria Quay, EH6 6QQ.
Get in the habit of regularly checking your baby or child's seat, especially the restraints. Ensure that all adults securing it in a car are following the manufacturer's instructions on fitting.

CITY CAR CLUB

An alternative to owning a car in Edinburgh is to join the City Car Club. This is run by a private company, but has the support of the City of Edinburgh Council. You pay for the time you use a car for, plus a mileage charge. There is a monthly membership fee (at the moment this starts from £11 per month, and is inclusive of insurance and breakdown cover, amongst other things). You can hire a car for as little as an hour up to a few days (although this is usually through a hire-car company). You can book a car a few weeks in advance, or even as little as half an hour before you need one – although the location and type of car available may obviously be restricted in this case. The Club has 15+ cars, of various sizes, and they are located in dedicated parking bays round the city, such as Marchmont, Bruntsfield, Canonmills, Gorgie, Stockbridge and Portobello.
The Club does not provide car seats for children, so you would need to provide your own.

Contact:

Smart Moves
31 Argyle Place EH9 1JT
Tel: 0845 458 1784
Email: edinburgh@smartmoves.co.uk
Web: www.smartmoves.co.uk

CAR HIRE AND CHILD SEATS

Most local car rental firms offer car seats for 9 mths-4 yrs, but cost and availability varies considerably. It is recommended to book the car seat at the same time as hiring the car.
See Yellow Pages for contact details or log on to www.yell.com.

ON FOOT

Built on seven hills, Edinburgh is pretty steep in places! It's not always the easiest city to negotiate with pushchairs or prams, or with young children in tow. It always helps if you give yourself plenty of time and have some idea of the route you plan to take. In the city centre much has been done to encourage the pedestrian, such as widening pavements and adding crossings.

ROAD SAFETY

When out with small children it makes a lot of sense to emphasise basic road safety even from an early age, and in particular to set a good example. It is well known that road accidents are the major cause of death and injury to children and they are most at risk when on foot and alone. The Royal Society for the

Prevention of Accidents (RoSPA) teaches the following basic rules of road safety to children:

- **never go out without an adult.**
- **always hold an adult's hand.**
- **STOP, LOOK, and LISTEN before you cross the road.**

The Children's Traffic Club in Scotland is a free club for children and parents of three-year-olds living in Scotland. Invitations to enrol are sent out by the local Health Board and parents/carers enrol their child by completing the registration card and returning it in the free post envelope provided. The invitation arrives shortly after the child's third birthday. Once enrolled, the child receives a membership certificate and a series of booklets, which contain activities designed to explore road safety. Advice is given on key points and suggestions are given for practice when out and about with the child. The materials are designed for use by parents with children. The club is administered by the Scottish Executive via the Scottish Road Safety Campaign from whom further information can be sought (see below). For advice about other road safety education matters. contact your local Road Safety Training Officer at Lothians and Borders police, Tel: 311 3019.

Scottish Road Safety Campaign

Heriot-Watt Research Park (North)
Riccarton, Currie
Edinburgh EH14 4AP
Tel: 0131 472 9200
Fax: 0131 472 9201
Email: enquiries@srsc.org.uk
Web: www.srsc.org.uk

ROAD SAFETY UNITS AND CONTACTS

Fife Police Headquarters Road Safety Unit

Detroit Road
Glenrothes
Fife KY6 2RJ
Tel: 01592 418 888
Fax: 01592 418 444
Email: Jane.Greer@fie.pnn.fife.police.uk

Lothian and Borders Road Safety Unit

Fettes Ave
Edinburgh EH4 1RB
Tel: 311 3066
Fax: 311 3113
Email: paul.rson@virgin.net (Paul Richardson)

Contacts for other areas in Scotland can be found on www.srsc.org.uk.

PROBLEMS WITH ROADS, PAVEMENTS, LIGHTING ETC

If you have experienced any problems with pavements, crossings or whatever, whether it is in the city centre or your local area, it's worth trying to do something about it. Write to, and encourage friends to write to, your local councillor, pointing out the dangers you and your children face and putting forward your preferred solution, or call CLARENCE (council helpline) on 0800 23 23 23.

TAXIS

Taxis are a fairly expensive way to travel in Edinburgh. Black cabs can be hailed in the street or at taxi ranks, and all charge standard fares. They take a maximum of 5 passengers. Not all black cabs are designed to accommodate wheelchairs, but those which are have the recognisable wheelchair logo prominently displayed. All black cabs are licensed with the City Council and their licence no. will be prominently displayed within the cab itself.

There are a variety of radio cab companies in Edinburgh for hire, details in the Yellow Pages. Some of these companies offer a range of vehicles, although unless you state how many people it's for the vehicle in question will probably be a saloon, licensed to carry four passengers.

Points to Note

All cabs and taxis should have licenses displayed and the drivers usually have ID badges.
Use the rear seatbelts: it's the law. Some styles of cabs have a pull-down child seat in the middle of the rear seat.
Irrespective of vehicle-type, they should operate under a meter system – so make sure your driver uses it, no matter what form of taxi or hire it is.

Some cab drivers will let you lift a pushchair into the cab with your child strapped in. This can save a lot of hassle, both on the journey and when you disembark! Remember to secure the pushchair while in transit.

TRAVELLING BY TRAIN

For all train times and fare enquiries, call the National Rail Enquiry Service, Tel: 08457 48 49 50
This a 24 hr service. operates a call-rotation system, so hold on if you don't get an answer straight away. Alternatively, visit www.nationalrail.co.uk.
If you are planning a journey, you could also check out Traveline (see above).

There are currently three main passenger service operators in and around Edinburgh. Their Customer Service numbers are as follows:

- **ScotRail Tel: 0845 601 5929**
- **GNER, Tel: 08457 225 333 (Mon-Fri 08.30-18.30)**
- **Virgin, Tel: 0121 654 7400**

STATIONS

Although there are around 10 stations in the Edinburgh area, there is limited use for trains within Edinburgh due to the current lack of suburban services. The following is an outline of the stations and the routes they serve.

Edinburgh Park
Opening imminently at the time of writing, this station is situated at the Edinburgh Park Business Park on the Western bounds of the city. It will create a stop between Haymarket and Linlithgow, as well as being a new stop on the Edinburgh-Bathgate route.

Edinburgh Waverley
The main station in Edinburgh and a principal station in the rail network. Trains run south from Waverley to England, and also serve other cities such as Glasgow, Aberdeen and Inverness. There are also connections to other routes, as well as busy local services to East and West Lothian and Fife.
The main station access for pushchairs is from Waverley Bridge. Other entrances, such as those from Market St and the station car park, have long flights of steps. Access to several of the platforms is by stairs or lifts. There is no drop off/pick up point for private cars.
The station provides many amenities on one level: the travel centre is inside the large, airy Victorian waiting hall – a great place for restless children, but it is always busy and there are automatic doors which allow easy exit! Within the bounds are the ticket and reservation counters, station, toilets, food court, cash machines etc. Out in the main concourse, there is WH Smiths, Boots the Chemist, Bureau de Change, hotel reservations desk, Hertz car rental (platform 7), luggage lockers, sandwich shops etc.
There is a charge to enter the toilets. There is a separate mothers' room for feeding and nappy-changing. The latter is usually kept locked, so ask the attendant for access. Fathers can have access to the toilet for the disabled for nappy-changing.

Haymarket

This station serves all points west and north. There are lots of steps to the platforms. The short trip between Waverley and Haymarket is popular as a playgroup outing. Snack bar on Platform 4.

South Gyle
A suburban halt serving all Fife trains. Tickets are obtained from the train conductor. Large car park on the southside, but quite a walk to the Edinburgh platform. Could be a struggle with a pushchair to get from one side to the other. Trains run regularly to Waverley.

Slateford, Westerhailes, Kingsknowe and Curriehill stations have hourly services to/from Glasgow Central via Shotts. Restricted Sunday services.

Musselburgh Station is served by services to/from North Berwick. Trains hourly, with a reduced service on Sunday.

THE TRAINS

Facilities on the trains themselves are improving. Most now have external and internal push buttons for sliding doors, so boarding with a pushchair and toddler in tow has become easier. There is usually adequate luggage space and pushchairs can be left folded up. Toilets on board are few, but at least one per train should include a fold-up nappy-change table.
One of the best ways to keep a child happy on board on a longer train journey is to feed him or her. Buffet trolleys operate on ScotRail Express and longer distance routes, but there are none on local services. These offer hot/cold drinks, sandwiches, crisps and confectionery. However, the range available can be extremely limited and everything is very expensive. It's far cheaper to take your own provisions.

FARES

As a general rule, under 5s travel free, on the understanding that they will give their seats up to fare paying passengers. An adult can be accompanied by up to two free under 5s.

A variety of special fares are available for families, including saver, cheap day returns and family railcard. Always ask to check the cheapest way to travel before buying your ticket. There is usually an abundance of leaflets with special deals available.

USEFUL POINTS OF CONTACT

Edinburgh and Scotland Tourist Information Centre

3 Princes St
Tel: 473 3800
Web: www.edinburgh.org

The friendly staff are happy to share and swap local knowledge with tourists and local people and can also draw on a huge database of attractions, tours and events. You'll glean lots of ideas for days out, activities and sports from the range of leaflets, guides and information sheets. They also stock a free monthly 'What's On' guide for Edinburgh and the Lothians. The web site has a special section for children put together by real experts — the pupils of the Royal High Primary School. Parents will find it useful too!

Scottish Tourist Board

23 Ravelston Ter EH4 3TP
Tel: 332 2433
Website: www.visitscotland.com

Tourist information for the whole of Scotland. Phone calls and letters only.

Walks & Country Places

Edinburgh is blessed with over 4,500 acres of parks, open spaces and woodlands where children and adults can relax or let off steam, without having to travel miles out into the country. The walks in this section include carefully tended parks and wild open hillsides. We have tried to give some indication of the terrain in terms of accessibility for pushchairs and small bikes; of course children can also be carried in a backpack or sling. Obviously conditions may vary on non-surfaced paths, particularly after rain.

More detailed information and maps may be found in Edinburgh City libraries and local bookshops. In particular a map of city cycle paths published by 'Spokes', the cyclists' organisation, is useful for walks where pushchair accessibility is needed. Happy tramping!

PARKS, HILLS, ESTATES & WOODS

The Braids

Grassy slopes and hills, good for kites, walking and sledging. Access and parking at the entrance to the Braid Hills Public Golf Course on Braid Hill Approach and along Braid Hill Dr. There are horses to be seen in fields nearby at Liberton Tower Farm.

Braidburn Valley Park
Pentland Ter, Comiston Rd

A stream runs through the middle of hilly slopes (which are well used for sledging during snow). Paths suitable for pushchairs. No play equipment. There is a 'fairy ring' of trees, ideal for children to run around and wear themselves out. The stream is suitable for fishing for tiddlers and is shallow enough for supervised paddlers near the 'fairy ring'.

The Hermitage of Braid and Blackford Hill Local Nature Reserve

The Hermitage of Braid: offers a taste of the countryside in the city and is ideal for pushchairs. A good flat entrance from Braid Rd (south of the mini roundabout) leads through a beautiful wooded valley beside the tumbling Braid Burn. There is a map at the entrance. At the heart of the valley is Hermitage House, a Ranger Centre with maps, leaflets and imaginative and informative activities for children of all ages. The Centre is open all year in the afternoons, 6 days/week (closed Sat). Picnic table on a flat grassy area in front of the house. Toilets inside the house and outside (although these are best used only in an emergency). If you take the right fork past the house there are a few steps up to an old icehouse, used to store ice in bygone days. The path follows on over bridges, excellent for 'Pooh Sticks', to the Lang Linn Bridge. Here you emerge from the wooded valley and can continue along to Blackford Glen Rd and eventually the foot of Liberton Brae. This is also an excellent walk for pushchairs. There are often cows in the fields across the burn and lots of bird life.

For those without pushchairs the Hermitage is riddled with steep twisty paths that are wonderful to explore. Bluebells in spring, bird boxes and inquisitive squirrels are all easy for tots to spot. At Lang Linn Bridge there are steps with a gate (tricky for pushchairs) and a stony path up to your left that will take you around the side of Blackford Hill to the pond.

The Ranger Centre often organises interest walks for families and can take playgroups and nurseries at quiet times. Contact the Countryside Ranger Service for details,

Tel: 447 7145
Email: ranger@cecrangerservice.demon.co.uk

Blackford Hill

Car parking at the Royal Observatory, Braid Rd and Midmar Dr; limited on street parking at Cluny Gdns for the pond, and at Blackford Glen Rd, Liberton. Maps of walks at the entrances. Several picnic sites, sledging in winter and popular for kite flying. Beware of the cliffs at the old quarry. Unfortunately the area is badly fouled by dogs, especially around the Observatory and at entrances.

The beautifully situated Blackford Pond, to your right as you enter from Cluny Gdns, contains ducks, moorhens, geese, coots and swans. The swans and geese can be very enthusiastic so keep children behind the low rail on the path. Sometimes there are squirrels to be seen too. There is a shelter on a landscaped path to the east side of the pond. Dogs are not allowed around the pond.

Bruntsfield Links and The Meadows

See Playgrounds and Parks

Cammo Estate

Main gate and Visitor Centre at Cammo Rd
Tel: 317 8797 (Barnton Ranger Service)

The estate was left to the National Trust in 1975. They made the house safe and feuded the estate to the City of Edinburgh Council. It is now managed to enhance the plant and wildlife environment, for use as a teaching resource and by the general public.

Cammo House is now just ruined remains, but its 100 acres of wildlife habitats in woodlands, meadows and marshes leave an estate of unusual character. There are snowdrops in spring and lots of butterflies in summer. Look out for nest boxes and their inhabitants in spring. The pond, originally built for curling, has a good range of pond life, including frogs, toads and insect larvae. At the far end of the pond reeds and other vegetation grows, providing cover for moorhen, mallard and very occasionally a kingfisher. There is also a walled garden. Most paths are accessible for pushchairs; a wheelchair and pushchair accessible trail has been created around approximately 1km of the estate. Other main paths have been upgraded.
The Visitor Centre in the lodge has toilets, including disabled, but no nappy changing surface; maps and leaflets about the park and displays. The Centre is staffed by the Ranger Service Tue to Fri, 14.00–16.00, and Sunday afternoon courtesy of the Friends of Cammo.

Cammo and the River Almond

Cammo Rd, Barnton

The paths along the River Almond can be joined from Cammo. These routes are not really suitable for pushchairs, as they are narrow, uneven and overgrown.
Start the walk on Cammo Rd. A signpost leads you through a gate on the right and down a rough wide path to the river. Here the riverbank is very steep. The path continues to follow the river upstream towards the airport, it can be very overgrown.
There are stepping stones about halfway along or turn up that path to the left near the bridge and you will eventually rejoin Cammo Rd again. Along this path you pass Craighall Temple – a locked tower, or turn right over Grotto Bridge. The river is very narrow here and looks spectacular after rain as the water thunders underneath. Just over the bridge is a cattle grid, which has been known to capture clambering youngsters! The path follows the river downstream and can be rough with some steep steps down to the water. It ends near the Cramond Brig Hotel. For a walk further downstream see Cramond, south: the River Almond Walkway. The Cammo Park leaflet mentioned in the previous entry also covers this area.

Corstorphine Hill Local Nature Reserve

Panoramic views of the city and beyond are offered at the 530ft summit. The terrain is varied, with a rocky and steep section – which includes a flooded quarry – between the Queensferry Rd and Clermiston Rd entrances, and large areas of woodland. Flora and fauna include conkers, acorns and pinecones, squirrels, badgers and foxes. There is also Clermiston Tower, built in 1851 to commemorate the centenary of Sir Walter Scott's birth. Access to the tower by arrangement with the Ranger Service or during Sundays in the summer courtesy of Friends of Corstorphine. Between the tower and the entrance on Clermiston Rd opposite Queen Margaret College, is the Walled Garden. The Friends of Corstorphine have restored the overgrown garden into a woodland walk for the community, allowing the less physically fit to be able to appreciate the garden as a microcosm of the vegetation found on the hill.
There are several routes to the summit of the hill: Clermiston Rd (3 paths: the one near the Capital Moat House is rough and steep); Queensferry Rd (steep and rugged); Craigcrook Rd (a long push, between new houses, up a fairly steep gradient, but a reasonably smooth path); Ravelston Dykes Rd (near Mary Erskine School and about 200 yards North of Murrayfield Golf Clubhouse) and from Cairnmuir Rd, at the junction with Kaimes Rd. This latter route is easiest for pushchairs, although muddy after rain, and there is car parking. There is a grassy slope on the left near this entrance – also good for sledging. The path to the summit follows the edge of the zoo where some animals may be seen before it joins the paths from Ravelston Dykes and Craigcrook entrances.

Craiglockhart Dell and Colinton Dell

Beautiful wooded glens with the Water of Leith and its walkway running through the centre (see separate entry). Plenty of paths to explore although those with pushchairs will have to search for flat routes. Cycling is only permitted on the main Water of Leith Walkway. Bridges for 'Pooh Sticks' and open grassed areas next to the river are ideal for picnics and games. Access includes Dell Rd, Colinton, Katesmill Rd, pathway from Lanark Rd near Dovecot Pk and behind the Tickled Trout pub on Lanark Rd at Slateford.

Craiglockhart Hill

Street parking is available at Craiglockhart Ter, Lockharton Cres and at Craiglockhart Sports Centre. Level paths from the sports centre and from Craiglockhart Ter are suitable for pushchairs and take you to the pond. The pond holds swans, ducks, moorhens and coots, the nests of some of which can be seen in early summer. There is a map of the area at Craiglockhart Ter and at the pond. Many interesting and attractive plants have been established to improve the area for bird and insect life. Off the level path steep paths, some with steps, go up through semi-natural woodlands to the top of the hill. The highest part is open and gives impressive views of the city and countryside beyond.

Cramond

The village is situated at the mouth of the River Almond. There are swans and seagulls to feed and lots of small boats to look at. Walks radiate in all directions from the yachting centre. There is a large car park on Cramond Glebe Rd, below Cramond Kirk and above the Cramond Inn. A ramp leads down to the esplanade. Below the Inn are public toilets. There are also two cafes serving teas and ice creams.

Cramond was home to an established Roman settlement. There is a partially excavated site in the upper car park, beside the 17th Century Cramond Kirk.

North – To Cramond Island

There is a newly upgraded causeway across the tidal mudflats out to Cramond Island, which is negotiable at low tide. Tide charts are pinned up at the start of the causeway monthly but often get torn down. Check the tide times with Forth Ports or the Ranger Service before setting out. Take a picnic to your own small uninhabited island. Good views of the Forth Bridges but keep an eye on your watch for returning.

South – The River Almond

About 1 1/2 miles, the walkway starts on the esplanade, near the yachting centre, and follows the river upstream on a wooded path. The path is wide and on the level, and is suitable for pushchairs and bikes, but can be muddy. The river is tidal up to Cockle Mill Cottages, where the path opens out into a grassy area, watch out for dog fouling. There is also a small car park, access from Whitehouse Rd via School Brae. The path continues up to Fair-a-Far Mill where there is a waterfall and a fish ladder. The mill is now a ruin and children will enjoy running through the arches and up a few steps. The river is railed at this point but toddlers can get underneath quite easily. People throw pennies into the top of the fall and children collect them later! The path continues up to the Cramond Brig Hotel and Haugh Park, but there is a steep flight of steps and pushchairs would have to be carried. See also Cammo and the River Almond, for a description of the route further upstream.

East – the Esplanade

A broad paved footpath runs for 2 miles from Cramond through Silverknowes to Granton Point West Shore Rd. An attractive area for promenading with the pram, roller-skating or for learning to ride a bike. Plenty of seats and shelters. Superb views across to Fife on clear days. Suitable for picnics on the Grassy Banks at Silverknowes where there is parking along Marine Drive – but look out for dog mess. You can also walk up to Lauriston Castle from Silverknowes.

Tide charts are available for reference in summer. Ice cream vans, pipe bands and entertainment over some summer weekends. The beach itself is sandy at Cramond and stony elsewhere. It can be oily and there are often pollution warnings about collecting shellfish. The beach is gently sloped but the tide can come in fast and maroon you on a sandbank – be prepared to paddle!

West - across the River Almond

There is no bridge across the Almond at Cramond, but it may be crossed by passenger ferry. Normally the Cramond Ferry is open from April to September 9.00 to 19.00 and October to March 10.00 to 16.00. It is closed on Fridays and from 13.00 to 14.00 for lunch. Passage costs 50p per person. No dogs or bicycles are allowed, and only small folding pushchairs can be carried. However at the time of writing the ferry is closed until further notice for essential repair work to the jetty. If you can cross by ferry, the land to the east of the river belongs to the Dalmeny Estate. There is a path to Dalmeny House, approximately 2 miles, but it is not negotiable with a pushchair. Look out for 'Eagle Rock', situated on the shoreline about 400 yards from the ferryman's cottage. Maintained by Historic Scotland it is thought that this rock may have been part of the Roman settlement. Children under supervision will enjoy exploring around the rock and the caves below. Better for pushchairs is the 4 1/2 mile shore walk to South Queensferry along a woodland path.

Dalmeny House and Estate

Tel: 331 1888
Web: www.dalmeny.co.uk

Take the A90 and then B924. There is a bus service from St Andrew Sq to Chapel Gate, 1 mile from the house.

House and estate are open from 14.00 to 17.30, Sun, Mon and Tue afternoons in July and August. While we'd not recommend Dalmeny House as a place to visit with young children, the estate itself is pleasant to walk around – fields, shore and woodland with cows, sheep, pheasants and a statue of a horse. There is a sheltered woodland walk through the rhododendrons and azaleas of the garden valley. No dogs allowed. Picnics only by prior arrangement. No fires.

The house can also be reached by the 4 1/2 mile Shore Walk from Long Craig Gate in South Queensferry to the ferry at

Cramond, (ferry closed for essential repair work to the jetty at the time of writing). The path is open all year round to pedestrians only. It is negotiable with a pushchair or manageable with small children in backpacks, and can be good fun if walking in a group: planning ahead and using 2 cars, one at either end of the route. This walk passes through several designated Sites of Special Scientific Interest – including nesting and feeding grounds for several rare species of birds, as well as giving wonderful views of the Forth. There are lovely beaches in the estate, particularly the ones near Barnbougle Castle and also just past Dalmeny House, known to locals as the 'shell-beds'. Gate closes 21.00 summer, 18.00 winter.

Figgate Burn Park

Entrances at Duddingston Rd and Hamilton Dr behind Portobello High School.

A strip of parkland with trees and grassy slopes along the Figgate Burn in Duddingston. The paths are easily negotiated and ideal for bikes. On Figgate Pond there are plenty of tame wildfowl to be fed. On raised ground to the north-east of the pond there is a children's playground where most of the equipment is better suited to school age children. Next to the Burn are the Craigentinny Carriage sidings, off the main railway line, which can be interesting for junior trainspotters, particularly when shunting is in progress. See *Playgrounds and Parks.*

Holyrood Park

Park Rangers' Office
Tel: 556 1761

Car parks at Dunsapie Loch, near the entrances at Duddingston Loch, Holyrood Palace and Meadowbank Ter.
A rugged park, including Arthur's Seat (823ft), Salisbury Crags, and three small lochs. A surfaced road, Queen's Dr runs around the park for approximately 3 miles. Apart from a small stretch of surfaced path from the Holyrood Palace entrance up Haggis Knowe towards St Anthony's chapel (about 200yds), all the other routes are rocky or on grass. The climb to Arthur's Seat is a steep one for youngsters (shortest route from Dunsapie Loch) but there is an excellent view at the top with a Trig Point indicating surrounding sites of interest. Lower down there are good views from Dunsapie Hill (523ft) – not quite a climb. It is possible to walk round St Margaret's Loch with a pushchair and there are ducks, geese and swans to be fed here. Rowing boats can be hired in the summer. In the south east of the park is Duddingston Loch, a bird sanctuary, where the geese and swans can be quite aggressive.

Leaving Queen's Dr, below Salisbury Crags and to the south-east of Pollock Halls is a cycle track and footpath, suitable for prams, known as the Innocent Railway (see *Railway Paths and Cycle Tracks, below*).

Inch Park

Old Dalkeith Rd, near the Cameron Toll Shopping Centre
A large area of grassland, with playing fields, deciduous trees, slopes for sliding, paved paths for pushchairs and learning to ride a bike. Ideal for letting off steam after a shopping session at Cameron Toll (there is an entrance from the car park). Large play area. See *Playgrounds and Parks.*

The Pentland Hills

Regional Park HQ
Tel: 445 3383
Email: rangerservice_phrp@yahoo.co.uk

A beautiful range of hills spreading along Edinburgh's southern edge. Supported by City of Edinburgh, Midlothian and West Lothian Councils and Scottish Natural Heritage. The Pentland Hills regional park consists of 2 country parks, reservoirs (no swimming permitted), nature reserves and other private areas. Within the Regional Park there are several areas of interest to parents with young children.

Bonaly

Where Bonaly Rd crosses the city bypass there is a fork in the road. The right turn, Torduff Rd (public vehicle access for only a few hundred yards and limited parking at the end) leads up to Torduff Reservoir and is surfaced but a long push from prams and small cyclists. At the reservoir you can turn left for a walk across to Bonaly Country Park (see below) – steps and a grassy path, but good views over the city. For pushchairs, a better walk is to follow the west side of the reservoir along to the end where there is a short push up to Clubbidean Reservoir, 3/4 mile. Here there is more space for picnics and there are sometimes anglers in boats to watch. The path alongside Clubbidean is rougher for pushchairs but energetic parents with backpacks may like to continue on to Currie, 1 1/2 miles.
Following Bonaly Rd, from the city bypass as far as it will go, brings you to a car park. This area is know as Bonaly Country Park and from here you can walk up into the hills. There is an information board with maps and a picnic area. Of the three paths up from here, the left is too steep for youngsters, the right takes you over Torduff Reservoir (see above) and up into the heather. The middle path, possible with pushchairs and for rea

sonable walkers leads up through a plantation of trees to Bonaly Reservoir.

Glencourse Reservoir

On the A702(T) Biggar Rd, 7 1/2 miles from the city centre; turn right at the Flotterstone Inn.

An Information Centre with displays and maps in the car park. The road up to Glencourse Reservoir is closed to public vehicles. Ideal for prams and cyclists. As you leave the car park, on your left next to the burn is a barbecue and children's area, dog free. Further along, off to the left across a footbridge is a wooded picnic area, and another up the hill in woods on the right. Several paths fork off across fields and up into the hills. At the reservoir, anglers in boats can often be seen. It is possible to follow the northern edge along to the end on a surfaced road. The water is fenced or walled off. Paths branch off to the right at intervals up to Castlelaw firing range and across the hills to Harlaw (unsuitable for youngsters). Lambs can be seen over the fences in spring.

Harlaw and Threipmuir Reservoirs

Harlaw Reservoir car park is reached by leaving Currie on Kirkgate (follow signs for Currie Old Kirk) or Balerno on Harlaw Rd; turn off at Harlaw Farm. There is an information board here. At the gate, turn right and follow a surfaced road about 100 yards to the reservoir. The former waterkeeper's cottage and garden are open as a Ranger Centre with maps, displays and leaflets. Toilet available. Picnic benches and pond in the wildlife garden. The path around the south side of Harlaw Reservoir has been upgraded and is ideal for pushchairs and bicycles. On the north side is a track (occasionally used by council vehicles), which can be reached by a small metal bridge or across the overflow in summer – fun for paddlers. The track (with paths off through the trees to explore), continues to the end of Harlaw Reservoir where it joins up with Threipmuir Reservoir by way of another overflow. To continue on around Harlaw, cross the footbridge here and turn left through the gap in the wall. The track follows the wall and over the bank on your right is Threipmuir Reservoir, not fenced. Turn left at the end of the wall to continue on around the south side of Harlaw. Those without pushchairs may like to negotiate the stiles further on for a walk back to the car park, along a lane across the fields.

It is possible to walk along Threipmuir from the overflow, keep to the right and do not cross the footbridge. This is an easy walk for pushchairs but you cannot link up with the car park at Red Moss (see below) as there are a series of kissing gates at the other end. It is not possible to walk all around the Threipmuir Reservoir. A variety of birds can be seen on this walk, keep your eyes peeled for herons and cormorants.

Car parking available also at Threipmuir and Red Moss Nature Reserve. Take 1st left in Balerno Village after the High School. Follow the road for approximately 2 miles out of the village past the animal sanctuary to the car park.

Hillend Country Park

Follow the Biggar Rd out just beyond Lothianburn Golf Course on the right and turn up to Hillend. The No 4 bus stops on the main road and there is a long path up to the ski centre. There are picnic tables up to the foot. There is a notice board with maps and general information on the Pentland Regional Park. At the top of the road there is the Hillend Ski Centre and a large car park. A chairlift at the artificial ski slope here may be used by non skiers. It is open 7 days a week. Tel: 445 4433 for opening hours. Adults - £1.40, Under 17s - 80p, Family Ticket (2 adults, 2 juniors)- £4.00; generally children taking a seat pay. No pushchairs. There are several bench type seats so you can tuck tots in between adults, a bar comes down to lap and foot height and keeps you safely in. Very active toddlers should not use the chairlift. There is a stop half way up to get off if a child becomes frightened. The ride up is exhilarating, sailing over skiers and golfers below. At the top there is a viewfinder on a cairn and there are paths through the heather which energetic tots, or parents with backpacks could cope with. The weather can change quickly though so don't stray too far from the chairlift. At the top of the lift are cameras and a tannoy so that the operators can check everybody is safely in before moving. Toilets in the ski centre reception and refreshments are available from the 'Hut on the Hill' portakabin.

Red Moss Wildlife Reserve and Bavelaw Bird Reserve, Balerno

Parking at Threipmuir – see Harlaw and Threipmuir Reservoirs. There is a picnic table here and information board with maps. A short footpath, unsuitable for pushchairs leads down to Threipmuir Reservoir and along to Harlaw (see relevant section). With a pushchair the best route is to turn left out of the car park and follow the road along towards a bridge. On your right is the Red Moss Nature Reserve. This area is boggy so keep to the boardwalk. Continue over the bridge and up a steep, tree lined hill. Bavelaw Bird Reserve is on your right and there is a bird hide on the shore, over a stile and along to a narrow boggy path. Note: the key is held at Balerno Post Office.

A signpost at the top of the hill gives walking options. Only the left continues to be suitable for pushchairs until you reach the stile opening onto the Pentland Hills. This walk is exposed and can be cold but worth it on a clear day for the views. There are sheep and cattle in the fields, waterfowl and fishermen on the reservoir below.

Swanston Village Farm

Access from Oxgangs Rd, by Swanston Rd over the city bypass.

A small picturesque village at the foot of the Pentlands near Fairmilehead. RL Stevenson lived at Swanston Cottage from 1867 to 1880. The whitewashed, thatched cottages of old Swanston village date from the 17th century and there is a mid-19th century farm with steadings. Beyond the village are grassy slopes with sheep grazing and lambs in springtime. Higher up is rougher ground. It is possible to walk over to Hillend but not with a pushchair. Nice for picnics.

Meadows Yard Local Nature Reserve

A small quiet reserve near Seafield (1 hectare). Access is via a steep flight of steps off Fillyside Rd, along which there is a regular bus service. The site has a narrow mulched path (so not great for pushchairs), running around an area of grasses, scrub and emergent trees. In the centre of the reserve is a small pond where on a warm summer day you may be fortunate to see a damselfly sunbathing. If not, butterflies abound in summer and in winter a mix of garden and scrub birds can be seen.

Portobello Beach and Promenade

The paved promenade runs for 1 3/4 miles from Seafield Rd to Morton St in Joppa. The west end of the beach is reached from Bath St. Here you will find an indoor amusement arcade with some children's rides, including a carousel, as well as the usual take away snacks. The quieter end of the beach is reached from Brunstane Rd. The beach is sandy, the City Council cleans it regularly and there is a no dog policy, but as on all beaches, vigilance is required and sandals are advisable for children. There are toilets at regular intervals along the promenade and information boards. Playgrounds can be found along the promenade at Straiton Place and at Tower Bank. See *Playgrounds and Parks*.

RAILWAY PATHS & CYCLE TRACKS

Railways were developed through Edinburgh by rival companies. The remains of some of these tracks have been developed into a network of cycle and footpaths which obviously supply flat walking, ideal for pushchairs. Spokes, the cyclists' organisation, publishes a map which shows them all. They include parts of the Water of Leith Walkway and the Innocent Railway. This is so called because horses, not steam engines, initially pulled the carriages. It runs from Holyrood Park (east of the Pollock Halls) to Craigmillar, walled between Prestonfield Golf Course and Duddingston Loch Nature Reserve; then on through Bingham to Musselburgh, following the main East Coast railway line, approximately 6 miles.

Another ex-railway cycle track starts from Balbirnie Pl in Roseburn where there is a map of the route. This metalled track crosses the Water of Leith with steep steps down to join the walkway and continues north to the old Barnton railway junction at Craigleith, where it divides. One branch goes to Davidson's Mains and the other branches again to Leith and Trinity. Here the cycle path passes along side St Marks Park which has a great new playground, and then through the centre of Victoria Park, which has two excellent playgrounds. (see *Playgrounds and Parks*).

For Spokes' contact details, see *Travel and Transport*

ROYAL BOTANIC GARDEN

East Gate on Inverleith Row and West Gate on Arboretum Pl
Tel: 552 7171

Car parking on 3 sides of the gardens (not Inverleith Row); easiest on Arboretum Pl
Opening times: Daily, except 25 Dec and 1 Jan
Apr-Aug: 9.30-19.00 (cleared at 18.45)
Sep-Oct: 9.30-17.00 (cleared at 16.45)
Nov-Mar: 9.30-16.00 (cleared at 15.45)
Admission: free

An immaculate, beautifully landscaped and well sign posted garden. Dogs are not allowed so there is no problem with dog fouling. There is no cycling allowed but there are cycle racks at the west gate. Abundant grassy areas, flat and sloped and tarred paths. There is a pond where you can feed the ducks, moorhen and swans, and where occasionally a heron can be seen. The shop at the west gate sells sunflower seeds to feed the very tame squirrels. The rockery area has a waterfall and lots of winding paths, some suitable for pushchairs. The Chinese garden has a pagoda next to a small pond and path winding up the slope with small bridges over a 'mountain stream'. Other themed areas, such as alpine, cryptogamic and herbaceous may interest the older child and parents; or just enjoy the extra space and gardens. Unfortunately no picnics are allowed.

The Glasshouse Experience
Daily, except 25 Dec and 1 Jan
Apr-Aug: 9.30-16.45
Sep-Oct: 9.30-16.45
Nov-Mar: *9.30-15.45*
Voluntary donation of £2.50 suggested.

You may be daunted by the suggested donation if you are a regular visitor or one who spends a few minutes in here looking at the fish. Staff stress that any donation is voluntary. There is only one entrance to the glasshouses – all other doors are exit only. Leaflets are available. Pushchairs can be left at the cash desk as the displays are on two levels – with quite a few sets of steps – and some paths between plants are quite narrow. Some ponds have no railings so hold on to active youngsters. There are old and new glasshouses, at various temperatures and humidities, and a small aquarium.

Inverleith House in the centre of the garden, houses a botanical art gallery with a programme of historical and contemporary exhibitions. No pushchairs or prams allowed.

Botanic Garden education staff lead guided tours and provide resource material for school parties. They are willing to give advice to playgroup and nursery teachers and adapt their materials to suit parties of younger children. Tel: 552 7175.

The shop at the West Gate has a range of goods suitable for younger children starting to learn about the environment. Toilets at the Glasshouses, Inverleith House and the West Gate. Nappy changing and feeding facility at the East Gate; ask the Park constabulary there to give you a key.

There is an ice cream kiosk at the West Gate and often an ice cream van parked across from the West Gate at the entrance to Inverleith Park. There are two cafés: The Terrace Café at the centre of the Gardens and Rachael's Tearoom at the East Gate. The Terrace Café is a popular meeting place for women and with small babies and toddlers, has nappy changing facilities and is a relaxed place to breastfeed. See *Eating Out: Edinburgh North.*

WATERWAYS

Union Canal

The Union Canal runs from the Lochrin Basin in Fountainbridge, access from Gilmore Pk and Leamington Rd. Alternatively there is a signposted car park just before the bypass at Calder Gdns off Calder Rd, from where you can walk into the city or out into the countryside. Hermiston also provides a convenient place to park. Thanks to the Millennium Link project the Union Canal now runs right through to Falkirk where the Millennium Wheel carries boats on to the Forth & Clyde Canal, thus connecting Edinburgh and Glasgow. The towpath through the city is on the north bank and is suitable for pushchairs, obviously children need close supervision. From the centre of the city and industrial buildings the canal passes suburban gardens and parks, and nesting swans can be seen. You may also see oarsmen from the rowing club. The canal is carried by the 12 arch Slateford Aqueduct over the Water of Leith and a long flight of steps lead down to the Water of Leith Walkway (see below). Beyond the bypass the canal offers an easy and delightful walk through open countryside, although you may have to negotiate steps to reach it.

See also The Bridge Inn, Ratho (*Places to Visit, Annual Events and Eating Out*) and the Canal Museum, Linlithgow, *Out of Town Trips*.

The Water of Leith Walkway

The Water of Leith rises in the Pentland Hills and runs through the villages of Balerno, Currie, Juniper Green and Colinton and into the heart of Edinburgh before flowing into the Firth of Forth at Leith. In its 24 miles it flows through wooded dells, past abandoned mills, elegant Georgian terraces and new housing developments, before opening up into a broad river surrounded by the buildings of Leith docks. It is designated an Urban Wildlife Site by the City of Edinburgh Council. Look out for herons, especially near weirs.

The walkway runs along most of the river in the City and most parts are negotiable with a pushchair. Unfortunately access is not always so easy and we have tried to list alternatives to steps, where they exist. Some sections are well used by dogs too. Keep an eye on young cyclists as the banks can be steep and there are not always railings, and watch out for exuberant cyclists racing ahead; pedestrians and dogs are not always aware of bikes behind them, and this can lead to collisions.

The brown water is due to peat. Giant hogweed a tall plant (up to 3m) with tiny white flowers has established itself on several stretches. Touching this plant or blowing through sections of its hollow stem may cause an allergic reaction and photosensitivity of the skin. These plants are routinely treated with weedkiller and hacked down but return each year. Along stretches of the river are raspberries and blackberries which should be safe to eat, but remember that dogs may have been there before you!

A comprehensive guide to the walkway complete with map and historical notes is available, price £2.50, from:

The Water of Leith Conservation Trust
24 Lanark Rd
Tel: 455 7367

Edinburgh City Libraries stock a good selection of books on the Water of Leith.
If you want to access parts of the route by bus, First Bus 66 and LRT 44 follow the Water of Leith from Balerno to Slateford along the A70 Lanark Rd.

Balerno to Juniper Green

The walkway begins to the north side of Balerno High School, Bridge Rd and follows the track of an old railway, making it ideal for pushchairs and cyclists. There are a number of access points along the route to Currie, Waulkmill Loan is easiest for pushchairs. At Currie Kirkgate there are steps up to the walkway, next to the bridge. Here it is better for pushchairs if you continue under the bridge and up the road to Currie Baptist Church, where there is access to the walkway via an old goods yard; you can park here too. The walkway continues for approx 1 1/2miles to Juniper Green. Easiest access is at Kinleith Mill, through the industrial estate off Blinkbonny Rd. There are also steps up from the walkway to Blinkbonny Rd bridge. There is a section here where a 20 feet wall drops sharply down to the river below so hold on to wandering tots. The path then crosses to the north side of the river again. Access in Juniper Green is from Baberton Loan, next to the Post Office where you can park.

Juniper Green to Slateford Inc Craiglockhart Dell and Colinton Dell

Along this attractive and peaceful section of the river the walkway continues on the old railway, passing under the city bypass and into a wooded dell; crossing the river several times. Good access next to Post Office in Juniper Green (see previous entry), West Mill Rd, Gillespie Rd by the bridge, or through Spylaw Park, Colinton where there is a good play area. Continuing on, the walkway enters an old railway tunnel, dimly lit but not as long as it looks and a superb place for echoes. Look out for a silhouette on the wall of a Balerno pug, the small engine specially designed for the steep sided Colinton Dell. The path emerges way above the river with other paths below. From Dell Rd, Colinton, down past the church, the walkway runs through the wooded Colinton and Craiglockhart Dells. This section is difficult for pushchairs as there are steps every so often (see separate entry). Access points include Katesmill Rd, at Redhall Mill and behind the Tickled Trout, on Lanark Rd at Slateford.

Slateford to Roseburn

The Water of Leith Heritage Centre is located on the Lanark Rd A70 at Slateford opposite the Tickled Trout pub. There is an exhibition where children can listen to the sounds of some of the wildlife they may see and look down onto a video of the river. Admission: Adults - £1.90, Children - £1.20 ,Under 5s free, Family Ticket - £5.00, Tel: 455 7367. Toilets and nappy changing facilities. There is limited parking at the centre. It is open 10.00-16.00 everyday from April to September; Wed – Sun, October to March. There is a flight of steps up to the Union Canal from Slateford for those without pushchairs. A flat pathway runs from Slateford to Gorgie Rd and the river can be followed through Saughton Park. See Playgrounds and Parks. The section beside Murrayfield Rugby Ground and Ice Rink can be accessed from Baird Dr and Riversdale Rd and provides an easy walk for pushchairs.

Roseburn to Dean Path

From Roseburn the path is accessed from Roseburn Cliff where shallow steps lead to a concrete path right next to the riverside. It is easy to follow to Belford Bridge. There are steps at the bridge so it is easier to leave the path by the back of the Hilton Hotel. There is also access to the Gallery of Modern Art via a steep and stepped path. From Belford Bridge the Dean Bank footpath follows a slow moving loop running in a deep and wooded glen. The path is surfaced and runs on the riverbank, a precarious few feet above the water. Some sections have a handrail about 3 ft high – useful for adults but small children can slip underneath quite easily. Access is from Dean Path, with steps a little way up the hill from Dean Village or for pushchairs a better option is at the footbridge along from Sunbury Mews in a modern housing development. There is access from an alleyway beside Damside in Dean Village but the cobbles can be slippy after wet weather and the walkway here is liable to flooding.

Dean Path to Stockbridge

This well railed and paved section runs along the south bank from Miller Row in Dean Village, to Saunders St in Stockbridge. As the river gushes beneath the dramatic Dean Bridge, it is hard to imagine the urban bustle only 10 mins walk away at the West End of Princes St. The depth of the steep wooded valley is emphasised by the views of the backs of Moray and Ainslie Pl. St Bernard's Well, a Georgian statue and temple, is halfway along the path and there are several flights of steps down to paddling and fishing spots. There are upper and lower routes between St Bernard's Well and the bridge at Saunders St. A new curved sloping path has been created to allow pushchair access direct to Saunders St.

Stockbridge to Warriston

There are steps down to the Deanhaugh Footpath next to Pizza Express in Stockbridge. Easier access from Haugh St or Falshaw Bridge at the other end of the pathway. At Falshaw Bridge turn left and immediately right onto Arboretum Ave. At the end of Arboretum Ave you reach the Rocheid Path with views across the river of the Colonies. Easiest exit from this path is via Inverleith Terrace Lane. If you cross the river the path becomes rather overgrown and there are steps up to Canonmills.

Warriston to Leith

If you want to continue to follow the river take Warriston Rd and follow the riverbank at the bridge. It is possible to take a pushchair along this path but hard pushing is sometimes required. An easier but less scenic route is to access the Warriston Cycleway from the corner of Canonmills and Broughton Rd. The two routes join at Connaught Pl where you can continue along the old railway line and rejoin the river after 500 metres. Or take the flight of steps up to Newhaven Road, cross the road, turn right and walk towards town, and after 50 metres a recently completed section of the walkway will take you across the river to Anderson Pl. Upon exiting at the road, turn left then right along West Bowling Green St and then rejoin the walkway where the sign indicates on the left side.

The scenery changes yet again as the now broad river enters the docks of Leith and you can treat yourselves to a well earned cup of coffee. There are plenty of buses to various destinations from the bottom of Leith Walk.

Index

A

B

C

F

G

N

NOTES

NOTES

NOTES

NOTES